CELEBRATING LITURGY YEAR B 1991

workbook
FOR LECTORS AND GOSPEL READERS

Graziano Marcheschi with Nancy Seitz Marcheschi

LITURGY TRAINING PUBLICATIONS

Acknowledgment

We wish to acknowledge Bill Burke and Fred Baumer whose work with *Workbook for Lectors and Gospel Readers* blazed a trail easy to follow.

Dedication

To Christine Boyd and Patti Seitz, for constant support when we knew we needed it, and especially for when we didn't know.

—*Nancy and Graziano Marcheschi*

Liturgy Training Publications
1800 North Hermitage Avenue
Chicago, Illinois 60622-1101
800-933-1800 FAX: 312-486-7094.

Editors: Elizabeth Hoffman and Peter Mazar
Editorial assistance: Theresa Pincich and Lorraine Schmidt
Cover art: Barbara Simcoe
Cover design: Ana M. Aguilar-Islas
Book design: Jane Kremsreiter

Printed in the United States of America.

ISBN 0-929650-16-6

CONTENTS

PASCHAL TRIDUUM

EASTERTIME

ORDINARY TIME

The Authors

GRAZIANO MARCHESCHI is well known for work in youth and adult retreats and parish missions. He directs the Anawim Players, a liturgical dance and drama company for which he writes much of the repertory. Graziano presents workshops on the ministries of the word at national gatherings on education and ministry. He also serves on the faculty of the Institute of Pastoral Studies of Loyola University, Chicago, and has taught at the Institute for Ministry of Loyola University, New Orleans. His original scripture dramas and prayer-poems are published by GIA Publications. Graziano holds an M.A. in drama from the University of Minnesota and is currently pursuing an M. DIV. degree.

NANCY SEITZ MARCHESCHI teaches music and performing arts to grades one through eight at St. Timothy grade school in Chicago where she also coordinates children's liturgies. She has danced professionally for most of her life. Nancy is choreographer and co-director of the Anawim Players and has created ritual and celebration experiences for many gatherings. She has done extensive work in the area of lector training and liturgy. Nancy holds a B.A. in drama from Loyola University of Chicago and is currently publishing her dance-prayers through GIA Publications. She teaches on the faculty of the Institute of Pastoral Studies of Loyola University, Chicago, and has taught at the Institute for Ministry of Loyola University, New Orleans. Nancy and her husband Graziano reside in Chicago with their daughters Chiara and Amanda.

PREFACE

Each year the Palm Sunday liturgy brings to our ears words from Isaiah which, though never intended as instructions for lectors, seem to say much about the ministry of proclamation. Listen to them now, removed from their context, and see if they say something to you about your work with the word: "The Lord God has given me a well-trained tongue that I might know how to speak to the weary a word that will rouse them." Without looking too hard, we can find in that verse a whole course in proclamation.

"The Lord God has given me . . ." Our ministry comes from God. It is the Lord who wants to communicate to the holy people we call church; it is God who has inspired these messages of hope and comfort, of challenge and surprising (sometimes shocking) truth. If we speak for God, let our ministry flow out of our relationship with God. Let it be rooted in prayer; let it reflect the joy and hope God's word brings to our lives.

"The Lord God has given me a *well-trained* tongue that I might *know how* to speak . . ." The work we do requires preparation and training. We are expected to employ all of our gifts in the act of proclamation. Besides our faith and obvious familiarity with the material, we bring to our task a command of the mechanics of good public reading: clear articulation, pausing, appropriate pacing, eye contact, personal involvement with the texts and all the other details that make an assembly want to listen instead of reading along in their missalettes.

"That I might know how to speak *to the weary* . . ." Many who gather in our churches each Sunday are indeed "weary." Not necessarily from overwork, but weary of heart and spirit, weary from worry about loved ones, weary from depression, from unanswered questions and unfulfilled lives, weary from pain, hopelessness and fear. To such as these you have been called to speak.

"A word that will *rouse* them." God's word is "living and effective, sharper than any two-edged sword"; it achieves the end for which God sends it. It is not a dead word. It is meant to change people—to erase the weariness, to fill the holes in their lives with hope and with God's healing comfort. You are the instrument through which that word is spoken. To be the kind of instrument that worthily proclaims the good news of salvation, you must be in love with the word and in love with the people to whom you speak it. Love them as the Lord loves them. Desire their good as God desires it.

Know that, whether you like it or not, you are part of every scripture you proclaim. Your listeners, no matter how hard they try, will be unable to divorce you from the message you speak. As the personality of each prophet is heard in every prophetic utterance, so your presence will color every passage you proclaim. It's unavoidable that the medium becomes part of the message.

You already know that the task you're about is immensely important. People's lives can change when they truly hear the word. Every nuance you reveal, every shade of meaning you share, helps that "hearing" to occur.

"When I found your words," said Jeremiah, "I devoured them; they became my joy and the happiness of my heart." If they become your joy, they can become ours as well.

Graziano Marcheschi

KEY

Transparency and Drama

"MIRROR, MIRROR ON THE WALL . . ." Mirrors do magic. They snap instant pictures of us. They make things disappear. One even comforted a queen each time she asked who was the fairest—until Snow White came along. Yes, mirrors do magic. But windows do miracles. While offering faint reflections of ourselves, they also point outward and bring outside worlds into our inside places. Solid and impenetrable, they still allow our sight to go beyond the place we're in and travel far away. The raindrops on the glass remind us that the window is there, yet somehow, as we look through, we become part of the raging storm outside. We see, hear and perhaps even feel it. We become the leaf caught in the whirlwind, yet we never get wet.

Mirrors show us ourselves, but like the walls they hang on, they can't let us through to other worlds. For all their magic, they can't compete with windows because they're more like walls.

WINDOWS. Lectors and gospel readers are not supposed to be walls; they're supposed to be windows. They can let us through, and point us outward, and help us see and hear and feel. Just like windows, we always know readers are there. But, at the same time, as we watch the realities they open up for us, we forget they're there and thrill at the marvelous display we see through them.

Many readers approach the task of proclamation with genuine humility. The last thing they may want to do, and the greatest thing they might fear, is becoming an obstacle—drawing more focus on themselves than on the living word they proclaim. Thank God for people of such sincerity and good will! You can be windows instead of walls. But "How" is the question.

ARTINESS. The talk in this *Workbook* of "oral interpretation," "dramatic pauses" and "creating characters" can smack of a world of theatrics, which may feel foreign to the ministry we share. We think of movie stars whose work draws attention to themselves. But we're trying to draw attention to the word, not ourselves. How can techniques that work for actors make our ministry more effective? We've all heard lectors who thought they were proclaiming Shakespeare: Over-articulating, with deepened voices and words rolling off the tongue, they sound "oh so sophisticated"—and possibly phony. Since they are more focused on how something is said than on what is said, we can stop believing them. We can look at them and see only them. They've become a wall because they're using a gimmick known as "artiness."

TRANSPARENCY. Like fine music or beautiful vestments, good proclamation can be good art. Avoiding artiness, therefore, cannot mean settling for mediocrity. The job of every good actor is to become transparent, to become lost in every role he or she is playing. Enjoyable as he was, every time he appeared on screen John Wayne played John Wayne. And it didn't matter if he was wearing cowboy boots or a green beret. He got away with it, and perhaps you loved it, but you never could forget you were watching John Wayne. Now think of a truly great actress or actor: Meryl Streep, Dustin Hoffman. When you watch these people on screen you can begin to forget them and start seeing only the characters they are creating. That's fine acting. And that's transparency.

That's also the lector's goal. And it is best achieved by skillful use of all the available reading techniques, not by ignoring them. Too many lectors think they're "getting out of the way" of scripture by being mediocre. They say they don't want to prevent scripture from being heard, but their mediocrity guarantees that it's not heard. The lector or gospel reader who is awkward or boring, who cannot differentiate one character in a reading from another, who reads too quickly or too slowly, who has too little energy and doesn't use the colorful words of a passage, who reads in a monotone without rising and falling dynamics and pacing, is the lector or gospel reader who draws attention to himself or herself. That person is a wall. The assembly sees only the reader and can't see beyond. But the really good lector—who utilizes appropriate techniques for the material being read—becomes transparent, like a window, and lets the assembly look through.

EXCELLENT READING. Though the assembly still sees the lector or gospel reader, they soon forget about him or her and enter the world they are drawn into. Technique alone won't get you to that point. In addition to technique, which is only good when it is not apparent, lectors and gospel readers must surrender to the reading—letting it read them—allowing its emotions to touch and move them before they in turn move the listeners. It's a goal that may take years to reach, but it's worth the effort because when you're truly excellent the assembly won't think of you as you read—they'll be too busy living in the world you've created.

By utilizing fully all the gifts you've been given by a generous God, you remind the assembly that God's word is alive right here and now. But the one who brings it to life is *you*. And that takes much time, energy, talent—and genuine humility.

Features of this Book

Scriptures

The readings appointed for each Sunday and holy day of Year B are provided and marked for stresses and pauses. Each set of readings is dated. The scriptures for the Third, Fourth and Fifth Sundays of Lent of Year A are also given; these readings are to be used in place of the Year B readings when the scrutinies are celebrated with the catechumens.

Lectionary number

Every edition of the lectionary gives a specific number to each set of readings for every Sunday and feast. We have included these numbers to help you find the readings in your lectionary. Always mark your place in the lectionary with one of its ribbons. *Please do not use this workbook at the lectern during worship.* That's what beautifully bound lectionaries are for.

Commentaries

In the far right and far left columns, commentaries on the readings are offered. These are intended to help you get a sense of the reading and to offer specific suggestions for proclamation.

Margin notes

Sometimes the margin notes introduce new ideas; other times they repeat information introduced in the commentary. Sometimes they are addressed to you as reader: *Slowly. Tenderly. Build!* Often they give hints as to how a person in the reading may have been thinking or feeling. At times words are defined and alternative translations are provided. Primarily these margin notes deal with motivation: what motivates the main people in the story, or the author of the text, or you as interpreter of their words.

Responsorial psalms

You may wonder why this workbook doesn't include the responsorial psalms. After all, the psalms *are* part of the liturgy of the word. However, the psalms are the domain of the cantor, not the lector. The foreword to the lectionary tells us that it is the cantor's role to lead the psalms—and that psalms are songs, not readings.

Pronunciation guide

Don't let unfamiliar names intimidate you. Refer to the pronunciation guide at the back of the book and practice the correct pronunciation.

Inclusive Language

What is inclusive language and why is it so important? Archbishop Raymond Hunthausen in a 1990 pastoral letter offered the following comments:

> Inclusive language, with respect to the liturgy, is a way of speaking and writing that does not give the impression of needlessly excluding certain persons. I urge each of us to be especially sensitive to the use of language that may be sexist, racist, clericalist or anticlericalist, anti-Semitic, as well as being offensive to the disabled.
>
> Most of our liturgical books were translated immediately after Vatican Council II, at a time when sensitivity to language that excludes or offends had not yet become part of our consciousness. Unfortunately, exclusive langauge is liberally scattered throughout our liturgical books. Though the issue of inclusive language is complex, we must try to be sensitive about how we address or speak of one another in the faith community and the way we refer to God. Care must be taken in choice of texts and in other pastoral adaptations, for often the integrity of the word of God or the very meaning of the rite may be at stake.
>
> Appropriate adaptation, in accord with liturgical guidelines, demands knowledge, time, energy and thought. Official changes in texts and translations may seem slow in coming, so our understanding and our patience are essential. There are instances when the language of impatience and protest can do more harm to the unity of the assembly than the use of exclusive langauge.

The readings throughout this workbook are from the New American Bible. Though the revised New Testament of the New American Bible is not yet approved for lectionary use, often citations from that version (designated "Rev. NAB") are given in the margin notes in an attempt to provide language that is less exclusive. These variations may be of use in settings where the scriptures are read or studied apart from the liturgy. The Revised NAB is undergoing further work, both to ensure inclusive language as much as possible and to present the texts in a way that will enable good proclamation. These revisions should be completed in the next few years.

Tools of the Trade

Preparing to Proclaim

Always read all three scriptures. Because the first readings have been chosen according to their relationship with the gospel passage, it is always important to look at those scriptures together. *Always read all three commentaries.* There are reading suggestions in each that can help you with your own passage. As you read the commentaries, refer to the sections of the scripture passage being discussed and make your own margin notations. *Read the scriptures again* using your margin notes and those printed in the text to remind you of the commentary suggestions. *Always read the scriptures aloud,* taking note of stress and pause suggestions. After several readings, alter the pause and stress markings to suit your own style and interpretation. *Form your prayer for the week around the scriptures you will proclaim on Sunday.* You may want to read the scriptures directly from the Bible, because that is the only way one can take note of the context of a particular passage.

Openings and closings

These are two of the three most critical moments in a reading (the third being the climax). First, establish eye contact with the assembly, then announce, from memory, "A reading from. . . ." Say "A (uh) reading from . . ." instead of "Ay reading." Pause (▪▪▪) and then begin the reading. Names of people are often the first words of a reading, so even when the context may not warrant a stress on the name, it is important to highlight it so that listeners don't miss who the subject is.

Pause (▪▪▪) at the end of the reading and establish eye contact before announcing (again, from memory) "This is the word (gospel) of the Lord." Your inflection should always signal that the reading is over.

"This is the word . . ." should never catch the assembly by surprise. End as if there were *no* "This is the word. . . ." Then, after a pause to establish eye contact with the assembly, add it on. Maintain eye contact while the assembly makes its response, and only then move away from the lectern.

Both approach and departure from the lectern should be made with reverence, neither too fast (suggesting you're in a hurry) nor too slow (appearing overly pious).

Build

"Build" refers to the vocal technique of increasing your intensity as you speak a certain word or sentence. Greater intensity has nothing to do with volume. It simply means you feel more strongly and communicate that stronger emotional involvement. That could be done by speaking more loudly, but a quieter voice might produce the same effect. The same is true of rate—sometimes "build" is achieved by speaking faster and sometimes by speaking slower. The point is to show greater intensity of feeling, more involvement, greater urgency. Lack of intensity is one of the "sins" of proclamation.

Whenever a word or idea is repeated ("Abraham, Abraham, . . ." "Rejoice in the Lord always! Again I say, rejoice!"), your intensity and urgency is always greater on the repetition. Without the "build" the repetition seems redundant and purposeless. People only repeat when they want to make a point, and they do that with the sound of their voice as well as with their words. But remember you can "build" the second "Abraham" by speaking it loudly or by speaking it quietly but with great energy. In a long passage you may need several "builds." In that case, increase to a certain level of intensity, then dip down and start up again.

Stress (italics)

The italics attempt to identify the operative words in a sentence, the ones that convey the meaning. Verbs do that best. They speak of action and intention. Next come nouns. Nouns are the people, places and things of a text—obviously important. Then there are color words like adverbs and adjectives. Stress these for variety or when they clarify the author's meaning.

The verb is generally more important in most verb-adverb combinations. In "He *looked* out at the people" ("looked" is the verb; "out" is the adverb), habit would have us stress *out*. To correct this, repeat the sentence several times without the adverb ("He looked at the people"), then reinsert the adverb and you should find yourself stressing the verb.

Context and variety determine whether a noun or adjective will be stressed. For example, "You shall be a glorious *crown* . . . a *royal* diadem." Prepositions are rarely stressed (unless you're saying: "He ran toward the wall and then *through* it!"). Don't hesitate to alter the stresses. But if you do, know why you're doing it.

If when reading a sentence it seems there are too many stresses, you're probably right. Italics do not always indicate the same degree of stress. When several words are italicized in a sentence, one or more may be subordinate. The passage "With their *hands* they will *support* you, that you may never *stumble* on a *stone*" contains four italicized words, but "support" and "stumble" receive the greater stress. No one way is the best way to accent a passage. When you combine the author's intent and the needs of your assembly—making the author's words as alive today as when they were first written—then you've found the best way to proclaim.

In any case, do not feel obligated to memorize all the stresses. The stress marks in this workbook are only suggestions. Feel free to disagree with them.

Units of thought

Many sentences contain more than one idea. Running too many words together blurs meaning and fails to distinguish ideas. Punctuation—meant for the eye, not the ear—does not always indicate clearly which words to group together or where to pause. You must identify the units of thought and use your voice to distinguish one from another. The listener is totally dependent on you for this organization of ideas.

The pause marks (▪ , ▪▪ , ▪▪▪) in the scripture texts serve two purposes: to divide the text into units that communicate a single image or thought and to indicate the lengths of pauses between these units.

Pauses

All pauses are not created equal. The pause marks indicate the suggested *length* of the pause between thought units. Hold a pencil in your hand as you read, and tap your book once for each box before speaking the next word. These single, double or triple beats will lend variety and help slow the pace of your reading.

If your pauses at the single boxes sound awkward, you're probably pausing too long. Though the double and triple boxes indicate pauses of more or less consistent duration, the single box can suggest pauses of varying lengths. Your sense of what's necessary must tell you what value to give the single pause. Some entire passages (and parts of others) move at a faster rate than other passages. There a single box might translate into a pause that's half as long as the standard pause or simply into the "stretching" (sustaining) of the word that occurs just before the box.

Pauses are never dead moments. You've heard of "pregnant pauses"—silences that say "something is going to happen." Something is always happening during a pause. Usually it is your effort to connect the previous thought with the next. During a pause you should be *thinking* "and then," "therefore," "however" or whatever connective fits the context.

Only practice will teach you how long to pause and how to fill your pauses. Too many pauses make a reading choppy; too few cause ideas to run into one another. Too long a pause breaks the flow; if pauses are too short, your listeners will be struggling to keep up with you. Most of the pauses in this book are only suggestions, but a substantial pause always follows "A reading from . . ." and a substantial pause always precedes "This is the word (gospel) of the Lord."

Pace

What's too fast and what's too slow? That depends on what you're reading, where and for whom. The larger the church, the larger the assembly and the more complex the text, the slower you must read. If you're going to make a mistake, better to be too slow than too fast. Your listeners have not spent time with this reading as you have. For them it's new. They need time to absorb it. They need time to catch your words and comprehend what you've said.

You'll read more slowly if you read ideas rather than words, if you share images rather than sentences. "Think" the ideas (as if for the first time) and "see" the images in your own mind before sharing them with the assembly. In real conversation you don't recite lists of ideas or arguments supporting a certain position. Your mind "thinks them up" one at a time. And it takes time for that to happen. Give yourself that time.

Dialogue, however, often moves at a faster pace than the rest of the passage—this helps the assembly hear the give-and-take going on between the speakers.

Ritardando

Ritardando refers to the practice, common in music, of becoming gradually slower as you approach the end of a piece. You do it almost every time you sing a song. On the last line you automatically slow down and expand the words. Many readings end the same way. But while the rate decreases, the intensity increases. Note how much more energy you invest in the measured last line of "Happy birthday toooo youuuuu."

Word value

The value of words is decided by the word itself: "Shock" is always a better word than "bean." "Shock" sounds like it means and immediately conjures images of terror and pain. "Bean" won't even make your mouth water. And the value of words is also decided by the context: The words "one, two, three . . ." don't mean much by themselves. But put in context they surely do: "If by the time I count to three everyone hasn't left the room, I'll detonate this bomb. One, two. . . ."

Literary Devices

Indirect quotations

Certain bits of narration may take on the flavor of dialogue. The narrator might report what a character said without quoting directly. When this occurs, read those indirect quotations not as the narrator but as the person who first spoke them. For example, in the passage, "The son grew angry at this and would not go in; but his father came out and began to plead with him," you might read "and would not go in" in the angry voice of the elder son, then conclude "and began to plead with him" as the patient father entreating his son.

Echoes

Some words are "echoes" of words that went before. For example: "You shall be a glorious crown . . . a royal diadem." Here, "diadem" echoes "crown," so it needs no stress. In such a case, emphasize the new idea.

Words that sound like they mean

These words require special emphasis. "Smashed," "vast," "in haste," "implore," "gleamed" evoke their meaning with their sound. Let them do their work. Reading "The wind *howled*" in the same manner as "The wind *blew*" would do the translator of scriptures a disservice.

Bodily Attitudes

Posture

Posture and body language become an unavoidable part of your proclamation. Whether you like it or not, your body speaks. Make sure it says what you want it to. When you speak, you become one with the word you proclaim. Don't let your face or body contradict the good news you announce.

Eye contact

Eye contact is your means of connecting with those to whom you minister. It tells them you know they are there and they are the reason *you* are there.

Eye contact says you care about your listeners and really want to share God's word with them. You should look at the assembly during the middle *and* at the end of every thought or sentence. That means you look down at the beginning, look up in the middle, look down quickly as you approach the end, and then look up again as you finish the sentence. This "down, up, down, up" pattern must not appear mechanical or choppy. Sustained eye contact works best. Better to sacrifice frequency of looking at the page for less frequent but more steady eye contact.

Gestures

Gestures should be rare. It's difficult to keep them from being distracting and appearing artificial. When a gesture is used (for a very good reason) it must be well rehearsed. To avoid a comic effect, gestures almost always *precede* the words they accompany. ("There he is!" followed by a pointing gesture always gets a laugh.) When in doubt, don't gesture.

Literary Forms

Have you ever heard a lector proclaim two readings that sounded alike? The first reading may have been from Genesis and the second from Paul, yet in sound, energy and mood one was a carbon copy of the other. Why? Because the lector had not learned that there are various forms of writing in the Bible and that each makes its own demands. Each reading, in fact, requires the lector to learn—and then communicate—the distinctive spirit of that reading. In this section we will consider four of those forms and their particular demands—stories, letters, prophetic writing and poetry.

LITERARY FORM: STORIES. God is the source of imagination and creativity. So it is no surprise that the inspired stories of scripture are among the most imaginative and powerful in all literature. They introduce us to the giants of our spiritual heritage. Stories must be told. You don't have to memorize them, but you do have to *tell* them.

Know the story. Know the context of the story—what precedes and follows it. Know the significance of the events for the character involved. Gain a clear sense of the chronology of the plot—how one event builds on another. Identify the climax and employ your best energy there. Don't throw away any good words.

Settings are extremely important. They give the context in which the action is to be played out. They make a difference. (For example, deserts feel different from mountaintops. Daytime moods are different from nighttime moods.) Settings are usually given at the beginning of a reading. Don't rush the description. Where a person in the story *is* tells us much about how he or she will *behave.*

The people in the story must be believable. You should understand their motivation—why they feel and act and speak as they do. Enter their minds and their emotions. Persons are often identified by their relationship to another: "the *parents* of this man who now could see," says John 9:18. Give stress to those identifying words. Sometimes you will need to change the inflection or tone of your voice for different speakers in the story.

The narrator is often a pivotal character. The narrator's voice is like the musical score of a film. Putting different pieces of music behind the same dialogue or action changes its mood dramatically. The narrator's voice with its timbre, pitch, rate and energy can make the same words convey very different moods or meanings. Sometimes the narrator is objective—not emotionally involved in the situation: "Jesus took Peter, John and James." But often the narrator has a subjective point of view and great interest in the events and characters of a story: "His face *changed* in appearance and his clothes became *dazzlingly white.*" Know the narrator's point of view and why he or she wants to tell the story.

Dialogue—what the people in a story say to each other and *how* they say it—is critical when telling a story. Learn to let the the speakers listen to and answer one another as in real conversation. Bring the dialogue to life and build suspense in the story, revealing one detail at a time.

LITERARY FORM: LETTERS. The first task is to know *who wrote* a letter and *who received* it. You have many biblical sources available from religious bookstores in which scholars present our knowledge of all the circumstances around a particular letter. Brief commentaries can be found in some Bibles as introductions to each of the letters. Remember that during Ordinary Time we usually read from a single letter for several Sundays in a row. Whether addressed to an individual, or to all the faithful of a particular city, or to all Christians everywhere, as the church we read these letters knowing they have a meaning and a message for us today.

The *tone* of each letter is a primary concern. A letter to a college friend will differ in tone from a letter of resignation. What remains the same, however, is the directness of delivery. Letters are like conversations. They require us to *visualize* the person we're addressing and to *want* to get our point across.

The *purpose* or intent of each letter is what dictates the tone. Often it is Paul who is writing. He is a complex figure. As teacher and spiritual leader, he is motivated by multiple concerns: to instruct, consolc, encourage, chastise, warn, settle disputes and more. When reading from one of his letters, be aware of what he is trying to accomplish.

Go *slowly* with the letters. It takes time for the assembly to catch the ideas you toss at them. In particular, Paul's theology can be tricky. His style is often a tangle of complex sentences. Many times his mood and purpose change within a single passage. Assuming Paul's role as "teacher," "disciplinarian," "companion on the journey"—or whatever—will help keep you from rushing. Love your listeners and desire their good as much as Paul and the other letter writers do.

LITERARY FORM: PROPHETIC WRITING. Being a prophet is never much fun. Some lectors know the feeling. The intensity of emotion and degree of urgency required in proclaiming the writing of the prophets make some lectors uncomfortable. But the urgency has to be there.

A pervasive theme of the Hebrew Scriptures is that *we are chosen.* With election comes responsibility. It was the job of the prophets to remind the chosen people about those responsibilities—not a popular task. Though you don't see them in the text, these words are often spoken with vocal exclamation points. One must work up courage to tell people what they don't want to hear. Once that energy starts flowing, it becomes a potent flood.

It's been said that in addition to troubling the comfortable, prophets were enlisted to comfort the troubled. With equal passion, the great seers spoke threat and consolation, indictment and forgiveness. You must do the same for the chosen people you call "parish."

The situation in which a prophet ministers is essential knowledge for the lector. Use resources to gain that information. All prophets didn't come from the same mold. Be attentive to style as well as to content. Often the prophet abruptly stops. Beware of the fast transitions, the instant climax and the frequent lack of conclusions.

LITERARY FORM: POETRY. The Hebrew Scriptures contain much poetry. Poetry is a marvelously effective and economical form of human communication. Rich with imagery and charged with emotion, poetry makes special demands on the proclaimer. Poetry, of course, appears in the psalms, in the Song of Songs, in many of the writings of the prophets, and even here and there in the gospels and letters and other parts of the Bible.

Take time. Poetry is gourmet food, eaten slowly and savored on the tongue, so go slowly with readings like this passage from Baruch: "The forest and every fragrant kind of tree have overshadowed Israel at God's command." You need to respond to the many images of poetry by letting yourself smell and feel as well as see the forests and fragrant trees.

Sound and meaning go hand-in-hand in poetry. Wordless music can create a mood, and so can the sound of poetry. Even in a language that you don't understand, poetry recited well should touch your emotions.

Rhythm is an essential element of poetry. It's what distinguishes poetry from prose. Rhythm teaches words to stretch, to balance and dance. As it slows and quickens, it reveals emotions and creates moods. Compare these two verses: "In times past, God spoke in fragmentary ways to our [ancestors] through the prophets" (Hebrews 1:1), and "For Zion's sake I will not be silent, for Jerusalem's sake I will not be quiet" (Isaiah 62:1). The first line is smooth and flat but the second has a rhythmic beat flowing through it that makes it exciting.

Repetition fills poetry. Yet instead of feeling redundant, the repetitions intensify our emotional experience. Each time Poe's "The Raven" repeats "nevermore" we become a bit more frightened. Hebrew poetry is masterful with repetition.

Ideas in poetry can be expressed in ways quite different from normal speech through a literary device called *parallelism.* This is a technique (also called "thought-rhyme") used to repeat, balance and develop ideas in a poem. For example, this is the first verse of Psalm 19:

> The heavens are telling the glory of God;
> and the firmament proclaims his handiwork.

Two parallel images express one idea. Since the two thoughts mean a similar thing, this is called synonymous parallelism. Antithetic parallelism uses opposing images to express one idea. Proverbs 15:15 says:

> Every day is miserable for the depressed,
> but a lighthearted person has a continual feast.

Contrasting ideas make a similar point. Keep your eyes open for these and other forms of parallelism. They remind us that poetry is different from everyday speech and make us aware of the power of repetition.

Studying the Gospel of Mark

This year, Year B, is the year during which the Gospel of Mark is proclaimed throughout the Sundays of Ordinary Time and on many of the Sundays in the liturgical seasons as well. Here's a list of fine resources on Mark:

Paul Achtemeier, *Invitation to Mark: A Commentary on the Gospel of Mark with Complete Text from the Jerusalem Bible.* Garden City NY: Image, 1978.

Daniel J. Harrington, "Mark," in *The New Jerome Biblical Commentary.* Edited by Raymond E. Brown, Joseph A. Fitzmeyer and Roland E. Murphy. Englewood Cliffs NJ: Prentice-Hall, 1990.

Daniel J. Harrington, *Mark.* New Testament Message, no. 4. Wilmington DE: Michael Glazier, 1979.

C. S. Mann, *Mark: A New Translation with Introduction and Commentary.* The Anchor Bible, vol. 27. Garden City NY: Doubleday, 1986.

Ched Myers, *Binding the Strong Man: A Political Reading of Mark's Story of Jesus.* Maryknoll NY: Orbis Books, 1988.

N. Perrin, "Mark, Gospel of," *The Interpreter's Dictionary of the Bible: An Illustrated Encyclopedia.* Supplementary volume. Nashville: Abingdon, 1976.

May the Lord
be in my heart
and on my lips
that I may
worthily proclaim
the good news
of salvation.

READING I "Oh, the seasons, they go round and round . . ." and eventually they get back to where they started. If we weren't such fallible human beings we might not need opportunities to start over again and again. Yet, as Isaiah reminds us, we are people who lose our shape and need the potter's hands to refashion us into the people we are called to be. Your voice alerts the assembly that a time of repentance and joyful expectation is here.

A penitent's hushed voice opens the reading with a humble statement of faith. Remorse enters as you ask "Why do you let us wander . . . and harden our hearts?" Is there a latent tendency in each of us to blame others for *allowing* us to hurt them?

The plea for God's "return" in power is spoken out of your own longing for God's coming to set things right in the world. Let the words "rend," "quaking" and "awesome deeds" make this prayer well up and spill out of you into the hearts of your listeners. You alternate between awe at God's greatness and a sense of sinfulness before a God who is rightly angry at people who have become "like polluted rags." Some hymnals change the classic lines "Amazing grace, how sweet the sound that saved a wretch like me," to read, ". . . that saved and *set me free*." But scripture affirms the healthiness of acknowledging our wretchedness before God, realizing we stand where we are only because of God's mercy. Today is a time for such acknowledgment, so let it ring in lines like "We have all withered . . . our guilt carries us away . . . you have hidden your face" and delivered us up "to our guilt." Remember that this poetry demands extra sensitivity to imagery and the *sound* of words.

"Yet" becomes a powerful declaration of divine love. There is not only groveling here. There is a sense of birthright: "you are our father," and we expect a child's due from a loving parent—the protection and guidance that come from a parent's nurturing hands.

READING II Scripture is so rich because it's so varied. Every time you think you've heard the entire message, you flip a page and discover there's much more to hear. With Isaiah we trembled before a God who saved "a wretch like me"; with Paul we rejoice "because of the favor [God] has bestowed on [us]." What a difference in moods! We "lack no spiritual gift," says Paul, for Christ will strengthen us so we "will be blameless on the day of our Lord." Mighty good news, particularly on a day when the gospel warns: "Be on guard!" Don't dilute Paul's good mood, for its contrast with the first reading and gospel sets out the paradoxes of comfort

DECEMBER 2, 1990

FIRST SUNDAY OF ADVENT

LECTIONARY #2

READING I Isaiah 63:16–17, 19; 64:2–7

A reading from the book of the prophet ▪ *Isaiah* ▪ ▪ ▪

Hushed and humble.

You, Lord, ▪ are our *father,* ▪ ▪
our *redeemer* you are named *forever.* ▪ ▪

Remorse and frustration at our unwillingness to do what we ought.

Why do you let us *wander,* O Lord, ▪
from your *ways,* ▪ ▪
and *harden* our *hearts* ▪ so that we
fear you *not?* ▪ ▪ ▪

A prayer; make it your own.

Return for the sake of your *servants,* ▪
the tribes of your *heritage.* ▪ ▪

Loudly. Suggest God's majesty and your awe.

Oh, that you would *rend* the heavens
and *come down,* ▪
with the mountains *quaking* before you, ▪ ▪
While you wrought awesome *deeds* we could not
hope for, ▪
such as they had not *heard* of from of *old.* ▪ ▪

Praise the God of power!

No ear has *ever* heard, ▪ no eye ever *seen,* ▪
any God but *you*
doing such deeds ▪ for those who *wait*
for him. ▪ ▪

Aware of sinfulness. Imploring.

Would that you might meet us doing *right,* ▪ ▪
that we were *mindful* of you in our ways! ▪ ▪ ▪

Honest admission of sins. "People" is more inclusive.

Behold, ▪ you are *angry,* ▪ and we are *sinful;* ▪ ▪
all of us have become like *unclean* men, ▪
all our good deeds are like *polluted* rags; ▪ ▪

Beautiful seasonal images.

We have all *withered* like leaves, ▪
and our guilt *carries* us away like the *wind.* ▪ ▪

With a sense of shame. Plurals make it inclusive: "There are none . . . who rouse themselves."

There is *none* who calls upon your name, ▪
who rouses himself to *cling* to you; ▪ ▪
For you have *hidden* your face from us ▪
and have *delivered* us up to our *guilt.* ▪ ▪ ▪

Sudden reversal. Claim the love of a merciful parent.

Yet, O Lord, ▪ ▪ you *are* our *father;* ▪ ▪
we are the *clay* ▪ and *you* are the *potter:* ▪ ▪
we are *all* the *work* of *your hands.* ▪ ▪ ▪

READING II 1 Corinthians 1:3–9

A reading from the first letter of *Paul* ▪ to the *Corinthians* ▪ ▪ ▪

Establish eye contact; greet your hearers with joy.

Grace and *peace* from God our Father ▪ and the *Lord* Jesus Christ. ▪ ▪ ▪

Slowly, one idea at a time.

Proud of his contribution to their growth.

A comforting promise.

Climax. Slowly and tenderly.

I *continually* thank my God for you ▪ because of the *favor* he has bestowed on you ▪ in *Christ Jesus,* ▪ in whom you have been *richly* endowed ▪ with every gift of *speech* and *knowledge.* ▪ ▪ Likewise, ▪ the *witness* I bore to Christ has been so *confirmed* among you ▪ that you lack *no* spiritual gift ▪ as you wait for the *revelation* of our Lord Jesus [Christ.] ▪ ▪ He will *strengthen* you to the *end,* ▪ so that you will be *blameless* on the day of our Lord Jesus Christ. ▪ ▪ God is *faithful,* ▪ and it was he who *called* you ▪ to *fellowship* with his Son, ▪ Jesus Christ our *Lord.* ▪ ▪ ▪

GOSPEL Mark 13:33–37

A reading from the holy *gospel* according to *Mark* ▪ ▪ ▪

The "disciples" are in the pews.

A frightening and sobering thought.

Rev. NAB says: "gatekeeper." "Watch . . . sharp eye" = indirect quote.

Start building the urgency.

"Dusk . . . dawn": don't rush. Each word has distinctive mood.

What kind of "sleep" might we be caught in?

Warning motivated by love.

Jesus said to his disciples: ▪ ▪ "Be *constantly* on the *watch!* ▪ ▪ *Stay awake!* ▪ ▪ You do not *know* ▪ when the appointed time will *come.* ▪ ▪ It is like a man traveling abroad. ▪ ▪ He *leaves* home and places his *servants* in charge, ▪ *each* with his own *task;* ▪ ▪ and he orders the man at the *gate* ▪ to watch with a *sharp* eye. ▪ ▪ Look *around* you! ▪ ▪ You do not *know* when the master of the house is *coming,* ▪ ▪ whether at *dusk,* ▪ at *midnight,* ▪ when the cock *crows,* ▪ or at *early* dawn. ▪ ▪ Do not let him come *suddenly* ▪ and catch you *asleep.* ▪ ▪ ▪ What I say to *you,* ▪ I say to *all:* ▪ ▪ *Be on guard!"* ▪ ▪ ▪

and threat, darkness and light, that are at the heart of Advent.

The first line is a formal greeting, like one you would place at the start of a letter. Immediately Paul becomes personal and emotional. He does it with a long sentence that contains several ideas, so go slow and look right at the assembly thinking of reasons for being grateful for each of them. Paul takes pride as well as joy in acknowledging that "the witness I bore to Christ has been so confirmed."

As we enter this season, we need to hear that God "will strengthen [us] to the end." You must believe this before you proclaim it. First, call on your own experience of God's faithfulness to find the conviction you'll need to remind your listeners that "God is faithful"; then, as if you were Paul, remind them—even, maybe especially, if they don't realize they've forgotten.

GOSPEL Jesus' universal call for watchfulness, punctuated by a brief parable, opens the Advent season. His announcement is meant to be a bit terrifying: "You do not know when the appointed time will come!" In an age when so much is known, from the secrets of the atom to the surprises of space, it seems a necessary and sobering reminder. Jesus' three exclamations will have their intended effect if you deliver them one at a time while looking at a different part of the assembly for each. You might even shake your head as you remind us the "appointed time" comes unexpectedly for individuals as well as for the world.

The parable convinces best through understatement. Employ an earnest, conversational tone that takes for granted the aptness of the analogy. Build the intensity of the conclusion, starting on "Look around you," again stressing that here is something we surely do not know. The four divisions of the night (dusk, midnight, cockcrow, dawn) help to emphasize the unexpected arrival of the master. Don't rattle off those time words. Use each word to create a different mood and to say all our expectations are unfounded.

Jesus' urgency is greater at the end than the beginning. Consider the kinds of "sleep" each of us falls into, and let the final warning wake us. After all, we are now even closer to the master's return.

READING I Sharpen your best storytelling skills for this reading and let yourself become the three great characters of the story as well as the editorializing narrator. (Review notes in the Key on "Eye Contact.")

Let your voice comment on the wrongness of what Adam has done even as you begin to narrate. God speaks the first question unemotionally, not knowing as yet of the transgression. Adam's answer is not full of panic. He is covering up, putting up a brave front. Let God's realization that something is wrong bloom on your face as you narrate, "Then he asked." God realizes what has happened, and doesn't want to know *who* told: The choices are few. The question is: *How* did you know you were naked? "You must have eaten, then . . ." Pause after you narrate, "the man replied . . ." Swallow hard and become Adam making his excuses. He can feel almost justified when saying, "so I ate it," if he has adequately blamed the woman.

On the next narration, slowly shift God's focus, and your body, to the woman. God's anger is controlled, tinged with sadness. Eve makes less of a defense and simply admits her weakness.

Shift focus and body again on the serpent narration and signal the wrath that is about to spill from God's mouth. God has been holding back; now the anger flows freely. Highlight the contrast in the last two comments to the serpent, "He will strike . . . *head*" (where he can do significant damage) "while you strike . . . *heel*" (where you can do no harm). Return to the narrator's persona. Then slowly, and with a sense of loss, speak to each of us who've inherited our first parents' mistake.

READING II There is a wonderful rhythm in the first line that adds to the exuberance of Paul's paean—his song of praise. Today is a special, holy day. Paul harkens us back to the beginnings of things but with a very different perspective from that of Reading I. The focus now is on original blessing, on goodness and love.

Slow down after the first sentence to explain why you're so excited. As you state your reasons let your energy and volume grow, giving "such was his will and pleasure" the feel of news too good to believe. Then burst into praise again with the last phrase.

Use the last paragraph to recapitulate all you've said. You've caught your breath. Now, more soberly, you make sure the point is clearly brought home. Subordinate the "who administers" clause and give greater emphasis to the last line.

DECEMBER 8, 1990

IMMACULATE CONCEPTION

LECTIONARY #689

READING I Genesis 3:9–15, 20

A reading from the book of *Genesis* ▪▪▪

Slowly, significantly . . . then a bit faster. Establish focus point for each character.

After *Adam* had *eaten* of the tree ▪ the Lord God *called* to the man and *asked* him, ▪▪ "Where are you?" ▪▪ He answered, ▪▪ "I *heard* you in the garden; ▪ but I was *afraid,* ▪ because I was *naked,* ▪ so I *hid* myself." ▪▪ Then he asked, ▪▪ "Who *told* you that you were naked? ▪▪ You have *eaten,* then, ▪ from the tree of which I had *forbidden* you to eat!" ▪▪ The man replied, ▪▪ "The *woman* whom you put here with me— ▪ *she* gave me *fruit* from the tree, ▪ and so I *ate* it." ▪▪ The Lord God then *asked* the woman, ▪▪ *"Why* did you *do* such a thing?" ▪▪ The woman answered, ▪▪ "The serpent *tricked* me into it, ▪ so I *ate* it." ▪▪▪

"He" = God. Slight pause before shifting back to narrator.

"And so . . ." = What else could I do?

Eve shows greater awareness of responsibility.

God's anger is fully vented.

Then the Lord God said to the *serpent:* ▪▪
"Because you have *done* this, ▪ you shall
be *banned*
from *all* the animals ▪
and from all the wild creatures; ▪▪
On your *belly* shall you crawl, ▪
and *dirt* shall you eat
all the days of your *life.* ▪▪
I will put *enmity* between you and the woman, ▪▪
and between *your* offspring and *hers:* ▪▪
He will strike at your *head,* ▪
while you strike at his *heel."* ▪▪▪

Not an anticlimax, but a way of drawing all into the drama.

The man called his wife *Eve,* ▪ because she became the *mother* of all the living. ▪▪▪

READING II Ephesians 1:3–6, 11–12

A reading from the letter of *Paul* ▪
to the *Ephesians* ▪▪▪

Don't hold back!

Building.

Praised be the *God* and *Father* of our *Lord* Jesus Christ, ▪ who has *bestowed* on us in Christ ▪ every spiritual *blessing* in the heavens! ▪▪ God *chose* us in him ▪ before the world *began,* ▪ to be *holy* and *blameless* in his sight, ▪▪ to be full of *love;* ▪▪▪

New build.

"And daughters" is more inclusive than "children." Perhaps shrug shoulders on "such was . . . pleasure."

likewise he *predestined* us through Christ Jesus to be his adopted *sons*— ▪ such was his *will* and *pleasure*— ▪ that all might *praise* the divine *favor* he has bestowed on us ▪ in his *beloved.* ▪▪▪

"Him" = Christ.

Subordinate this clause.

"To hope in Christ": Ritardando.

In him we were *chosen;* ▪ for in the *decree* of God, ▪ who administers *everything* according to his will and counsel, ▪ we were predestined to *praise* his *glory* ▪ by being the *first* ▪ to *hope* in *Christ.* ▪▪▪

GOSPEL Luke 1:26–38

A reading from the holy *gospel* according to *Luke* ▪▪▪

The angel *Gabriel* was sent from *God* ▪ to a town of Galilee named *Nazareth,* ▪ to a *virgin* betrothed to a man named *Joseph,* ▪ of the house of *David.* ▪▪ The virgin's name ▪ was *Mary.* ▪▪ Upon arriving, ▪ the angel *said* to her: ▪▪ *"Rejoice,* O highly *favored* daughter! ▪▪ The *Lord* is with you. ▪ *Blessed* are you among women." ▪▪▪ She was *deeply troubled* by his words, ▪ and *wondered* what his greeting *meant.* ▪▪ The angel *went on* to say to her: ▪▪ "Do not *fear,* Mary. ▪ You have found *favor* with God. ▪ You shall *conceive* and bear a *son* ▪ and give him the name ▪ *Jesus.* ▪▪ *Great* will be his dignity ▪ and he will be called *Son* of the *Most High.* ▪▪ The Lord God will *give* him the throne of *David* his father. ▪▪ He will *rule* over the house of Jacob *forever* ▪ and his *reign* will be without *end."* ▪▪▪

Pause and let your face express what you describe.

Persuade as well as inform.

Rev. NAB: "since I have no relations with a man."

Reassuring.

Mary said to the angel, ▪ "How can this *be* ▪ since I do not *know* man?" ▪▪ The angel answered her: ▪▪ "The *Holy Spirit* will come upon you ▪ and the power of the *Most High* will *overshadow* you; ▪▪ hence, ▪ the holy offspring to be born ▪ will be called *Son* of *God.* ▪▪ Know that *Elizabeth* your kinswoman ▪ has conceived a *son* in her old age; ▪ she who was thought to be *sterile* ▪ is now in her *sixth month,* ▪▪ for *nothing* is impossible with God." ▪▪▪

Emphasis on "nothing" (not even a virgin birth). Almost a whisper.

Looking at assembly.

Mary said: ▪ "I am the *maidservant* of the Lord. ▪ Let it be *done* to me as you *say."* ▪▪ With that ▪▪ the angel *left* her. ▪▪▪

GOSPEL For emotional intensity and drama this story rivals today's first reading. To do justice to the reading and the young woman of Nazareth whose feast we celebrate you must bring these characters to life with voice and body. There is no dispassionate narrator in this passage. Throughout the evangelist manifests emotional involvement. The opening sentence sets the historical and geographical scene. All the information is important: "from God" (supernatural origin) "to Nazareth" (what good can come from there?) "a virgin" (makings of a miracle!) "Joseph . . . of David" (the Royal House) "Mary" (the central character—speak her name with tenderness and affection).

As the angel, speak with authority but without shouting and with enough energy to frighten a young girl caught unawares. Become Mary as you narrate how deeply troubled she was, letting your face convey her puzzlement. In the next lines the angel both comforts Mary and subtly persuades her to accept her divine selection.

As narrator you might anticipate Mary's confusion by shaking your head during the narration, then speaking Mary's line as a genuine and important question. Make the angel's response gentle and calm and straightforward. Great truth often requires great simplicity. The angel's mood and tempo pick up when referring to Elizabeth. This is an angelic guarantee that God is powerful and will do what was promised. As God's representative, the angel's own credibility is at stake.

Mary's *fiat* can be almost a whisper. The story is told. Look right at your assembly, pause briefly after "that" and tell them the angel left.

READING I It's easy to remember that much of Isaiah is poetry when you realize that at least a half dozen popular hymns have been inspired by this passage alone. Remember that in poetry sound and meaning are Siamese twins, inextricably joined. What you say and how you say it are equally important, for meaning lies both in the words themselves and in the sound they create when spoken.

The Father-God addressed in last week's first reading now responds—even teaching you how to read: "Give comfort to my people. . . . Speak tenderly." Last week's call to conversion and Peter's warnings today about destruction might overwhelm us were they not balanced by the tenderness of passages like this. A message of newness and fresh starts dominates the passage: "Guilt is expiated," winding ways are made straight! That calls for a tone of joy—and relief, given Peter's admonitions in the second reading.

From the tenderness of the first paragraph build to a muted intensity in the voice that "cries out . . . prepare the way of the Lord!" Suggest how incredible it is that these events will occur, remembering that these are poetic images that are not literal prophecies of what will happen to mountains but of what, even more incredibly, will happen to human hearts. Believe it, you say, "for the mouth of the *Lord* has spoken."

Isaiah insists you "cry out" as on a mountaintop. Translate that instruction into intensity rather than volume, belief rather than decibels. Only if you truly believe God renews hearts can you become a "herald of good news!"

Isaiah's images are related to each other. God's "strong arm" is the same one that "gathers the lambs"; God's "reward" and "recompense" (stressed instead of the prepositions "with" and "before") are the comfort of "his bosom." Images of strength are interwoven with images of tenderness. Together they become the fabric of reassurance and new life the Lord wants to wrap around us.

READING II Because this is a letter, a personal and direct tone is appropriate. Certainly any passage addressed to "dear friends" requires increased eye contact and a tone suggesting familiarity with those addressed. Pay attention to the time words "day" and "a thousand years," letting their sound suggest the length of time described. Reason with your listeners that what looks like "delay" is instead *"generous patience."*

Pause after "come to repentance," then slowly and quietly, like a thief moving in on the loot, speak of the coming of the day of the Lord. Suddenly, like the thief springing on

DECEMBER 9, 1990

SECOND SUNDAY OF ADVENT

LECTIONARY #5

READING I Isaiah 40:1–5, 9–11

Remember that in poetry sound and meaning are often synonymous.

A reading from the book of the prophet ▪ *Isaiah* ▪ ▪ ▪

Comfort, ▪ give comfort to my *people,* ▪
says your God. ▪ ▪

"Tenderly" conveys how you should sound.

Speak *tenderly* to Jerusalem, ▪ and *proclaim* to her ▪
that her service is at an *end,* ▪
her *guilt* is *expiated;* ▪ ▪

Hushed intensity. Convince us.

Indeed, ▪ she has *received* from the hand of the Lord ▪
double for all her sins. ▪ ▪ ▪

More important to build intensity than volume.

A voice *cries* out: ▪ ▪
In the *desert* prepare the *way* of the Lord! ▪ ▪
Make *straight* in the wasteland ▪ a *highway* for our God! ▪ ▪
Every *valley* shall be *filled* in, ▪
every *mountain* and *hill* shall be made *low;* ▪ ▪

Our "rough" and "rugged" hearts will be transformed.

The *rugged* land shall be made a *plain,* ▪
the *rough* country, ▪ a *broad* valley. ▪ ▪
Then the *glory* of the Lord shall be *revealed,* ▪

"All people" is more inclusive.

and *all* mankind shall *see* it together; ▪ ▪
for the mouth of the Lord has *spoken.* ▪ ▪ ▪

Speak to Zion and Jerusalem.

Go up onto a *high* mountain,
Zion, ▪ *herald* of glad tidings; ▪ ▪
Cry out at the *top* of your voice,
Jerusalem, ▪ herald of *good news!* ▪ ▪
Fear *not* to cry out ▪
and *say* to the cities of Judah: ▪ ▪
Here is your *God!* ▪ ▪

Images of power and tenderness blend together.

Here comes with *power*
the Lord God, ▪
who *rules* by his *strong* arm; ▪ ▪

Don't emphasize prepositions.

Here is his *reward* with him, ▪
his *recompense* before him. ▪ ▪

Slow and gentle.

Like a *shepherd* he feeds his flock; ▪ ▪
in his *arms* ▪ he *gathers* the lambs, ▪ ▪
Carrying them in his *bosom,* ▪
and *leading* the ewes with *care.* ▪ ▪ ▪

READING II 2 Peter 3:8–14

A reading from the second letter of *Peter* ▪ ▪ ▪

First establish eye contact, then speak.

Stretch the words "years" and "thousand."

Like a loving teacher.

"Day of the Lord . . ."—slowly, then get louder and faster.

Slowly.

This point ▪ must *not* be *overlooked,* dear friends. ▪ ▪ In the *Lord's* eyes, ▪ *one* day is as a thousand *years* ▪ and a *thousand* years are as a *day.* ▪ ▪ The Lord does not *delay* in keeping his promise— ▪ though some *consider* it "delay." ▪ ▪ *Rather,* ▪ he shows you generous *patience,* ▪ since he wants *none* to *perish* ▪ but *all* to come to *repentance.* ▪ ▪ The day of the Lord will come like a *thief,* ▪ and on that day the heavens will *vanish* with a *roar;* ▪ ▪ the elements will be destroyed by *fire,* ▪ and the earth and all its *deeds* ▪ will be made *manifest.* ▪ ▪ ▪

Note rewording in commentary.

Persuasive.

Joy.

The "effort" is not without joy.

Since *everything* is to be destroyed in this way, ▪ what sort of *men* must you *not* be! ▪ ▪ How *holy* in your conduct and devotion, ▪ *looking* for the coming of the day of God ▪ and trying to *hasten* it! ▪ ▪ *Because* of it, ▪ the heavens will be destroyed in *flames* ▪ and the elements will *melt* away in a *blaze.* ▪ ▪ What we *await* ▪ are *new* heavens and a new *earth* ▪ where, ▪ according to his *promise,* ▪ the *justice* of *God* will reside. ▪ ▪ So, beloved, ▪ while *waiting* for this, ▪ make *every effort* to be found without *stain* or *defilement,* ▪ ▪ and at *peace* in his sight. ▪ ▪ ▪

GOSPEL Mark 1:1–8

The *beginning* of the holy *gospel* according to *Mark* ▪ ▪ ▪

The beginning of "good news!"

Use John's voice.

Build energy.

Insistent.

Here begins the *gospel* of *Jesus Christ,* ▪ the *Son* of *God.* ▪ ▪ In *Isaiah* the prophet, ▪ it is *written:* ▪ ▪
"I send my *messenger* before you ▪
to *prepare* your way: ▪ ▪
a *herald's* voice in the desert, ▪ *crying,* ▪ ▪
'Make *ready* the way of the Lord, ▪
clear him a *straight* path.'" ▪ ▪ ▪

Stress importance of John's role.

Amazed at success.

Despite this, people came to him.

John's voice.

Contrast "water" (not much) with "the Holy Spirit" (everything!).

Thus it was that *John* the *Baptizer* appeared in the desert ▪ proclaiming a baptism of *repentance* ▪ which led to the *forgiveness* of *sins.* ▪ ▪ All the Judean *countryside* and the people of *Jerusalem* went out to him in *great* numbers. ▪ ▪ They were being *baptized* by him in the *Jordan River* ▪ as they *confessed* their sins. ▪ ▪ John was clothed in *camel's* hair, ▪ and wore a leather *belt* around his waist. ▪ ▪ His food was *grasshoppers* and wild *honey.* ▪ ▪ The *theme* of his preaching was: ▪ ▪ "One more *powerful* than I is to come *after* me. ▪ ▪ I am not *fit* to stoop and untie his *sandal* straps. ▪ ▪ *I* have baptized you in *water:* ▪ ▪ *he* will baptize you ▪ in the *Holy Spirit.*" ▪ ▪ ▪

the object, increase your volume and tempo for "on that day . . . with a roar." Then go slower again when you tell us our layers of cover-ups will be removed and all our deeds "made manifest."

The second paragraph starts awkwardly. Instead of "what sort of men must you not be," the Revised NAB says "what sort of persons ought you to be." "How" is dropped and the question answered: You should be "Holy in your conduct . . . looking for the coming of the day of God . . . and trying to hasten it." The image of fiery destruction should be convincing and unsettling. But then comfort comes to the fore as you explain why everything must melt in a blaze: so that a new heaven and earth can replace the old! Speak that sentence slowly, with joy, as if watching that new world being born. Remain upbeat for the last sentence as you tell us that in our waiting, and even in our struggle to live "without stain," we anticipate the joy of that future world.

GOSPEL The gospel is good news. We've heard that thousands of times and we've told our people that as many times. When we say "Here begins the gospel of Jesus" we must sound like we know that what we're about to share is good news for all; it's good news worth sharing!

Quote Isaiah with the awareness that you are identifying his "messenger" with John the Baptizer. In fact, you can use John's voice to speak the Isaian quote, the same voice you'll employ later to say, "One more powerful than I. . . ." There is excitement in the announcement, the same excitement you might employ to alert a crowd that a long-awaited hero has arrived.

John was a pivotal character in the messianic drama. Describe his "baptism of repentance" aware of the import of his activity, and relate with humble awe the success of this strange man's ministry: "*All* the Judean countryside . . . in *great* numbers . . . *confessed* their sins!" The fascination with his attire and diet serves to accentuate his success, for your tone insinuates: "How could such a man attract such crowds?"

John speaks for himself about the one to come after him. Make his voice insistent, as if he must convince the crowds that he is *not* who they think he is. He need not be the lunatic of some biblical films; instead give his voice a humble yet strong quality as he asserts his unworthiness to "untie his sandal straps." The final sentence is the climax. It is not simply a statement of facts but a qualitative comparison: I have given you a glass of water, John says, but he will serve you the wine of the Spirit!

READING I Cause and effect readings are marvelous if the author has constructed a bridge to move you from one side to the other. Unfortunately the lectionary editors have dismantled Isaiah's bridge (the second part of verse 2 through verse 10 are skipped) and pulled the two shores right alongside each other, requiring an instantaneous transition.

The first nine lines announce the wonderful things God's Spirit has done *to* you and *through* you: "You" meaning yourself in the persona of the prophet and as proclaimer speaking to the "lowly" and "brokenhearted" in the pews of your church. The assertions about God's Spirit being upon you, anointing you and sending you must be spoken humbly: You know what you say is true because you've been shaken to your core by the experience; now share the news aware that your selection was the result not of your worthiness but of God's mercy.

A growing conviction charges your voice when you speak of healing and "liberty" and "release," your eyes meeting others in the assembly who need to be convinced that God is this generous. Pause, perhaps shutting your eyes as if to envision all you've announced coming true, then launch into the expression of joy that comprises the second half of the reading.

There are few things more pathetic than a lector who says "I rejoice" with no energy and a glum expression! Your tone should say, "I can hardly believe I've been so lucky!" Sense God's goodness surrounding you even as you speak: Communicate wedding day joy and exploit the rich imagery of crowns and jewels and new life springing from a fertile earth. It's all beautiful and glowing and too wonderful to hold in. So don't.

READING II Please don't paste on a Pollyanna smile and tell us to rejoice and pray and give thanks! Paul's time words (always, never, constant) are the key to his message. He doesn't call for blindness to life's trials; on the contrary, he asks us to keep our eyes open and rejoice anyway. When speaking each admonition, remember that you're asking us to rejoice even if a loved one has died, to give thanks even if we are unemployed, to keep praying even as we dine on the bitter dish of failure. Only one who has suffered and clung to faith could ask the near impossible of us, and no doubt with a hushed and humble voice.

Continue instructing, imagining there is imminent danger that we might do precisely what you're asking us to avoid. You know the importance of the spirit, prophecies,

DECEMBER 16, 1990

THIRD SUNDAY OF ADVENT

LECTIONARY #8

READING I Isaiah 61:1–2, 10–11

A reading from the book of the prophet ▪
Isaiah **▪▪▪**

Speak for Isaiah and yourself, humbly but with excitement and growing joy.

The *spirit* of the Lord *God* is upon me, ▪
because the Lord has *anointed* me; ▪▪
He has *sent* me to bring *glad tidings*

Address the "lowly" in your assembly.

to the *lowly,* ▪
to *heal* the *brokenhearted,* ▪▪
To proclaim *liberty* to the *captives* ▪
and *release* to the *prisoners,* ▪▪

With conviction.

To announce a year of *favor* from the Lord ▪

Pause.

and a day of *vindication* by our God. ▪▪▪

I rejoice *heartily* in the Lord, ▪

Smile. Imagine promises coming true.

in my God is the *joy* of my soul; ▪▪
For he has *clothed* me with a robe of *salvation,* ▪

"Wrapped" sounds like it means.

and *wrapped* me in a mantle of *justice,* ▪▪
Like a *bridegroom* adorned with a *diadem,* ▪

Pause, then new build.

like a *bride* bedecked with her *jewels.* ▪▪
As the earth brings forth its *plants,* ▪
and a *garden* makes its growth *spring* up, ▪▪
So will the Lord God make *justice* and *praise*

Are you still smiling?

spring up before *all* the *nations.* ▪▪▪

READING II 1 Thessalonians 5:16–24

Short reading = slow reading.

A reading from the first letter of *Paul* ▪
to the *Thessalonians* ▪▪▪

Use pauses. Recall the times it's hard to follow these instructions.

Rejoice always, ▪▪ *never* cease praying, ▪▪ render *constant* thanks; ▪▪ such is God's *will* for you in Christ *Jesus.* ▪▪▪

Don't speed up. Convince us this is important.

Do not *stifle* the spirit. ▪▪ Do not despise *prophecies.* ▪▪ *Test everything;* ▪▪ retain what is *good.* ▪▪ *Avoid* any semblance of *evil.* ▪▪▪

A prayer. Visualize someone for whom you pray.

May the God of *peace* make you *perfect* in holiness. ▪▪ May you be preserved *whole* and *entire,* ▪▪ *spirit,* ▪ *soul,* ▪ and *body,* ▪ *irreproachable* at the coming of our Lord Jesus Christ. ▪▪ He who *calls* us is *trustworthy,* ▪▪ therefore he *will* do it. ▪▪▪

GOSPEL John 1:6–8, 19–28

A reading from the holy *gospel* according to *John* ▪ ▪ ▪

Speak of John with familiarity and love.

Dropping "men" is more inclusive.

There was a man named *John* sent by God, ▪ who came as a *witness* to testify to the *light,* ▪ so that *through* him all men might *believe*— ▪ ▪ but only to *testify* to the light, ▪ for he himself was *not* the light. ▪ ▪ ▪

Use character placement technique. Change vocal quality for John and priests.

The testimony John *gave* when the Jews sent *priests* and *Levites* from Jerusalem to ask ▪ ▪ *"Who are* you?" ▪ ▪ was the absolute statement, ▪ ▪ "I am not the *Messiah."* ▪ ▪ They questioned him *further,* ▪ ▪ *"Who,* then? ▪ *Elijah?"* ▪ ▪ "I am *not* Elijah," ▪ he answered. ▪ ▪ "Are you the *prophet?"* ▪ ▪ *"No,"* ▪ he replied. ▪ ▪ ▪

Veiling hostility.

Aware of enormity of role.

Finally they said to him: ▪ ▪ *"Tell* us who you are, ▪ so that we can give some *answer* to those who *sent* us. ▪ ▪ What do you have to *say* for yourself?" ▪ ▪ He said, ▪ quoting the prophet *Isaiah,* ▪ ▪ "I am ▪
'a *voice* in the desert, ▪ *crying* out: ▪ ▪
Make *straight* the way of the Lord!'" ▪ ▪ ▪

Less veiling, more hostility. Baptizing will be nothing compared to what the Messiah will do.

Like a prayer.

An aside, as if these were familiar locations.

Those whom the *Pharisees* had sent proceeded to question him *further:* ▪ ▪ "If you are *not* the Messiah, ▪ nor *Elijah,* ▪ nor the *prophet,* ▪ ▪ why do you *baptize?"* ▪ ▪ John *answered* them: ▪ ▪ "I baptize with *water.* ▪ ▪ There is one *among* you whom you do not *recognize*— ▪ the one who is to come *after* me— ▪ ▪ the strap of whose sandal I am not *worthy* to *unfasten."* ▪ ▪ ▪ This happened in *Bethany,* ▪ across the *Jordan,* ▪ where John was *baptizing.* ▪ ▪ ▪

testing everything; persuade us to do what you ask by convincing us of the importance of each caution.

If the entire passage were a letter to a distant loved one, the final sentences would be your prayerful salutation. Again you're asking the impossible, only now of God, who is to make us "perfect in holiness." The last sentence gives meaning to all that preceded. Why have you asked so insistently for the impossible? Because the one who calls us "is *trustworthy* . . . [and] will do it!" Of course, only if you have placed your own trust in God can you convincingly ask us to do the same.

GOSPEL If a person can embody a season, then certainly John embodies Advent. Even his effort to assert who he is anticipates our own struggle to hang on to the identity of this slippery season that the commercial world has stolen from us and turned into a time of garish superficialities. John's simple self-identification tells us the purpose of Advent: not frenzied shopping and partying, but making "straight the way of the Lord." In a culture which has surrendered its precious symbols of trees, wreaths, lights and music to a commercial system that uses them to hawk their goods, we *need* to hear a voice crying out the nature of this season. So John makes a second appearance in as many weeks saying the raised "voice" must be our own, calling attention to the "one among [us]" who still goes unrecognized.

The stress in the passage goes to the efforts to identify. That requires slow and insistent reading. John was an enigma. Layer by layer you approach the core of his identity—a witness, but not the light, not the Messiah, not Elijah and not the prophet—but a voice, a voice proclaiming boldly to prepare for one who will be far greater than himself.

The priests' voice becomes increasingly frustrated while John's remains strong but unemotional. There is emotion, however, when he says who he is; the emotion coming from his awareness of the magnitude of his responsibility—speak as if it were on your shoulders to turn around this materialistic culture of ours in one Advent season.

Missing or ignoring his point, the questioners persist with barely concealed hostility: "Why do you baptize?" Minimizing his own ministry, he urges and prays that they look about and recognize the disguised God among them.

READING I Today, as always, it's best to start with the gospel. A divine messenger tells Mary she is chosen and comforts her with reassurance that God's plan will produce a ruler who will reign forever from David's throne. God is the initiator; God makes the promises: Mary listens in awed silence to guarantees of future blessings. David is another story. *He* initiates. He thinks *he* can do something for *God.* God questions David, who must listen in humbled silence as God speaks.

Narrate the opening as if you were David surveying your comfortable kingdom, reviewing your triumphs and deciding it's time to show some appreciation by doing God a big favor. Speak with presumption in David's voice, so that God's reaction will not seem capricious and unjust.

God rejects David's idea and reminds him that he is where he is because of divine favor. Like a scolded schoolboy David must listen to God listing how *"I"* did this and *"I"* did that for you. With energy, enthusiasm and pride God goes on to list what else will be done for David. Like a teacher whom the student wanted to honor God says, "No, you won't honor me, I'm going to honor you." The revelation in the last line is the best. Precede it with a pause and then, with love for this impulsive student, say that God won't be outdone in generosity.

READING II If Paul weren't compelled to say six things on the way to his making a point, proclaiming this passage would be much easier. Here he uses 76 words to say: Praise God! If only the economy of his "Amen" characterized the rest of his writing; after all, how many passages require you to plan your *breathing*? But enough complaining; let's roll up our sleeves and get working!

The message is simple:

To him who is able to strengthen you in the gospel which I proclaim when I preach Jesus Christ, the gospel which reveals the mystery [which was] hidden for many ages but [is] now manifested through the writings of the prophets, and [which was—this same gospel] at the command of the eternal God, made known to all the Gentiles that they may believe and obey—*to him,* the God who alone is wise, *may glory be given through Jesus Christ unto endless ages. Amen.*

Everything from the first to the second "to him" is parenthetical. Even the phrase after the second "to him" is parenthetical; only the italics represent Paul's main point. While winding round the clauses, remember where you're headed. Don't rush toward the goal or

DECEMBER 23, 1990

FOURTH SUNDAY OF ADVENT

LECTIONARY #11

READING I 2 Samuel 7:1–5, 8–11, 16

A reading from the second book of *Samuel* ▪ ▪ ▪

Assume David's confident attitude.

When *King David* was settled in his *palace,* ▪ and the Lord had given him *rest* from his enemies on *every* side, ▪ he said to *Nathan* the prophet, ▪ ▪ "Here

A touch of condescension.

I am living in a house of *cedar,* ▪ while the *ark* of *God* dwells in a *tent!"* ▪ ▪ Nathan *answered* the

Sincerely approve the plan.

king, ▪ ▪ *"Go,* ▪ do *whatever* you have in mind, ▪ for the Lord is *with* you." ▪ ▪ But that *night* the Lord

Anticipate God's disapproval.

spoke to Nathan and said: ▪ ▪ *"Go,* ▪ tell my servant *David,* ▪ ▪ 'Thus says the *Lord:* ▪ ▪ Should *you* build *me* a house to dwell in?' ▪ ▪

Here's what I've done for you!

"'It was *I* who took you from the *pasture* and from the care of the *flock* ▪ to be *commander* of my people *Israel.* ▪ ▪ *I* have been with you *wherever* you went, ▪ and I have *destroyed* all your *enemies* before

Here's what I will do for you. You love this impetuous king.

you. ▪ ▪ And I will make you *famous* like the *great* ones of the earth. ▪ ▪ I will fix a *place* for my people Israel; ▪ ▪ I will *plant* them so that they may *dwell* in their place without further *disturbance.* ▪ ▪ Neither shall the *wicked* continue to *afflict* them as they did

"Since the time . . . Israel": spoken as an aside.

of *old,* ▪ since the time I first appointed *judges* over my people Israel. ▪ ▪ I will give you *rest* from *all*

Pause. Best promise is last.

your enemies. ▪ ▪ The Lord *also* reveals to you ▪ that *he* will establish a house for *you.* ▪ ▪ Your *house*

Again, convey God's love for David.

and your *kingdom* shall endure *forever* before me; ▪ ▪ your *throne* shall stand *firm* forever.'" ▪ ▪ ▪

READING II Romans 16:25–27

Short reading = slow reading. Decide where you'll catch your breath.

A reading from the letter of *Paul* ▪ to the *Romans* ▪ ▪ ▪

Stress "him" and "gospel."

To *him* who is able to *strengthen* you in the *gospel* ▪ which I *proclaim* when I preach *Jesus Christ,* ▪ the gospel which reveals the *mystery* ▪ *hidden* for many ages ▪ but now *manifested* through the writings of the *prophets,* ▪ *and,* ▪ at the command of the eternal *God,* ▪ made known to all the *Gentiles* ▪ that they may *believe* and *obey—* ▪ ▪ to *him,* ▪ the God who *alone* is wise, ▪ may *glory* be given through *Jesus Christ* ▪ unto *endless* ages. ▪ ▪ *Amen.* ▪ ▪ ▪

You're still talking about "the gospel."

Main point and climax.

Breathe and shift focus before "Amen."

GOSPEL Luke 1:26–38

A reading from the holy *gospel* according to *Luke* ▪ ▪ ▪

The angel *Gabriel* was sent from *God* ▪ to a town of Galilee named *Nazareth,* ▪ to a *virgin* betrothed to a man named *Joseph,* ▪ of the house of *David.* ▪ ▪ The virgin's name ▪ was *Mary.* ▪ ▪ Upon arriving, ▪ the angel *said* to her: ▪ ▪ *"Rejoice,* O highly *favored* daughter! ▪ ▪ The *Lord* is with you. ▪ *Blessed* are you among women." ▪ ▪ ▪ She was *deeply troubled* by his words, ▪ and *wondered* what his greeting *meant.* ▪ ▪ The angel *went on* to say to her: ▪ ▪ "Do not *fear,* Mary. ▪ You have found *favor* with God. ▪ You shall *conceive* and bear a *son* ▪ and give him the name ▪ *Jesus.* ▪ ▪ *Great* will be his dignity ▪ and he will be called *Son* of the *Most High.* ▪ ▪ The Lord God will *give* him the throne of *David* his father. ▪ ▪ He will *rule* over the house of Jacob *forever* ▪ and his *reign* will be without *end."* ▪ ▪ ▪

Comfort even before you frighten her. Use the pauses.

Pause and let your face express what you describe.

Persuade as well as inform.

Mary said to the angel, ▪ "How can this *be* ▪ since I do not *know* man?" ▪ ▪ The angel answered her: ▪ ▪ "The *Holy Spirit* will come upon you ▪ and the power of the *Most High* will *overshadow* you; ▪ ▪ hence, ▪ the holy offspring to be born ▪ will be called *Son* of *God.* ▪ ▪ Know that *Elizabeth* your kinswoman ▪ has conceived a *son* in her old age; ▪ she who was thought to be *sterile* ▪ is now in her *sixth month,* ▪ ▪ for *nothing* is impossible with God." ▪ ▪ ▪

Fear dominates again.

Rev. NAB: "since I have no relations with a man."

Reassuring.

Emphasis on "nothing" (not even a virgin birth).

Almost a whisper.

Mary said: ▪ "I am the *maidservant* of the Lord. ▪ Let it be *done* to me as you *say."* ▪ ▪ With that ▪ ▪ the angel *left* her. ▪ ▪ ▪

Looking at assembly.

you'll create a muddle. Your tone says: We're still moving toward the point . . . we're almost there . . . not yet . . . right around the corner . . . now . . . no wait . . . *here* it is! Do all that with a smile, deep joy and the awareness that you are singing praise to a great and generous God.

GOSPEL Consult the commentary for the Immaculate Conception gospel for further insights into this reading.

As noted in the commentary on the first reading, Mary stands in contrast to David, yet with both characters the same point is made: God is in control and only when we yield to God's sovereignty can God's power be released in our lives and lead us to glory.

On the feast of the Immaculate Conception this gospel serves to highlight the theme of Mary's selection by God. Today its purpose is different. Who better than Mary illustrates Advent's pervasive theme of waiting? Waiting often involves a cycle of becoming afraid and being comforted until the anticipated event arrives. That tells us much about how to proclaim this gospel passage. Place your emphasis on Mary's "deeply troubled" responses to the angel's greeting and to the announcement that she will bear a child ("How can this be . . .?"). Equal emphasis goes to the angel's reassurances: "Do not fear . . . the Holy Spirit will come upon you."

Mary speaks her "yes" without understanding its implications, but with a simple acknowledgement (not void of fear) that as God's servant she will do what she's asked.

READING I Imagine a friend, who had given up hope of ever conceiving a child, confiding in you that she is pregnant. Then she swears you to secrecy. Finally something happens that convinces you that, permission or not, you must share the news. Speak to and about such a person as you proclaim the song that is tonight's first reading. The prophet is full of news that can't be withheld, and all of it is good.

Twice in the passage ("silent . . . quiet," "crown . . . diadem") an idea is stated in the first of a pair of lines and immediately repeated, with slightly different words, in the second. This repetition becomes a redundancy only if you render both lines with the same inflection, color and energy. Stress different parts of the parallel structures and you'll achieve both emphasis and variety.

Let words like "vindication," "victory" and "glory" contrast with the gloom and disappointment that would have been had the womb remained barren. Let the joy continue to build, all the while visualizing the growing child. "No more shall . . ." briefly changes the mood and recalls the hopelessness of the "forsaken" and "desolate" days. But immediately the painful memories are dismissed in favor of images of hope and joy.

Speak the last six lines slowly and with much effort to persuade, giving the second line of each couplet the greater emphasis and conviction. But stress "you" the final three times it appears.

READING II Paul is in a setting much like yours. He is not writing a letter, but addressing an assembly in a worship space: responding to the synagogue officials' request that anyone with an exhortation for the people should speak. Today's passage ends, however, where that exhortation begins. Our text is really Paul's introduction, his warm-up. Rather than the fervor usually required for Paul, you can exercise some reserve. In preparing to announce the good news of Jesus, Paul first briefly reviews salvation history. The review is important for us as well. So call your assembly to listen, knowing they are among the "others who reverence our God."

Speak of Egypt with a sense that your listeners know the story but can profit from a reminder. David, too, is well known. Paul's point is that God provided kings to watch over Israel. As God, speak of David with pride, but with less emotion than if David were the central character of the passage. The next sentence gets as close as any is going to get to being the climax of the passage, so turn up the energy a bit.

DECEMBER 24, 1990

CHRISTMAS VIGIL

LECTIONARY #13

READING I Isaiah 62:1–5

A reading from the book of the prophet ▪
Isaiah **▪ ▪ ▪**

You can't hold it in!

For *Zion's* sake I will *not* be silent, ▪ ▪
for *Jerusalem's* sake I will not be *quiet,* ▪
Until her *vindication* shines forth like the *dawn* ▪
and her *victory* like a burning *torch.* ▪ ▪

Nations shall behold your vindication, ▪
and all *kings* your *glory;* ▪ ▪
You shall be called by a *new* name ▪
pronounced by the mouth of the *Lord.* ▪ ▪
You shall be a glorious *crown* in the *hand*
of the Lord, ▪
a *royal* diadem held by your *God.* ▪ ▪

Past hopelessness recalled. "Men" can be "people."

No more shall men call *you* ▪ *"Forsaken,"* ▪ ▪
or your *land* ▪ *"Desolate,"* ▪ ▪

Present joy!

But you *shall* be called ▪ *"My Delight,"* ▪ ▪
and your *land* ▪ *"Espoused."* ▪ ▪

"You!"

For the Lord *delights* in *you,* ▪
and makes your land his *spouse.* ▪ ▪

Tender marriage imagery.

As a young man *marries* a virgin, ▪

"You!"

your *Builder* shall marry *you;* ▪ ▪
And as a bridegroom *rejoices* in his bride ▪

"You!"

so shall your *God* ▪ rejoice in *you.* ▪ ▪ ▪

READING II Acts 13:16–17, 22–25

A reading from the *Acts* of the *Apostles* **▪ ▪ ▪**

Include entire assembly with eye contact.

Rev. NAB says: "our ancestors."

With pride.

[When *Paul* came to Antioch Pisidia, ▪ he entered the *synagogue* there] ▪ and motioning to them for *silence,* ▪ he began: ▪ ▪ "Fellow *Israelites* ▪ and you others who *reverence* our God, ▪ *listen* to what I have to say! ▪ ▪ The *God* of the people Israel once *chose* our *fathers.* ▪ ▪ He made this people *great* during their sojourn in the land of *Egypt,* ▪ and 'with an *outstretched* arm' ▪ he *led* them out of it. ▪ ▪ God raised up David as their *king;* ▪ ▪ on *his* behalf he testified, ▪ ▪ 'I have found *David* ▪ son of Jesse ▪

to be a man after my own *heart* ▪ who will fulfill my *every* wish.' ▪ ▪ ▪

Set off the word "Jesus" with pauses.

"According to his *promise,* ▪ God has brought forth from this man's *descendants* ▪ *Jesus,* ▪ a *savior* for Israel. ▪ ▪ John heralded the *coming* of Jesus ▪ by proclaiming a baptism of *repentance* to *all* the people of Israel. ▪ ▪ As John's career was coming to an *end,* ▪ he would say, ▪ ▪ 'What you *suppose* me to be ▪ I am *not.* ▪ ▪ Rather, ▪ look for the one who comes *after* me. ▪ ▪ I am not *worthy* ▪ to unfasten the *sandals* on his feet.'" ▪ ▪ ▪

John is insistent.

Slow down last sentence.

But immediately Paul returns to his summary. Keep the reading from fizzling out by speaking as John on the final sentences. John can sound a bit frustrated, perhaps even irritable. Then shift mood suddenly for the last line. Give it sincerity and great humility. Allow that famous line to echo in your listeners' minds long after you have finished.

GOSPEL Matthew 1:1–25

The beginning of the holy *gospel* according to *Matthew* ▪ ▪ ▪

Without rushing. Solemnly.

A family record of *Jesus Christ,* ▪ son of *David,* ▪ son of *Abraham.* ▪ ▪ ▪ *Abraham* was the father of *Isaac,* ▪ Isaac the father of *Jacob,* ▪ Jacob the father of *Judah* and his brothers. ▪ ▪

Renew the energy every few lines. The pronunciation guide in the back of this book will come in handy for rehearsal.

Judah was the father of *Perez* and *Zerah,* ▪
whose *mother* was *Tamar.* ▪ ▪
Perez was the father of *Hezron,* ▪
Hezron the father of *Ram.* ▪ ▪
Ram was the father of *Amminadab,* ▪
Amminadab the father of *Nahshon,* ▪
Nahshon the father of *Salmon.* ▪ ▪
Salmon was the father of *Boaz,* ▪
whose *mother* was *Rahab,* ▪ ▪
Boaz was the father of *Obed,* ▪
whose *mother* was *Ruth.* ▪ ▪
Obed was the father of *Jesse,* ▪
Jesse the father of *King David.* ▪ ▪
David was the father of *Solomon,* ▪
whose *mother* had been the wife of *Uriah.* ▪ ▪
Solomon was the father of *Rehoboam,* ▪
Rehoboam the father of *Abijah,* ▪
Abijah the father of *Asa.* ▪ ▪
Asa was the father of *Jehoshaphat,* ▪
Jehoshaphat the father of *Joram,* ▪
Joram the father of *Uzziah.* ▪ ▪
Uzziah was the father of *Jotham,* ▪
Jotham the father of *Ahaz,* ▪
Ahaz the father of *Hezekiah.* ▪ ▪
Hezekiah was the father of *Manasseh,* ▪
Manasseh the father of *Amos,* ▪
Amos the father of *Josiah.* ▪ ▪ ▪

Recognize these more familiar names.

GOSPEL This genealogy lends solemnity to the liturgy of the word. To achieve a proclamation that can hold the assembly will be challenging, but worth the effort.

If you were to glance at your family tree, doubtless certain names would leap out at you provoking a smile of recognition while others would leave your face blank. It's not necessary here that each name be read with a distinctive quality. The rhythm of the repetitions is like a litany. Let the more familiar names cause you to slow down, as images of that character's life color the way you speak the name. There should be enough familiar names to sustain interest throughout the reading. This is not the genealogy of one nuclear family, but of all God's people. Read with that awareness. (If two voices are employed for the genealogy as a means of sustaining interest—not a bad idea—then a solo third voice should read the nativity account that follows the genealogy.)

A more intimate tone is appropriate for the birth story. You are describing a delicate situation, so you must speak of it delicately. The sentence about Mary has a "bad news—good news" quality. "She was found with child," *but* "through the power of the Holy Spirit."

Communicate Joseph's sensitivity by taking time on the "upright man" clause and inserting a brief pause before the word "quietly." Assuming the character of the angel, let your tone convince and reassure a hurt and frightened Joseph that he should have "no fear."

Shift from persuasion to proclamation, and let the prophet's voice announce the coming of Emmanuel. Be sure to take time with the name's translation. The final sentences are somewhat anticlimactic but contain important information. Conclude the story simply, but sustain your eye contact for a moment after speaking the name "Jesus."

Josiah became the father of *Jechoniah* and his
brothers ▪ at the time of the
Babylonian exile. ▪▪
After the Babylonian exile ▪
Jechoniah was the father of *Shealtiel,* ▪
Shealtiel the father of *Zerubbabel.* ▪▪
Zerubbabel was the father of *Abiud,* ▪
Abiud the father of *Eliakim,* ▪
Eliakim the father of *Azor.* ▪▪
Azor was the father of *Zadok,* ▪
Zadok the father of *Achim,* ▪
Achim the father of *Eliud.* ▪▪
Eliud was the father of *Eleazar,* ▪
Eleazar the father of *Matthan,* ▪
Matthan the father of *Jacob.* ▪▪
Jacob was the father of *Joseph* ▪
the *husband* ▪ of *Mary.* ▪▪
It was of *her* ▪ that Jesus who is called the
Messiah ▪ was *born.* ▪▪▪
Thus the total number of *generations* is: ▪▪

Deliberate redundancy. Stress "fourteen" each time.

from Abraham to David, ▪ *fourteen*
generations; ▪▪
from David to the Babylonian *captivity,* ▪
fourteen generations; ▪▪
from the Babylonian captivity to the *Messiah,* ▪
fourteen generations. ▪▪▪

A third solo voice may take over here if two readers proclaimed genealogy.

The bad news: "found with child." The good news: "through the . . . Holy Spirit."

Painful for Joseph.

Speak the angel's words tenderly yet powerfully.

Now this is how the *birth* of Jesus Christ came about. ▪▪ When his mother *Mary* was engaged to *Joseph,* ▪ but before they *lived* together, ▪ she was found with *child* ▪▪ through the power of the *Holy Spirit.* ▪▪ *Joseph* ▪ her husband, ▪ an *upright* man *unwilling* to expose her to the *law,* ▪ decided to *divorce* her ▪ *quietly.* ▪▪ Such was his intention ▪ when *suddenly* the angel of the Lord appeared in a *dream* ▪ and said to him: ▪▪ *"Joseph,* ▪ son of David, ▪ have no *fear* about taking Mary as your *wife.* ▪▪ It is by the *Holy Spirit* that she has *conceived* this child. ▪ She is to have a *son* ▪ and you are to name him ▪ *Jesus* ▪ because he will *save* his people from their *sins."* ▪▪▪ All this happened ▪ to *fulfill* what the Lord had said through the prophet: ▪▪

"The *virgin* shall be with *child* ▪
and give birth to a *son,* ▪▪
and they shall call him ▪ *Emmanuel,"* ▪

"God is with us." Climax of reading.

a name which means ▪ *"God is with us."* ▪▪▪

Emphasis on "any."

As he had been instructed.

When Joseph awoke ▪ he *did* as the angel of the Lord had *directed* him ▪ and *received* her into his home as his *wife.* ▪▪ He had no relations with her at *any* time before she bore a son, ▪ whom he *named* ▪ *Jesus.* ▪▪▪

[Shorter: Matthew 1:18–25]

DECEMBER 25, 1990

CHRISTMAS MIDNIGHT

LECTIONARY #14

READING I Isaiah 9:1–6

A reading from the book of the prophet ▪ *Isaiah* ▪ ▪ ▪

Create the contrasts.

The people who walked in *darkness* ▪
have seen a *great light;* ▪ ▪
Upon those who dwelt in the land of *gloom* ▪
a *light* has *shone.* ▪ ▪
You have brought them abundant *joy*
and *great* rejoicing, ▪
As they rejoice before you as at the *harvest,* ▪
as men make *merry* when dividing *spoils.* ▪ ▪

"Men" could be "victors."

Slow. For the *yoke* that *burdened* them, ▪
Slow. the *pole* on their *shoulder,* ▪
Slow. And the *rod* of their *taskmaster* ▪
Faster. you have *smashed,* ▪ as on the day of Midian. ▪ ▪
Slow. For every *boot* that tramped in *battle,* ▪
Slow. every *cloak* rolled in *blood,* ▪
Faster. will be *burned* as fuel for flames. ▪ ▪ ▪

Gently.

For a *child* is born to us, ▪ a *son* is *given* us; ▪
upon his shoulder *dominion* rests. ▪ ▪

Regally. Each title is different.

They name him ▪ *Wonder-Counselor,* ▪
God-Hero, ▪
Father-Forever, ▪ *Prince* of *Peace.* ▪ ▪

The sense of this sentence is: His dominion (which he exercises) from David's throne and over (David's) kingdom, (and) which he confirms and sustains by judgment and justice both now and forever, is vast and forever peaceful.

His dominion is *vast*
and *forever peaceful,* ▪
From *David's* throne, ▪ and over his *kingdom,* ▪
which he *confirms* and *sustains* ▪
By *judgment* and *justice,* ▪
both *now* and *forever.* ▪ ▪ ▪

Persuade.

The *zeal* of the Lord of hosts ▪ *will do* this! ▪ ▪ ▪

READING I We are fortunate to have so much of Isaiah in the lectionary. Isaiah had not only the gift of prophecy, but of poetry as well. The first half of the reading is full of contrasts: light and darkness, oppression and freedom. You'll need first to draw clear, sharp pictures, then make quick shifts to the contrasting image. Capture the feelings of hopelessness and depression in the "darkness" and "gloom" lines through a slow and measured delivery and appropriate facial expression. Then, like the switching on of a lamp, brighten your face and your vocal delivery on the two "light" lines. Continue building the joy through the next sentence.

The sobering images of burdens and oppression require you to resume a somber mood. Build slowly through the "yoke," "pole" and "rod" images, increasing your intensity, but not your pace; then "smash" the images with the final line of the sentence, increasing your rate and intensity. Repeat the pattern on "tramped," "blood" and "burned."

Begin the final section of the passage with warmhearted affection for the newborn child. Then immediately sound a note of majesty and authority as you sing the praises of the ideal monarch you describe; sustain that tone throughout the "dominion" sentence, which is awkward but replete with royal imagery. You have prophesied the glorious reign of a future, ideal king who will liberate the people from all oppression. Use the final line to convince your listeners this will occur.

READING II This reading begins with a "birth announcement." Paul's "grace" is the same dark-dispelling "light" of Isaiah's reading. Herald this good news, then, with enthusiasm and high energy.

This reading might look like another of Paul's lists of dos and don'ts. But it is really much more. Paul is proclaiming the consequences of the Messiah's advent; the effect on us of light shining in our darkness. Read the second sentence not as an exhortation of what we *should do* but as an announcement of what we *can* do now that grace has appeared.

"Eager" in the last line needs strong emphasis. It captures the mood of the entire reading. Our awareness of the "appearing" (in Latin, *"adventus,"* in Greek, *"epiphaneia"*) does not leave us unmoved. Instead it makes us eager to respond.

GOSPEL In the *Peanuts* Christmas special, Charlie Brown struggles against his friends' commercialism but fails to create a true Christmas spirit among them. He finally shouts his frustration in an almost cosmic question: "Does anybody know what Christmas is all about?" Matter-of-factly Linus replies, "I do." Standing center stage in a pool of light, he begins: "And there were in the same country shepherds abiding in the fields. . . ."

Through an ordinary childish voice the familiar poetry of the King James Version conveyed the solemnity and holiness of the night. The words said it all. Linus simply spoke them. But he spoke them as only a child could, without the technical tricks of a trained orator but with a sense of conviction born of belief.

That is your challenge tonight: to allow your belief in the truth of this story to color your telling of it. It should not be flat or sound like the evening news but be infused with a quiet intensity. Luke writes with the conviction of an editorial writer giving details about Jesus' birth that add a human dimension to the birth narrative of the Son of God.

Go very slowly, then, one phrase at a time, to allow the words to do their work. Their familiarity is comforting and reassuring. There is a sacredness in the cadences, a sense of wonder wrought by the imagery. This passage conjures up a nostalgia that few other scriptures can. Consider using the Revised New American Bible translation that restores many of the familiar phrases rendered awkwardly by the NAB.

READING II Titus 2:11–14

A reading from the letter of *Paul* ▪ to *Titus* ▪ ▪ ▪

"The grace of God" = Isaiah's "great light." "Men" can be dropped for inclusive reading.

All this is now possible for us.

Don't slow down. High energy.

The grace of God has *appeared,* ▪ offering *salvation* to all men. ▪ ▪ It trains us to *reject* godless ways ▪ and *worldly* desires, ▪ and live *temperately,* ▪ *justly,* ▪ and *devoutly* in this age ▪ as we await our *blessed hope,* ▪ the *appearing* of the glory of the *great God* ▪ and of our *Savior* ▪ Christ Jesus. ▪ ▪ It was he who *sacrificed* himself for us, ▪ to *redeem* us from all *unrighteousness* ▪ and to *cleanse* for himself a people of his *own,* ▪ *eager* ▪ to do what is *right.* ▪ ▪ ▪

GOSPEL Luke 2:1–14

A reading from the holy *gospel* according to *Luke* ▪ ▪ ▪

Tell the story carefully, with a voice filled with wonder.

Significantly.

In those days ▪ Caesar Augustus published a *decree* ▪ ordering a *census* of the *whole world.* ▪ ▪ This *first* census took place while *Quirinius* was governor of *Syria.* ▪ ▪ Everyone went to *register,* ▪ *each* to his own town. ▪ ▪ And so *Joseph* ▪ went from the town of *Nazareth* in Galilee ▪ to *Judea,* ▪ to David's town of *Bethlehem—* ▪ because he was of the *house* and *lineage* of David— ▪ to register with *Mary,* ▪ his espoused *wife,* ▪ who was with *child.* ▪ ▪ ▪

Rev. NAB says: "the time came for her to have her child."

Rev. NAB says: "the inn."

While they were there ▪ the days of her confinement ▪ were *completed.* ▪ ▪ She gave birth to her *first-born son* ▪ and wrapped him in *swaddling* clothes ▪ and laid him in a *manger,* ▪ because there was *no room* for them in the place where *travelers* lodged. ▪ ▪ ▪

Boldly.

Subdued fear.

Quiet intensity.

Rev. NAB places "and lying in a manger" at the end of the sentence.

Rev. NAB says: "Glory *to God in the* highest."

There were *shepherds* in the locality, ▪ living in the *fields* ▪ and keeping night watch by *turns* over their flock. ▪ ▪ The *angel* of the Lord *appeared* to them, ▪ as the *glory* of the Lord *shone* around them, ▪ and they were very much *afraid.* ▪ ▪ The angel *said* to them: ▪ ▪ "You have nothing to *fear!* ▪ I come to proclaim *good news* to you— ▪ tidings of great *joy* to be shared by the *whole people.* ▪ ▪ This day in David's city ▪ a *savior* has been born to you, ▪ the *Messiah* and *Lord.* ▪ ▪ Let this be a *sign* to you: ▪ ▪ in a *manger* ▪ you will find an *infant* ▪ *wrapped* in swaddling clothes." ▪ ▪ *Suddenly,* ▪ there was with the angel a *multitude* of the heavenly host, ▪ *praising God* and saying, ▪ ▪

"Glory to God in high heaven, ▪
peace on earth ▪ to those on whom his
favor *rests."* ▪ ▪ ▪

DECEMBER 25, 1990

CHRISTMAS DAWN

LECTIONARY #15

READING I Isaiah 62:11–12

A reading from the book of the prophet ▪ *Isaiah* ▪ ▪ ▪

"Behold" is a better exclamation.

See, ▪ the Lord *proclaims*
to the *ends* of the earth: ▪ ▪
Say to daughter *Zion,* ▪

Bold proclamation.

your *savior comes!* ▪ ▪

No stress on prepositions.

Here is his *reward* with him, ▪
his *recompense* before him. ▪ ▪

Attitude of reconciliation.

They shall be called the *holy* people, ▪
the *redeemed* of the Lord, ▪

"Frequented" = Frih-kwén-ted. ("i" as in "it") ("e" as in "let"). Ritardando. Reassuring.

and *you* shall be called ▪ *"Frequented,"* ▪
a city that is *not forsaken.* ▪ ▪ ▪

READING II Titus 3:4–7

A reading from the letter of *Paul* ▪ to *Titus* ▪ ▪ ▪

Announce salvation, then reason why.

When the *kindness* and *love* of God our Savior *appeared,* ▪ he *saved* us, ▪ not because of any righteous *deeds* we had done, ▪ but because of his *mercy.* ▪ ▪ He saved us through the *baptism* of new birth ▪ and *renewal* by the *Holy Spirit.* ▪ ▪ This Spirit

Enjoy the word "lavished."

he *lavished* on us through Jesus Christ our *Savior,* ▪ that we might be *justified* by his *grace* ▪ and

"In . . . life" = Ritardando.

become *heirs,* ▪ in hope, ▪ of *eternal* life. ▪ ▪ ▪

READING I A short reading requires slow pacing. The Lord has two announcements: The Savior comes; Jerusalem will be renowned. God has chosen you today to make those proclamations. Try substituting "Behold" for "see"; it works better as an exclamation. Then imagine the imperative "say" addressed first of all to *you* as proclaimer, and speak boldly for the Lord asking others to also speak in God's name. Though "reward" and "recompense" are synonyms echoing each other, stress both these words rather than either of the prepositions "with" or "before."

The last four lines of the poem have a softer tone. Speak to an outcast who is being taken back: one who was desolate who is being restored to a position of honor. The last line calls for a very slow delivery, which assures more than it informs your listeners. (Make sure you rehearse the pronunciation of "frequented.")

READING II This reading is straightforward, well reasoned and carefully balanced. Though this is not a songlike poem like the first reading, it too requires a slow and measured delivery. Begin with a stress on the first word "When" and see how that changes the intonation of the whole clause, forcing you to place extra emphasis on "he saved us." Now the well-reasoned balance begins. We were saved *not* because of deeds *but* because of mercy. "He saved us through the *baptism* of new birth and *renewal* by the Spirit."

Christmas Day is a good time to think about abundant generosity. The word "lavished" more than captures the spirit of Christmas giving. Use that word for all it's worth, and rouse your early morning worshipers with the news of God's munificence. A build on "be justified" and "become heirs" will show just how lavish our God is.

GOSPEL This gospel contains a powerful irony: Simple shepherds are the first invited to witness the Christ. Jesus' humanity and our oneness with him is powerfully communicated here.

Though the shepherds' dialogue is rather dignified and formal, they are humble folk who've just conversed with angels. Imagine your own excitement and the anticipation of something even more astonishing on the other side of the hill. Capture that feeling when you speak as the shepherds. Let the words "in haste" tell you how that phrase should be delivered, but slow down as you mention Mary and Joseph. Pause briefly then as if you had been searching and suddenly spotted the child. Let the phrase "and the baby" escape from your lips, then go slowly again to the end of the sentence. Speak "understood" with great significance, giving it all the hindsight that two thousand years can offer.

Try speaking of the shepherds' report with quiet exhilaration. That will set the mood for the next sentence about Mary, which should be characterized by dignity and reverence, letting hindsight once again lend added significance and weight to her pondering. Use a build to keep "glorifying" and "praising" from sounding the same in the final sentence, which speaks about us as well as the shepherds.

GOSPEL Luke 2:15–20

A reading from the holy *gospel* according to *Luke* ▪ ▪ ▪

Breathless excitement.

When the angels had *returned* to heaven, ▪ the *shepherds* said to one another: ▪ ▪ "Let us go over to *Bethlehem* ▪ and *see* this event which the Lord has made *known* to us." ▪ ▪ They went in *haste* ▪ and found *Mary* and *Joseph,* ▪ ▪ and the *baby* lying in the manger; ▪ ▪ once they *saw,* ▪ they *understood* what had been *told* them concerning this child. ▪ ▪ All who *heard* of it ▪ were *astonished* at the report *given* them by the shepherds. ▪ ▪ ▪

"They . . . haste" sounds like what it says. Pause, then slow down on "lying . . . manger."

Brief pause after "things."

Mary *treasured* all these things ▪ ▪ and *reflected* on them in her heart. ▪ ▪ The shepherds returned, ▪ *glorifying* and *praising* God ▪ for all they had *heard* and *seen,* ▪ in *accord* with what had been told them. ▪ ▪ ▪

Two different words. Build.

And us, too!

FROM THE KEY

Preparing to Proclaim. *Always read all three scriptures.* Because the first readings have been chosen according to their relationship with the gospel passage, it is always important to look at those scriptures together. *Always read all three commentaries.* There are reading suggestions in each that can help you with your own passage. As you read the commentaries, refer to the sections of the scripture passage being discussed and make your own margin notations. *Read the scriptures again* using your margin notes and those printed in the text to remind you of the commentary suggestions. *Always read the scriptures aloud,* taking note of stress and pause suggestions. After several readings, alter the pause and stress markings to suit your own style and interpretation. *Form your prayer for the week around the scriptures you will proclaim on Sunday.* You may want to read the scriptures directly from the Bible, because that is the only way one can take note of the context of a particular passage.

Openings and closings. These are two of the three most critical moments in a reading (the third being the climax). First, establish eye contact with the assembly, then announce, from memory, "A reading from. . . ." Say "A (uh) reading from . . ." instead of "Ay reading." Pause (▪ ▪ ▪) and then begin the reading. Names of people are often the first words of a reading, so even when the context may not warrant a stress on the name, it is important to highlight it so that listeners don't miss who the subject is.

Pause (▪ ▪ ▪) at the end of the reading and establish eye contact before announcing (again, from memory) "This is the word (gospel) of the Lord." Your inflection should always signal that the reading is over.

"This is the word . . ." should never catch the assembly by surprise. End as if there were *no* "This is the word. . . ." Then, after a pause to establish eye contact with the assembly, add it on. Maintain eye contact while the assembly makes its response, and only then move away from the lectern.

Both approach and departure from the lectern should be made with reverence, neither too fast (suggesting you're in a hurry) nor too slow (appearing overly pious).

DECEMBER 25, 1990

CHRISTMAS DAY

LECTIONARY #16

READING I Isaiah 52:7–10

A reading from the book of the prophet ▪ *Isaiah* ▪▪▪

How *beautiful* upon the mountains ▪
are the *feet* of him who brings *glad* tidings, ▪
Announcing *peace,* ▪ bearing *good news,* ▪
announcing *salvation,* ▪ and *saying* to Zion, ▪▪
"Your *God* is *King!"* ▪▪▪

The Inclusive Language Lectionary *says "the messenger" instead of "him."*

Hark! ▪▪ Your *watchmen* raise a cry, ▪
together they *shout* for joy, ▪
For they see *directly,* ▪ before their *eyes,* ▪
the Lord *restoring* Zion. ▪▪
Break out together in *song,* ▪
O *ruins* of Jerusalem! ▪▪
For the Lord *comforts* his people, ▪
he *redeems* Jerusalem. ▪▪
The Lord has *bared* his holy arm
in the sight of *all* the nations; ▪▪
All the ends of the earth will *behold* ▪
the *salvation* of our God. ▪▪▪

The Inclusive Language Lectionary *says "sentries."*

Right in front of their eyes!

Quieter.

You know all this is true.

Climax.

Ritardando.

READING II Hebrews 1:1–6

A reading from the letter to the *Hebrews* ▪▪▪

In times *past,* ▪ God spoke in *fragmentary* and *varied* ways to our fathers ▪ through the *prophets;* ▪▪ in this, ▪ the *final* age, ▪ he has spoken to *us* through his *Son,* ▪ whom he has made *heir* of all things ▪ and *through* whom he first *created* the universe. ▪▪ This Son is the *reflection* of the Father's *glory,* ▪ the *exact* representation of the Father's being, ▪ and he *sustains* all things by his powerful *word.* ▪▪▪ When the Son had *cleansed* us from our sins, ▪ he took his seat at the *right* hand of the Majesty in heaven, ▪ as far *superior* to the angels as the *name* he has inherited is superior to *theirs.* ▪▪

To which of the *angels* did God ever say, ▪▪
"You are my *son;* ▪▪ today I have *begotten* you"? ▪▪
Or again, ▪▪
"I will be his *father,* ▪ and he shall be my son"? ▪▪

"Ancestors" is more inclusive.

Emphasize parallel words: "times past" / "final age," "fathers" / "us" and "prophets" / "Son."

From a hymn. More spirited.

Nouns are the key words, not pronouns.

READING I How rich and varied is the literary heritage from which we draw the lectionary readings. Beautiful poetry from an enthronement hymn comprises the first reading. Reading II is excerpted from one of the most distinguished works of the New Testament, while the sublime poetry of John's gospel completes the triad. What a privilege to give vocal life to this beautiful literature!

Think of a joyous event that captures the imagination of the masses: the home team winning the Super Bowl or the royal wedding of Charles and Diana. A news anchor trying to describe the mood of the celebrating crowds would be hard pressed to find adequate words. Isaiah has found words to say that a merciful God comforts and restores a fallen people. Become the news anchor and let Isaiah write your copy. Because you're the commentator, not one of the revelers, start with a reserved exhilaration, but build your energy to a climax in "Your God is King!"

Now the sentinels in their watchtowers pick up the joyous cry of the messenger. Describe that excitement by being excited yourself that God has come to save. Use the repetition in "they see directly, before their eyes" to emphasize the wonder of God's presence.

If you picture a glorious God healing and restoring the most blighted areas of your city, you'll find the right energy to call the city (Jerusalem and yours) to song! If you also recall the ways God has healed and restored you, you'll find the appropriate shift to an intense but intimate tone while saying: "For the Lord comforts. . . ." The last four lines must be spoken with the conviction of an eyewitness who knows these things are true: the news anchor summarizing an event that has been personally as well as publicly moving.

READING II Imagine a presidential news conference where a momentous decision was announced. You as a recognized expert are called upon to comment on the situation and the Chief Executive's handling of it. Your objective is instruction; your tone, didactic; your subject, of highest importance. That's what the author of Hebrews is doing: speaking in an authoritative way on the subject of God's revelation. Step-by-step the author sets up the argument, carefully balancing the ideas: "In times past" God spoke to [*ancestors*] through *prophets,* "in this age" he has spoken to us through the *Son.* Give vocal contrast to the words that balance each other. Continue the lecture precisely articulating these theological points to establish a foundation for your further arguments.

The next paragraph begins an argument designed to lead to a "therefore," which doesn't occur till chapter two and is not part of today's reading. Work against an anticlimactic ending by asking the questions in a way that indicates the answer is obvious to all. But make the final sentence strong, letting your stress of the word "worship" indicate what an extraordinary statement this is.

GOSPEL This is a beautiful but familiar passage, so we have two primary objectives: Convey the beauty without letting the familiarity cause anyone to tune out, thinking, "I already know this passage." The reading is beautifully balanced and moves along almost effortlessly through the use of staircase parallelism (where the last word of one phrase becomes the first word of the next). Communicating the meaning of the text will be relatively easy, particularly if you utilize the words designated for stress. The emphasis goes not to the repeated word but to the word introducing a new idea. Poetry, however, is as concerned with communication of feeling as of meaning. By focusing your energies on showing the emotion in this reading you will create a freshness that should hold even those who already know this passage.

The gospel of John begins as Genesis begins. Of course this is intentional, and of course you should punctuate it. Then continue through the poetry segment as if speaking of someone you know well and love deeply.

The John the Baptist narration need not lose the caring tone you've established, for the "light" here still refers to the one to whom you are strongly bonded. Maintaining this tone will be less jarring than switching to a dispassionate "narrator" voice.

The next poetry segment can move at a faster pace than the first. Create a new build with each of the three sentences, but build also and breathe at the end of each short line. Speak the next narration with less emotion but strong conviction. Build your intensity on the "not," "not," "nor" phrases, then almost whisper "but by God."

Read the "Word became flesh" passage as if you were witnessing the birth of a child with all its attendant awe and joy. Carry the joy through the next John narration and climax it on the line "love following upon love."

The last paragraph will feel anticlimactic. In balancing "law" and "Moses" with "love" and "Jesus," don't become didactic. Reveal, rather, how fortunate we are to have received the revelation of God in Jesus.

And again ▪ when he leads his *first-born* into the
world, ▪ he says, ▪▪
Strong conclusion.
"Let all the angels of God ▪ *worship* him." ▪▪▪

GOSPEL John 1:1–18

The beginning of the holy *gospel* according to *John* ▪▪▪

Echoes of Genesis.
In the *beginning* ▪ was the *Word;* ▪▪
Slowly.
the Word was in God's *presence,* ▪
Ritardando: "and the . . ."
and the *Word was God.* ▪▪
Stress new idea.
He was *present* to God in the beginning. ▪
OK to stress prepositions.
Through him ▪ all things came into *being,* ▪
and *apart* from him ▪ *nothing* came to be. ▪▪
Rev. NAB *says: "and this life was the light of the human race."*
Whatever came to be in him, ▪ found *life,* ▪
life for the *light* of men. ▪▪
The light *shines* on in darkness, ▪
a darkness that did *not* overcome it. ▪▪▪
There was a man named *John* sent by *God,* ▪ who
came as a *witness* ▪ to testify to the *light,* ▪ so that
Dropping "men" is more inclusive.
through him all men might *believe*— ▪ but only to
testify to the light, ▪ for he himself was *not* the
light. ▪▪ The *real* light which gives light to *every*
"One" is more inclusive.
man ▪ was *coming* into the world. ▪▪
Stress these prepositions also.
He was *in* the world, ▪
Faster pace.
and *through* him the world was *made,* ▪
yet the world did not *know* who he was. ▪▪
To his *own* he came, ▪
yet his own did not *accept* him. ▪▪
Any who *did* accept him ▪
he *empowered* to become *children* of God. ▪▪
These are they who *believe* in his name— ▪ who
Achieve emphasis through whisper. "Anyone's" is more inclusive.
were begotten not by *blood,* ▪ not by carnal *desire,* ▪
nor by man's *willing* it, ▪ but by God. ▪▪▪
The Word became *flesh* ▪
As if witnessing the awe-filled birth.
and made his *dwelling* among us, ▪▪
and we have *seen* his glory: ▪
the glory of an only *Son* coming
from the Father, ▪
filled with enduring *love.* ▪▪▪
Joy.
John *testified* to him by *proclaiming,* ▪▪ "This is *he*
of whom I said, ▪▪ 'The one who comes *after* me
Try a slight pause after "was."
ranks *ahead* of me, ▪ for he *was before* me.'" ▪▪
Of his *fullness*
we have all had a *share*— ▪
love following upon *love.* ▪▪
Balance "law" and "love," "Moses" and "Jesus."
For while the *law* was a gift through *Moses,* ▪ this
enduring *love* came through *Jesus Christ.* ▪▪ No one
Avoid didactic tone.
has ever *seen* God. ▪ It is God the only *Son,* ▪ *ever* at
the Father's side, ▪ who has *revealed* him. ▪▪▪

[Shorter: John 1:5, 9–14]

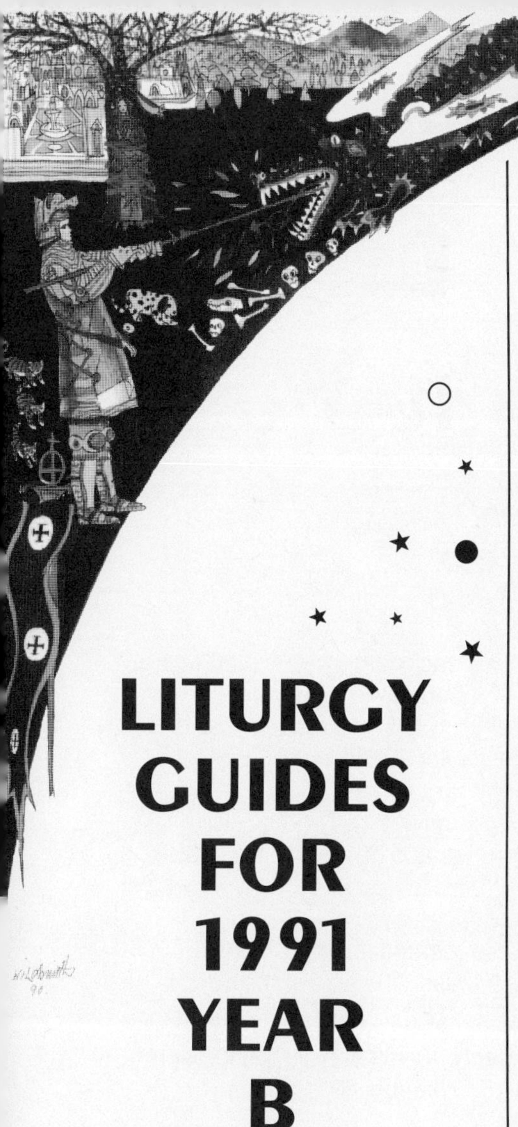
Detail from 1991 Liturgical Calendar.

LITURGY GUIDES FOR 1991 YEAR B

1991 LITURGICAL CALENDAR has vibrant, full color art by Brian Wildsmith. The seasons have distinctive colors and the Sundays, feasts and holy days are clearly indicated. Great as a gift, for a teaching aid, and for anyone working with the liturgy. Quantity prices make it affordable for all parish families. Order extras for each classroom and the sacristy.

Poster size *(26 × 26 inches)*
Single copies: **$6.00 each**.
2–9 copies: **$5.00 each.**.
10–24 copies: **$4.00 each**.
25 or more copies: **$2.00 each**.

NOW AVAILABLE TO USE IN CONJUNCTION WITH POSTER CALENDAR IN CLASSROOM OR COMMITTEE:

Notebook size *(11 × 17 inches)*
Pack of 25: **$7.00 per pack of 25**.
250 or more: **$5.00 per pack of 25**.
[Sorry, we cannot ship less than a pack.]

1991 SOURCEBOOK FOR SUNDAYS AND SEASONS contains season-by-season and Sunday-by-Sunday notes on the celebration of Mass with practical suggestions for keeping the seasons. A wealth of useful texts, notes on the order of Mass, and suggestions for music and worship decor make this a unique resource. Put the *Sourcebook* side by side with *Workbook for Lectors and Gospel Readers* as study tools for planning seasons and Sundays. Use the card below to order the 1991 *Sourcebook*.

Single copies: **$5.95 each**.
5 or more copies: **$4.50 each**.

Three convenient ways to order

CALL: 1-800-933-1800
(Minimum phone order $20.00)

FAX: 312-486-7094
(Minimum order $20.00)

MAIL: Send the card below. Include check for order under $20.

(To inquire about orders or payments call 1-800-933-4779.)

Use this card to order additional 1991 books only.

To order 1992 books early, use the card placed further on in this book.

PLACE POSTAGE HERE

LTP

LITURGY TRAINING PUBLICATIONS
Reorder Department
1800 North Hermitage Avenue
Chicago IL 60622-1101

1991 At Home with the Word

This is a book for:

- individuals and families
- parish groups (Renew, Christ Renews His Parish, Cursillo, Bible study and the catechumenate)
- high school or college catechesis
- liturgy planners, homilists, catechumenate teams
- those confined to their homes who wish to read the scriptures each week with the church
- ministers of communion to the sick

A wonderful, inexpensive Advent or Christmas gift from the parish to each household!

How can we prepare to listen well to the scriptures each Sunday? How can those readings be present in the homes of parishioners to be read and discussed during the week?

At Home with the Word has the three readings for each Sunday of 1991. The translation is taken from the acclaimed *Lectionary for the Christian People,* based on the Revised Standard Version. The readings are followed by short, thought-provoking and discussion-starting comments and questions. Each week a special set of lively notes suggests all sorts of ways to accept the challenge of the gospel and act on it at home, in the parish and in our world.

At Home with the Word includes beautifully illustrated seasonal psalms, daily home prayers, as well as the prayers of the Mass. The size of the book is 8 × 10 inches.

Single copies: **$5.95 each**; 2–9 copies: **$3.25 each**; 10–99 copies: **$2.50 each**; 100–499 copies: **$2.00 each**; 500–999 copies: **$1.75 each**; 1000 or more copies: **$1.50 each**.

Get the best deal! Check with the parish staff and organizations. Order together to receive the best discount.

Use this card to order 1991 (Year B) books and calendars only.

To order 1992 (Year C) books early, use the card placed further on in this book.

☐ Please send ______ copies of 1991 *At Home with the Word.* $5.95 each. = ______

☐ Please send reprint license forms for 1991 *At Home with the Word.*

☐ Please send ______ copies of 1991 *Workbook for Lectors and Gospel Readers.* $8.00 each. = ______

☐ Please send ______ copies of 1991 *Manual para proclamadores de la palabra.* $8.00 each. = ______

☐ Please send ______ copies of *A Well-Trained Tongue.* *(See description on page 177.)* $6.95 each. = ______

☐ Please send ______ copies of 1991 *Sourcebook for Sundays and Seasons.* $5.95 each. = ______

☐ Please send ______ copies of 1991 *Liturgical Calendar, Poster Size* (26 × 26). $6.00 each. = ______

☐ Please send ______ packs of 1991 *Liturgical Calendar, Notebook Size* (11 × 17). *[Packs of 25 only]* $7.00 pack. = ______

Total = ______

Read carefully and choose your method of payment.

$ ______ Full payment enclosed. If sending full payment with order, add 5% for shipping and handling. (10% outside US and Canada.) Minimum of $2.00. US funds only.

$ ______ Bill me. Minimum "bill me" order is $20. 10% for shipping and handling will be added to the bill. (15% outside US and Canada.)

Bill to ______

Account # ______

Address ______

City, State, Zip ______

Phone ______/______

Send to/Attention ______

Street Address ______

(We ship UPS. Give only street address please. No PO Boxes.)

City, State, Zip ______

Date ordered ___/___/___. To avoid duplication of orders, please keep a copy for your records.

THANK YOU FOR YOUR ORDER!

DECEMBER 30, 1990

THE HOLY FAMILY

LECTIONARY #17B

READING I Sirach 3:2–6, 12–14

A reading from the book of *Sirach* ▪ ▪ ▪

Addressed to adolescents.

First chiasma.

"Sons and daughters" is more inclusive.

Second chiasma.

Addressed to young adults.

Third chiasma.

Addressed to mature adults. "My child" is more inclusive.

Visualizing someone you know.

One phrase at a time. Evenly, without a build.

The Lord sets a *father* in *honor* over his children; ▪ ▪
a *mother's authority* he *confirms*
over her sons. ▪ ▪
He who *honors* his father *atones* for sins; ▪ ▪
he stores up *riches* who *reveres* his mother. ▪ ▪
He who honors his father is *gladdened*
by *children,*
and when he *prays* he is *heard.* ▪ ▪
He who *reveres* his father will live a *long* life; ▪ ▪
he *obeys* the Lord who brings *comfort*
to his *mother* ▪ ▪
My *son,* ▪ take *care* of your father
when he is *old;* ▪ ▪
grieve him *not* as long as he lives. ▪ ▪
Even if his mind *fails,* ▪ be *considerate*
with him; ▪ ▪
revile him not in the fullness
of your *strength.* ▪ ▪
For *kindness* to a father will not be *forgotten,* ▪
it will serve as a *sin offering*— ▪ ▪
it will take *lasting* root. ▪ ▪ ▪

READING I Sirach calls on you to preach a lesson on the right relationship of children to parents, and it's a lecture addressed to children of all ages. The exclusive language of this passage is difficult to remedy; try recasting some of it in the second person plural. For example, "You who honor your fathers atone for sins; you store up riches when you revere your mothers."

The first lines might be addressed to the youngsters and adolescents in the crowd, those still under the direct authority of parents. Pick out one or two in the assembly and speak convincingly to them. The next six lines might be aimed at the young adults, those leaving the nest or soon to become parents themselves. Remind them that the parent-child bond changes but never breaks.

Notice three times in these lines we encounter a literary device common in biblical writing: the chiasma—a cross-parallel where the word order of two balanced ideas is reversed. An ordinary parallel would look like this: "The one who a) reveres b) father c) atones for sin; the one who a) reveres b) mother c) stores up riches." A chiasma reverses the a-b-c sequence. Usually the phrase out of the expected sequence (". . . a mother's authority," ". . . stores up riches," ". . . obeys the Lord") receives the emphasis. This literary device produces interesting prose. Take advantage of it in your proclamation.

The last six lines address mature adults faced with the care of aging parents. You know people with this responsibility. Without a preachy tone, remind them of love's demands. You won't overdo it if, as you begin "even if his mind fails," you picture someone you know who has grown senile. Imagine a period after each phrase in the last sentence. Don't build from one phrase to the next, but speak with deep-felt conviction.

READING II Though Paul's specific prescription for the family doesn't occur till the end of the passage on this Christmastime Sunday, the entire text can be addressed to family members. Imagine yourself entering a home in the midst of a family argument. After calling for silence and demanding attention, you begin. Scan their faces as you speak, variously chiding, instructing, pleading. Any list is difficult. Give variety to the five virtues listed by directing each to a different face in the assembly.

The advice of the first lines brings healing. The next eight lines give instructions for growth. Change your tone from peacemaker to counselor (keeping yourself humble by speaking to yourself as well). You'll need a sense of authority and influence, but even more a tone of genuine concern.

The second paragraph focuses on the duties rather than the rights of family members. Avoid the suggestion of superiority of one member over another by emphasizing each one's responsibility to the others. The word "love" connotes myriad duties of husband to wife and can be stretched for that purpose. True love requires its own brand of "submission." All the instructions receive equal emphasis, including the last. Just like the "fathers," you don't want to sound like a nag. So, again, speak as you would to your own family whom you love so much.

GOSPEL Several years ago some friends had a baby whose face was badly deformed at birth. They found it difficult to speak with friends about this. The doctors prescribed a series of surgeries which promised to correct most of the problems. With resignation and fragile hope they set out on the journey, which continues still, to undo nature's damage. Many times along that road friends and family, through comforting hands and words, provided hope that the couple thought they'd lost; and as each surgery succeeded it was those same loved ones who raised the loudest cheers of joy.

The gospel of the last Sunday of Advent was filled with promises made to Mary about the child she was asked to bear. She gave birth to a boy who, in the words of a poem, "was born not with a crown but with a price on his head." Only the eyes of faith could assure Mary that this child was destined "to rule over the house of Jacob." So God's mercy sends Simeon and Anna to provide the reassurance human eyes could not.

This passage begins by drawing attention to Mary and Joseph's keen observance of the law and its dictates. Speak the quotations

READING II Colossians 3:12–21

A reading from the letter of *Paul* ▪ to the *Colossians* ▪▪▪

Peacemaker. Goal is healing.

Because you are God's *chosen* ones, ▪ *holy* and *beloved,* ▪▪ *clothe* yourselves with heartfelt *mercy,* ▪▪ with *kindness,* ▪ *humility,* ▪ *meekness,* ▪ and *patience.* ▪▪ *Bear* with one another; ▪▪ *forgive* whatever *grievances* you have against one another. ▪▪ Forgive as the *Lord* has forgiven *you.* ▪▪ Over *all* these virtues put on *love,* ▪ which *binds* the rest together and makes them *perfect.* ▪▪ Christ's *peace* must reign in your *hearts,* ▪ since as members of the *one body* you have been *called* to that peace. ▪▪ Dedicate yourselves to *thankfulness.* ▪▪ Let the *word* of Christ, ▪ *rich* as it is, ▪ *dwell* in you. ▪▪ In *wisdom* made perfect, ▪ *instruct* and *admonish* one another. ▪▪ Sing *gratefully* to God from your *hearts* ▪▪ in *psalms,* ▪ *hymns,* ▪ and *inspired* songs. ▪▪ *Whatever* you do, ▪ whether in *speech* or in *action,* ▪▪ do it in the *name* of the *Lord Jesus.* ▪▪ Give *thanks* to God the Father through him. ▪▪▪

Stress goes to new idea: "as the Lord *has forgiven* you."

Counselor. Goal is instruction for growth.

Duties, not rights, for both husbands and wives.

You who are *wives,* ▪▪ be *submissive* to your husbands. ▪▪ This is your *duty* in the Lord. ▪▪ *Husbands,* ▪▪ *love* your wives. ▪▪ Avoid any *bitterness* toward them. ▪▪ You *children,* ▪▪ *obey* your parents in *everything* as the *acceptable* way in the Lord. ▪▪ And *fathers,* ▪▪ do not *nag* your children ▪ lest they *lose heart.* ▪▪▪

Equal emphasis on each instruction.

GOSPEL Luke 2:22–40

A reading from the holy *gospel* according to *Luke* ▪▪▪

Note repeated references to "the law." Parents model fidelity to the covenant for their son.

When the day came to *purify* them according to the law of *Moses,* ▪ Mary and Joseph brought Jesus up to *Jerusalem* ▪ so that he could be presented to the *Lord,* ▪ for it is written in the *law* of the Lord, ▪▪ "Every *first-born male* shall be *consecrated* to the Lord." ▪▪ They came to offer in *sacrifice* "a pair of turtledoves or two young pigeons," ▪ in accord with the *dictate* in the law of the Lord. ▪▪▪

Quote the law in the voice of Joseph or Mary.

Tell it like a favorite story.

There *lived* in Jerusalem at the time a certain man named *Simeon.* ▪▪ He was *just* and *pious,* ▪ and awaited the *consolation* of Israel, ▪ and the *Holy Spirit* was upon him. ▪▪ It was *revealed* to him by the Holy Spirit ▪ that he would not experience *death* until he had *seen* the *Anointed* of the Lord. ▪▪ He

Note repeated references to Spirit.

Reference to "law."

came to the *temple* now, ▪ *inspired* by the Spirit; ▪▪ and when the parents *brought in* the child Jesus to perform for him the customary *ritual* of the law, ▪ he *took* him in his arms and *blessed* God in these words: ▪▪

Assume Simeon's voice. Slow, with deep-down peace.

"*Now,* ▪ Master, ▪ you can *dismiss* your
servant in *peace;* ▪▪
you have *fulfilled* your word. ▪▪
For my eyes have *witnessed* your saving *deed* ▪
displayed for all the *peoples* to *see:* ▪▪
A revealing *light* to the *Gentiles,* ▪
the *glory* of your people *Israel.*" ▪▪

Wide-eyed.

The child's father and mother were *marveling* at what was being *said* about him. ▪▪ Simeon *blessed* them and said to *Mary* his mother: ▪▪ "This child is destined to be the *downfall* and the *rise* of *many* in Israel, ▪ a *sign* that will be *opposed* ▪ and you yourself shall be *pierced* with a *sword* ▪ so that the thoughts of many *hearts* may be laid *bare.*" ▪▪▪

More quietly but with authority.

With love and respect.

There was also a certain *prophetess,* ▪ *Anna* by name, ▪ daughter of Phanuel of the tribe of Asher. ▪▪ She had seen *many* days, ▪ having lived seven years with her *husband* after her marriage ▪ and then as a *widow* until she was *eighty-four.* ▪▪ She was *constantly* in the temple, ▪ worshiping *day* and *night* in *fasting* and *prayer.* ▪▪ Coming on the *scene* at this moment, ▪ she gave *thanks* to God ▪ and *talked* about the child to all who looked forward to the *deliverance* of *Jerusalem.* ▪▪▪

Respect for her piety.

Slower. Imagine her taking the child in her arms.

Reference to "law."

When the pair had *fulfilled* all the prescriptions of the law of the Lord, ▪ they *returned* to Galilee and their own town of *Nazareth.* ▪▪ The child grew in *size* and *strength,* ▪ filled with *wisdom,* ▪ and the *grace* of God was upon him. ▪▪▪

Said with hindsight and "faith-sight."

[Shorter: Luke 2:22, 39–40]

from the law the way Mary or Joseph might have quoted them to remind each other of their responsibilities.

Introduce Simeon as you imagine Mary or Joseph might have described him when recounting these events to a neighbor. There is reverence and affection in every word. Simeon speaks his prayer calmly, not with lottery-winning excitement, but with the profound peace of one who has waited many years. His prophecy is authoritative and uncompromising; he is too old and has waited too long to be anything else. Again in the voice of Mary or Joseph speak of Anna and her strange words with amazement.

The encounter is soon over and the parents must cling to these prophetic words as they watch their boy grow, for though he was "filled with wisdom and the grace of God," it would be many years before another prophet, named John, would recognize him for who he was.

READING I It's New Year's Day. Many people are making promises to others, to themselves, to God. God makes a promise, too, and you get to speak it. This is a prayer familiar to many from posters, plaques and prayer cards. But it's probably as cherished as it is familiar.

The priesthood of the Hebrews derived from Aaron and his sons, and here God gives them an instrument through which blessings can flow down to the people. Teach the blessing to your assembly as God teaches it to Moses—speaking with the expectation that your listeners will appropriate their priestly roles and pass the blessing on to family and friends. "Teaching" it does not mean dictating in a slow monotone. It means capturing the emotional power of the words and of the action of blessing. Teach them to say it with compassion, with generosity, with love. How might Mary, or any parent, speak these words to a child leaving home? (If extending your hand while speaking the words of blessing would dissipate any of your intensity and warm-heartedness, don't do it. Otherwise, try it.)

The lines before and after the blessing need a contrasting quality. God is direct. "I will bless them" sounds like a chief executive who wants subordinates to know she or he means business.

READING II Good old Paul! He never can make up his mind whether to teach or inspire. In this passage he does both, teaching first. Your task is to distinguish each point in the long first sentence from every other. Clarify Paul's meaning by using the commas and brief pauses (the Revised NAB deletes "forth" and adds a comma after "Son" in the second clause). This Marian day demands that "born of a woman" not be glossed over since it highlights Mary's role in the birth of Jesus. Paul wants to convince. You must do the same. Doubtless there are some in your church who don't believe or feel that they truly are God's children.

The second sentence bridges Paul's instructional and inspirational agendas. It starts with legal language, and then climaxes the reading with a cry of "Daddy." That's a possible translation of "Abba," so give "Father!" that quality.

Speak the last two sentences as if looking in the face of someone who has just inherited a great fortune and you've been chosen to give them the good news. (You have!)

Note: This passage will sound more exclusive than most if the masculine language is not adjusted, especially on this solemnity of a woman.

JANUARY 1, 1991

MARY, MOTHER OF GOD

LECTIONARY #18

READING I Numbers 6:22–27

A reading from the book of *Numbers* ▪▪▪

Slowly. Giving directions.

The *Lord* said to Moses: ▪▪ "Speak to *Aaron* and his sons ▪ and *tell* them: ▪▪ This is how you shall *bless* the Israelites. ▪▪ Say to them: ▪▪

Take time.

The Lord *bless* you and *keep* you! ▪▪

Tenderly.

The Lord let his face *shine* upon you, ▪
and be *gracious* to you! ▪▪
The Lord look upon you *kindly* ▪

"And . . . peace": ritardando.

and *give* you *peace!* ▪▪

God means it. Sound like it.

"I will bless": Ritardando.

"So shall they invoke my *name* upon the Israelites, ▪▪ and *I will bless* them." ▪▪▪

READING II Galatians 4:4–7

A reading from the letter of *Paul* ▪
to the *Galatians* ▪▪▪

Clarifying.

Mentally insert: "who was born."

Rev. NAB says: "receive adoption." ". . . and daughters" is more inclusive.

"Children" and "child" are more inclusive.

When the *designated* time had come, ▪ God sent forth his *Son* ▪ born of a *woman,* ▪ born under the *law,* ▪ to *deliver* from the law ▪ those who were *subjected* to it, ▪ so that we might receive our *status* ▪ as adopted sons. ▪▪ The *proof* that you are sons ▪ is the fact that God has sent forth into our *hearts* ▪ the *spirit* of his Son ▪ which *cries* out ▪▪ *"Abba!"* ▪ *("Father!").* ▪▪▪ You are no longer a *slave* ▪ but a *son!* ▪▪ And the fact that you *are* a son makes you an *heir,* ▪ by *God's* design. ▪▪▪

GOSPEL Luke 2:16–21

A reading from the holy *gospel* according to *Luke* ▪ ▪ ▪

Remembering, not witnessing.

The shepherds went in *haste* to Bethlehem ▪ and *found* Mary and Joseph, ▪ and the baby ▪ lying in the manger; ▪ ▪ once they *saw,* ▪ they *understood* what had been *told* them concerning this child. ▪ ▪ All who *heard* of it ▪ were *astonished* at the report *given* them by the shepherds. ▪ ▪ ▪

Seeing is believing.

Visualize what Mary "treasured" and "reflected on."

Mary *treasured* all these things ▪ and *reflected* on them in her heart. ▪ ▪ The shepherds *returned,* ▪ *glorifying* and *praising* God for all they had heard and seen, ▪ in accord with what had been *told* them. ▪ ▪ ▪

Pause and make transition.

When the eighth day arrived for his *circumcision,* ▪ the name *Jesus* was given the child, ▪ the name the *angel* had given him ▪ *before* he was conceived. ▪ ▪ ▪

Significantly.

Ritardando.

GOSPEL This is the gospel from the Christmas Mass at Dawn (see that commentary). Here it is again with the addition of verse 21, an important text signaling Christ's incorporation into the people of Israel. But that's the ending. We're still celebrating the Christmas mystery, and it should be a joy to retell the familiar Lucan narrative.

Give more time to the "once they saw" realization, letting the elapsed time add depth to the shepherds' insight. In fact, you might speak the whole first paragraph from Mary's perspective as, years later, she reflects on these events. Speak of Mary's "treasuring" as you would speak of your own mother reflecting on your childhood.

A new idea is introduced in the last sentence. Given the biblical significance of naming, the use of the passive voice here may well be fortuitous and significant. Jesus' name has a divine, not human origin. Mary and Joseph's authority over Jesus is transitory. The Son of God remains under the aegis of his heavenly Father. Take time, therefore, with the last clause of the sentence.

FROM THE KEY

Stress (italics). The italics attempt to identify the operative words in a sentence, the ones that convey the meaning. Verbs do that best. They speak of action and intention. Next come nouns. Nouns are the people, places and things of a text—obviously important. Then there are color words like adverbs and adjectives. Stress these for variety or when they clarify the author's meaning.

The verb is generally more important in most verb-adverb combinations. In "He *looked* out at the people" ("looked" is the verb; "out" is the adverb), habit would have us stress *out.* To correct this, repeat the sentence several times without the adverb ("He looked at the people"), then reinsert the adverb and you should find yourself stressing the verb.

Context and variety determine whether a noun or adjective will be stressed. For example, "You shall be a glorious *crown* . . . a *royal* diadem." Prepositions are rarely stressed (unless you're saying: "He ran toward the wall and then *through* it!"). Don't hesitate to alter the stresses. But if you do, know why you're doing it.

If when reading a sentence it seems there are too many stresses, you're probably right. Italics do not always indicate the same degree of stress. When several words are italicized in a sentence, one or more may be subordinate. The passage "With their *hands* they will *support* you, that you may never *stumble* on a *stone"* contains four italicized words, but "support" and "stumble" receive the greater stress. No one way is the best way to accent a passage. When you combine the author's intent and the needs of your assembly—making the author's words as alive today as when they were first written—then you've found the best way to proclaim.

In any case, do not feel obligated to memorize all the stresses. The stress marks in this workbook are only suggestions. Feel free to disagree with them.

READING I This is one of those readings that should leave you tired after you've read it. The emotional intensity of these words is great. Your emotional involvement with them must be as great. Express it through your vocal vibrance, facial mobility and, especially, the expression in your eyes. If you are the medium through which this message will be proclaimed, you will inevitably become part of the message. There are two people communicating to the assembly: Isaiah (the author) and you (the interpreter). Don't create a conflict between Isaiah's message and yours by making *what* you proclaim be in conflict with *how* you proclaim.

So what is the *how?* Exuberantly, with vitality and veracity (honest emotions). Start boldly, rousing the populace, announcing good news. Briefly lower the energy as you remind your listeners that many still stumble in darkness without reason for rejoicing. "But upon you" resumes the fervent exhilaration that carries through to the end of the reading.

The second paragraph reveals the consequences of God's action for Jerusalem. You are overwhelmed by the city's good fortune. Can you keep a smile off your face, a sparkle out of your eyes? Let the last line suggest to you the spirit of this whole reading.

P.S. A friend of mine introduced himself to a fellow pilgrim in Jerusalem as a priest from America. He heard the pilgrim reciprocate by introducing himself as the monarch of an Eastern kingdom. Suddenly Isaiah's prophecy became surprisingly literal.

READING II The challenge here will be to avoid making Paul appear vain. From prison he is asserting his unique role as apostle to the gentiles. In the first sentence he is asking for recognition of this special office. There's an implied "Right?" at the end of the sentence and the expectation of a resounding "Yes!"

In the second paragraph you are presiding at the reading of a will, preparing to reveal each one's share of the inheritance. You must speak slowly and carefully to avoid misunderstandings. The seal is broken, the contents about to be read. "It is no less than this . . ." introduces the announcement and comes out quickly. Then speak slowly as you enumerate the provisions of the "will." You are speaking not to those whose inheritance must now be shared (the Jews) but to those who've been added to the will (the gentiles). You are persuading them of their good fortune while at the same time rejoicing over it with them.

JANUARY 6, 1991

THE EPIPHANY OF THE LORD

LECTIONARY #20

READING I Isaiah 60:1–6

A reading from the book of the prophet ▪ *Isaiah* ▪▪▪

Begin boldly.

Rise up in *splendor,* Jerusalem! ▪
Your *light* has come, ▪
the glory of the Lord *shines* upon you. ▪▪

Slower.

See, ▪ *darkness* covers the earth, ▪
and *thick clouds* cover the *peoples;* ▪▪
But upon *you* ▪ the Lord *shines,* ▪
and over you appears his *glory.* ▪▪

Be convincing.

Nations shall *walk* by your light, ▪
and *kings* by your *shining* radiance. ▪▪
Raise your eyes and *look* about; ▪
they all *gather* and come to *you:* ▪▪
Your *sons* come from afar, ▪
and your *daughters* in the arms
of their nurses. ▪▪

Maintain the intensity.

Then ▪ you shall be *radiant* at what you see, ▪
your heart shall *throb* and *overflow,* ▪▪

Such good fortune!

For the *riches* of the sea shall be *emptied* out
before you, ▪▪
the wealth of *nations* shall be brought to *you.* ▪▪
Caravans of camels shall *fill* you, ▪

"Dromedaries" = "camels."

dromedaries from *Midian* and *Ephah;* ▪▪
All from *Sheba* shall come ▪
bearing ▪ *gold* and *frankincense,* ▪
and *proclaiming* ▪ the *praises* of the Lord. ▪▪▪

READING II Ephesians 3:2–3, 5–6

A reading from the letter of *Paul* ▪ to the *Ephesians* ▪▪▪

Expecting agreement.

Stress "gave" to avoid stressing "me."

Stress "revealed," not "me." Rev. NAB uses "human beings" in place of "men."

I am sure you have heard of the *ministry* ▪ which *God* in his goodness ▪ *gave* me ▪ in your regard. ▪▪ God's secret *plan,* ▪ as I have briefly *described* it, ▪ was *revealed* to me, ▪ *unknown* to men in *former* ages ▪ but now ▪ revealed by the *Spirit* to the holy

Simultaneously persuading and rejoicing.

apostles and *prophets.* ▪▪ It is no less than this: ▪▪ in Christ Jesus the *Gentiles* ▪ are now *co-heirs* with the *Jews,* ▪▪ members of the same *body* ▪ and *sharers* of the *promise* ▪ through the preaching of the *gospel.* ▪▪▪

GOSPEL Matthew 2:1–12

A reading from the holy *gospel* according to *Matthew* ▪▪▪

Signal that Herod is the bad guy.

Magi are open and sincere.

After Jesus' *birth* ▪ in Bethlehem of Judea ▪ during the reign of King *Herod,* ▪ *astrologers* from the east arrived one day in Jerusalem ▪ *inquiring,* ▪▪ *"Where* is the newborn *king* of the *Jews?* ▪▪ We observed his *star* at its rising ▪ and have *come* to pay him *homage."* ▪▪ At this news ▪ King Herod became greatly *disturbed,* ▪ and with him *all* Jerusalem. ▪▪ Summoning all of the *chief priests* and *scribes* of the people, ▪ he *inquired* of them ▪ *where* the *Messiah* was to be *born.* ▪▪ "In *Bethlehem* of *Judea,"* they informed him. ▪ "Here is what the *prophet* has written: ▪▪

A gathering storm.

Speak "Summoning . . . born" in the persona of Herod.

As one of the priests, explaining.

'And *you,* ▪ *Bethlehem,* ▪ land of Judah, ▪
are by no means *least* among the princes
of Judah, ▪
since from you shall come a *ruler* ▪
who is to *shepherd* my people Israel.'" ▪▪

Sugarcoated malice.

Herod called the astrologers *aside* ▪ and found out from *them* ▪ the exact *time* of the star's *appearance.* ▪▪ Then he sent them to Bethlehem, ▪ after having *instructed* them: ▪▪ "Go ▪ and get *detailed information* about the child. ▪▪ When you have *discovered* something, ▪ report your findings to *me* ▪ so that I may *go* and offer him homage *too."* ▪▪

After their audience with the king, ▪ they *set out.* ▪▪ The *star* ▪ which they had observed at its *rising* ▪ *went ahead* of them ▪ until it came to a *standstill* over the place where the *child* was. ▪▪ They were *overjoyed* at seeing the star, ▪ and on *entering* the house, ▪ *found* the child with *Mary* his mother. ▪▪ They *prostrated* themselves and did him *homage.* ▪▪ Then they opened their *coffers* ▪ and *presented* him with gifts of *gold,* ▪ *frankincense,* ▪ and *myrrh.* ▪▪▪

Speak "not to return to Herod" as an angel.

They received a *message* in a *dream* ▪ not to *return* to Herod, ▪ so they went back to their *own* country ▪ by *another* route. ▪▪▪

GOSPEL Here's another passage that requires your best skills as a storyteller to unravel a tale of intrigue and malice peopled by kings and priests, astrologers and angels and, not least of all, by yourself as narrator.

Let your narrator voice comment on all the action and characters, starting with a note of suspicion even as you speak Herod's name. The Magi are upbeat and eager. Let them stress "King of the Jews," for it is those words that will perk up Herod's ears.

Convey Herod's fear over the threat to his throne as you tell of his becoming "disturbed" and of his angry "summoning of the priests." The Isaiah quote is spoken not as the prophet, but in the persona of a priest and with a guardedly didactic tone.

Herod sugarcoats his malice when speaking to the Magi. Suggest how convincing he was even as you describe how he "found out the exact time." You can speak the lines more as Herod than as narrator. Herod succeeds in seducing the Magi. After all, it took a dream to later warn them away from him.

The story progresses straightforwardly to the point of entering the "house." Now slow down and visualize the scene as you tell it. Exploit the word "prostrated." People don't hear it much. It's a rich word that expresses well the awe that filled the Magi. The final sentence says both "phew!" and "ha ha." In the nick of time (phew!) the necessary information was kept from the villain Herod (ha ha!).

READING I As a proclaimer of the word you perform two tasks: First, you read the words of scripture, which is relatively simple; second, and more importantly, you draw us into the scripture and draw out for us the scripture's meaning. The second part is trickier because it involves more than pronouncing words: it involves enlivening them in a way that evokes a response from us. Proclaimers don't share information in the way a newscaster does; they persuade us to respond in a certain way to the information.

The first reading invites us to feel a certain way about God's servant. It shares some information about him—he has God's spirit, he will bring forth justice—but what's important is the feeling and conviction which that news evokes—joy and hope that our own eyes will be opened, confinement brought to an end. Let your tone complement the intent of the writing rather than contradict it by sounding flat or unenthused.

In the first paragraph God speaks of the servant in the third person. The servant will be God's representative, so God proudly introduces him, listing the fine qualities that will make his ministry successful. Note that "Until he establishes justice . . ." finishes the thought begun in the two preceding clauses. "The coastlands will wait . . ." stands alone as a separate thought.

In the second paragraph God addresses the servant in the first person. Instead of a public forum where God displays this model servant, the two are in private conference where God gives final words of encouragement before the servant embarks on his ministry. Stress the repeated "I" and the verbs: It is God who has "called," "grasped" and "formed" the servant for the task. Because God is with him the servant *can* open eyes and bring light to those in darkness. Your tone must be persuasive, and your words an invitation to rejoice!

JANUARY 13, 1991

THE BAPTISM OF THE LORD

LECTIONARY #21

READING I Isaiah 42:1–4, 6–7

Let your sound match the moods of the passage.

A reading from the book of the prophet ▪
Isaiah **▪▪▪**

God presents the "servant" with pride.

Here is my *servant* whom I *uphold,* ▪
my *chosen* one ▪ with whom I am *pleased,* ▪▪▪
Upon whom I have put my *spirit;* ▪▪
he shall bring forth *justice* to the nations, ▪

He will be gentle, not loud or pushy.

Not *crying* out, ▪ not *shouting,* ▪
not making his voice heard in the *street.* ▪▪

He will treat the weak and poor with kindness. "A bruised reed . . . on the earth" = one clause.

A *bruised* reed he shall not *break,* ▪
and a *smoldering* wick he shall not *quench,* ▪
Until he establishes *justice* on the earth; ▪▪

"Wait" = energetic, earnest longing.

the coastlands will *wait* for his teaching. ▪▪▪

Shift to first person.

I, ▪ the Lord, ▪ have *called* you for the *victory* of justice, ▪▪

Be brave. Have no fear.

I have *grasped* you by the hand; ▪▪
I *formed* you, ▪ and set you
as a *covenant* of the people, ▪
a *light* for the nations, ▪▪

Speak to the "servant."

To *open* the eyes of the *blind,* ▪
to bring out *prisoners* from *confinement,* ▪▪

Ritardando: "those who live in darkness."

and from the *dungeon,* ▪ those who *live* in *darkness.* ▪▪▪

READING II Acts 10:34–38

Catch a breath, then take on the character of Peter.

A reading from the *Acts* of the *Apostles* ▪ ▪ ▪

Peter addressed *Cornelius* ▪ and the people assembled at his *house* ▪ in *these* words: ▪ ▪ "I *begin* to see how *true* it is ▪ that God shows *no* partiality. ▪ ▪ *Rather,* ▪ the man of *any* nation ▪ who *fears* God and acts *uprightly* ▪ is *acceptable* to him. ▪ ▪ This is the *message* he has sent to the sons of *Israel,* ▪ ▪ 'the good news of *peace*' ▪ proclaimed through *Jesus Christ* ▪ who is Lord of *all.* ▪ ▪ I take it you *know* what has been reported all over Judea about Jesus of Nazareth, ▪ beginning in *Galilee* with the baptism *John* preached; ▪ ▪ of the way God *anointed* him with the *Holy Spirit* and *power.* ▪ ▪ He went about doing *good works* ▪ and healing *all* who were in the grip of the *devil,* ▪ ▪ and *God* was *with* him. ▪ ▪ ▪

Few words to make big point. "Person" is more inclusive.

Pace quickens slightly. "Sons and daughters" is inclusive.

Not conversational but remembered with awe.

Spoken with affection.

GOSPEL Mark 1:7–11

Short reading = slow reading.

A reading from the holy *gospel* according to *Mark* ▪ ▪ ▪

Asking us to remember.

The theme of *John's* preaching was: ▪ ▪ "One more *powerful* than I is to come *after* me. ▪ ▪ I am not *fit* to stoop and untie his *sandal* straps. ▪ ▪ *I* have baptized you in *water;* ▪ ▪ *he* will baptize you in the *Holy Spirit.*" ▪ ▪ ▪

Your tone signals that the remembering is over.

During that time, ▪ *Jesus* came from Nazareth in Galilee ▪ and was *baptized* in the Jordan by *John.* ▪ ▪ *Immediately* ▪ on *coming up* out of the water ▪ he saw the sky *rent* in two ▪ and the *Spirit* descending on him like a *dove.* ▪ ▪ Then a *voice* came from the heavens: ▪ ▪ "You are my beloved *Son.* ▪ ▪ On *you* ▪ my favor rests." ▪ ▪ ▪

Anticipate excitement over the apparition.

See it happening in your mind's eye.

Loving and reassuring.

READING II You've got to hand it to Peter. He could be so wrong, and he could be so honest about admitting it. Peter had always believed that the salvation Jesus brought was for Jews alone; gentiles were unclean and had no share in the Kingdom. Inspired by a vision he comes to the home of the gentile Cornelius and realizes that *anyone* who "fears God and acts uprightly" can be a disciple of Jesus. Imagine Peter putting palm to forehead, gesturing disbelief of his own thick-headedness. I was so wrong, he says, but now I see the truth! His stresses would naturally go to phrases like: "*no* partiality . . ." "of *any* nation . . ." "lord of *all.*"

The rest of the passage is Peter's proclamation of the gospel of Jesus, the good news of *universal* salvation. Having just made one realization, Peter's mind starts making connections. He gains momentum as the excitement of his realization explodes in his mind. How ironic, he seems to say, that the message sent to "the sons [and daughters] of *Israel*" was that Jesus is "Lord of *all.*" As he continues he has two reasons to be excited: He is sharing great news with new believers, and the great news *is* his friend and Lord, Jesus. Sounds like what you'll be doing on Sunday, doesn't it?

GOSPEL Twice in Advent we heard John's self-abasement: "One more powerful than I is to come after me." There it served the purpose of heightening the expectation for the Messiah. Now it serves as a review; a step backwards before the next forward step which is the descent of the Spirit. You remind us of what John had prophesied (in one breath he referred to *both* baptism and the Spirit) so we will better appreciate what's about to happen.

As the omniscient narrator who knows more than the characters in your story, narrate the arrival of Jesus on the scene, your voice anticipating the excitement that's but one immersion in the river away. Descriptions which start with "immediately" should be narrated as if they were happening even as you speak. Your eyes widen like John's as you see the Spirit hovering like a dove over Jesus. You're given few words to narrate an extraordinary event, so you don't rush; create the awed excitement of a great miracle. The better you visualize the scene the better the assembly will be able to see it with you.

Finally, the "voice." It is the voice of God speaking of a "beloved son." Does that call for thunder or for tenderness? Remembering that this baptism will eventually lead to the cross, perhaps it should sound like the voice that spoke to Mary years before: "Do not be afraid. You have found favor with God."

READING I If you know children, you know how unremarkable this event is. A child awakens in the night, mumbles something about hearing noises and is sleepily encouraged to return to sleep. Parents learn not to take such occurrences too seriously for the child's sake as well as their own. Assuming Eli understands children, he would not overreact to the boy's nocturnal mumblings.

Another point. Often a pivotal event seems quite ordinary as it occurs, and only later does its profound significance strike us. As narrator you understand the significance of this divine call for Samuel's life and the life of Israel. Samuel is *not* aware and Eli is slow to catch on.

Now prepare to tell your story, and tell you must, for this has more the feel of "Once upon a time" than "Dan Rather reporting . . ." Setting is important: the temple—where a young boy would be easily overwhelmed by the magnificence of the space and where Eli is aware of the special presence of God. Characters are important: Samuel—young, naive, sleepy; Eli—tired but patient, suddenly aware. Suspense is important: "*Again* the Lord called Samuel. . . . The Lord called Samuel *again*, for the *third* time. . . ." The turning point ("*Then* Eli understood") and the climax ("*Speak*, for your servant is listening") are the most important moments, deserving your best energy.

The first two times Samuel goes to Eli he speaks with no wider awareness than that of a sleepy child. Both times Eli is calm and gentle. The third time Samuel is more insistent, perhaps a bit whiny. Suddenly Eli comprehends. His advice is almost whispered, as if he doesn't want God to overhear.

The presence of the Lord is manifest in the authoritative way you call out "Samuel," remembering to build the repetition of the name. Samuel responds in a child's awed and humble (maybe frightened) voice.

After a pause, convince us this child grew into a sturdy tree that bore good fruit.

JANUARY 20, 1991

SECOND SUNDAY IN ORDINARY TIME

LECTIONARY #66

READING I 1 Samuel 3:3–10, 19

Be aware of the setting. Narrator understands significance of these events.

A reading from the first book of *Samuel* ▪▪▪

Samuel was sleeping in the temple of the Lord ▪ where the *ark* of God was. ▪▪ The *Lord* ▪ *called* to *Samuel,* ▪▪ who answered, ▪▪ "*Here* I am." ▪▪

A good boy doing what he's told.

He ran to *Eli* and said, ▪▪ "Here I *am.* ▪ You *called* me." ▪▪ "I did *not* call you," ▪ Eli said. ▪▪ "Go back to *sleep.*" ▪▪ So he *went* back to sleep. ▪▪

Eli is not annoyed.

Narrator enjoys the suspense.

Again the Lord called Samuel, ▪ who *rose* and went to *Eli.* ▪▪ "Here I *am,*" ▪ he said. ▪▪ "You *called* me." ▪▪ But he *answered,* ▪▪ "*I* did not call you, my son. ▪▪ *Go* back to sleep." ▪▪

Concerned for the boy, Eli calms him.

At *that* time Samuel was not *familiar* with the Lord, ▪ because the Lord had not *revealed* anything to him as *yet.* ▪▪

Important aside. Note stress on "yet."

The Lord called Samuel *again,* ▪ for the *third* time. ▪▪ *Getting* up and going to *Eli,* ▪ he said, ▪▪ "*Here* I am. ▪▪ You *called* me." ▪▪ *Then* ▪ Eli *understood* ▪ that the *Lord* was calling the youth. ▪▪

Samuel: tired and whiny. Eli's realization: slowly.

So he *said* to Samuel, ▪▪ "Go to *sleep,* ▪ and *if* you are called, ▪ reply, ▪▪ '*Speak,* Lord, ▪ for your servant is *listening.*'" ▪▪

Hushed.

When Samuel *went* to sleep in his place, ▪ the Lord *came* and *revealed* his presence, ▪ *calling* out as before, ▪▪ "*Samuel,* ▪ *Samuel!*" ▪▪ Samuel answered, ▪▪ "*Speak,* ▪ for your servant is *listening.*" ▪▪▪

God's presence is awesome. Build on second "Samuel."

Excited, but fearful.

Samuel *grew* up, ▪ and the *Lord* was *with* him, ▪ not permitting *any* word of his to be *without effect.* ▪▪▪

Speak with pride.

READING II 1 Corinthians 6:13–15, 17–20

A blunt message requires sustained eye contact and love for those addressed.

Contrast "immortality" and "Lord."

This is good news.

Reason with intensity.

"Person" and "one's" are more inclusive.

Don't defile the Spirit!

"You are not. . . . in your body": with intensity.

A reading from the first letter of *Paul* ▪ to the *Corinthians* ▪ ▪ ▪

The *body* is not for *immorality;* ▪ ▪ it is for the *Lord,* ▪ and the *Lord* is for the *body.* ▪ ▪ God, ▪ who *raised* up the Lord, ▪ will raise *us* also by his *power.* ▪ ▪ ▪

Do you not *see* that your bodies are members of *Christ?* ▪ ▪ Whoever is *joined* to the Lord ▪ becomes one *spirit* with him. ▪ ▪ ▪ *Shun* lewd conduct. ▪ ▪ Every *other* sin a man commits is *outside* his body, ▪ but the fornicator sins against his *own* body. ▪ ▪ You must *know* that your body is a *temple* of the Holy Spirit, ▪ who is *within*— ▪ the Spirit you have received from *God.* ▪ ▪ You are not your *own.* ▪ ▪ You have been *purchased,* ▪ and at what a *price!* ▪ ▪ So *glorify* God in your *body.* ▪ ▪ ▪

GOSPEL John 1:35–42

Name these as familiar locations.

Intense, perhaps hushed.

"Heard" with more than their ears.

A playful exchange.

Convey their excitement as they follow.

Great joy and awe.

Jesus does not give away the difference this name change will make.

A reading from the holy *gospel* according to *John* ▪ ▪ ▪

John was in *Bethany* ▪ across the *Jordan* ▪ with two of his *disciples.* ▪ ▪ As he watched *Jesus* walk by he said, ▪ ▪ *"Look!* ▪ ▪ There is the *Lamb* of *God!"* ▪ ▪ The two disciples *heard* what he said, ▪ and *followed* Jesus. ▪ ▪ When Jesus turned around and *noticed* them following him, ▪ he asked them, ▪ ▪ "What are you *looking* for?" ▪ ▪ They *said* to him, ▪ ▪ "*Rabbi* (which means *Teacher*), ▪ where do you *stay?"* ▪ ▪ "Come and *see,"* ▪ he answered. ▪ ▪ So they *went* to see where he was lodged, ▪ and *stayed* with him that day. ▪ ▪ (It was about *four* in the afternoon.) ▪ ▪ ▪

One of the two who had *followed* him after hearing *John* ▪ was Simon Peter's *brother* ▪ *Andrew.* ▪ ▪ The *first* thing he did was *seek* out his brother Simon and *tell* him, ▪ ▪ "We have found the *Messiah!"* ▪ (which means the *Anointed*). ▪ ▪ He *brought* him to Jesus, ▪ who *looked* at him and said, ▪ ▪ "You are *Simon,* ▪ son of *John;* ▪ ▪ your name shall be *Cephas* ▪ (which is rendered *Peter*)." ▪ ▪ ▪

READING II Sometimes strong words are best, and rarely is Paul afraid to use them. The Corinthians thought sexuality was an area of no rights or wrongs, so Paul quickly steps in to set things straight. But instead of finger-wagging he offers persuasive arguments for moral behavior based on his respect for the body's sacredness.

Paul knows what he wants to say. His clear message here is that any lewd conduct is incompatible with the dignity we are given by oneness with Christ. Fornicators sin against their own selves and against the Spirit who dwells within them. Bad enough! Worse is that we don't have a *right* to violate ourselves for we are not our *own;* at great "price," God has "purchased" us.

Imagine the emotional intensity of this reading as a graph with five peaks: "The body is not for *immorality,*" "Do you not *see,*" "*Shun* lewd conduct," "You must *know*" and "You are not your *own* . . . so *glorify* God in your body." In between are moments of ascending or descending intensity leading to the next key phrase.

You don't need to be angry to speak hard sayings, but you don't have to lace them with honey, either. After all, what you say is offered for the good of your listeners.

GOSPEL Andrew Greeley writes about Chicago as if all of his readers had been there. They haven't, but that doesn't keep him from writing about the place as if they had. Scripture often assumes a familiarity with certain geographical sites which your reading tone must not contradict. So speak of Bethany and the Jordan as you might about a city and a river your listeners know.

John speaks of Jesus with an intensity, a certainty and with such a fixed and reverent gaze that his seven words become enough persuasion to turn Andrew and friend into John's *ex*-disciples. A fascinating exchange ensues between Jesus and the disciples; each party speaks coyly, revealing less than the other wants to know. Don't overdramatize Jesus' invitation. Relate the episode from the viewpoint of the evangelist who, doubtless, heard about the event from both men (unless *he* was the unnamed disciple).

Now the story is rolling. The identity of one man is given—Andrew—which leads to the introduction of another major character, Peter. Andrew's testimony combines certainty and disbelief, familiarity and awe.

Here a pivotal event is disguised in ordinary clothing: Jesus' address to Peter contains no life-altering overtones, and there was no way Peter could have known then that by changing his name Jesus was changing his destiny.

READING I Read the whole book of Jonah and get reacquainted with this reluctant prophet (it's just two pages!). Actually this is the *second* time "The word of the Lord came to Jonah"; his encounter with the whale made him more disposed to heed God's directive to "set out." You'll disappoint your whole assembly if you rattle off this story like it was a report of the Secretary of State's trip to Yugoslavia. It's a great tale that deserves color, variety, texture *and* your awareness of what precedes and follows this episode.

"Jonah made ready" only because of the whale of an inducement God provided—and his close call moved Jonah's feet—but *not* his heart. That knowledge colors your narration. Jonah does the Lord's "bidding," but not with much enthusiasm.

Describe the city's enormity from Jonah's perspective as he dreads the prospect of *walking* through it for "three (long!) days." But the message of destruction he relishes; he can't wait for the devastation. Shout his threats forcefully. Then speak with Jonah's incredulity as you recount the people's repentance.

Imagine yourself a Ninevite upon whom it gradually dawns that the promised destruction is cancelled: Start slowly, a phrase at a time. "When God saw [look right] by their actions [look left] how they turned from their evil way [look front] he *repented* [exploding with the good news, you announce it to the terrified fellow citizens around you] of the evil that he threatened to do to them; [pause, look at assembly, then slowly and with a smile] he did not carry it out."

READING II It's happening everyday all around us. It's inevitable. Often we ignore it, but the world as we know it *is* passing away! Does the fact that Paul wrote these words to a community that expected the imminent return of Jesus and the end of the world render them meaningless to us? Of course not. In a no less dramatic way, our world *is* coming to an end. Almost daily, it seems, governments change, species disappear, friends and relatives die. We don't live in the same world we were born into, and when we die it will be different still.

In the first and last lines Paul rings the bell and flicks the lights that signal the end is near. Individual lives are short and we mustn't spend our lives worrying about the things of this world. Coax us, in the character of Paul, and call us to live as people who know that after baptism into Christ nothing remains the same; every relationship, every emotion, every transaction changes.

JANUARY 27, 1991

THIRD SUNDAY IN ORDINARY TIME

LECTIONARY #69

READING I Jonah 3:1–5, 10

A colorful story; don't mute its tones.

A reading from the book of the prophet ▪ *Jonah* ▪▪▪

God's voice = powerful and compassionate.

Jonah's exaggerated perspective.

Forcefully, with relish.

With amazement.

The word of the *Lord* came to *Jonah* ▪ saying: ▪▪ "*Set* out for the great city of *Nineveh,* ▪ and *announce* to it the message that I will *tell* you." ▪▪ So Jonah made *ready* ▪ and *went* to Nineveh, ▪ according to the Lord's *bidding.* ▪▪ Now Nineveh was an enormously *large* city; ▪▪ it took *three* days to go through it. ▪▪ Jonah *began* his journey through the city, ▪ and had gone but a *single* day's walk announcing, ▪▪ "*Forty* days more ▪ and Nineveh shall be *destroyed,*" ▪▪ when the people of Nineveh *believed* God; ▪▪ they proclaimed a *fast* ▪ and *all* of them, ▪ *great* and *small,* ▪ put on *sackcloth.* ▪▪▪

Speak as a Ninevite who can't believe God relented.

Ritardando: "he did not carry it out."

When God *saw* by their *actions* ▪ how they *turned* from their evil way, ▪ he *repented* of the evil that he had threatened to do to them; ▪▪ he did *not* carry it out. ▪▪▪

READING II 1 Corinthians 7:29–31

"The time is short" and so is this reading: Go slow.

A reading from the first letter of *Paul* ▪ to the *Corinthians* ▪▪▪

"Brothers and sisters" is more inclusive.

Compassionate advice, not cold orders. Contrast: "wives . . . none," "weep . . . not," "rejoice . . . not," "buyers . . . nothing," "use . . . not."

Look at assembly, realizing you are among the "we."

I *tell* you, brothers, ▪ the time is *short.* ▪▪ From *now* on ▪ those with *wives* should live as though they had *none;* ▪▪ those who *weep* ▪ should live as though they were *not* weeping, ▪▪ and those who *rejoice* ▪ as though they were *not* rejoicing; ▪▪ *buyers* should conduct themselves as though they owned *nothing,* ▪ and those who make use of the *world* ▪ as though they were *not* using it, ▪▪ for the world as *we* know it ▪ is *passing* away. ▪▪▪

GOSPEL Mark 1:14–20

A reading from the holy *gospel* according to *Mark* ▪ ▪ ▪

"Arrest" affects opening mood.

After John's *arrest,* ▪ Jesus appeared in *Galilee* ▪ proclaiming God's *good news:* ▪ ▪ "This is the time of *fulfillment.* ▪ ▪ The *reign* of God is at *hand!* ▪ ▪ *Reform* your lives ▪ and *believe* in the good news!" ▪ ▪ ▪

Strength and determination.

Emphasize occupational reference.

Invitation: energetic and exciting! "Men and women" is more inclusive.

Emphasize familial relationship.

Again awed and admiring.

As he made his way along the *Sea* of *Galilee,* ▪ he observed *Simon* and his brother *Andrew* casting their *nets* into the sea; ▪ ▪ they were *fishermen.* ▪ ▪ Jesus *said* to them, ▪ ▪ "Come *after* me; ▪ ▪ I will make you fishers of *men."* ▪ ▪ They immediately *abandoned* their nets ▪ and became his *followers.* ▪ ▪ Proceeding a little *farther* along, ▪ he caught sight of *James,* ▪ *Zebedee's* son, ▪ and his brother *John.* ▪ ▪ They *too* were in their boat putting their *nets* in order. ▪ ▪ He *summoned* them on the spot. ▪ ▪ They *abandoned* their father Zebedee, ▪ who was in the boat with the *hired* men, ▪ and *went* off in his *company.* ▪ ▪ ▪

This kind of urgent plea for changed behavior always must be spoken with compassion. Stress all the opposites: "*wives . . .* had *none,*" "*weep . . . not* weeping," etc. And never lose the urgency: Some people listening to you may not live long enough to hear this scripture again.

GOSPEL "Good news" preceded by bad. "After John's arrest" is an opening that casts a deliberate shadow and suggests that as Jesus follows John in ministry, so will he follow him in death. It also sets the mood for Jesus' proclamation: He announces the kingdom fully aware of the price he'll pay, steeled and sober in his delivery.

As you narrate the call of the apostles, imagine yourself there watching these people give up everything to follow a person with nothing. Last week's gospel from John, which revealed that some of them were already disciples of the Baptist (Andrew, maybe John), lends credence to the immediacy of their response to Jesus, but it does not detract from the marvel of that instant decision.

Mark uses the two sets of brothers to make points about the price of discipleship: It costs everything—livelihood, as in the case of Simon and Andrew, and family, as in James and John's case. That suggests the areas of stress in your reading: In the first case emphasize references to "fish" and "nets" and "fishermen"; in the second, stress the references to Zebedee. (To make Christ's call more inclusive, opt for "fishers of men and women" instead of "people" and preserve the familiarity of this classic phrase.)

Jesus' words ring with zeal and strength and a sense of excitement, for he needs to capture these men's imaginations before he can win their allegiance. In preparing to proclaim, it may be helpful to remember how Christ won your allegiance.

READING I A good proclaimer helps an assembly understand both individual words and the sense they make when put together. This results from the proper use of pauses and stresses and the grouping of words into thought units. Deuteronomy could be a confusing muddle if you don't "lift out" its meaning for your listeners.

At Horeb the Israelites were so intimidated by the divine presence, manifested in fire and thundering voice, that they asked that God not "speak" directly to them again but, instead, through a human intermediary. Pleased with the request, God decides to grant it.

Moses announces God's decision: "A prophet like *me* [in human form]" God will raise up from "your own kinsmen [kin]." Then he reviews the reasons for God's decision: "This is exactly what you *requested* . . . when you said . . ." Here he quotes the people and assumes their trembling, panicked voices. (They meant it when they said "lest we *die*," for it was believed no mortal could survive God's presence.)

God's voice finishes the passage. God says, I'll give you what you need. But intermediaries can bring problems: Some may not "listen to my words which he speaks in my name." They will answer for such disrespect, God says sternly. A more serious problem is the prophet who abuses his office and speaks "an oracle I have not commanded." God's remedy is uncompromising and blunt: "He shall die."

READING II Out of context, parts of this passage make little sense and may even alienate some listeners. But read the first and last sentences, which frame the reading, and you'll see Paul's tone is very pastoral. He's trying to be helpful, to give good advice for hard times. We would differ from Paul on the role marriage plays in devoting ourselves (or not) to the Lord. If you were expecting the end of the world, wouldn't you tell your loved ones to focus only on the essentials and simplify their lives? That's what Paul is trying to do. Who wouldn't agree that a less complicated life appears easier to live than one laden with the responsibilities of children, home and spouse?

The first sentence sets Paul's premise; pause, then share his advice—stressing his contrasts. Speaking slowly and noting the stresses will reveal Paul's meaning, for it's a simple message. More important is his tone. He is pointing to higher things, while remaining firmly rooted in reality. He's solicitous and unusually flexible in his options. He's not

FEBRUARY 3, 1991

FOURTH SUNDAY IN ORDINARY TIME

LECTIONARY #72

READING I Deuteronomy 18:15–20

A reading from the book of *Deuteronomy* ▪ ▪ ▪

With authority. Like a business person setting things in order. "Kin" is more inclusive.

Moses spoke to the people, saying: ▪ ▪ "A prophet like *me* will the *Lord,* your *God,* ▪ *raise* up for you ▪ from among your own *kinsmen;* ▪ ▪ to *him* you shall *listen.* ▪ ▪ This is exactly what you *requested* of the Lord, your God, ▪ at *Horeb* ▪ on the day of the *assembly,* ▪ when you said, ▪ ▪

Speak as the Israelites.

'Let us not again hear the *voice* of the Lord, our God, ▪ ▪ nor see this great *fire* any more, ▪ lest we *die.*' ▪ ▪ And the *Lord* said to me, ▪ ▪

God's voice: generous and in charge.

'This was *well* said. ▪ ▪ I will *raise* up for them a prophet like *you* from among their *kinsmen,* ▪ and will put *my words* into his mouth; ▪ ▪ he shall *tell* them all that I *command* him. ▪ ▪

Dropping "man" and substituting "them" for "him" is more inclusive.

If any man will *not* listen to my words ▪ which he speaks in my *name,* ▪ I *myself* will make him *answer* for it. ▪ ▪

Slower. Great privelege = great responsibility.

But if a prophet *presumes* to speak in my name ▪ an oracle that I have *not* commanded him to speak, ▪ or speaks in the name of *other* gods, ▪ ▪

Eye contact for added emphasis.

he shall *die.*'" ▪ ▪ ▪

READING II 1 Corinthians 7:32–35

A reading from the first letter of *Paul* ▪
to the *Corinthians* ▪ ▪ ▪

Explain how we can be "free of all worries."

I should like you to be *free* of all *worries.* ▪ ▪

Stress the contrasts.

The *unmarried* man is busy with the *Lord's* affairs, ▪ concerned with *pleasing* the Lord; ▪ ▪ but the *married* man is busy with this *world's* demands ▪ and is occupied with pleasing his *wife.* ▪ ▪ This means he is *divided.* ▪ ▪

He's calling each of us to total commitment to Christ.

The *virgin*— ▪ indeed, *any* unmarried woman— ▪ is concerned with things of the *Lord,* ▪ in pursuit of *holiness* in *body* and *spirit.* ▪ ▪ The *married* woman, ▪ on the other hand, ▪ has the cares of this *world* to absorb her ▪ and is concerned with pleasing her *husband.* ▪ ▪

Eye contact.

I am going into this with you for your own *good.* ▪ ▪ I have *no* desire to place *restrictions* on you, ▪ but I *do* want to promote what is *good,* ▪

Sincerely. Look directly at assembly.

what will help you to devote yourselves *entirely* to the *Lord.* ▪ ▪ ▪

GOSPEL Mark 1:21–28

A reading from the holy *gospel* according to *Mark* ▪ ▪ ▪

"Capernaum" = "Ka-pér-nay-um"

Suggest his spellbinding authority.

[In the city of *Capernaum,*] ▪ Jesus entered the *synagogue* on the sabbath ▪ and began to *teach.* ▪ ▪ The people were *spellbound* by his teaching ▪ because he taught with *authority* ▪ and not like the *scribes.* ▪ ▪ ▪

Much energy. Fast rate.

"Sharply" sounds like it means.

Sustain intensity.

With awe.

Your tone approves this phenomenon.

Ritardando: "throughout . . . Galilee."

There *appeared* in their synagogue a man with an *unclean spirit* ▪ that *shrieked:* ▪ ▪ "What do you *want* of us, Jesus of Nazareth? ▪ ▪ Have you come to *destroy* us? ▪ ▪ I *know* who you are— ▪ the *Holy* One of *God!"* ▪ ▪ Jesus rebuked him *sharply:* ▪ ▪ "Be *quiet!* ▪ ▪ Come *out* of the man!" ▪ ▪ At that ▪ the unclean spirit *convulsed* the man *violently* ▪ and with a loud *shriek* ▪ came out of him. ▪ ▪ All who looked on were *amazed.* ▪ ▪ They began to *ask* one another: ▪ ▪ "What does this *mean?* ▪ ▪ A completely *new* teaching in a spirit of *authority!* ▪ ▪ He gives *orders* to unclean *spirits* ▪ and they *obey* him!" ▪ ▪ From *that* point on ▪ his reputation *spread* throughout the surrounding region of Galilee. ▪ ▪ ▪

legislating "restrictions," only offering opinions for our "own good." Read this chapter in Corinthians and you'll see Paul cares about his listeners; then let your voice say he would care about us, too.

GOSPEL Sometimes a single word jumps out of a passage to tell us how to read it. "Spellbound" leaps from this page, a powerful word that describes Jesus' influence on his audience. As teller of the "greatest story ever told" you must employ every storytelling skill to narrate this exciting tale. The Key discusses "transparency" and the difference between "walls" and "windows" (page v). Good readers become transparent by utilizing, not hiding, their gifts and employing oral interpretation techniques so their listeners see not them, but *through* them. It's important to remember that as we discuss the dramatic possibilities of this text.

Speak the first paragraph with the authoritative tones that characterized Jesus' teaching. That mood-setting is essential for the unfolding action which follows.

The possessed man "shrieked," but you don't have to. Suggest the compulsion with which he speaks, the uncontrolled flow of his exclamations. He's loud; he's fast; he's intense; he's on the offensive and defensive at the same time; he's afraid. Jesus matches his volume and energy and we hear (and see on your face) the "authority" that set him apart from the scribes.

Narrate the exorcism as if you were watching it now, capturing the terrible energy of this bizarre event. Without losing the energy go right on to narrate the amazement of the onlookers, filling their question with awe. You needn't try for three different onlooker voices, but do vary the energy, intensity and rate of their comments.

As you inform us of his growing "reputation," your tone acknowledges how proper and predictable was that spreading fame.

READING I When our pain becomes so great that the only thing we can *do* about it is *talk* about it, we discover, amazingly, that talking about it *does* something for us. The "mystery" part of the paschal mystery is that the complete darkness of death and the full joy of the resurrection are closely related. Plumbing the depths of misery is not necessarily bad. This passage is a marvel of misery, oozing with pain, anxiety and depression, and Job shows no embarrassment in expressing it.

Today's gospel will balance this reading with images of healing and hope. Here, focus on life's futility: Life is as demeaning as forced military service ("drudgery") and as hopeless as slavery. Speak these lines with conviction, even anger.

Job looks at his life and sees "months of misery" filled with "troubled *nights*" and "*days*" that vanish as quickly as his "hope." Speak of those lonely nights and desperate days like a terminally ill person who is very depressed. The despair of the last line can be spoken quietly and sincerely. Surely there's been a time when such an emotion wanted to rule your heart: Remember that time and share it. Then the gospel will even more strongly surprise us with its good news.

READING II Once again Paul is expressing strong emotions about subjects near and dear to him: the gospel and himself. Again, he's a bit on the defensive, and his defensiveness is derived from those who questioned his status as an apostle. Having made his point that one who labors is worthy of recompense, he moves on to assert that he labors for the gospel because he is "under compulsion" and has "no choice." Therefore he can't even "boast" about what he does, for he would be ruined if he did *not* do it!

That Paul feels strongly and that these are intensely personal issues for him are the keys to your proclamation. He is not bragging; he is persuading skeptics. Preaching the gospel "willingly," he says, is its own reward; but even if he were unwilling, he couldn't escape the fact that he's been "entrusted with a charge," a responsibility that he simply can't evade. Yet, though he is compelled to preach, he does so freely, expecting nothing in return, without even exercising "the authority the gospel gives [him]." There is argumentativeness in his tone, but also joy that comes from feeling free of indebtedness to others.

The second paragraph is full of balances which should be proclaimed clearly: "not bound to anyone" balances "the slave of all"; "I have made myself *all*" balances "to save

FEBRUARY 10, 1991

FIFTH SUNDAY IN ORDINARY TIME

LECTIONARY #75

READING I Job 7:1–4, 6–7

Stretch words to create plaintive sound.

A reading from the book of *Job* ▪▪▪

Job spoke, ▪ saying: ▪▪

"Human life" is more inclusive. "Drudgery" = forced military service. Recast in plural: "We are slaves, . . . hirelings. . . ."

Is not man's life on earth a *drudgery*? ▪▪
Are not his *days* those of a *hireling*? ▪▪
He is a *slave* who longs for the *shade*, ▪
a hireling who *waits* for his wages. ▪▪

"Told off for me" = "assigned to me."

So *I* have been assigned *months* of *misery*, ▪
and *troubled* nights have been told off
for me. ▪▪

Fast and anxious.

If in *bed* I say, ▪▪ "*When* shall I *arise*?" ▪▪

Slowly. "Drags on" sounds like it means. Faster again. "Restlessness" sounds like it means.

then the night *drags* on; ▪▪
I am filled with *restlessness* until the dawn. ▪▪▪

My *days* are swifter than a *weaver's shuttle*; ▪▪

Hopelessness.

they come to an end without *hope*. ▪▪
Remember ▪ that my life is like the *wind*; ▪▪

Long pause before "This is the Word of the Lord."

I shall not see *happiness* again. ▪▪▪

READING II 1 Corinthians 9:16–19, 22–23

A reading from the first letter of *Paul* ▪
to the *Corinthians* ▪▪▪

Very personal and direct.

Preaching the *gospel* is not the subject of a *boast*; ▪▪ I am under *compulsion* and have no *choice*. ▪▪ I am

Less emotion, more reasoning.

ruined if I do *not* preach it! ▪▪ If I do it *willingly*, ▪ I *have* my recompense; ▪▪ if *unwillingly*, ▪ I am nonetheless entrusted with a *charge*. ▪▪ And this *recompense* of mine? ▪▪ It is simply *this*, ▪▪ that

Animated and a bit defensive.

when *preaching* I offer the gospel *free* of charge ▪ and do not make *full* use of the authority the gospel *gives* me. ▪▪▪

Although I am not *bound* to anyone, ▪ I made myself the *slave* of all ▪ so as to *win* over as many as

He's a willing slave motivated by love.

possible. ▪▪ To the *weak* ▪ I became a *weak* person ▪

Stress the balances.

"Men" can be "people."

Ritardando: "in the hope . . . blessings."

with a view to *winning* the weak. ▪▪ I have made myself *all* things to *all* men ▪ in order to *save* at least *some* of them. ▪▪ In *fact,* ▪ I do all that I do for the *sake* of the gospel ▪ in the hope of having a *share* in its *blessings.* ▪▪▪

GOSPEL Mark 1:29–39

A reading from the holy *gospel* according to *Mark* ▪▪▪

Like a friend telling a familiar story.

Don't rush. Don't overdramatize.

Shift moods.

Upon leaving the *synagogue,* ▪ *Jesus* entered the house of *Simon* and *Andrew* ▪ with James and John. ▪▪ Simon's *mother-in-law* lay *ill* with a fever, ▪ and the *first* thing they did ▪ was to *tell* him about her. ▪▪ He *went* over to her ▪ and *grasped* her hand and *helped* her up, ▪ and the fever *left* her. ▪▪ She *immediately* began to *wait* on them. ▪▪▪

Suggest Jesus' power without overdramatizing.

Change the mood.

Childlike excitement.

Energized and upbeat.

See in your mind's eye what you describe.

After sunset, ▪ as *evening* drew on, ▪ they brought him *all* who were ill ▪ and those *possessed* by demons. ▪▪ Before long ▪ the *whole town* was gathered outside the door. ▪▪ Those whom he *cured,* ▪ who were variously *afflicted,* ▪ were *many,* ▪ and so were the *demons* he expelled. ▪▪ But he would not *permit* the demons to *speak,* ▪ because they *knew* him. ▪▪▪ Rising *early* the next morning, ▪ he went off to a *lonely* place in the *desert;* ▪▪ there he was absorbed in *prayer.* ▪▪ Simon and his companions managed to *track* him down; ▪▪ and when they *found* him, ▪ they told him, ▪▪ "Everybody is *looking* for you!" ▪▪ He *said* to them: ▪▪ "Let us move on to the *neighboring* villages ▪ so that I may proclaim the good news *there* also. ▪▪ *That* is what I have *come* to do." ▪▪ So he went into their *synagogues* ▪ *preaching* the good news ▪ and expelling *demons* throughout the *whole* of Galilee. ▪▪▪

at least *some*"; and so on. His freedom has allowed him to *choose* the slavery of willing service. Paul's service to the weak and to all is a sign of his great love, which you should convey throughout this paragraph. Paul loves willingly, for he knows that service without love offers *no* share in the gospel's blessings.

GOSPEL Mark's gospel is distinctive in its simplicity. He says much with few words and makes the amazing events of the kingdom appear commonplace. Don't embellish Mark's simplicity as you read; instead, let the understatement speak with its own eloquence. As long as you don't rush, and as long as you *use* all the words to tell the story, Mark's images will come to life and weave their magic.

As the narrator, become someone who knew and dearly loved Jesus. Familiarity will then color expressions like "Simon's mother-in-law," "the first thing they did," "grasped her hand," "She immediately began to wait on them." When first you saw that miracle it may have amazed you; now, in memory, it evokes a smile, raised eyebrows and a gentle nodding of the head.

The time references expand Mark's condensation and create unique moods for each episode. "Sunset" and "evening" suggest the tired part of a day suddenly made tumultuous by the arrival of the sick and possessed. Don't work too hard to convince us that "the whole town" sought him out. This, too, has become commonplace. Jesus' power to silence demons is mentioned in a way that suggests you've come to take that power for granted.

"The next morning" creates a mood of rapt silence which is suddenly broken by the disciples' exclamation. Energized by his prayer, Jesus is firm in his decision to "move on." The last sentence is an understatement delivered simply and with total belief: The good news is Jesus did what he came to do!

READING I Note there are three major attitude shifts in the passage. The first twelve lines are full of urgent pleading. A God on the verge of vengeance makes a final call for conversion. The urgency is high. "Even now" (late as it is), says the Lord, it's not too late. The words, though always important individually, *combine* here to create a climate of entreaty. Use the individual words—"fasting," which is different from "weeping," which is different from "mourning"—to build your importunity. Words like "rend" and "return" add to the effect. Convince your listeners that the God who urges is in fact "merciful" and "relenting."

A shift occurs at "Blow the trumpet in Zion!" Your pertinacity has paid off. The people respond. The trumpet sounds the call to repentance. Become the ruler of the people, having made your own inner conversion, now calling the masses to do the same—while there is time! You're used to giving orders; give them! "Proclaim!" "Call!" "Gather!" "Notify!" "Assemble!" Rushing won't work. Speak urgently, yes, but with conviction and authority. Slow down on "children" and "bridegroom," making it clear that penitence now takes precedence over all else (even honeymoons).

The last two lines present good news and the final shift. It's no longer time for shouting. Let the words "concern" and "pity" tell you how to speak: quietly, slowly—as the compassionate God who forgives.

READING II Paul picks up where Joel left off. Only now he enlists each of us—as proclaimers, as God's people—to announce to the world an insistent call to conversion. As Christians each of us is a representative of Christ. Through us Christ does his work, with us he accomplishes the "ministry of reconciliation" (spoken of in an earlier part of this letter). But we can best call others to reconciliation by first being reconciled ourselves. Hence you implore us in Christ's name. Today is no day for holding back. There's too much at stake. "We might become the very holiness of God."

You just implored, now you must "beg." Are you willing to let your voice convey that much urgency, that much concern? Do you care enough about your listeners to make unmistakable the message that reconciliation can be lost and to declare the good news that "now" it is offered again, "now" is the "acceptable time" to act? Your delivery on the two phrases following "For he says . . ." should be slow, measured and careful, striving to be understood. The two "nows" are explosive and your rate faster.

FEBRUARY 13, 1991

ASH WEDNESDAY

LECTIONARY #220

READING I Joel 2:12–18

A reading from the book of the prophet ▪ *Joel* ▪ ▪ ▪

Even *now,* ▪ says the Lord, ▪ ▪
Pleading. *return* to me with your *whole* heart, ▪
Three different responses. with *fasting,* ▪ and *weeping,* ▪ and *mourning;* ▪ ▪
Rend your *hearts,* ▪ not your *garments,* ▪
and *return* to the Lord, ▪ your God. ▪ ▪
For *gracious* and *merciful* is he, ▪
slow to anger, ▪ *rich* in kindness, ▪
and *relenting* in punishment. ▪ ▪
Voice full of hope. Perhaps he will *again* relent ▪
and leave behind him a *blessing,* ▪
Offerings and *libations*
for the Lord, ▪ your *God.* ▪ ▪ ▪

Pause. Major attitude shift. Blow the *trumpet* in Zion! ▪
Use the imperative verbs. proclaim a *fast,* ▪
call an *assembly;* ▪ ▪
Gather the people, ▪
notify the congregation; ▪ ▪
Assemble the elders, ▪
Slowing a bit. gather the *children*
and the *infants* at the breast; ▪ ▪
Let the *bridegroom quit* his room, ▪
and the *bride* her *chamber.* ▪ ▪
Between the *porch* and the *altar* ▪
let the *priests,* ▪ the *ministers* of the Lord, ▪
Try stretching the word. *weep,* ▪
Be the voice of all the people. And *say,* ▪ ▪ *"Spare,* O Lord, ▪ your *people,* ▪
and make *not* your heritage a *reproach,* ▪
with the nations *ruling* over them! ▪ ▪
The sarcastic voice of non-believers. *Why* should they say among the peoples, ▪ ▪
'Where is their *God?'"* ▪ ▪ ▪

Pause. Another attitude shift. Then ▪ the Lord was stirred to *concern* for his land ▪
and took *pity* on his people. ▪ ▪ ▪

READING II 2 Corinthians 5:20—6:2

A reading from the second letter of *Paul* ▪ to the *Corinthians* ▪▪▪

First establish eye contact, then speak. Make "implore" sound like what it means. "Be reconciled" for your own good!

We are *ambassadors* for *Christ,* ▪▪ *God* as it were ▪ *appealing* through *us.* ▪▪ We *implore* you, ▪ in *Christ's* name: ▪▪ be *reconciled* to God! ▪▪▪ For *our* sakes ▪ God made *him* ▪ who did not *know* sin ▪ to *be* sin, ▪ so that in *him* ▪ *we* might become the very *holiness* of God. ▪▪▪

Take pause after "says" and after "heard you." Longer pause after "helped you."

Ritardando: ". . . is the day of salvation." Build second "now."

As your fellow workers ▪ we *beg* you *not* to receive the grace of God in *vain.* ▪▪ For he says, ▪▪ "In an *acceptable* time I have *heard* you; ▪▪ on a day of *salvation* ▪ I have *helped* you." ▪▪▪ *Now* is the acceptable time! ▪▪ *Now* ▪ is the *day* of *salvation!* ▪▪▪

GOSPEL Matthew 6:1–6, 16–18

A reading from the holy *gospel* according to *Matthew* ▪▪▪

A warning to people you care about.

With a sense of frustration.

Convince listeners that this is do-able.

Jesus said to his disciples: ▪▪ "Be on *guard* against performing religious acts for people to *see.* ▪▪ *Otherwise* ▪ expect *no* recompense from your heavenly Father. ▪▪ When you give *alms,* for example, ▪ do not blow a *horn* before you in synagogues and streets ▪ like *hypocrites* looking for *applause.* ▪▪ You can be *sure* of this much, ▪ they are *already* repaid. ▪▪ In *giving* alms ▪ you are not to let your *left* hand know what your *right* hand is *doing.* ▪▪ Keep your deeds of mercy *secret,* ▪ and your *Father* ▪ who *sees* in secret ▪ will *repay* you. ▪▪▪

Such wasted energy!

Here's the better way.

"One" is more inclusive.

"When you are *praying,* ▪ do not *behave* like the hypocrites ▪ who love to *stand* and pray in *synagogues* ▪ or on *street corners* in order to be *noticed.* ▪▪ I give you my *word,* ▪ they are *already* repaid. ▪▪ Whenever *you* pray, ▪ go to your room, ▪ *close* your door, ▪ and pray to your Father in *private.* ▪▪ Then your *Father,* ▪ who *sees* what no *man* sees, ▪ will *repay* you. ▪▪▪

Not sarcasm, but regret.

You are proud of those who will heed this advice.

Ritardando: "will repay you."

"When you *fast,* ▪ you are not to look *glum* as the *hypocrites* do. ▪▪ They *change* the appearance of their *faces* so that others may *see* they are fasting. ▪▪ I *assure* you, ▪ they are *already repaid.* ▪▪ When *you* fast, ▪ see to it that you *groom* your hair and *wash* your face. ▪▪ In *that* way ▪ *no one* can see you are fasting ▪ but your *Father* who is *hidden;* ▪▪ and your Father who *sees* what is hidden ▪ will *repay* you." ▪▪▪

GOSPEL How do we proclaim a reading in which Jesus attacks the religious insincerity of certain members of his society? We proclaim it in a way that suggests that all are members of that group and with a humility that allows us to look first at ourselves. The words are there and must be read, but you might best serve the scripture by underplaying the lines referring to the hypocrites, avoiding any mocking sarcasm in your tone.

Anger, not sarcasm, characterizes Jesus' attitude toward those who deceive others, and themselves, about the quality of their personal piety. In Zeffirelli's *Jesus of Nazareth* this scene depicts a fiery Jesus hurling words of accusation like a zealous prosecutor summing up to the jury. You might make yours an intense but less strident anger born of the realization that hypocrisy is as self-destructive as it is self-aggrandizing. You are warning your listeners about a potential trap. Let your voice say: Don't go near; you'll fall in!

The other thing you are saying is "Do it right and God will reward you." There is reassurance, encouragement, even joy in that refrain. And note that a refrain is what you have at the end of each paragraph—slightly reworded each time, but saying the same thing: The Father *sees* and will repay. Rather than varying the stresses, hit those same three words each time, capitalizing on the ability of refrains to draw us deeper into an idea and intensify our experience. Speak with real concern for the spiritual welfare of your listeners. Be worried about the choices they will make.

READING I Times and places of origin are important. We enshrine our presidents' birthplaces, mark anniversaries of famous "firsts" such as the walk on the moon, and remember where and when we pledged ourselves to our spouse. In Israel "covenant" was a key concept, so its origins were of pivotal importance. Unlike the narrower, more demanding covenants made with Abraham and Moses, this covenant with Noah embraces all humankind and asks nothing in return for God's promise of eternal exemption from destruction by flood. This first covenant between God and people is a key moment in human history that the Genesis author wants remembered, so the technique of refrain is employed to aid our memories.

Recall how the singing swells in church every time a refrain recurs and you'll realize what effective aids to memory refrains are. A God who has wiped the slate clean and wants to start fresh, says: "I am now establishing my covenant . . . I will establish my covenant . . . This is the sign . . . of the covenant . . . I set my . . . bow to serve as a sign of the covenant . . . I will recall the covenant . . ." In those refrains God's *initiative* is blatant, God's good will palpable; the repetitions serve to reinforce that. The fact that the repeated references to covenant say the same thing over and over is no reason to rush them. In songs you spend the same amount of time on refrains each time they recur. Do the same here. Use them like a caress to stroke God's people with tenderness, to persuade them about the sincerity of God's forgiveness. In other words, let your voice and attitude become the "bow" promising unending fidelity.

READING II Peter's message is so well-reasoned and logical, you'd think Paul was his ghostwriter. Peter begins by answering the question of "why Christ died" but interjects an aside ("a just man [person] for the sake of the unjust") before answering: "so that he could lead you to God." Start with high energy, dip slightly on the aside, and renew the energy for the answer; this way the question and answer will be connected and the aside subordinated.

Peter rivals Paul here in his use of balances. He compares "life" with "death," "fleshly" with "spirit," "eight" with "you" and "stain" with "conscience." Emphasizing these parallel ideas will help your listeners understand. In light of the first reading, the reference to Noah should be especially highlighted. Peter describes the "patient" mercy

FEBRUARY 17, 1991

FIRST SUNDAY OF LENT

LECTIONARY #23

READING I Genesis 9:8–15

A reading from the book of *Genesis* ▪ ▪ ▪

The introduction signals that good news is coming.

God said to *Noah* and to his *sons* with him: ▪ ▪ *"See,* ▪ I am now establishing my *covenant* with you ▪ and your *descendants* after you ▪ and with every living *creature* that was *with* you: ▪ ▪ all the *birds,* ▪ and the various tame and wild *animals* ▪ that were *with* you and *came out* of the ark. ▪ ▪ I will establish my *covenant* with you, ▪ that *never* again shall all bodily creatures be *destroyed* ▪ by the waters of a *flood;* ▪ ▪ there shall *not* be another flood to *devastate* the earth." ▪ ▪ God *added:* ▪ ▪ "This is the *sign* that I am giving for *all ages* to come, ▪ of the covenant between *me* and *you* ▪ and *every* living creature with you: ▪ ▪ I set my *bow* in the clouds ▪ to *serve* as a *sign* of the covenant between *me* and the *earth.* ▪ ▪ When I bring *clouds* over the earth, ▪ and the bow *appears* in the clouds, ▪ I will *recall* the covenant I have made between *me* and *you* and *all* living beings, ▪ so that the waters shall never *again* become a flood ▪ to *destroy* all mortal beings." ▪ ▪ ▪

Don't rush. Naming creatures shows compassion for all creation.

Strong and loving.

With conviction.

As if to remove any doubt.

A guarantee!

"I will recall": God is given human qualities in this section. It's a repetition, but with renewed energy.

READING II 1 Peter 3:18–22

Connect Peter's questions and answers. "Man" can be "person."

Contrast "fleshly" and "spirit."

"Spirits in prison" refers to the dead. Emphasis on God's patient mercy.

"You" contrasts with "eight" above.

See Rev. NAB translation in commentary. "Stain" parallels "conscience."

Strong ending.

A reading from the first letter of *Peter* ▪ ▪ ▪

This is *why* Christ died for sins ▪ *once* for all, ▪ a *just* man for the sake of the *unjust:* ▪ ▪ so that he could *lead* you to *God.* ▪ ▪ He was put to *death* insofar as *fleshly* existence goes, ▪ but was given *life* in the realm of the *spirit.* ▪ ▪ It was in the *spirit* also that he went to *preach* to the spirits in *prison.* ▪ ▪ They had *disobeyed* as long ago as *Noah's* day, ▪ while God *patiently* waited until the *ark* was built. ▪ ▪ At *that* time, ▪ a *few* persons, *eight* in all, ▪ *escaped* in the ark through the *water.* ▪ ▪ *You* are now saved by a *baptismal* bath which corresponds to this *exactly.* ▪ ▪ This *baptism* is no removal of physical *stain,* ▪ but the *pledge* to God of an irreproachable *conscience* through the *resurrection* of Jesus Christ. ▪ ▪ He went to *heaven* and is at God's *right hand,* ▪ with angelic rulers and powers *subjected* to him. ▪ ▪ ▪

GOSPEL Mark 1:12–15

Short reading = slow reading.

Use each word for color, texture, mood.

Contrast "beast" and "angels."

"Arrest" contrasts with rest of paragraph.

Urgency. Shift focus on each exclamation.

You, too, are a believer.

A reading from the holy *gospel* according to *Mark* ▪ ▪ ▪

The *Spirit* sent Jesus out toward the *desert.* ▪ ▪ He *stayed* in the wasteland *forty* days, ▪ put to the *test* there by *Satan.* ▪ ▪ He was with the *wild beasts,* ▪ and *angels* waited on him. ▪ ▪ ▪

After John's *arrest,* ▪ Jesus appeared in *Galilee* ▪ proclaiming God's *good news:* ▪ ▪ "This is the time of *fulfillment.* ▪ ▪ The *reign* of *God* is at *hand!* ▪ ▪ *Reform* your lives ▪ and *believe* in the good news!" ▪ ▪ ▪

God bestowed on Noah, then builds his enthusiasm as he asserts that same mercy is extended to us.

The Revised NAB translates "This baptism . . . through the resurrection of Jesus Christ" as "[This baptism] is not a removal of dirt from the body but an *appeal* to God for a clear conscience, through the resurrection of Jesus Christ." Jesus and the resurrection are the heart of Peter's message. Christ's victory over death gives us power in our own struggles, and hope that we will join him in "heaven" where he rules "at God's right hand" and over the angelic powers. That's a strong message that requires a strong ending.

GOSPEL Among the evangelists Mark was always insisting on "just the facts." This bare-bones gospel is ample proof of that. Even though his is the shortest gospel Mark often provides details the longer-winded evangelists leave out. And, as life has taught us, less is often more. So today, do what every cook who has been caught short of food for unexpected guests learns to do: Serve less but serve it well.

"Well" here means slowly; not in slow motion of course, but in a way that lets you visualize the scene as you speak and that alerts the assembly to this stylized, dramatic rendering of the climactic encounter between two epic personalities. Stress the key words: "desert," "wasteland," "forty days," "test" and "Satan." Only Mark mentions the "wild beasts," a reference which adds to the surreal quality of the scene.

The second paragraph begins with an ominous reference to John's arrest that foreshadows Jesus' own destiny. Yet, even with that awareness, Mark presents a vital, energetic Christ boldly proclaiming the good news of the kingdom. Slow your delivery of his three exclamations by addressing each to a different part of the assembly. Proclaim as Jesus did, by inviting your assembly to believe *with* you that God's reign can overwhelm and transform your life.

READING I This reading is also proclaimed during the Easter Vigil. See that commentary for further analysis.

Abraham responds with a naive and ironic "Ready" to God's terrible request to "Take your *son,*" made all the more gut-wrenching by the powerful emphasis: "your *only* one, whom you *love.*" The rest of God's command is underplayed. Without embellishment, the words themselves can speak the horror.

Describe Abraham's work with altar and wood the same way you would imagine him doing it: numbly, steeled against the anguish that will follow, containing his emotion to avoid alarming his young son. The action with the knife is narrated one phrase at a time. Speaking it in one breath would make him seem heartless.

God removes the sinister mask to reveal compassionate concern: "Do not do the *least* thing!" From a shocked "Yes, Lord?" Abraham's mood resolves into relief as he spies and then prepares the ram.

The "Lord's messenger" speaks for the Lord who emphatically promises ("I *swear* by *myself)* the gift of a homeland peopled with countless descendants. For a man who entered old age with no heir to carry on his name this is great comfort, as is the promise of "blessing" for each of us who are Abraham's *spiritual* heirs.

READING II One of the most comforting lines of scripture opens this reading. To prevent its being missed, take a substantial pause after introducing the Letter to the Romans, and with sustained eye contact speak the line from memory. That line contains all Jesus came to reveal about the Father: God loves us, is on our side and longs to see us happy!

Paul's second question flows from his first: If God loves us *so* much, enough to be willing to sacrifice his son for us, is it possible that "he would not grant us" every single thing we need? Your attitude should convey Paul's conviction that the answer is obvious.

The next questions are somewhat playful, asked with consummate confidence, the way a child perched safely in a tree might look down at playmates and say, "Who's going to take my ball away, you?" The God who *"justifies"* won't condemn; Christ who won our salvation won't take it back. There is tremendous gratitude (and pride) in the description of Jesus who died, no, "was *raised up,*" and who now sits in glory interceding for us.

FEBRUARY 24, 1991

SECOND SUNDAY OF LENT

LECTIONARY #26

READING I Genesis 22:1–2, 9, 10–13, 15–18

A reading from the book of *Genesis* ▪ ▪ ▪

"Test" signals bad news.

"Ready" = ironically eager.

God put Abraham to the *test.* ▪ ▪ He *called* to him, ▪ ▪ *"Abraham!"* ▪ ▪ *"Ready!"* ▪ he replied. ▪ ▪ Then God said: ▪ ▪ "Take your son *Isaac,* ▪ your *only* one, ▪ whom you *love,* ▪ and *go* to the land of Moriah. ▪ ▪ There you shall *offer* him up as a *holocaust* ▪ on a height that I will *point out* to you." ▪ ▪ ▪

God's voice: strong and unyielding. Don't overdramatize.

Suggest a stoic Abraham.

One phrase at a time, as if difficult to speak.

Sudden and strong. Build on the second "Abraham!"

When they *came* to the place of which God had *told* him, ▪ Abraham built an *altar* there ▪ and arranged the *wood* on it. ▪ ▪ Then he *reached* out ▪ and took the *knife* ▪ to *slaughter* his son. ▪ ▪ But the Lord's messenger *called* to him from heaven, ▪ ▪ *"Abraham,* ▪ *Abraham!"* ▪ ▪ *"Yes,* Lord," ▪ he answered. ▪ ▪ "Do *not* lay your hand on the boy," ▪ said the messenger. ▪ ▪ "Do not do the *least* thing to him. ▪ ▪ I *know* now how *devoted* you are to God, ▪ since you did not *withhold* from me your own *beloved* son." ▪ ▪ ▪ As Abraham *looked* about, ▪ he spied a *ram* caught by its horns in the thicket. ▪ ▪ So he went and *took* the ram ▪ and offered it up as a *holocaust* ▪ in *place* of his son. ▪ ▪ ▪

Compassionate voice.

With a sense of relief.

Strong declaration.

This is a lifelong dream fulfilled.

Look at assembly. They are included in this "blessing."

Again the Lord's messenger called to Abraham from heaven ▪ and said: ▪ ▪ "I *swear* by *myself,* ▪ declares the Lord, ▪ that because you *acted* as you did in not *withholding* from me your beloved *son,* ▪ ▪ I will *bless* you *abundantly* ▪ and make your *descendants* as *countless* as the *stars* of the sky and the *sands* of the seashore; ▪ ▪ your descendants shall take *possession* of the gates of their *enemies,* ▪ and *in* your descendants ▪ *all* the *nations* of the earth shall find *blessing*— ▪ ▪ *all* this ▪ because you *obeyed* my command." ▪ ▪ ▪

READING II Romans 8:31–34

A reading from the letter of *Paul* ▪ to the *Romans* ▪▪▪

Memorize first line. Express comfort.

Answer is obvious, right!

Pause as if awaiting reply.

Don't rush. Allow time for silent reply.

Your joyous tone says: "Of course not!"

If *God* is for us, ▪ who can be *against* us? ▪▪ Is it *possible* ▪ that he who did not spare his *own Son* ▪ but *handed* him over for the sake of us *all* ▪ will not *grant* us all things *besides?* ▪▪ Who shall bring a *charge* against God's *chosen* ones? ▪▪ God, ▪ who *justifies?* ▪▪ Who shall *condemn* them? ▪▪ Christ *Jesus,* ▪ who *died* ▪ or rather was *raised* up, ▪ who is at the *right* hand of God ▪ and who *intercedes* for us? ▪▪▪

GOSPEL Mark 9:2–10

Extra long pause.

A reading from the holy *gospel* according to *Mark* ▪▪▪

Pause; then slowly.

Incredulous.

Peter can't believe his eyes.

Enthusiastic joy.

An aside—you know the feeling.

"Overshadowing" intensifies the awe. Gentle and loving.

Jesus took *Peter,* ▪ *James* ▪ and *John* off by themselves with him ▪ and led them up a high *mountain.* ▪▪ He was *transfigured* before their eyes ▪ and his clothes became *dazzlingly* white— ▪ *whiter* than the work of any *bleacher* could make them. ▪▪ *Elijah* appeared to them ▪ along with *Moses;* ▪▪ the two were in *conversation* with *Jesus.* ▪▪ Then *Peter* spoke to Jesus: ▪▪ *"Rabbi,* ▪ how *good* it is for us to *be* here. ▪▪ Let us erect three *booths* on this site, ▪ one for *you,* ▪ one for *Moses,* ▪ and one for *Elijah."* ▪▪ He hardly knew what to *say,* ▪ for they were all overcome with *awe.* ▪▪ A *cloud* came, ▪ *overshadowing* them, ▪ and out of the cloud a *voice:* ▪▪ "This is my *Son,* ▪ my *beloved.* ▪▪ *Listen* to him." ▪▪ *Suddenly* ▪ looking around ▪ they no longer saw *anyone* with them— ▪▪ only *Jesus.* ▪▪▪

Speak as if you hear it but it doesn't register.

And so do we! Extra long pause before: "This is the gospel. . . ."

As they were coming *down* the mountain, ▪ he *strictly* enjoined them ▪ not to *tell* anyone what they had seen ▪ *before* the Son of Man had *risen* from the *dead.* ▪▪ They *kept* this word of his to *themselves,* ▪ though they continued to *discuss* what ▪▪ "to *rise* from the *dead"* ▪ meant. ▪▪▪

GOSPEL Mark's breathless account of the transfiguration poses challenges to those who read it. How do you do justice to so significant an event with so few words? Can you make transitions in mood with a single word like "suddenly?" Will the mystery and awe that greeted the disciples on the mountain touch the disciples who sit in the pews? Unfortunately none of these questions can be dismissed, because they raise issues that deal directly with the purpose for which you read: that the person of Jesus might be proclaimed, that who he was might shape who we are and will become.

One sentence and the curtain rises on this drama. So make that first sentence raise the curtain slowly. Pause before and after it, then, as if seeing it yourself, say "He was transfigured," pausing after each word. Though he seems in a hurry, Mark takes time to attest to the whiteness of "his clothes"; Elijah and Moses, representing the prophets and the law of Israel, are seen, amazingly, to be "in *conversation*" with Jesus.

"And here *I* am *witnessing* all this," Peter must be thinking, as he fumbles for something to do. Let yourself become Peter expressing first unbridled joy in words that echo through the ages: "How good it is for us to be here!" and then his sudden inspiration to build the booths. Mark's aside is not condescending; it suggests his understanding of the overwhelming nature of the event.

The "cloud" brings a mood of even greater awe, but the voice surprises us with its tenderness and love. Mark's trademark "Suddenly" then breaks the mood and everything is over.

Jesus' demand for secrecy sounds like something heard by the apostles while they are deeply absorbed in something else. They're pondering the mystery of rising "from the dead." Generations later, though we know what it meant for Jesus, don't we all still wonder what it will mean for us? Let that question linger before announcing "This is the gospel of the Lord."

READING I A parent or teacher makes rules out of love for children who need the wisdom that comes with age. God does the same for us. The scriptures view the Law as liberating us from the tyranny of our weaknesses. God's *love*, not God's anger, shows us the better way. The phrase "God delivered all these commandments" suggests something awaited, maybe longed for, that will enable us to live and love. God's reminder that "I . . . brought you out of . . . slavery" tells the people that a concerned and loving God is speaking. That tone dominates your entire reading.

The injunction to worship only the Lord reflects God's awareness that worshiping other gods means adopting their *values* rather than the values contained in the commandments. God is jealous for the people's welfare; he sternly admonishes them to resist the allurements of other gods. God doesn't want to threaten punishment, but all actions have consequences. Though God is eager to shower mercy "down to the thousandth generation," your tone warns that God's justice will give us what we deserve.

God knows our needs; resting and communing with our God is foremost among them. Like a mama telling her son, "Eat, it's good for you!", you command sabbath observance, noting that God's concern extends even to the "slave," the "beast" and the "alien."

Respect for father and mother is linked to "long life." Tenderly, looking at the parents before you, call us to that respect.

The "shall not" commandments call us to live in peace with each other. Looking at different parts of the assembly, quicken your pace and increase your intensity until the last two injunctions. Read these slowly, letting your tone suggest the futility of desiring what is not ours. This is no list of do's and don't's; it's more a "Christmas list" and each commandment is a gift God has for us.

READING II No wise person looking for a savior would climb the hill of Calvary to interview the man hanging on the cross. And yet our "foolish" faith tells us that is where true wisdom and power are to be found. Where we least expect, where human eyes see only defeat and folly, Paul insists we find the greatest wisdom and incomparable strength. He offers the baffling sign of the cross. No wonder this crucified messiah was a "stumbling block" to Jews and an "absurdity" to everyone else.

Speak of what Jews demand and Greeks look for as reasonable positions; then proudly announce that "we preach" an admittedly unreasonable position that,

MARCH 3, 1991

THIRD SUNDAY OF LENT

LECTIONARY #29

READING I Exodus 20:1–17

A reading from the book of *Exodus* ▪ ▪ ▪

The commandments are delivered as gifts of love.

Your tone says: "I am the Lord who loves you."

God delivered all these *commandments:* ▪ ▪ *"I,* the Lord, ▪ am your *God,* ▪ who brought you out of the land of *Egypt,* ▪ that place of *slavery.* ▪ ▪ You shall not have *other* gods besides *me.* ▪ ▪ You shall not carve *idols* for yourselves in the shape of anything in the *sky* above ▪ or on the *earth* below ▪ or in the *waters* beneath the earth; ▪ ▪ you shall not *bow down* before them ▪ or *worship* them. ▪ ▪ For *I,* ▪ the Lord, your *God,* ▪ am a *jealous* God, ▪ inflicting *punishment* for their *fathers'* wickedness ▪ on the *children* of those who *hate* me, ▪ down to the *third* and *fourth* generations; ▪ ▪ but bestowing *mercy* down to the *thousandth* generation, ▪ on the children of those who *love* me ▪ and *keep* my commandments. ▪ ▪ ▪

Great disdain for false gods and what they stand for.

"Fathers can be "ancestors."

Gentle and persuasive.

Firm and uncompromising. "Him" can be "the one."

"You shall not take the *name* of the Lord, your God, ▪ in *vain.* ▪ ▪ For the Lord will not leave *unpunished* ▪ him who *takes* his name in vain. ▪ ▪ ▪

Let your tone say: "This is reasonable. It's not too much to ask."

"Remember to keep *holy* the *sabbath* day. ▪ ▪ *Six* days you may labor and do *all* your work, ▪ ▪ but the *seventh* day is the *sabbath* of the Lord, ▪ your *God.* ▪ ▪ *No* work may be done then ▪ either by *you,* ▪ or your *son* or *daughter,* ▪ or your male or female *slave,* ▪ or your *beast,* ▪ or by the *alien* who lives with you. ▪ ▪ In six days the Lord made the *heavens* and the *earth,* ▪ the *sea* and *all* that is in them; ▪ ▪ but on the *seventh* day ▪ he *rested.* ▪ ▪ That is why the Lord has *blessed* the sabbath day ▪ ▪ and made it *holy.* ▪ ▪ ▪

The sabbath is extended to all.

Fast and intense, then, suddenly, slower and calm.

Caress the words "blessed" and "holy."

Don't rush.

"Honor your *father* and your *mother,* ▪ that you may have a *long* life ▪ in the land which the Lord, your God, ▪ is *giving* you. ▪ ▪

Faster pace.

"You shall not *kill.* ▪ ▪

"You shall not commit *adultery.* ▪ ▪

"You shall not *steal.* ▪ ▪

"You shall not bear *false witness* against your *neighbor.* ▪ ▪

Slower. Suggesting: "Don't spend your energy coveting these things."

"You shall not *covet* your neighbor's *house.* ▪ ▪ You shall not *covet* your neighbor's *wife,* ▪ nor his male or female *slave,* ▪ nor his *ox* or *ass,* ▪ nor *anything* else that *belongs* to him." ▪ ▪ ▪

[Shorter: Exodus 20:1–3, 7–8, 12–17]

READING II 1 Corinthians 1:22–25

Short reading, so go slow!

A reading from the first letter of *Paul* ▪ to the *Corinthians* ▪ ▪ ▪

Contrast "signs" and "wisdom."

Jews and Greeks and everyone in the pews are "called."

Rev. NAB is clearer and inclusive: "For the foolishness of God is wiser than human wisdom, and the weakness of God is stronger than human strength." Slowly.

Jews demand *"signs"* ▪ and Greeks look for *"wisdom,"* ▪ ▪ but *we* preach *Christ crucified,* ▪ ▪ a *stumbling* block to Jews, ▪ and an *absurdity* to Gentiles; ▪ ▪ but to those who are *called,* ▪ Jews and Greeks *alike,* ▪ Christ is the *power* of God ▪ *and* the *wisdom* of God. ▪ ▪ For God's *folly* ▪ is *wiser* than men, ▪ ▪ and his *weakness* ▪ more *powerful* than men. ▪ ▪ ▪

GOSPEL John 2:13–25

A reading from the holy *gospel* according to *John* ▪ ▪ ▪

Upbeat. No hint of what's to come.

Sudden shift. Your voice tenses.

Release the anger.

Anger and force no one could resist.

In the disciples' voices.

As the Jewish *Passover* was near, ▪ Jesus went up to *Jerusalem.* ▪ ▪ In the *temple* precincts ▪ he came upon people engaged in selling *oxen,* ▪ *sheep* and *doves,* ▪ and others seated ▪ changing *coins.* ▪ ▪ He made a [kind of] *whip* of cords ▪ and *drove* them all *out* of the temple area, ▪ sheep and oxen *alike,* ▪ and *knocked over* the moneychangers' tables, ▪ *spilling* their coins. ▪ ▪ He *told* those who were selling *doves:* ▪ ▪ *"Get* them *out* of here!" ▪ ▪ *Stop* turning my Father's *house* into a *marketplace!"* ▪ ▪ His disciples *recalled* the words of Scripture: ▪ ▪ *"Zeal* for your house *consumes* me."▪ ▪ ▪

On the offensive.

A dare they don't understand.

Sinister contempt.

Quietly. No contempt for adversaries. Compassion for the misunderstood Jesus.

At this the Jews *responded,* ▪ ▪ "What *sign* can you show us *authorizing* you to do these things?" ▪ ▪ *"Destroy* this temple," ▪ was Jesus' answer, ▪ ▪ "and in *three* days I will *raise* it up." ▪ ▪ They *retorted,* ▪ ▪ "This temple took *forty-six years* to build, ▪ and *you* are going to 'raise it up in *three days*'!" ▪ ▪ *Actually* he was talking about the temple of his *body.* ▪ ▪ Only *after* Jesus had been raised from the dead ▪ did his disciples *recall* that he had said this, ▪ and come to *believe* the Scripture ▪ and the *word* he had spoken. ▪ ▪ ▪

Suggest superficiality of this belief.

Caution, anger, sadness.

Ritardando: "Of what was . . ." "Man's" can be "the human."

While he was in *Jerusalem* during the Passover festival, ▪ many *believed* in his name, ▪ for they could *see* the signs he was performing. ▪ ▪ For *his* part, Jesus would not *trust* himself to them ▪ because he *knew* them *all.* ▪ ▪ He needed *no one* to give him testimony about *human nature.* ▪ ▪ He was *well* aware ▪ of what was in man's *heart.* ▪ ▪ ▪

understandably, trips people up. "But to those who are called" is spoken tenderly.

The last sentence summarizes Paul's thesis. It's one of those statements that would have stopped people in their tracks when they first heard it. Let your slow and earnest delivery and your careful balance of opposites ("folly" and "wiser") make us hear it again for the first time.

GOSPEL Some tempers work like traffic lights: They start out green and turn yellow before blazing red. But others are like railroad signals; dark and silent one second, ringing and flashing red the next. John would persuade us Jesus' temper was of the second sort.

We have no clue until the whip starts flailing that Jesus is the least bit disturbed. Narrate the first sentence in an upbeat mood as Jesus approaches the holy city at festival time. Your voice tenses as you mention the "selling [of] oxen, sheep and doves" and the "changing [of] coins." The train is roaring toward the crossing but still no signal warns of its approach. The "whip" is made with jaws clenched tightly, then suddenly lights begin to flash. Spill the anger as you tell of animals being driven out while tables are dumped of their coins. By the time Jesus speaks, his temper is fully released, a runaway train that no one could stop. Quote scripture ("Zeal . . . ") not as the enraged Jesus but as the disciples commenting, with nodding heads, on Jesus' tirade.

The bystanders respond with anger and disdain, trying to eyeball Jesus into retreat. He holds his ground and dares them to "destroy this temple." Go ahead, he seems to say, I dare you. And in three days you can watch me raise it up! Now they think they have him. Their scorn contrasts "forty-six years to build" with "three days . . . to raise it up."

Without malice toward the detractors, the evangelist takes over explaining what Jesus meant and when it was finally understood.

The last paragraph is surprising. We don't expect such caution from Jesus. Suggest the superficiality of belief that's based solely on "signs" and you'll make Christ's wariness more understandable. The three final sentences start with a too-many-times-burned caution that sparks momentarily into anger and resolves finally into sadness about what lies in the human heart.

READING I The first reading often serves to set the stage for the gospel. *"Thirst," "drink"* and *"water,"* first introduced in the Exodus account, become the central images of John's story. Perhaps water is a ubiquitous image in the scriptures because, being so essential to our survival, it serves as a powerful symbol of God's place in our lives. The wandering Israelites thirst not only for water but also for reassurance that "the Lord is in [their] midst."

That lack of certainty, which turns to fear and borders on despair, characterizes the encounter between Moses and the people. Recall the last time you were uncertain of how to get to a certain destination and asked your passenger's opinion about which way to turn. When that advice sent you in the wrong direction, did you resist or yield to the temptation to say, "Why did I listen to you? I knew we shouldn't go this way. Now we're worse off than before." The grumbling of the Israelites, though surprising after the miracles they've witnessed, demonstrates the very human tendency to blame someone for whatever difficulty we find ourselves in. But however human, it is still obnoxious. Fill their dialogue with fear and anger, leaving no room for sympathy. Moses calls out loudly to God, fearing what the people might do to him, but also frustrated that he's been put in such a difficult situation.

It's hard to imagine that God would be anything but saddened and angered by the people's lack of faith. Yet God is merciful and tolerates much human weakness. Make God sound frustrated, angry at first but gradually melting into a tone of loving reassurance. The expectant tone with which you narrate "This Moses did . . ." should suggest that water did indeed flow.

Regret characterizes the final narration. The last line is a reminder that Lent calls each of us to trust that God will always be "in our midst."

READING II You've had an argument with friend or spouse. The anger tears your stomach while you pout. Finally you pick up the phone or find the one you've wronged and speak the words that wrestled with your tongue. And peace moves back into your heart. Paul says the same thing happens to the Christian who has been "justified by faith." We are no longer separated from God but instead are given "access by faith" to the divine presence. We now stand before a God who allows us to boast—boast that one day we will share in the glory of God. This hope is a free gift of God that, though tasted, is as yet unattained. It will not "leave us disappointed," however, because it is based on

MARCH 3, 1991

THIRD SUNDAY OF LENT, YEAR A

Editor's note: *Lenten Sunday liturgies which include a celebration of the rite of scrutiny of the Rite of Christian Initiation of Adults also include this set of readings from Year A. These readings replace the readings for Year B.*

LECTIONARY #28

READING I Exodus 17:3–7

As "narrator," shift focus to take in whole assembly. As "people," face left to address Moses. "Grumbled" sounds like it means.

As Moses, focus front over heads of assembly. Afraid and somewhat angry.

As God, again face left where you earlier placed Moses. Start angry, end reassuring.

Let us know the miracle happened.

"Massah" = Maś-uh, "Meribah" = Mér-i-bah (i as in "it"). With regret over the lack of faith.

A reading from the book of *Exodus* ▪ ▪ ▪

In their *thirst* for water, ▪ the people *grumbled* against Moses, ▪ saying, ▪ ▪ *"Why* did you ever make us *leave* Egypt? ▪ ▪ Was it just to have us *die* here of *thirst* with our *children* and our *livestock?"* ▪ ▪ So Moses *cried* out to the Lord, ▪ ▪ "What shall I *do* with this people? ▪ ▪ A little *more* and they will *stone* me!" ▪ ▪ The Lord *answered* Moses, ▪ ▪ *"Go* over there in *front* of the people, ▪ along with some of the *elders* of Israel, ▪ holding in your *hand,* ▪ as you go, ▪ the *staff* with which you *struck* the *river.* ▪ ▪ *I* will be standing there in *front* of you ▪ on the *rock* in *Horeb.* ▪ ▪ *Strike* the rock, ▪ and the *water* will *flow* from it ▪ for the people to *drink."* ▪ ▪ *This* Moses *did,* ▪ in the *presence* of the *elders* of Israel. ▪ ▪ The place was called *Massah* and *Meribah,* ▪ because the Israelites *quarreled* there and *tested* the Lord, ▪ saying, ▪ ▪ "Is the *Lord* in our *midst* ▪ or *not?"* ▪ ▪ ▪

READING II Romans 5:1–2, 5–8

Support this theology with emotional intensity, with joy at your own salvation.

Christ is the key that makes it all possible.

Speak with confidence and authority. "Love of God" = God's love for us, not ours for God.

A reading from the letter of *Paul* ▪ to the *Romans* ▪ ▪ ▪

Now that *we* have been *justified* by *faith,* ▪ we are at *peace* with God through our *Lord Jesus Christ.* ▪ ▪ Through *him* we have gained *access* by *faith* to the *grace* in which we *now stand,* ▪ and we boast of our *hope* for the *glory* of *God.* ▪ ▪ And *this hope* will *not* leave us *disappointed,* ▪ because the *love* of *God* has been *poured* out in our *hearts* ▪ through the *Holy Spirit* who has been *given* to us. ▪ ▪ At the *appointed*

"Godless men": Rev. NAB says "the ungodly." "Just man . . . good man": "Person" is more inclusive.

time, ▪ when we were *still powerless,* ▪ Christ *died* for us *godless* men. ▪▪ It is *rare* that *anyone* should lay down his *life* for a *just* man, ▪ though it is *barely possible* that for a *good* man someone *may* have the *courage* to *die.* ▪▪ It is *precisely* in *this* that God *proves* his *love* for us: ▪▪ that while *we* were *still sinners,* ▪ Christ *died* for *us.* ▪▪▪

Climax. Be persuasive.

GOSPEL John 4:5–42

Tell the story as if you'd lived it.

A reading from the holy *gospel* according to *John* ▪▪▪

"Had to pass": theological, not geographical necessity, for he could have taken a customary bypass route.

(1) Jesus had to pass through *Samaria,* ▪ and his journey *brought* him to a Samaritan town named *Shechem* ▪ near the plot of *land* which *Jacob* had given to his son *Joseph.* ▪▪ This was the site of *Jacob's well.* ▪▪ Jesus, ▪ *tired* from his journey, ▪ *sat* down at the well. ▪▪

(2) The *hour* was about *noon.* ▪▪ When a Samaritan *woman* came to *draw* water, ▪ Jesus *said* to her, ▪▪ "Give me a *drink.*" ▪▪ (His disciples had gone off to the *town* to buy *provisions.*) ▪▪ The Samaritan woman *said* to him, ▪▪ *"You* are a *Jew.* ▪▪ How can you ask *me,* ▪ a *Samaritan* and a *woman,* ▪ for a *drink?*" ▪▪ *(Recall that Jews* have *nothing* to do with *Samaritans.)* ▪▪ Jesus *replied:* ▪▪

Convey his tiredness when Jesus speaks.

An aside. Quieter. In voice of narrator.

Strong, almost arrogant.

Aside. Spoken with voice of the woman.

As if he had a sly smile on his face.

(3) "If only you *recognized* God's *gift,* ▪
and *who* it is that is *asking* you for a drink, ▪
you would have asked *him* instead, ▪
and he would have *given* you ▪ *living* water." ▪▪

She challenges him. Almost mocking.

"Sir," ▪ *she challenged* him, ▪▪ "you don't have a *bucket* ▪ and this well is *deep.* ▪▪ Where do you expect to *get* this *flowing* water? ▪▪ *Surely* you don't pretend to be *greater* than our ancestor *Jacob,* ▪ who *gave* us this well and *drank* from it with his *sons* and his *flocks?*" ▪▪ *Jesus replied:* ▪▪

Persuasive and authoritative.

(4) "Everyone who drinks *this* water ▪
will be *thirsty* again. ▪▪
But *whoever* drinks the water *I* give him ▪
will *never* be thirsty; ▪▪
no, ▪ the water *I* give
shall become a *fountain* within him, ▪
leaping up to provide *eternal life.*" ▪▪

Dropping "him" is more inclusive.

"That person" is more inclusive.

She takes him literally. She wants this magic water.

The woman *said* to him, ▪▪ *"Give* me this water, sir, ▪ so that I won't grow *thirsty* and have to keep *coming* here to *draw* water." ▪▪

Calmly. An innocent request. Slowly.

(5) He *told* her, ▪▪ *"Go,* ▪ call your *husband,* ▪ and then come *back* here." ▪▪ "I *have* no husband," ▪ replied the woman. ▪▪ "You are *right* in saying you

God's love for us that "has been poured out in our hearts through the Holy Spirit."

Turn that Pauline theology into meaningful and impassioned communication. Remember the feeling of peace that comes when you make up with a loved one. Realize that though we were the ones who did wrong, it was God who took the first step at reconciliation. Rejoice as you would if someone gave you their friendship and then lavished you with gifts as well, expecting nothing in return. That's what God has done and Paul is expressing his excitement.

For Paul, God's great love for us is proven by the fact that God reached out to us while we were still "godless . . . still sinners!" "Look," he argues (always trying to persuade), "when is anyone willing to die for even a good person? Well, all right, *maybe* for a *really* good person someone might find the courage to die. But Christ died while we were still sinners. That proves God loves us!" First convince yourself of that. And then, as does the woman at the well in today's gospel passage, convince friends and neighbors.

GOSPEL This is a long gospel. Use it in its entirety. Editing, no matter how judicious, will weaken the story.

As homilist you have many things with which to be concerned. As gospel reader, however, your only concern is the story. As story this is a wonderful piece of literature. Study it carefully and use your vocal skills to bring the narrative to life. There are three acts to this drama, each with a distinctive mood. First is the sometimes pointed, sometimes ironic repartee between Jesus and the woman. Second is the return of the apostles, characterized by their surprise and confusion and by Jesus' urgency. Third is the enthusiastic response of the Samaritans.

(1, 2) Remember Jesus is truly tired. The sun is hot. Although he needs a cool drink he has to wait to draw water, for he has no bucket. Jesus shatters custom both by speaking to a woman in public and by associating with a Samaritan. The woman is an obviously strong character. She's not intimidated by this Jew who asks for water. She, too, is countercultural. After all, she's a woman who has lived with more than one man to whom she was not married. The second aside can be spoken with her almost sarcastic voice.

(3) Jesus couldn't expect the woman to know who he is. His comment is something of a teaser, used to hold her and rouse her curiosity. But, because of his fatigue, the dialogue is rather low-key. Obviously she misses his tone and the point, for she chal-

lenges him to come up with this "flowing water."

(4, 5) Jesus is persuasive in his next discourse. She becomes excited, but only because of her misunderstanding. She makes her request with a quickened tempo. Without revealing his motivation, Jesus makes a seemingly innocent request of her: "Call your husband." Caught off guard, she speaks slowly, tentatively. Jesus now drops his mask and speaks plainly. The first two sentences express strong feeling as he helps her face her sinfulness without driving her away. But his last sentence conveys compassion and lacks condemnation.

(6) All arrogance is gone as she forces her mouth to speak the words, "you are a prophet." Her question about worship shifts the conversation to a less embarrassing subject. Jesus works hard to answer, his intensity building. Reason, inspire, persuade!

(7) The woman, touched by Jesus' words, begins to suspect his identity. There's an implied question in her statement. Jesus rewards her by revealing himself to her—a gesture of respect and love.

(8) The return of the disciples suddenly changes the mood. They are surprised by what they see. The woman, transformed by her encounter and freed of all shame, runs off to share her excitement.

(9, 10) The disciples are genuinely concerned about Jesus but completely miss his point. They shrug their shoulders as they ask the question. But Jesus does not let them walk away confused. His explanation is a summary of his whole career. There are two exclamation points in this passage. Jesus urgently wants his friends to understand what he is all about. "Listen. . . . Open!"

Jesus "exclaimed" . . . so speak with strong feeling.

have *no* husband!" ▪ Jesus exclaimed. ▪▪ "The *fact* is, ▪ you have had *five,* ▪ and the man you are living with *now* is *not* your husband. ▪▪ What you *said* is *true* enough." ▪▪

Perhaps she's changing the subject. To be more inclusive change "men ought to" to "people should."

(6) *"Sir,"* ▪ answered the woman, ▪▪ "I can *see* you are a *prophet.* ▪▪ *Our ancestors* worshiped on this *mountain,* ▪ but *you* people claim that *Jerusalem* is the place where men *ought* to worship God." ▪▪ Jesus told her: ▪▪

One day none of this will matter.

"Believe me, woman, ▪
an hour is *coming* ▪
when you will *worship* the Father
neither on this *mountain*
nor in Jerusalem. ▪▪▪

But for now, it is the Jews who follow the better way and are channels of the covenant promise.

You people worship what you do *not* understand, ▪
while *we understand* what we worship; ▪▪
after all, ▪ *salvation* is from the *Jews.* ▪▪

Yet a still better way is coming.

Yet an hour is *coming,* ▪ and is *already here,* ▪
when *authentic* worshipers
will *worship* the Father in *Spirit* and *truth.* ▪▪
Indeed, ▪ it is just *such* worshipers
the Father *seeks.* ▪▪▪
God is *Spirit,* ▪
and those who *worship* him ▪
must worship in *Spirit* and *truth."* ▪▪▪

A hidden question here.

(7) The *woman* said to him: ▪▪ "I *know* there is a *Messiah* coming. ▪▪ (This term means *Anointed.*) ▪▪ When he *comes,* ▪ he will *tell* us *everything."* ▪▪

Gospel climaxes here.

Jesus replied, ▪▪ *"I* who *speak* to you am *he."* ▪▪▪

Change of mood . . . surprise.

(8) His *disciples,* ▪ *returning* at this point, ▪ were *surprised* that Jesus was speaking with a *woman.* ▪▪ No one put a *question,* however, ▪ such as ▪▪ "What do you *want* of him?" ▪ or ▪ "Why are you *talking* with her?" ▪▪

Ask questions as if spoken by disciples.

The woman then *left* her water jar and *went* off into the town. ▪▪ She said to the *people:* ▪▪ *"Come* and *see* someone who told me *everything* I ever *did!* ▪▪ Could this not be the *Messiah?"* ▪▪ With that ▪ they *set* out from the town to *meet* him. ▪▪▪

Insistent.

(9) Meanwhile the disciples were *urging* him, ▪▪ *"Rabbi,* ▪ *eat* something." ▪▪ But he *told* them: ▪▪
"I have *food* to eat
of which you do not *know."* ▪▪

Confused.

At this the disciples said to one another, ▪▪ "You do not suppose anyone has *brought* him something to eat?" ▪▪ Jesus *explained* to them: ▪▪

With energy and urgency.

(10) "Doing the *will* of him who *sent* me
and *bringing* his work to *completion*
is my *food.* ▪▪
Do you not have a *saying:* ▪▪

"Reapers . . . collect their wages and gather" is more inclusive.

"Person" is more inclusive.

You are one of those who believed.

Strong finish!

'Four months *more*
and it will be *harvest'?* ▪▪
Listen to what I say: ▪▪
Open your eyes and *see!* ▪▪
The fields are *shining* for harvest! ▪▪
The *reaper* already *collects* his wages
and gathers a *yield* for *eternal life,* ▪
that sower and reaper may *rejoice* together. ▪▪
Here we have the saying *verified:* ▪▪
'One man *sows;* ▪ another *reaps.'* ▪▪
I sent you to *reap*
what you had not *worked* for. ▪▪
Others have done the labor, ▪
and *you* have come into their *gain."* ▪▪▪

(11) Many Samaritans from that town *believed* in him on the strength of the woman's *word* of testimony: ▪▪ "He told me *everything* I ever *did."* ▪▪ The *result* was that, ▪ when these Samaritans *came* to him, ▪ they *begged* him to *stay* with them awhile. ▪▪ So he stayed there *two days,* ▪ and through his *own* spoken word many *more* came to faith. ▪▪ As they told the *woman:* ▪▪ "No *longer* does our faith depend on *your* story. ▪▪ We have heard for *ourselves,* ▪ and we *know* that this really *is* the *Savior* of the world." ▪▪▪

[Shorter: John 4:5–15, 19–26, 39, 40–42]

(11) The Samaritans believed "on the strength of the woman's word." Stress that narration and speak her line as she did. Their enthusiastic response is conveyed by the word "begged." Remember, as narrator you are one of these who "came to faith." Speak with energy and excitement. The last sentence is your personal statement of faith spoken slowly and with deep conviction.

FROM THE KEY

Inclusive Language. What is inclusive language and why is it so important? Archbishop Raymond Hunthausen in a 1990 pastoral letter offered the following comments:

"Inclusive language, with respect to the liturgy, is a way of speaking and writing that does not give the impression of needlessly excluding certain persons. I urge each of us to be especially sensitive to the use of language that may be sexist, racist, clericalist or anti-clericalist, anti-Semitic, as well as being offensive to the disabled.

Most of our liturgical books were translated immediately after Vatican Council II, at a time when sensitivity to language that excludes or offends had not yet become part of our consciousness. Unfortunately, exclusive langauge is liberally scattered throughout our liturgical books. Though the issue of inclusive language is complex, we must try to be sensitive about how we address or speak of one another in the faith community and the way we refer to God. Care must be taken in choice of texts and in other pastoral adaptations, for often the integrity of the word of God or the very meaning of the rite may be at stake.

Appropriate adaptation, in accord with liturgical guidelines, demands knowledge, time, energy and thought. Official changes in texts and translations may seem slow in coming, so our understanding and our patience are essential. There are instances when the language of impatience and protest can do more harm to the unity of the assembly than the use of exclusive langauge."

The readings throughout this workbook are from the New American Bible. Though the revised New Testament of the New American Bible is not yet approved for lectionary use, often citations from that version (designated "Rev. NAB") are given in the margin notes in an attempt to provide language that is less exclusive. These variations may be of use in settings where the scriptures are read or studied apart from the liturgy. The Revised NAB is undergoing further work, both to ensure inclusive language as much as possible and to present the texts in a way that will enable good proclamation. These revisions should be completed in the next few years.

READING I The author of Chronicles is frustrated over the people's refusal to remain faithful to the covenant and to heed the voices of God's messengers. How would you speak about a city council who ignored years of admonitions to prepare for an earthquake or hurricane they knew was inevitable? How would you say, "they mocked [our] messengers . . . despised [our] warnings . . . and scoffed" at all we said? Remember, your every word reflects conviction that this fate was self-generated. The "anger of the Lord" is a consequence of freely chosen behavior.

The Chaldean atrocities are intentionally listed. Don't gloss over them, but let them do their work of shocking us with graphic detail. As you speak of the destruction of people, places and "precious objects," you must hurt as though the home of your childhood or the homes of your relatives were being pillaged. Jeremiah's voice isn't righteous; it's an echo in which we now recognize the truth—bitter as it is to swallow.

The sovereign God uses an earthly king to fulfill Jeremiah's words. Ironically this pagan is more responsive to God's promptings than was Israel. God has *not* forgotten the covenant, and mercy is God's method. Cyrus's voice is charged with simple sincerity, not pomposity. The last phrase is a blessing, undeserved but generously imparted.

MARCH 10, 1991

FOURTH SUNDAY OF LENT

LECTIONARY #32

READING I 2 Chronicles 36:14–17, 19–23

A reading ▪ from the second book of *Chronicles* ▪ ▪ ▪

Head-shaking frustration.

Almost angry.

All the *princes* of Judah, ▪ the *priests* and the *people* ▪ added *infidelity* to *infidelity,* ▪ practicing all the *abominations* of the nations ▪ and *polluting* the Lord's *temple* ▪ which he had *consecrated* in Jerusalem. ▪ ▪ ▪

God did everything possible.

"Fathers" can be "ancestors."

You can hardly believe it yourself.

Such atrocities are not unknown in our day.

Pain in your voice at such loss.

Subjugation and humiliation.

The land will rest for 70 years to compensate for desecrated sabbaths.

Early and *often* did the Lord, ▪ the God of their *fathers,* ▪ send his *messengers* to them, ▪ for he had *compassion* on his people and his *dwelling* place. ▪ ▪ But they *mocked* the messengers of God, ▪ *despised* his warnings, ▪ and *scoffed* at his prophets, ▪ until the *anger* of the Lord against his people was so *inflamed* ▪ that there was no *remedy.* ▪ ▪ Then he brought up *against* them the king of the *Chaldeans,* ▪ who *slew* their young men in their own *sanctuary* building, ▪ sparing neither young *man* nor *maiden,* ▪ neither the *aged* nor the *decrepit;* ▪ ▪ he delivered *all* of them over into his *grip.* ▪ ▪ *Finally,* ▪ their enemies *burnt* the house of God, ▪ tore down the *walls* of Jerusalem, ▪ set all its palaces *afire,* ▪ and *destroyed* all its precious *objects.* ▪ ▪ Those who *escaped* the sword ▪ he carried *captive* to *Babylon,* ▪ where they became his and his sons' *servants* ▪ until the kingdom of the *Persians* came to power. ▪ ▪ All this was to *fulfill* the word of the Lord spoken by *Jeremiah:* ▪ ▪ "Until the land has *retrieved* its lost sabbaths, ▪ during all the time it lies *waste* ▪ it shall have *rest* ▪ while *seventy* years are fulfilled." ▪ ▪ ▪

Strong, with authority.

Sincere, not pompous.

"Let them go and may their God be with them" is more inclusive. As a blessing.

In the first year of *Cyrus,* ▪ king of *Persia,* ▪ in order to *fulfill* the word of the Lord spoken by Jeremiah, ▪ the Lord *inspired* King Cyrus of Persia ▪ to issue this *proclamation* throughout his kingdom, ▪ both by word of *mouth* and in *writing:* ▪ ▪ "Thus says Cyrus, ▪ king of Persia: ▪ ▪ 'All the *kingdoms* of the earth ▪ the *Lord,* ▪ the God of heaven, ▪ has *given* to me, ▪ ▪ and he has also *charged* me to build him a *house* in *Jerusalem,* ▪ which is in *Judah.* ▪ ▪ *Whoever,* therefore, ▪ among you ▪ belongs to any *part* of his people, ▪ let him *go* up, ▪ and may his *God* be with him!'" ▪ ▪ ▪

READING II Ephesians 2:4–10

A reading from the letter of *Paul* ▪ to the *Ephesians* ▪▪▪

Core of the passage.

More comfort than instruction.

God is *rich* in *mercy:* ▪▪ because of his great *love* for us ▪ he brought us to *life* with *Christ* ▪ when we were *dead* in *sin.* ▪▪ By this *favor* you were saved. ▪▪ Both *with* and *in* Christ Jesus ▪ he *raised* us up ▪ and gave us a place in the *heavens* ▪ that in the ages to *come* ▪ he might display the great *wealth* of his favor, ▪ *manifested* by his *kindness* to us in Christ Jesus. ▪▪

Stronger and more direct than above. Not scolding.

I *repeat,* ▪ it is owing to his *favor* ▪ that *salvation* is *yours* ▪ through *faith.* ▪▪ This is not your *own* doing, ▪ it is God's *gift;* ▪▪ neither is it a *reward* for anything you have *accomplished,* ▪ so let no one *pride* himself on it. ▪▪

"So let none pride themselves" is more inclusive.

Rejoice over this gift.

We are truly his *handiwork,* ▪ *created* in Christ Jesus to lead the *life* of *good deeds* ▪ which God *prepared* for us ▪ in *advance.* ▪▪▪

READING II When a child complained about the allowance she received for the "work" she did at home, her parents reminded her that she was not paid for doing household chores. Each family member was expected to complete his or her fair share. The allowance, they insisted, was freely given, not earned.

Paul asserts the same thing here. Yes, we were "created . . . to lead the life of good deeds," but it is by God's "favor [we] were saved," not through any merit of our own. Paul even repeats it: "It is owing to his favor that salvation is yours." It's a free gift, pure and simple.

The tone of the passage is set in the first five words: "God is rich in mercy." Speak gently and tenderly of a God who lavishes on us the richest gift of all, salvation. Convey the solicitousness of a God who sought us out "when we were dead in sin" that we might have new life. God's "great love" motivates God's saving action in our lives. Let us hear that love in every sentence, in every pause; and let us see it in your eyes.

Sometimes we persuade with insistent energy, assuming a courtroom manner. Today let your energy be the kind that convinces children they are loved even when they bring home poor report cards or make the last out in a game. There is profound joy in knowing that salvation "is not your own doing." Convince us of that, but make sure the first person you persuade is yourself.

FROM THE KEY

Pauses. All pauses are not created equal. The pause marks indicate the suggested *length* of the pause between thought units. Hold a pencil in your hand as you read, and tap your book once for each box before speaking the next word. These single, double or triple beats will lend variety and help slow the pace of your reading.

If your pauses at the single boxes sound awkward, you're probably pausing too long. Though the double and triple boxes indicate pauses of more or less consistent duration, the single box can suggest pauses of varying lengths. Your sense of what's necessary must tell you what value to give the single pause. Some entire passages (and parts of others) move at a faster rate than other passages. There a single box might translate into a pause that's half as long as the standard pause or simply into the "stretching" (sustaining) of the word that occurs just before the box.

Pauses are never dead moments. You've heard of "pregnant pauses"—silences that say "something is going to happen." Something is always happening during a pause. Usually it is your effort to connect the previous thought with the next. During a pause you should be *thinking* "and then," "therefore," "however" or whatever connective fits the context.

Only practice will teach you how long to pause and how to fill your pauses. Too many pauses make a reading choppy; too few cause ideas to run into one another. Too long a pause breaks the flow; if pauses are too short, your listeners will be struggling to keep up with you. Most of the pauses in this book are only suggestions, but a substantial pause always follows "A reading from . . ." and a substantial pause always precedes "This is the word (gospel) of the Lord."

GOSPEL In an age when atrocities make daily headlines, we hear that "God so loved the world." The world is not evil; God sent the Son not to condemn but to save it. God gave Christ as a gift so that he might usher us into the realms of "eternal life."Jesus speaks words of assurance and comfort to Nicodemus; assume your assembly needs the same assurance.

That each person *chooses* salvation or condemnation is a concept we often stubbornly resist. We still want to pin the blame on God. Present Christ's reasoning slowly and clearly, without harshness, but with the pain Jesus must have felt at knowing that some prefer darkness to the light he freely offers. Utilize a different tone on each of the last two sentences. A furrowed brow might accompany your explanation that those who "hate the light" don't "come near it." But an ingenuous joy characterizes your assertion that true believers aren't afraid to reveal that their "deeds are done in God."

GOSPEL John 3:14–21

A reading from the holy *gospel* according to *John* ▪ ▪ ▪

Think of the assembly as Nicodemus.

Jesus said to *Nicodemus:* ▪ ▪
"Just as Moses *lifted* up the serpent
in the desert, ▪ ▪
so must the *Son* of *Man* be lifted up, ▪ ▪
that all who *believe* ▪
may have *eternal life* in him. ▪ ▪

It's so simple!

Tenderly. Slowly.

Yes, ▪ God so *loved* the world ▪
that he gave his *only Son,* ▪
that whoever *believes* in him may *not die* ▪
but may *have* eternal life. ▪ ▪ ▪
God did not send the Son into the world
to *condemn* the world, ▪
but that the world might be *saved*
through him. ▪ ▪
Whoever *believes* in him *avoids*
condemnation, ▪

Avoid harshness.

but whoever does *not* believe is *already*
condemned ▪

Rev. NAB says: "Because he has not believed. . . ." You could say "Because of not believing. . . . "

for not believing in the name of God's
only Son. ▪ ▪ ▪
The *judgment* in question is this: ▪ ▪
the *light* came into the world, ▪

With regret. "Men" can be "people."

but men loved *darkness* rather than light ▪
because their *deeds* were *wicked.* ▪ ▪

Make the pronouns and verbs plural: "everyone" = "all," "hates" = "hate" "he" = "they," etc.

Everyone who practices *evil* ▪
hates the light; ▪ ▪

Don't pause. Speak like the one afraid.

he does not come *near* it ▪
for fear his *deeds* will be *exposed.* ▪ ▪

Smile. With joy.

But he who acts in *truth* ▪
comes into the light, ▪
to make clear
that *his* deeds ▪ are done in *God."* ▪ ▪ ▪

MARCH 10, 1991

FOURTH SUNDAY OF LENT, YEAR A

Editor's note: *Lenten Sunday liturgies which include a celebration of the rite of scrutiny of the Rite of Christian Initiation of Adults also include this set of readings from Year A. These readings replace the readings for Year B.*

LECTIONARY #31

READING I 1 Samuel 16:1, 6–7, 10–13

A reading from the first book of *Samuel* ▪ ▪ ▪

A simple command spoken with authority.

The Lord said to *Samuel:* ▪ ▪ "I am sending you to *Jesse* of Bethlehem, ▪ for I have *chosen* my *king* from among his *sons.*" ▪ ▪

A natural assumption. He thinks his job is nearly done.

God corrects Samuel like a patient teacher. To be more inclusive try this adjustment: "not as you see does God see, for you see. . . ."

As Jesse and his sons *came* to the *sacrifice,* ▪ Samuel looked at *Eliab* and *thought,* ▪ ▪ "*Surely* the Lord's *anointed* is here before him." ▪ ▪ But the *Lord* said to Samuel: ▪ ▪ "Do not *judge* from his *appearance* or from his lofty *stature,* ▪ because I have *rejected* him. ▪ ▪ Not as *man* sees does *God* see, ▪ because man sees the *appearance* ▪ but the *Lord* looks into the *heart.*" ▪ ▪

Stress the number of sons not chosen.

Exasperated, almost worried.

His tone says: But he couldn't be the one!

Delight in the description.

Describe the anointing slowly. But "rushed" sounds like it means!

In the *same* way Jesse presented *seven* sons before Samuel, ▪ but Samuel *said* to Jesse, ▪ ▪ "The *Lord* has not chosen any *one* of these." ▪ ▪ Then Samuel *asked* Jesse, ▪ ▪ "Are these *all* the sons you have?" ▪ Jesse *replied,* ▪ ▪ "There is still the *youngest,* ▪ who is tending the sheep." ▪ ▪ Samuel *said* to Jesse, ▪ "*Send* for him; ▪ ▪ we will not *begin* the sacrificial banquet until he *arrives* here." ▪ ▪ Jesse *sent* and had the young man *brought* to them. ▪ ▪ He was *ruddy,* ▪ a youth *handsome* to behold ▪ and making a *splendid* appearance. ▪ ▪ The *Lord* said, ▪ ▪ "*There*— ▪ *anoint* him, ▪ for *this* is *he!*" ▪ ▪ Then Samuel, ▪ with the horn of *oil* in hand, ▪ *anointed* him in the midst of his *brothers;* ▪ ▪ and from *that* day on, ▪ the *spirit* of the Lord *rushed* upon *David.* ▪ ▪ ▪

READING I American politics are not unlike the situation described here. We look at candidates in a primary and think we see the obvious front-runner. But God's ways (and the ways of the American electorate) are not always our ways. Often an unexpected "dark horse" emerges to run away with the race. It helps to have a sense of humor when observing the American political process. Samuel, too, needs a sense of humor to deal with the situation God has given him. He is sent to recognize one among seven brothers whom God has "chosen" to be king. He doesn't know who he's looking for, yet he's the seer who must announce God's choice to the anxious family. Not an enviable position!

God's directive should be spoken with authority. "It's a simple task," God says, "go do it." Start the second paragraph slowly, using your inflection to make up for the verses missing from this passage. Samuel has invited Jesse's family to a sacrifice where he can survey the sons and select the "Lord's anointed." Eliab seems the obvious choice. "Not so," says God, to Samuel's assumption. Speak as God with the tone of a patient and loving teacher. Samuel has been set up by God to fail at first. God uses the opportunity to teach a valuable lesson about God's ways and ours.

Suggest the lengthy, tedious and somewhat embarrassing process of receiving *seven* sons for approval and needing to reject each one. Exasperated, perhaps doubting himself, Samuel asks: "Are these *all* the sons?" Jesse's reply betrays his belief that David couldn't possibly be the right choice. Samuel gets excited. "Thank God there's another . . . maybe this one?" Take time to describe David. Convey Samuel's relief at seeing this young man who glowed from God's favor shining within him. Stress "ruddy," "handsome" and "splendid." God speaks with authority and pride. Convey God's pleasure, and your own as narrator, as you describe the anointing. "Rushed" is one of those great words that surprises and communicates. But remember, the Spirit rushes, not you.

READING II All lives experience transition. Physical, emotional, intellectual growth are part of what it means to be human. Paul adds another category: spiritual growth. Think of your progress in one of the other areas of development when you read what Paul says here about moving from darkness to light. Once you were a child, now you're an adult. Once you were ignorant, now you know. Once you were without Christ, now you have him. So act like it! Be an adult, use your knowledge, *live* like a *Christian.* It's Paul the teacher at the podium once again.

Paul explains *why* we should live as children of light: Because goodness and justice and truth grow in the light and they are what "pleases the Lord." Make no mistake about it. With energy and urgency Paul continues: "Take no part . . . It is shameful . . . such deeds are condemned." Imagine yourself writing to a young person who's away at school for the first time, reminding them to use their newfound freedom responsibly, warning them that shameful behavior eventually comes to light.

The tone of the last four lines is very different. After focusing on the dangers of living in the dark, Paul sings an invitation to embrace instead the light that is Christ. Pause before "That is why . . ." and muster a hushed intensity that erupts on the word "Awake."

"Arise" builds the energy and leads to the joyous promise that "Christ will give you light." This is a promise embraced by today's blind man in the gospel and all of us who once were in darkness.

GOSPEL Again we have a long gospel and again we have a classic story. Recognize and value the literary beauty of the writing and the power of the story form. Don't undermine those values by shortening the text.

This gospel could easily be divided into vocal parts. That's fine when all readers are excellent. Often, however, division is used as a quick and easy method of sustaining interest in a long reading. The reality is that it is neither quick nor easy to get three people to read well together; the power of the story is lost if the readers assume that greater numbers automatically make a better reading. One fine reader who can create the various characters and moods will sustain the assembly's interest and better maintain the integrity of the story.

The narrator is important. Though this person has no strong emotional lines, emotional involvement is necessary. The several parenthetical asides give the narrator the sound of an eyewitness-turned-believer, relating the story to other believers. Imagine

READING II Ephesians 5:8–14

The good news of the opening and closing sentences undergirds your teaching tone in the body of this reading. "Darkness" = not having Christ; "light" = having him.

A reading from the letter of *Paul* ▪ to the *Ephesians* ▪ ▪ ▪

"Goodness," "justice," "truth" are three different virtues and should sound like it.

Strong directives, but don't lose the joy.

There was a time when you were *darkness,* ▪ but *now* ▪ you are *light* in the *Lord.* ▪ ▪ *Well,* then, ▪ *live* as *children* of light. ▪ ▪ *Light* produces every kind of *goodness* ▪ and *justice* and *truth.* ▪ ▪ Be *correct* in your judgment of what *pleases* the Lord. ▪ ▪ Take *no* part in *vain* deeds done in *darkness;* ▪ ▪ rather, ▪ *condemn* them. ▪ ▪ It is *shameful* even to *mention* the things these people do in *secret;* ▪ ▪ but when such deeds are *condemned,* ▪ they are *seen* in the light of *day,* ▪ and all that then *appears* is *light.* ▪ ▪ That is *why* we read: ▪ ▪

Pause. Shift to more joyful tone. These lines are taken from an early baptismal hymn.

"*Awake,* O sleeper, ▪
arise from the *dead,* ▪
and *Christ* will give you *light.*" ▪ ▪ ▪

GOSPEL John 9:1–41

Be aware of who you are as narrator.

A reading from the holy *gospel* according to *John* ▪ ▪ ▪

Stress "blind from birth" for it is later questioned.

Disciples genuinely curious, not arrogant.

Jesus' answer is surprising.

(1) As Jesus *walked* along, ▪ he saw a *man* who had been *blind* from *birth.* ▪ ▪ His disciples *asked* him, ▪ ▪ "*Rabbi,* ▪ was it *his* sin or his *parents'* that *caused* him to be born *blind?*" ▪ ▪ "*Neither,*" ▪ answered Jesus: ▪ ▪

"It was *no* sin, ▪ either of *this* man
or of his parents. ▪ ▪
Rather, ▪ it was to let God's *works*
show forth in him. ▪ ▪
We *must* do the deeds of him who
sent me ▪ while it is *day.* ▪ ▪

With urgency and hope.

The *night* comes on
when *no* one can work. ▪ ▪
While *I* am in the world ▪
I am the *light* of the world." ▪ ▪

Odd behavior. Describe one detail at a time.

(2) With that Jesus *spat* on the ground, ▪ *made mud* with his saliva, ▪ and *smeared* the man's *eyes* with the mud. ▪ ▪ Then he *told* him, ▪ ▪ "*Go,* ▪ wash in the *pool* of *Siloam.*" ▪ ▪ (This *name* means "*One* who has been *sent.*") ▪ ▪ *So the man went* off and *washed,* ▪ and *came* back able to *see.* ▪ ▪ ▪

Convey the wonder of the crowd.

(3) His *neighbors* and the people who had been *accustomed* to see him *begging* began to *ask,* ▪ ▪ "Isn't this the fellow who used to *sit* and *beg?*" ▪ ▪ Some were

"It was he" and "it was not . . . him" are spoken in voices of the excited neighbors.

Hold back on emotions.

Now emotion is expressed.

Suddenly realizes he's almost forgotten about finding the miracle worker.

There's trouble ahead!

He's careful not to say too much.

Strong emotions on both sides.

Almost reluctantly he makes this public declaration of faith.

Obviously, "The Jews" are the religious leaders. Every character in this story is a Jew.

Leaders now impatient and short-tempered.

They are eager to please but reluctant to say too much.

No disrespect.

Explain their seeming lack of parental concern.

For them this is a given.

Beggar is growing bolder.

Half sarcastic, half hoping for their conversion.

claiming it *was* he; ▪ ▪ others maintained it was *not* but someone who *looked* like him. ▪ ▪ The man *himself* said, ▪ ▪ *"I'm* the *one,* ▪ all right." ▪ ▪ They *said* to him then, ▪ ▪ *"How* were your eyes *opened?"* He answered: ▪ ▪ "That *man* they call *Jesus* made *mud* and *smeared* it on my *eyes,* ▪ telling me to go to *Siloam* and *wash.* ▪ ▪ When I *did* go and wash, ▪ I was able to *see."* ▪ ▪ "Where *is* he?" ▪ they asked. ▪ ▪ He replied, ▪ ▪ "I have *no idea."* ▪ ▪ ▪

(4) Next, ▪ they *took* the man who had been born blind ▪ to the *Pharisees.* ▪ ▪ (Note that it was on a *sabbath* that Jesus had *made* the mud paste and *opened* his eyes.) ▪ ▪ The Pharisees, in turn, ▪ began to *inquire* how he had *recovered* his sight. ▪ ▪ He *told* them, ▪ ▪ "He put *mud* on my eyes. ▪ ▪ I *washed* it off, ▪ and *now* I can *see."* ▪ ▪ This prompted some of the Pharisees to *assert,* ▪ ▪ "This man *cannot* be from *God* because he does not *keep* the *sabbath."* ▪ ▪ Others *objected,* ▪ ▪ "If a man is a *sinner,* ▪ how can he perform *signs* like *these?"* ▪ ▪ They were *sharply divided* over him. ▪ ▪ Then they addressed the blind man *again:* ▪ ▪ "Since it was *your* eyes he opened, ▪ what do *you* have to say about him?" ▪ ▪ "He is a *prophet,"* ▪ he replied. ▪ ▪ ▪

(5) The Jews *refused* to believe that he had *really* been born blind and had *begun* to see, ▪ until they *summoned* the *parents* of this man who now could see. ▪ ▪ "Is this your *son?"* ▪ they asked, ▪ ▪ "and if so, ▪ do you *attest* that he was *blind* at *birth?* ▪ ▪ How do you *account* for the fact that he *now* can *see?"* ▪ ▪ His parents *answered,* ▪ ▪ "We *know* this is our son, ▪ and we know he *was* blind at birth. ▪ ▪ But *how* he can see *now,* ▪ or *who* opened his eyes, ▪ we have *no idea.* ▪ ▪ Ask *him.* ▪ ▪ He is *old* enough to speak for *himself."* ▪ ▪ (His parents *answered* in this fashion because they were *afraid* of the Jews, ▪ who had already *agreed* among themselves that *anyone* who acknowledged *Jesus* as the *Messiah* ▪ would be *put* out of the *synagogue.* ▪ ▪ That was *why* his parents said, ▪ ▪ "He is of *age—* ▪ ask *him."*) ▪ ▪

(6) A *second* time they *summoned* the man who had been born blind and *said* to him, ▪ ▪ "Give *glory* to *God!* ▪ ▪ *First* of all, ▪ we *know* this man is a *sinner."* ▪ ▪ *"I* would not know whether he is a *sinner* or *not,"* ▪ he answered. ▪ ▪ "I know *this* much: ▪ ▪ I was *blind* before; ▪ ▪ *now* I can *see."* ▪ ▪ They persisted: ▪ ▪ "Just *what* did he *do* to you? ▪ ▪ *How* did he open your eyes?" ▪ ▪ "I have *told* you *once,* ▪ but you would not *listen* to me," ▪ he answered them. ▪ ▪ *"Why* do you want to hear it *all over* again? ▪ ▪ Do not tell me ▪ *you* want to become his disciples

a grandfather speaking to his wide-eyed grandchildren about some great person he once knew.

(1) The disciples innocently reflect the accepted wisdom of the day when asking their question. Without arrogance they assume some sin has caused the blindness. They want to know whose. Jesus' answer is a surprise—all the more forcefully delivered because it is so unexpected. He knows that the time for him to "show forth" God's works is growing shorter. He speaks of the advance of night with both urgency and hope.

(2) Deliver the mud paste narration with energy, one phrase at a time. Jesus speaks with an authority the beggar cannot question. The narrator conveys the wonder of the crowd when the blind man comes back able to see.

(3) The neighbors are astounded. Their voices are excited. Each is an authority. Each claims to know the truth. The beggar answers the skeptical neighbors who ask "How . . . ?" by stating the facts without editorial comment, revealing his excitement only on "I . . . see." He surprises even himself as he realizes he doesn't know the whereabouts of (nor has he seen) Jesus.

(4) Imagine him now swept along by the swelling crowd. You signal the anticipated controversy with the aside regarding the Sabbath. The beggar plays it cool, relying on an unemotional enumeration of the facts. A few Pharisees overreact out of fear and jealousy while their more sincere colleagues ridicule them, insisting no "sinner" could do such things. The skeptics question the beggar, hoping to hear something with which to discredit Jesus. Recognizing the risk, the beggar goes ahead and calls Jesus a prophet.

(5) Suggest the belligerence of the leaders in the next narration. They fear being deceived. The parents fear for their safety, so they say only what they must and volunteer nothing. The parenthetical statement is the narrator's attempt to explain why the parents seemed so uncaring. Fear can cause unexplainable behavior.

(6) The second summons is born of anger and frustration. The assumption that Jesus is a sinner is spoken as a given. But the beggar won't have it. "I don't make your assumptions," he says. "But here's what I do know [and can safely say]." The tension mounts. Gradually the beggar yields his defenses and releases some sarcasm. His response to their scorn is, "Well, this is news!" Openly mocking at first, he launches into a sincere lecture without even realizing it. Their response is swift and harsh.

(7) Your tone suggests Jesus' concern when he seeks out the beggar. His question is an invitation. Tired and somewhat defeated, the beggar asks for information. Gently, tenderly, Jesus obliges. A long pause precedes the profession of faith as the beggar remembers the voice, examines the face and then responds. This compassionate Jesus can also face facts. Some will reject him. There is real judgment in the final speech, but it is spoken with genuine regret. Jesus is the good shepherd who would not lose any sheep.

Sustained energy, variety and careful attention to the very real characters who populate this story will make its telling effective and rewarding. No doubt it will take practice. No doubt it will be worth it.

Angry reproach.

No longer worried about consequences to himself.

Anger and contempt.

too?" ▪▪ They retorted *scornfully,* ▪ *"You* are the one who is that man's *disciple.* ▪▪ *We* are disciples of *Moses.* ▪▪ We know that *God* spoke to Moses, ▪ but we have *no* idea where *this* man *comes* from." ▪▪ He came *back* at them: ▪▪ *"Well, this* is *news!* ▪▪ You do not *know* where he *comes* from, ▪ yet he *opened* my *eyes.* ▪▪ We *know* that God does not hear *sinners,* ▪ but that if someone is *devout* ▪ and *obeys* his will ▪ he *listens* to him. ▪▪ It is *unheard* of that anyone ever *gave* sight to a person *blind* from *birth.* ▪▪ If *this* man were *not* from *God,* ▪ he could *never* have done such a thing." ▪▪ *"What!"* ▪ they exclaimed, ▪▪ "You are *steeped* in *sin* from your *birth,* ▪ and *you* are giving *us* lectures?" ▪▪ With that ▪ they *threw* him out *bodily.* ▪▪▪

Jesus, the good shepherd, seeks out the new lamb.

Pause. Realize, then respond.

With pained honesty.

(7) When Jesus *heard* of his expulsion, ▪ he *sought* him out and *asked* him, ▪▪ "Do you *believe* in the *Son of Man?"* ▪▪ He *answered,* ▪▪ "Who *is* he, sir, ▪ that I *may* believe in him?" ▪▪ "You have *seen* him," ▪ Jesus replied. ▪▪ "He is *speaking* to you *now."* ▪▪ ("I *do* believe, ▪ *Lord,"* ▪ he said, ▪▪ and *bowed* down to *worship* him. ▪▪ *Then* Jesus said:) ▪▪

"I *came* into this world to *divide* it, ▪
to make the sightless *see*
and the *seeing blind."* ▪▪

Some of the Pharisees around him *picked* this up, ▪ saying, ▪▪ "You are not counting *us* in with the *blind,* are you?" ▪▪ To which Jesus *replied:* ▪▪

"If you *were* blind
there would be *no sin* in that. ▪▪
'But we *see,'* you say, ▪
and your sin *remains."* ▪▪▪

[Shorter: John 9:1, 6–9, 13–17, 34–38]

MARCH 17, 1991

FIFTH SUNDAY OF LENT

LECTIONARY #35

READING I Jeremiah 31:31–34

A reading from the book of the prophet ▪ *Jeremiah* ▪ ▪ ▪

Joyous good news.

Brief glance at past wrongdoing. "Fathers" can be "ancestors."

By permitting the Babylonian exile.

Renewed energy and joy.

Speak this as if it were the tenderest gesture of love imaginable.

"Kinsmen" can be "relatives" or "family."

Be amazed at God's willingness to forgive and forget.

The days are *coming,* ▪ says the Lord, ▪ when I will make a *new* covenant with the house of Israel and the house of Judah. ▪ ▪ It will not be like the covenant I made with their *fathers* ▪ the day I took them by the *hand* to lead them forth from the land of *Egypt:* ▪ ▪ for they *broke* my covenant, ▪ and I had to show myself their *master,* ▪ says the Lord. ▪ ▪ But *this* is the covenant which I will make with the house of Israel *after* those days, ▪ says the Lord. ▪ ▪ I will place my law *within* them, ▪ and *write* it upon their *hearts:* ▪ ▪ I will be their *God,* ▪ and they shall be my *people.* ▪ ▪ *No longer* will they have need ▪ to *teach* their friends and kinsmen how to *know* the Lord. ▪ ▪ *All,* ▪ from *least* to *greatest,* ▪ shall *know* me, ▪ says the Lord, ▪ for I will *forgive* their evildoing ▪ and *remember* their sin *no more.* ▪ ▪ ▪

READING II Hebrews 5:7–9

Short reading = slow reading.

A reading from the letter to the *Hebrews* ▪ ▪ ▪

Offer Christ as a model for us.

"And he was heard . . .": a logical consequence.

Make your listeners know they're included.

In the days when Christ was in the *flesh,* ▪ he offered *prayers* and *supplications* ▪ with loud *cries* and *tears* to God, ▪ who was able to *save* him from death, ▪ ▪ and he was *heard* ▪ because of his *reverence.* ▪ ▪ *Son* though he *was,* ▪ he learned *obedience* from what he suffered; ▪ ▪ and when *perfected,* ▪ he became the *source* of eternal salvation ▪ for *all* who *obey* him. ▪ ▪ ▪

READING I It happens to all of us at one time or another: Someone wrongs us, then grace enables us to let go of the hurt and move ahead, inviting the wrongdoer to move ahead with us. Focused on *what will be,* we quickly review the past, careful not to reawaken the old hurts in order to let the newness of what will come stand in stark contrast with what has been. "I know it's been painful between us," we might say, "but the past is done, and tomorrow can be different."

God's voice exuberantly announces miraculous good news: "I will make a new covenant." Then, like a wronged lover perhaps, God winces at the memory of the infidelity: "It will not be like the covenant" made at Zion that "they broke." Speak with regret for Israel's sinfulness and the punishment (exile) it brought upon them.

Suddenly the clouds of memory part and the sun's new light pours in: "But *this* is the covenant . . . " (that phrase seals shut the door to the past): "I will place my law *within* them [stress that preposition] and write it upon their *hearts.*"

With total belief, say that teaching will become unnecessary; "least to greatest" will know the Lord without instruction, you insist, because they will be so impressed with a God who first forgives and then forgets.

READING II When children are frightened by bad dreams or bullies or a medical emergency, a good parent can often allay their fear by telling a story of when he or she was in a similar situation: "Did I ever tell you about the time I cut *my* thumb carving a jack-o'-lantern? I had to get stitches, too, and I was *soooo* afraid!" The technique not only distracts the children, it tells them someone else survived such an ordeal and offers hope that they might, too. Parent or not, the author of Hebrews knows this strategy and applies it well for the sake of any who might be reticent about approaching Christ in the midst of human woe, who fear his judgment rather than anticipate his sympathy toward human weakness.

Address your listeners like a parent encouraging a child not to be afraid to do what God's own son was willing to do: to offer "prayers and supplications with loud cries and tears." Your stresses would then go to the nouns ("when *Christ* was in the flesh . . . ") and the pronouns ("*he* offered prayers . . . and *he* was heard . . . "), though, of course, not every pronoun is stressed.

Every short passage should be read slowly and demands that you have your images set in your mind *before* you speak the first word. This short passage demands that you believe, like Jesus, that we, too, can find blessings in our sufferings as we also seek to be perfected.

GOSPEL Even back then, it seems, who you knew made a difference. The Greeks approach the only two apostles with Greek names asking for an audience with Jesus. So unusual is this request from a gentile that the apostles pass the decision to Jesus. But he makes no direct response; his focus is on "the hour" that has "come."

The remainder of the passage is suffused with the paradoxes that distinguish the Christian faith: Death leads to life; clinging to life is a sure way to lose it; defeat in the world's eyes means glorification in God's.

Jesus announces his own passing and the necessity for that "hour" to come. He is at once teacher and student, teaching and learning about the need to surrender to the will of God. Therefore Jesus can't be flippant or didactic; he must *feel* all he says and understand its full import, like someone on a deathbed consoling relatives who have gathered, instead of being consoled by them.

Even for Jesus the reality of death is overwhelming. "My soul is troubled . . . " is how John speaks of Jesus' anguish. Knowing he came for the very crisis he fears, Jesus resolves to accept it by asking God to make the moment of his death into a moment of glory.

The voice "from the sky" is like thunder—that means it should grab attention and impress those who hear it. The crowd responds with animated, though uncomprehending, excitement. Jesus' final words suggest resignation, inner peace and excitement over what his being "lifted up" will mean for "all men [people]." Because you, unlike the crowds, understand that Jesus' death makes possible salvation for all, you can narrate the parenthetical sentence with knowing significance rather than regret. After all, "this statement of his" also indicated the sort of life he would offer to each of us.

GOSPEL John 12:20–33

A reading from the holy *gospel* according to *John* ▪ ▪ ▪

Tell us this is unusual.

Among those who had come up to worship at the feast of *Passover* ▪ were some *Greeks.* ▪ ▪ They approached *Philip,* ▪ who was from *Bethsaida* in *Galilee,* ▪ and put this *request* to him: ▪ ▪ "*Sir,* ▪ we should like to see *Jesus.*" ▪ ▪ Philip went to tell *Andrew;* ▪ ▪ Philip and Andrew in turn ▪ came to inform *Jesus.* ▪ ▪ Jesus *answered* them: ▪ ▪

Reflect their uncertainty about what to do.

"The hour has *come* ▪
for the Son of Man to be *glorified.* ▪ ▪

As if reassuring loved ones who are about to lose you.

I solemnly *assure* you, ▪
unless the *grain* of *wheat* falls to the earth
and *dies,* ▪
it *remains* just a grain of wheat. ▪ ▪
But *if* it dies, ▪
it produces much *fruit.* ▪ ▪

Use of plurals is more inclusive: "Those who love their life lose it . . ."

The man who *loves* his life ▪
loses it, ▪ ▪
while the man who *hates* his life in this world ▪
preserves it to life *eternal.* ▪ ▪

"If any would serve me, let them follow me."

If anyone would *serve* me, ▪
let him *follow* me; ▪ ▪
where *I* am, ▪
there will my *servant* be. ▪ ▪

Gentle and sincere.

Anyone who serves me, ▪
the Father will *honor.* ▪ ▪

Genuine turmoil.

My soul is *troubled* now, ▪
yet what should I *say*— ▪ ▪

Implied is: "No, I won't say that; instead I'll say . . ."

Father, ▪ *save* me from this hour? ▪ ▪
But it was for *this* that I *came* to this hour. ▪ ▪
Father, ▪ *glorify* your name!" ▪ ▪

Strong and commanding.

Then a *voice* came from the *sky:* ▪ ▪
"I *have* glorified it, ▪
and will glorify it *again.*" ▪ ▪

Excited and confused.

When the *crowd* of bystanders *heard* the voice, ▪ they said it was *thunder.* ▪ ▪ *Others* maintained, ▪ "An *angel* was speaking to him." ▪ ▪ *Jesus* answered, ▪ ▪ "That voice did not come for *my* sake, ▪ but for *yours.* ▪ ▪

Jesus is at peace.

"Now has *judgment* come upon this world, ▪
now will this world's *prince* be *driven* out, ▪
and *I* ▪ once I am *lifted up* from earth— ▪

"Men" can be "people."

will draw *all* men to *myself.*" ▪ ▪
(This *statement* of his ▪ indicated the sort of *death* he was going to die.) ▪ ▪ ▪

MARCH 17, 1991

FIFTH SUNDAY OF LENT, YEAR A

Editor's note: *Lenten Sunday liturgies which include a celebration of the rite of scrutiny of the Rite of Christian Initiation of Adults also include this set of readings from Year A. These readings replace the readings for Year B.*

LECTIONARY #34

READING I Ezekiel 37:12–14

Great urgency and sincerity throughout.

A reading from the book of the prophet ▪ *Ezekiel* ▪ ▪ ▪

"O my . . . graves" = slowly. "And . . . rise from them" = faster.

Slower again.

Note different stress. Energy no less than before.

Imagine looking into eyes of one who needs these promises. Long pause before breaking mood and saying "This is. . . ."

Thus says the Lord *God:* ▪ ▪ O my *people,* ▪ I will open your *graves* ▪ and have you *rise* from them, ▪ and *bring* you back to the land of *Israel.* ▪ Then you shall *know* that I *am* the Lord, ▪ when I *open* your graves and have you *rise* from them, ▪ O my people! ▪ ▪ I will put my *spirit* in you that you may *live,* ▪ and I will *settle* you upon your *land;* ▪ ▪ thus you shall *know* that I am the *Lord.* ▪ ▪ I have *promised,* ▪ and I *will* do it, ▪ says the Lord. ▪ ▪ ▪

READING II Romans 8:8–11

Read slowly, logically, but with joy.

A reading from the letter of *Paul* ▪ to the *Romans* ▪ ▪ ▪

The good news! Let all know it applies to them.

"He" can be "that person."

Your tone says: How sad this would be!

See rephrasing in commentary. Good news again!

Hope of new life for the body as well as the spirit.

Those who are in the *flesh* cannot *please* God. ▪ ▪ But *you* are *not* in the flesh; ▪ ▪ you are in the *spirit,* ▪ since the Spirit of God *dwells* in you. ▪ ▪ If anyone does not *have* the Spirit of *Christ,* ▪ he does not *belong* to Christ. ▪ ▪ If Christ *is* in you, ▪ the body is indeed *dead* because of *sin,* ▪ while the *spirit lives* ▪ because of *justice.* ▪ ▪ If the *Spirit* of him who raised *Jesus* from the *dead* dwells in *you,* ▪ then *he* who raised *Christ* from the dead ▪ will bring *your* mortal bodies to life *also* ▪ through his *Spirit* dwelling *in* you. ▪ ▪ ▪

GOSPEL John 11:1–45

A reading from the holy *gospel* according to *John* ▪ ▪ ▪

Speak familiarly of these places and people. Avoid melancholy.

(1) There was a certain man named *Lazarus* who was *sick.* ▪ ▪ He was from *Bethany,* ▪ the village of *Mary* and her sister *Martha.* ▪ ▪ (This *Mary* whose brother Lazarus was sick ▪ was the one who *anointed* the Lord

READING I God speaks directly, urgently in this text. It is God's voice, not the prophet's that we hear. The exclamation "O my people" frames God's first promise, which is also stated twice in those two sentences. "I will open your graves" must be spoken slowly and significantly so that the impact of these strange words will not be lost. Quicken the pace on "and have you rise . . . ," your excitement and sudden exclamation suggesting the movement of the bodies from their graves. Speak more slowly for the rest of the sentence, your tone confident and assuring. There is no anger or arrogance, only a burning love that seeks to convince the people for their own good, not for God's vindication. The stresses are somewhat different, but your energy is no less when you refer, the second time, to opening graves and rising from them.

God's second promise is spoken with great intensity and sincerity. Imagine speaking to victims of violence. Your words must be so reassuring, so full of truth that they can believe you *will* be their strength and their protection if they dare face life again. Such an intense image and delivery will require a longer pause before you announce "This is the word. . . ." Don't hold back, for many wounded hearts wait to hear these words of comfort.

READING II Here is a message of hope and promise echoing the words of Ezekiel in Reading I. Speak Paul's lines with enthusiasm and joy. He starts with bad news, then immediately qualifies with "But you are not" part of that bad news. He then announces the "good news" of life in the Spirit.

You will want to move slowly through this passage but without diminishing your enthusiasm. You are making points that you think are very logical: "You are not in the *flesh* [because] you are in the *spirit* [and that is true because] the Spirit of God dwells in you." "Flesh" is all those things that focus us on self rather than on God and others. You rejoice that those to whom you speak are not trapped in such self-centeredness. Use Paul's contrasting words to make and emphasize his points, especially contrasting "body," "dead" and "sin" with "spirit," "lives" and "justice." A clearer reading of that sentence is given by the revised NAB: "If Christ is in you, *although* the body is dead because of sin, the spirit is alive because of righteousness." You can achieve the same clarity with the present text by simply adding "although" before "the body" and dropping the word "while."

Paul concludes by announcing that the same spirit who makes it possible for Christians to live holy lives will also bring their "mortal bodies to life" on the last day. Ezekiel and John unite with Paul in proclaiming that good news.

GOSPEL This powerful story speaks both of what happened in Jesus' day and of what happens now. Almost daily, death finds us. Whether in the guise of a failed relationship or a great loss, we drink life's pain and enter dark tombs with large stones rolled across them. And Jesus still comes to call us forth. Your listeners will hear that message only if the historical story is well told. So, first of all, be a storyteller and tell the whole story (the long form) remembering that the telling is a sacramental moment during which the eternal Word is enfleshed. (Such sacred moments should not be edited!)

(1) Your narrator is not someone who watches these events as they unfold, but a believer who is relating the story some time after it has taken place. With the advantage of hindsight, the tale is told. The opening lines are not melancholy. The narrator knows the people and the village being described and speaks familiarly of perfume and hair-dried feet. The sisters' message is spoken with their voices, concerned but not panicked—for Jesus can heal. Jesus' response is low-key. He knows they won't comprehend his words.

(2) Convince your listeners of Jesus' great love for Martha and her family. Jesus' delay does not surprise you for you know the end of the story, but you emphasize it to evoke questions from your audience. The apostles fear what waits in Jerusalem and don't hide it. The suggestion that Jesus is acting irresponsibly is also in their tone. Jesus answers like one who knows his wisdom is beyond that of his followers. There's no agitation in his voice. His tone is more direct when he tells them Lazarus is "asleep." But that just leaves them scratching their heads. The announcement of Lazarus's death is spoken simply, without emotion. The simplicity will hint at the depth of feeling that lies within. Peter's grandstanding at the washing of the feet at the Last Supper is no less overplayed than Thomas's impetuosity here.

(3) Sustain both interest and energy as you narrate the arrival at Bethany. These are important details. The energy increases as Martha runs out to meet Jesus. She is hurt and angry. "Even now . . ." does not signal an abrupt change in her mood. She states her expectation that Jesus can and *should* do something. Jesus' response is intentionally cryptic and *not* what Martha wants to hear. From intimate conversation between Jesus and Martha we shift to Jesus' public proclamation that he is the source of life. Martha

Use voices of Mary and Martha.

Low-key.

Emphasize this to make listeners wonder why he didn't go. You already know.

Fear! For Jesus and themselves.

Recast in plural to be inclusive: "Those walk by day do not . . ."

Confused: If this is true, why do we have to go there?

Simply. Holding emotions in check.

Youthful impetuosity.

Keep narration lively.

Suggest Martha's agitation.

Hurt and anger and the expectation that still he should do something.

This is not what she wanted to hear.

Jesus speaks for all to hear.

"That person" is more inclusive.

with *perfume* ▪ and dried his *feet* with her *hair.)* ▪ ▪ ▪ The sisters sent *word* to Jesus to *inform* him, ▪ ▪ *"Lord,* ▪ the one you *love* is *sick."* ▪ ▪ Upon *hearing* this, ▪ Jesus said: ▪ ▪

"This *sickness* is not to *end* in *death;* ▪ ▪
rather ▪ it is for *God's glory,* ▪
that *through* it the *Son* of God may
be *glorified."* ▪ ▪ ▪

(2) Jesus *loved* Martha and her sister and Lazarus *very much.* ▪ ▪ Yet, after *hearing* that Lazarus was sick, ▪ he *stayed* on where he was for *two days* more. ▪ ▪ *Finally* he said to his *disciples,* ▪ ▪ "Let us *go* back to Judea." ▪ ▪ *"Rabbi,"* ▪ protested the disciples, ▪ ▪ "with the Jews only *recently* trying to *stone* you, ▪ you are going back up there *again?"* ▪ ▪ Jesus answered: ▪ ▪

"Are there not twelve hours of *daylight?* ▪ ▪
If a man goes *walking* by *day* he does
not *stumble,* ▪
because he *sees* the world *bathed* in light. ▪ ▪
But if he goes walking at *night* ▪
he *will* stumble, ▪
since there is *no light* in him." ▪ ▪

After uttering these words, ▪ he *added,* ▪ ▪ "Our *beloved* Lazarus has fallen *asleep,* ▪ but I am going there to *wake* him." ▪ ▪ At *this* the disciples *objected,* ▪ ▪ *"Lord,* ▪ if he *is* asleep his life will be *saved."* ▪ ▪ Jesus had been speaking about his *death,* ▪ but *they* thought he meant *sleep* in the sense of *slumber.* ▪ ▪ Finally Jesus said *plainly,* ▪ "Lazarus is *dead.* ▪ ▪ For *your* sakes I am *glad* I was not there, ▪ that you may come to *believe.* ▪ ▪ In any event, ▪ let us *go* to him." ▪ ▪ Then *Thomas* ▪ (the name means *"Twin"*) ▪ said to his fellow disciples, ▪ ▪ "Let us *go* along, ▪ to *die* with him." ▪ ▪ ▪

(3) When Jesus *arrived* at Bethany, ▪ he found that Lazarus had *already* been in the tomb *four days.* ▪ ▪ The village was not *far* from Jerusalem—just under *two* miles— ▪ and *many* Jewish people had come out to *console* Martha and Mary over their brother. ▪ ▪ When Martha *heard* that *Jesus* was coming ▪ she went to *meet* him, ▪ while *Mary* sat at *home.* ▪ ▪ Martha *said* to Jesus, ▪ ▪ *"Lord,* ▪ if you had *been* here, ▪ my brother would *never* have *died.* ▪ ▪ Even *now,* ▪ I am *sure* that God will give you *whatever* you ask of him." ▪ ▪ "Your brother will *rise* again," ▪ Jesus assured her. ▪ ▪ "I *know* he will rise again," ▪ Martha replied, ▪ ▪ "in the *resurrection* on the last day." ▪ ▪ Jesus told her: ▪ ▪

"I am the resurrection and the life: ▪ ▪
whoever *believes* in me, ▪
though he should *die,* ▪ will come to *life;* ▪ ▪

Martha forgets her needs and states her faith . . . quietly.

and whoever is *alive* and believes in *me* ▪
will *never die.* ▪ ▪
Do *you* believe this?" ▪ ▪ *"Yes,* Lord," ▪ she replied. ▪ ▪ "I have *come* to believe that you are the *Messiah,* ▪ the *Son* of *God:* ▪ ▪ *he* who is to *come* into the world." ▪ ▪ ▪

Whisper.

Suggest Mary's excitement.

Buzzing gossip of the crowd.

"Fell at his feet" sounds like it means.

Slowly and quietly.

Like whining kids.

Slowly. Building toward climax.

(4) When she had *said* this ▪ she went back and *called* her sister *Mary.* ▪ ▪ "The *Teacher* is here, ▪ *asking* for you," ▪ she whispered. ▪ ▪ As *soon* as Mary *heard* this, ▪ she got up and *started* out in his direction. ▪ ▪ (*Actually* Jesus had not yet *come* into the village ▪ but was *still* at the spot where Martha had *met* him.) ▪ ▪ The *Jews* who were in the house with Mary ▪ *consoling* her ▪ saw her get up *quickly* and *go* out, ▪ so they *followed* her, ▪ thinking she was going to the *tomb* to *weep* there. ▪ ▪ When Mary *came* to the place where *Jesus* was, ▪ *seeing* him, ▪ she *fell* at his feet and *said* to him, ▪ ▪ *"Lord,* ▪ if *you* had been here ▪ my *brother* would never have *died."* ▪ ▪ ▪ When Jesus *saw* her *weeping,* ▪ and the Jewish folk who had *accompanied* her *also* weeping, ▪ he was *troubled* in *spirit,* ▪ *moved* by the *deepest* emotions. ▪ ▪ ▪ *"Where* have you *laid* him?" ▪ he asked. ▪ ▪ *"Lord,* ▪ *come* and *see,"* ▪ they said. ▪ ▪ Jesus began to *weep,* ▪ which caused the *Jews* to remark, ▪ ▪ *"See* how much he *loved* him!" ▪ ▪ But *some* said, ▪ ▪ "He *opened* the eyes of that *blind* man. ▪ ▪ Why could he not have done *something* to *stop* this man from *dying?"* ▪ ▪ ▪ Once again ▪ *troubled* in *spirit,* ▪ Jesus *approached* the tomb. ▪ ▪

With authority.

Practical concern about the stench.

A gentle reproach.

Look up. Loudly.

(5) It was a *cave* with a *stone* laid across it. ▪ ▪ *"Take* away the stone," ▪ Jesus directed. ▪ ▪ Martha, ▪ the dead man's sister, ▪ *said* to him, ▪ ▪ *"Lord,* it has been *four* days now; ▪ ▪ *surely* there will be a *stench!"* ▪ ▪ Jesus replied, ▪ ▪ "Did I not *assure* you that if you *believed* you would *see* the *glory* of *God?"* ▪ ▪ They then *took* away the stone and Jesus *looked upward* and said: ▪ ▪

"Father, I *thank* you for having *heard* me. ▪ ▪
I know that you *always* hear me ▪
but I have said this for the sake of the *crowd,* ▪
that *they* may believe that you *sent* me." ▪ ▪

Pause before "Lazarus." Go slowly; this is the climax.

(6) Having *said* this, ▪ he called *loudly,* ▪ ▪ *"Lazarus,* ▪ *come out!"* ▪ ▪ ▪ The *dead* man *came* out, ▪ *bound* hand and foot with linen strips, ▪ his face *wrapped* in a cloth. ▪ ▪ *"Untie* him," ▪ Jesus told them, ▪ ▪ "and let him go *free."* ▪ ▪ ▪

Quietly, slowly, but building the energy.

(7) This caused *many* of the Jews who had come to *visit* Mary, ▪ and had *seen* what Jesus *did,* ▪ to put their *faith* in him. ▪ ▪ ▪

[Shorter: John 11:3–7, 17, 20–27, 33–45]

then lays aside her own agenda and quietly makes her declaration of faith.

(4) Martha's whisper initiates a scene of growing intensity and excitement. Imagine, and let your voice suggest, Mary jumping to her feet. Suggest, too, the curiosity and buzzing conversation of the crowd. Mary's exclamation is pure sorrow, not reproach. That, together with the mourning of the crowd, releases Jesus' own emotions that you should speak of slowly and with much emphasis. You've played the next scene every time you've visited a funeral home: "Where have you laid him?" "Come and see."

(5) "It was a cave" is the haunting introduction to the place of reversal and victory. Jesus speaks with authority, but Martha's concern betrays her lack of confidence that a miracle will occur. Jesus gently reproaches, reminding her who he is. Lift your eyes as you pray, speaking the prayer so that even the whole crowd of mourners would be able to hear it.

(6) Pause after "he called loudly" and with power and authority speak the name of a friend you wish to call back to life. Though the name comes out "Lazarus," in your mind see someone you love who needs new life in Jesus. Ezekiel's vision comes to life before you. Take time with the description and enjoy it. It's an awesome and beautiful sight.

(7) The last three lines are spoken quietly, your energy building on each phrase. A good proclamation of this story will leave you tired. So will rehearsing it many times. But this is fine literature, and the assembly deserves no less than our best effort.

PROCESSION GOSPEL Every year this day comes to confront our vacillating natures. In many ways Palm Sunday is the most honest day of the year, for today we do somersaults and expose both sides of our mercurial characters. We would like to identify ourselves exclusively with the exultant crowds who rejoice at Jesus' coming, padding the road with their cloaks. But our hearts were minted with two sides, and the coin is easily flipped to reveal a capacity for darker motives and Good Friday menace.

Fresh from a miracle, the crowd pursues Jesus—perhaps expecting added fireworks. But Jesus is not distracted by their jubilant mood; instead he is focused on preparations for his entry into the city. Though Mark makes no mention of the Zechariah prophecy, which Christ's entry fulfills, Jesus' careful attention to details makes the scene an intentional reenactment of the prophecy (see Zechariah 9:9). In typical fashion, however, Jesus upends the people's expectations: I'll be your Messiah, he acknowledges, but on my terms; not in regal splendor but as one of the lowly, riding an ass.

Mark's geography is important: The Mount of Olives was popularly associated with the coming of the Anointed One; Jerusalem, of course, suggests all that will unfold there in just a matter of days. Jesus instructs the disciples calmly and with full confidence, making no great display of his foreknowledge of the colt and its availability.

The disciples are amazed to find things as Jesus described, his prescience accurate even to the question posed by the bystanders. There is rebuke in that question, so your narration of the disciples' reply should suggest both the timidity of their response and your surprise that they "let them take it."

The scene builds as cloaks start flying and Jesus' path is padded with branches. Capture the mood of Jesus engulfed by the crowd, looking behind and before him as the chant begins to swell, perhaps forgetting for a moment the reversal that awaits just a few days down the road. The more jubilant the "Hosannahs," the more striking the paradox of the curses the crowds will soon hurl at Jesus. The final line is a prayer that becomes as poignant as it is ironic when we remember Jesus will soon ask his Father to save him from the fate this same crowd will help engineer.

READING I The first six lines of this passage should have special meaning for you as a lector. They are a prayer of thanks for the ministry you are privileged to exercise. Isaiah's Suffering Servant also speaks these words with gratitude for God's special call—a call

MARCH 24, 1991

PASSION (PALM) SUNDAY

LECTIONARY #37B

PROCESSION GOSPEL Mark 11:1–10

A reading from the holy *gospel* according to *Mark* ▪ ▪ ▪

"Bethphage" = "Beth-fay-gee." These are important code words.

As the *crowd* drew near *Bethphage* and *Bethany* on the *Mount* of *Olives,* ▪ close to *Jerusalem,* ▪ Jesus sent off two of his *disciples* with the *instructions:* ▪ ▪ "Go to the village *straight* ahead of you, ▪ and as soon as you *enter* it ▪ you will find tethered there a *colt* ▪ on which *no* one has ridden. ▪ ▪ *Untie* it and bring it *back.* ▪ ▪ If anyone *says* to you, ▪ ▪ 'Why are you *doing* that?' ▪ ▪ say, ▪ ▪ 'The *Master* needs it ▪ but he will send it *back* here at *once.*'" ▪ ▪ So they *went* off, ▪ and *finding* a colt tethered out on the street near a *gate,* ▪ they *untied* it. ▪ ▪ Some of the *bystanders* said to them, ▪ ▪ "What do you *mean* by untying that colt?" ▪ ▪ They answered as Jesus had *told* them to, ▪ and the men let them *take* it. ▪ ▪ They *brought* the colt to Jesus ▪ and threw their *cloaks* across its back, ▪ and he *sat* on it. ▪ ▪ *Many* people spread their cloaks on the *road,* ▪ while *others* spread *reeds* which they had cut in the fields. ▪ ▪ Those *preceding* him ▪ as well as those who *followed cried* out: ▪ ▪

Straightforward. Don't overstate Jesus' foreknowledge of events.

Reveal disciples' surprise.

Question: reproachful. Answer timid; then surprise again.

Convey the mounting excitement.

Build intensity and volume on the two "blessed" statements. Retain intensity, but lower volume on final line.

"Hosannah! ▪ ▪
Blessed be he who *comes*
in the *name* of the *Lord!* ▪ ▪
Blessed be the *reign* of our father David
to *come!* ▪ ▪
God *save* him from on *high!"* ▪ ▪

READING I Isaiah 50:4–7

A reading from the book of the prophet ▪ *Isaiah* ▪ ▪ ▪

Let your entire presence express the gratitude.

The Lord God has *given* me
 a *well-trained* tongue, ▪
That I might know how to *speak* to the *weary*
 a *word* that will *rouse* them. ▪ ▪
Morning after morning
 he opens my *ear* that I may *hear;* ▪ ▪

Proud and grateful for God-given strength to endure.

And I have not *rebelled,* ▪
 have *not* turned back. ▪ ▪

"Beat" and "plucked" sound like they mean. "Plucked my beard" is a grave insult.

I gave my *back* to those who *beat* me, ▪
 my *cheeks* to those who *plucked*
  my beard; ▪ ▪
My *face* I did not *shield*
 from *buffets* and *spitting.* ▪ ▪ ▪

The voice of hope in the face of adversity.

The *Lord God* is my *help,* ▪
 therefore I am not *disgraced;* ▪ ▪

"Flint" sounds like it means. Speak with rock-like confidence.

I have *set* my face like *flint,* ▪
 knowing that I shall *not* be
  put to *shame.* ▪ ▪ ▪

READING II Philippians 2:6–11

A reading from the letter of *Paul* ▪ to the *Philippians* ▪ ▪ ▪

A command given with a smile. Persuasive.

Your *attitude* must be *Christ's:* ▪ ▪

Moderate tempo.

 though he was in the form of *God* ▪
 he did not deem *equality* with God
 something to be *grasped* at. ▪ ▪
Rather, ▪ he *emptied* himself ▪

Stress on humility and the reality of pain endured. Rev. NAB says: "coming in human likeness; and found human in appearance."

 and took the form of a *slave,* ▪
 being *born* in the *likeness* of *men.* ▪ ▪
He was *known* to be of human estate, ▪
 and it was thus that he *humbled* himself, ▪

Slower tempo.

 obediently accepting even *death,* ▪
 death on a *cross!* ▪ ▪ ▪

Turning point. Sudden tempo shift: faster and louder.

Because of this, ▪
 God highly *exalted* him ▪
 and *bestowed* on him the *name*
 above *every other* name, ▪ ▪
So that at *Jesus'* name ▪

Slower here.

 every *knee* must bend
 in the *heavens,* ▪ on the *earth,* ▪

Suddenly faster.

 and *under* the earth, ▪
 and every *tongue proclaim* ▪
 to the *glory* of *God* the *Father:* ▪ ▪

Ritardando: "Jesus . . . Lord."

 JESUS CHRIST IS LORD! ▪ ▪ ▪

that is bitter as well as sweet. Speak with pride and joy about knowing how to speak to the *"weary"* (carry a clear image in your mind of who the weary are in your community) a word that will *"rouse* them." (Rouse them more with your attitude of joyous enthusiasm than with loudness of voice.)

Thinking of someone who has suffered for acting rightly (a friend who chooses to be gossiped about rather than gossiping about her detractors) will help you proclaim the next six lines. The section stresses the freedom with which the Servant endured the abuse of others. Though the pain suggested is intense, note that it is spoken of in the past tense.

The last four lines acknowledge God's help. Here's the reason why the Servant was strong in facing opposition. He is filled with a God-given confidence that he will not "be put to shame." He stands strong, solid and ready. The confidence in your voice is a rock ready to be struck and ready to make sparks.

READING II This beautiful hymn of praise almost begs to be sung. Indeed, a simple chanting of Paul's words would be powerful. (But we'll assume that's not your gift. All the gifts you do have, however, must be summoned to do justice to this reading.) Like a piece of music, the passage moves through several tempos. Your sensitivity to these will lend variety to the proclamation and allow you to build to a closing crescendo.

The first line is an order, delivered with a smile on your face that *gently* persuades. Next comes an explanation of *why* we should imitate Christ. He did not grasp on to his "equality with God" but allowed himself to be "emptied," becoming like one of us. In typical Christian irony, emptying leads to filling; humility to glorification. Christ accepted death; yes, even the most humiliating form of death imaginable, "death on a cross."

That realization leads us to the turning point of the reading: "Because of this. . . ." Speak with a quickened tempo of Christ's exaltation by God. Note the striking similarity with Isaiah's Servant Song of the first reading. Paul's servant also did not rebel ("he emptied himself") and offered his back for beating (he accepted "even death . . . on a cross") and thus he was not disgraced ("God highly exalted him"). Speak of that exaltation as a reward, greatly deserved. Take time to say that the universe ("heavens . . . earth . . . and under") must join the praise. The last line is not capitalized by accident. There the praise peaks. Your voice is both instrument and amplifier playing slowly and majestically in praise of Lord Jesus.

PASSION The concept of remembrance is an essential and cherished part of Jewish life. Remembering animates the community by bringing to the present events and realities of the past. Our liturgy is based on that concept: We remember Jesus and in the remembering he is present among us. Storytelling also employs this concept. Even when we already know a story, we relive it only one moment and event at a time, so we can hope, at any given point in the telling, that events might unfold differently *this* time than they did the last time we heard the story. When we take a theater seat to watch *Romeo and Juliet* we already know that the lovers will be dead; but inevitably, as the scenes unfold, a secret, mysterious longing tempts us to believe that this time Juliet might awaken and the families reconcile before it's too late. The first people on whom stories work their magic, of course, are the storytellers themselves, who are as much victims of their storytelling as any listener; they, too, sink into the details of the story and laugh and cry and hope that things will work out for the best. As teller of the Passion narrative, you become the story's victim by being the first to feel the fear and tears, the love and hate, the anger and the pathos and the guilt in all its scenes.

Mark's Passion contrasts with the one we read on Good Friday. John presents a regal Jesus in charge of his destiny, reigning from the cross, who surrenders his life with no outcry or regret. Mark's is a darker tale of abandonment and woe, presenting a Jesus who is resigned to the ironic necessity that his glorification will come only after and through his suffering and death. "Abandoned," "denied," "accused," "rejected" and "mocked" are the action words of Mark's narrative. Like Matthew's account, which it parallels so closely, Mark's is a description of the painful passage the Messiah must make before he enters his glory. He paints in Rembrandt shades and shadows that intensify as the drama progresses. Luke shows a healing, compassionate Christ moving toward Calvary; John, a sovereign lord; but Mark's Jesus is Isaiah's silent, suffering servant who finds vindication from the unlikeliest source—a Roman soldier who declares him God's son only when he hangs dead and disgraced from a cross reserved for criminals. This is a sad, intense and ironic Passion. The strong emotions here should not be diminished; they will heighten the dramatic reversal of Christ's ultimate vindication.

A parish's best readers should be enlisted for the Passion proclamation. If you divide the text into parts, don't designate only one reader as narrator; narration can be shared

PASSION Mark 14:1—15:47

The *Passion* of our *Lord Jesus Christ* ▪ according to *Mark* ▪ ▪ ▪

Proximity of festival adds urgency to their scheming.

"Trick" and "kill" sound as harsh as their meaning.

Self-serving caution.

(1) The feasts of *Passover* and *Unleavened Bread* ▪ were to be observed in *two* days' time, ▪ and therefore the chief *priests* and *scribes* ▪ began to look for a way to *arrest* Jesus by some *trick* ▪ and *kill* him. ▪ ▪ Yet they pointed out, ▪ ▪ *"Not* during the *festival,* ▪ or the people may *riot."* ▪ ▪ ▪

Suggest her confidence despite the whispers.

Build the anger.

Are their motives pure?

With affection.

Assuring her and teaching them.

(2) When Jesus was in *Bethany* ▪ reclining at table in the house of *Simon* the *leper,* ▪ ▪ a *woman* entered ▪ carrying an alabaster jar of *perfume* ▪ made from *expensive* aromatic nard. ▪ ▪ *Breaking* the jar, ▪ she began to *pour* the perfume on his *head.* ▪ ▪ Some were saying to themselves *indignantly:* ▪ ▪ "What is the *point* of this extravagant *waste* of perfume? ▪ ▪ It could have been *sold* for over *three hundred* silver pieces and the money given to the *poor."* ▪ ▪ They were *infuriated* at her. ▪ ▪ But *Jesus* said: ▪ ▪ "Let her *alone.* ▪ ▪ Why do you *criticize* her? ▪ ▪ She has done me a *kindness.* ▪ ▪ The *poor* you will *always* have with you ▪ and you can be *generous* to them whenever you *wish,* ▪ but you will *not* always have *me.* ▪ ▪ She has *done* what she *could.* ▪ ▪ By perfuming my *body* ▪ she is *anticipating* its preparation for *burial.* ▪ ▪ I *assure* you, ▪ wherever the *good news* is proclaimed *throughout* the world, ▪ what *she* has done ▪ will be *told* in her *memory."* ▪ ▪ ▪

You can hardly believe he would do it.

Patting him on the back.

(3) Then *Judas Iscariot,* ▪ one of the *Twelve,* ▪ went off to the *chief priests* ▪ to *hand* Jesus *over* to them. ▪ ▪ *Hearing* what he had to say, ▪ they were *jubilant* ▪ and promised to give him *money.* ▪ ▪ He for *his* part ▪ kept looking for an *opportune* way to hand him over. ▪ ▪ ▪

Unaware of what's coming, they're in a mood to celebrate.

Unemotional and assured. Does not betray his concern.

Faster pace. Amazed at Jesus' accuracy.

(4) On the *first* day of Unleavened Bread, ▪ when it was *customary* to sacrifice the *paschal lamb,* ▪ his *disciples* said to him, ▪ ▪ *"Where* do you wish us to go to prepare the Passover *supper* for you?" ▪ ▪ He sent *two* of his disciples with these *instructions:* ▪ ▪ "Go into the *city* ▪ and you will come upon a *man* carrying a *water* jar. ▪ ▪ *Follow* him. ▪ ▪ Whatever house he *enters,* ▪ say to the *owner,* ▪ ▪ 'The *Teacher* asks, ▪ ▪ Where is my *guestroom* where I may eat the *Passover* with my *disciples?'* ▪ ▪ Then he will *show* you an *upstairs* room, ▪ spacious, ▪ furnished, ▪ and all in *order.* ▪ ▪ *That* is the place you are to get *ready* for us." ▪ ▪ The disciples *went* off. ▪ ▪ When they *reached* the city ▪ they found it *just* as he had *told* them, ▪ and they *prepared* the Passover supper. ▪ ▪ ▪

"Dark" sets mood for revealing the betrayer.

(5) As it grew *dark* ▪ he *arrived* with the Twelve. ▪ ▪ They *reclined* at table, ▪ and in the *course* of the meal Jesus said, ▪ ▪ "I give you my *word,* ▪ *one* of you is about to *betray* me, ▪ yes, ▪ one who is *eating* with me." ▪ ▪ They began to say to him *sorrowfully,* ▪ one by one, ▪ ▪ *"Surely* not *I!"* ▪ ▪ He said, "It is one of the *Twelve—* ▪ a man who *dips* into the dish with me. ▪ ▪ The Son of Man is going the way the *Scripture* tells of him. ▪ ▪ Still, ▪ *accursed* be that man by whom the Son of Man is *betrayed.* ▪ ▪ It were *better* for him ▪ had he *never* been born." ▪ ▪ ▪

Hard to speak these words.

Afraid and defensive.

Great sadness.

Change mood.

Not as ritual prayer, but as words spoken to friends.

(6) During the meal ▪ he took *bread,* ▪ *blessed* and *broke* it, ▪ and *gave* it to them. ▪ ▪ *"Take* this," ▪ he said, " this is my *body."* ▪ ▪ He likewise took a *cup,* ▪ gave *thanks* ▪ and *passed* it to them, ▪ ▪ and they all *drank* from it. ▪ ▪ He said to them: ▪ ▪ "This is my *blood,* ▪ the blood of the *covenant,* ▪ to be *poured out* on behalf of *many.* ▪ ▪ I solemnly *assure* you, ▪ I will *never* again drink of the *fruit* of the *vine* ▪ until the day when I drink it in the *reign* of *God."* ▪ ▪ ▪

Sense of loss and longing for reunion.

(7) After singing *songs* of *praise,* ▪ they walked out to the *Mount* of *Olives.* ▪ ▪

Convincingly but without anger.

Jesus then *said* to them: ▪ ▪ "Your *faith* in me shall be *shaken,* ▪ for *Scripture* has it, ▪ ▪
'I will *strike* the shepherd ▪
and the *sheep* will be *dispersed.'* ▪ ▪
But after I am *raised* up, ▪ I will go to Galilee *ahead* of you." ▪ ▪ *Peter* said to him, "Even though *all* are shaken in faith, ▪ it will *not* be that way with *me."* ▪ ▪ Jesus answered, ▪ ▪ "I give you my *assurance,* ▪ ▪ this *very* night ▪ before the cock crows *twice,* ▪ you will *deny* me *three* times." ▪ ▪ But Peter kept reasserting *vehemently,* ▪ ▪ "Even if I have to *die* with you, I will *not* disown you." ▪ ▪ They *all* said the *same.* ▪ ▪ ▪

Assurance and hope.

He's convinced.

Not trying to persuade, but preparing him for the inevitable.

A little hurt and a lot of love.

(8) They went then to a place named *Gethsemani.* ▪ ▪ "Sit down here while I *pray,"* ▪ he said to his disciples; ▪ ▪ at the *same* time he took along with him *Peter,* ▪ *James,* ▪ and *John.* ▪ ▪ Then he began to be *filled* with *fear* and *distress.* ▪ ▪ He said to them, ▪ ▪ "My heart is filled with *sorrow* to the point of *death.* ▪ ▪ *Remain* here and stay *awake."* ▪ ▪ He advanced a *little* ▪ and *fell* to the ground, ▪ *praying* that if it were *possible* ▪ this hour might *pass* him by. ▪ ▪ He kept saying, ▪ ▪ *"Abba* ▪ (O Father), ▪ you have the *power* to do *all* things. ▪ ▪ *Take* this cup *away* from me. ▪ ▪ But let it be as *you* would have it, ▪ not as *I."* ▪ ▪ When he *returned* ▪ he found them *asleep.* ▪ ▪ He said to *Peter,* ▪ ▪ *"Asleep,* Simon? ▪ ▪ You could not stay awake for even an *hour?* ▪ ▪ Be on *guard* ▪ and pray that *you* may not be put to the *test.* ▪ ▪ The *spirit* is

Containing his grief.

Absolute terror.

Wanting to say "No." Don't rush his acceptance.

Disappointed and upset.

No anger, but a warning.

with all the readers. Dialogue sounds natural if at least two readers take on the dialogue lines. Someone designated "Speaker" can't carry on a two- or three-way conversation with himself or herself. Avoid assigning a role to the assembly. Proclamation can't happen when everyone is forced to read along with the proclaimers. Whatever resource you utilize for dividing up the lines, use this commentary, and your prayer time, to plumb the depths of the text, the characters and their motivations.

(1) The Conspiracy. Echoes of the procession gospel reverberate here. The priests and scribes have observed Jesus' immense popularity; their hostile scheming stands in sharp contrast with the crowd's affection. The sound of words like "trick" and "kill" suggests the daggers of hate these leaders would plunge into Jesus. Their calculated caution only intensifies the feeling of malice.

(2) The Anointing at Bethany. The mood here is of "calm before the storm," and Jesus knows it. He *wants* to enjoy the company of his friends and the attention and tender ministry given him by the woman. Let your narration be as soothing as the perfume poured on Jesus' head. The "indignant" comments of the onlookers should be whispered, their tone a violent contrast with the comfort of the ointment. The intensity of expressions like "extravagant waste" and "infuriated" suggests motives beyond financial concern. Perhaps jealousy or greed fuel these harsh comments. While ministry to the poor is a constant responsibility for the disciples, this is the last opportunity they'll have to minister to Jesus. The woman seems to know this and in Jesus' voice we hear his gratitude, not only for the kindness done, but for the vision and understanding that allows her, and not his disciples, to intuit the road of suffering he's about to walk.

(3) The Betrayal. "One of the Twelve" (a phrase often paired with Judas' name) expresses the shock of Jesus' betrayer coming from the ranks of his most intimate friends. Mark supplies no motive, but your voice should suggest some turmoil and ambivalence in Judas. The priests are jubilant, promising "money," and he becomes even more determined to find an "opportune way" to betray his friend.

(4) Passover Preparations. Still unaware of the events that will soon descend upon them, the disciples appear in a festive mood inquiring about preparations. As in the procession gospel, Jesus has prescient knowledge of the details of the celebration: He speaks, not with emotion, but with confidence, like "the Teacher" he calls himself instructing his pupils. "When they reached

the city . . ." is spoken in a faster pace, as if by the disciples who are amazed and delighted to find things "just as he told them."

(5) The Betrayer: Cloaked in darkness, Jesus and friends secretly enter the city. "In the course of the meal" Jesus finally speaks of his betrayer. There is pain in his voice as he speaks of being betrayed by one who is *eating* with him. Sudden panic ensues as one by one they deny their guilt. Without melodrama or self-pity Jesus insists that one *is* guilty and names the action that will identify him. Though resigned to his fate, Jesus laments with knotted-throat and clenched-jaw control that it will be one of his own who opens the door for Scripture's fulfillment.

(6) The Lord's Supper. Jesus wipes the bitter taste of betrayal from his lips and says: "Take this . . . this is my body . . . my blood." There's love in those words, for his friends and for all who will be drawn to this meal. The cup from which Jesus will "never again drink" seems filled with fear and sorrow, but he quickly shifts focus to a time when drinking and fellowship will be renewed in "the reign of God." Though the meal ends in song, Jesus' joy is muted by his realization that these friends will soon scatter.

(7) Peter's Denial Foretold. On the Mount of Olives, where David had fled in an earlier age and wept upon discovering that he'd been betrayed by a trusted adviser, Jesus prophesies his best friends' cowardice. While he must convince them that they *will* do what they now feel is inconceivable, he doesn't let judgment infect his voice. You will abandon me, he says, that's certain. But immediately he offers hope of resurrection and assurance of reunion. Peter vehemently and naively asserts his fidelity. Jesus counters his bravado with a tone that says: You *will* fail, but I'll love you just the same.

(8) Gethsemani. Darkness closes in around Jesus, who still wears a brave face as he instructs the disciples to sit down. Only his most trusted friends are allowed to see the mask of courage slipping. Fear and distress threaten to overwhelm Jesus and he confesses the sorrow in his heart. He asks his friends for support through their presence and watchfulness. Suddenly, alone, the full weight of his grief thrusts him to the ground. There's no mistaking Jesus' desire to reject his fate, but the word "Abba" immediately hints the possibility of acceptance; his intimate relationship with the Father makes possible a trust that says "as *you* would have it, not as I." The fortitude with which he predicted Peter's denial is not in evidence when Jesus returns to find the disciples

willing ▪ but *nature* is *weak.*" ▪▪ Going *back* again ▪
he began to pray in the *same* words. ▪▪ Once *again* he
found them *asleep* on his return. ▪▪ They could *not*
A weak excuse.
keep their eyes *open,* ▪ nor did they know what to *say*
to him. ▪▪ He returned a *third* time and said to
Not angry. Resigned and ready.
them, ▪▪ "*Still* sleeping? ▪▪ Still taking your *ease?* ▪▪
It will have to *do.* ▪▪ The *hour* is on us. ▪▪ You will
Look up and "see" the mob coming, then say: "Rouse yourselves . . ."
see that the Son of Man is to be *handed* over into the
clutches of *evil* men. ▪▪ *Rouse* yourselves and *come*
along. ▪▪ *See!* ▪ My *betrayer* is *near.*" ▪▪▪

(9) Even while he was still *speaking,* ▪ *Judas,* ▪ one of
Contrast "one of the Twelve" with "swords and clubs."
the *Twelve,* ▪ made his *appearance* accompanied by
a crowd with *swords* and *clubs;* ▪▪ these people had
been sent by the *chief priests,* ▪ the *scribes,* ▪ and the
elders. ▪▪ The betrayer had arranged a *signal* for
Whispered.
them, ▪ saying, ▪▪ "The man I shall *embrace* is the
one; ▪▪ *arrest* him and *lead* him away, ▪ taking *every*
precaution." ▪▪ He then went *directly* over to him ▪
Pause before and after "Rabbi."
and said, ▪▪ "*Rabbi!*" ▪ and *embraced* him. ▪▪ At
this, they laid *hands* on him and *arrested* him. ▪▪
Faster pace.
One of the *bystanders* drew his *sword* and *struck* the
Suggest Peter's fury.
high priest's slave, ▪ cutting off his *ear.* ▪▪ Addressing
himself to them, ▪ Jesus said, ▪▪ "You have come out
Strong and confident.
to arrest me armed with *swords* and *clubs* ▪ as if
Shaming them for their cowardice.
against a *brigand.* ▪▪ I was within your reach *daily,* ▪
teaching in the temple precincts, ▪ yet you *never*
arrested me. ▪▪ But *now,* ▪ so that the Scriptures may
Stops mid-sentence.
be *fulfilled. . . .*" ▪▪ With that, ▪ all *deserted* him and
fled. ▪▪ There was a young man *following* him ▪ who
was covered by *nothing* but a linen *cloth.* ▪▪ As they
"Him" = Jesus.
seized him ▪ he left the cloth behind and ran off
naked. ▪▪▪

Signal the approaching danger.
(10) Then they led Jesus off to the *high priest,* ▪ and
all the *chief* priests, ▪ the *elders* and the *scribes* came
Hesitant and afraid.
together. ▪▪ *Peter* followed him at a *distance* right
into the high priest's *courtyard,* ▪ where he found a
seat with the temple *guard* and began to *warm*
himself at the *fire.* ▪▪ The chief priests with the
whole Sanhedrin were busy soliciting *testimony*
Frustration.
against Jesus that would lead to his *death,* ▪ but they
could not *find* any. ▪▪ *Many* spoke against him
falsely under oath ▪ but their *testimony* did not
agree. ▪ *Some,* for instance, ▪ on taking the *stand,* ▪
They quote him in slow cadences.
testified falsely by *alleging,* ▪▪ "We heard him
declare, ▪ 'I will *destroy* this temple made by *human*
hands,' and 'In *three* days I will construct another ▪
Narrator enjoys their failure.
not made by human hands.'" ▪▪ *Even* so, ▪ their
testimony did *not* agree. ▪▪▪

Taking charge.
(11) The high priest *rose* to his feet before the court ▪
and began to *interrogate* Jesus: ▪▪ "Have you *no*
Trying to provoke him.
answer to what these men *testify* against you?" ▪▪

High priest is amazed.

Forceful and loud.

Calmly. Regally.

He jumps at the opportunity.

They're convinced he's a liar and blasphemer.

But Jesus remained *silent:* ▪ ▪ he made *no* reply. ▪ ▪ Once *again* the high priest interrogated him: ▪ ▪ "Are you the *Messiah,* ▪ the *Son* of the *Blessed One?*" ▪ ▪ Then Jesus *answered:* ▪ ▪ "I *am;* ▪ ▪ and you will *see* the Son of Man seated at the *right* hand of the *Power* ▪ and *coming* with the *clouds* of *heaven.*" ▪ ▪ ▪ At that the high priest *tore* his robes and said: ▪ ▪ "What further *need* do we have of *witnesses?* ▪ ▪ You have heard the *blasphemy.* ▪ ▪ What is your *verdict?*" ▪ ▪ They all *concurred* in the verdict ▪ *"guilty,"* ▪ ▪ with its sentence of *death.* ▪ ▪ Some of them then began to *spit* on him. ▪ ▪ They *blindfolded* him and *hit* him, ▪ saying, ▪ ▪ "Play the *prophet!*" ▪ ▪ while the officers *manhandled* him. ▪ ▪ ▪

Tension throughout the scene.

Simple curiosity.

He denies and pauses, then challenges with question.

Insulted, she's determined to identify him.

Adamant.

In a rage, cursing.

As a haunting memory. Underplayed . . . as if remembering tears, not shedding them.

(12) While *Peter* was down in the *courtyard,* ▪ one of the *servant* girls of the high priest came along. ▪ ▪ When she *noticed* Peter warming himself, ▪ she looked more *closely* at him and said, ▪ ▪ "You *too* were with *Jesus* of *Nazareth.*" ▪ ▪ But he *denied* it: ▪ ▪ "I don't know what you are *talking* about! ▪ ▪ ▪ What are you *getting* at?" ▪ ▪ Then he went out into the *gateway.* ▪ ▪ At that *moment* ▪ a *rooster* crowed. ▪ ▪ The *servant* girl, ▪ keeping an *eye* on him, ▪ started *again* to tell the bystanders, ▪ ▪ *"This* man is *one* of them." ▪ ▪ Once *again* he denied it. ▪ ▪ A little *later* the *bystanders* said to Peter once more, ▪ ▪ "You are *certainly* one of them! ▪ ▪ You're a *Galilean,* ▪ are you *not?*" ▪ ▪ He began to *curse,* ▪ and to *swear,* ▪ "I don't even *know* the man you are talking about!" ▪ ▪ Just then ▪ a *second* cockcrow was heard ▪ and Peter recalled the *prediction* Jesus had made to him, ▪ ▪ "Before the cock crows *twice* ▪ you will *disown* me *three* times." ▪ ▪ He *broke* down and began to *cry.* ▪ ▪ ▪

Official and businesslike.

Pause after "interrogated him" to study Jesus.

Calm and in control.

More intense now.

Register Pilate's surprise.

(13) As soon as it was *daybreak* the chief priests, ▪ with the elders and scribes ▪ (that is, the *whole Sanhedrin*), ▪ reached a *decision.* ▪ ▪ They *bound* Jesus, ▪ *led* him away, ▪ and handed him over to *Pilate.* ▪ ▪ Pilate *interrogated* him: ▪ ▪ *"Are* you the *king* of the Jews?" ▪ ▪ *"You* are the one who is saying it," ▪ Jesus replied. ▪ ▪ The chief *priests,* ▪ meanwhile, ▪ brought many *accusations* against him. ▪ ▪ Pilate interrogated him *again:* ▪ ▪ *"Surely* you have *some* answer? ▪ ▪ See how *many* accusations they are *leveling* against you." ▪ ▪ But greatly to Pilate's *surprise,* ▪ Jesus made *no* further response. ▪ ▪ ▪

Suggest hope of release.

(14) Now on the occasion of a *festival* ▪ he would *release* for them *one* prisoner— ▪ *any* man they asked for. ▪ ▪ There was a prisoner named *Barabbas* ▪ jailed along with the *rebels* who had committed *murder* in the uprising. ▪ ▪ When the crowd came up

asleep. He's disappointed and upset. Twice more he'll pray before recovering his fortitude, and he needs their support. Further, he knows each person must eventually face "the test," so he urges them to strengthen their weak natures against that time of trial. The feebleness of the excuse that "they could not keep their eyes open" explains why, surprised and ashamed, the disciples didn't know "what to say" to Jesus. Steeled by his third time at prayer, Jesus returns and responds philosophically to the sight of the disciples "still taking [their] ease." He knows he must face his "hour" alone, and now he is ready. He rouses and urges them to witness the handing over of "the Son of Man" into the "clutches of evil men." Having vanquished fear, Jesus looks up and announces calmly, "My betrayer is near."

(9) The Betrayal and Arrest. Judas is identified as one of the intimate "twelve" in the same sentence that describes his arrival with "swords and clubs." Draw attention to those contrasting realities. There is contrast, too, in the tone of his whispered instructions to the chief priests and his salutation to Jesus. That greeting must be preceded by a pause, suggesting the effort with which Judas forced the word out of his mouth before he embraces Jesus.

The pace quickens as the bystander responds with swordplay. Jesus ignores this violence as he ignored Judas' embrace. He speaks to the mob instead, not to dissuade but to indict them for the cowardice that made them seek him under the cover of darkness. Midsentence he stops to watch his friends desert him. The young man who sheds his linen cloth and flees naked, is symbolic of Christ's *total* abandonment: Early in his ministry the disciples left everything to follow Jesus, now they leave everything to forsake him.

(10) Jesus before the Sanhedrin. The tone of the next section is dominated by the mood of the priests who've waited for this moment to have it out with Jesus. The festering malice you hint at in the opening sentence will explain Peter's fearful following "at a distance" as he approaches the high priest's house. Suggest his tenuous presence among the temple guard as he warms himself at the fire. *"All"* the priests and the *"whole"* Sanhedrin gather to condemn Jesus; their frustration and anger grow as they try and fail to gather evidence to convict. The narrator enjoys telling how even the perjured testimony "did not agree." Remember that while the malice is real, it emanates less from evil hearts than from blinded hearts, hearts convinced that Jesus is a fraud.

(11) The Verdict. Assume the character of

the high priest who takes charge, thinking he can *provoke* a response from Jesus. More silence provokes another salvo from the priest. Suggest that Jesus *decided* to answer, for his own reasons, not because of the priest, and give the answer dignity and authority. At last, something! And just what the priests needed. Like vultures hungering for their prey, they fall upon Jesus with their verdict and "its sentence of *death*." Use the verbs to suggest the fury with which they degraded this sanctimonious blasphemer who has finally fallen into their grip.

(12) Peter's Denial. Peter's fear and guilt dominate this section; in the courtyard he, too, is being tried, ending up as his own judge and jury. The persistent servant girl is at first simply curious, but quickly becomes insistent as she, and the bystanders, see through Peter's feigned ignorance and resent his taking them for fools. Peter initially avoids the girl's question, then, sensing her eyes still upon him, he assaults her with the challenge, "What are you getting at?" Next he denies Jesus. Finally he curses. The cockcrow slaps Peter to his senses. Gripped by guilt he recalls Jesus' prophecy in wide-eyed horror. Imagine him telling the story in a homily to newly converted Christians, recalling for them his guilt-induced pain and tears.

(13) Jesus before Pilate. Your tone resembles that of a jury foreman announcing the decision reached by "the *whole* Sanhedrin." Pilate's entrance is abrupt. Perhaps he's been pried from his bed to deal with this troublemaker. First he questions Jesus because he has to, but by the second inquiry the priests' adamant accusations have piqued his interest.

(14) The Sentence of Death. As narrator allow yourself to hope that here the tide will change; that *Jesus* might be the "man they asked for." Even Pilate seems hopeful that the custom might provide the means for releasing Jesus. He's like a magician forcing a card, pretending not to know of the jealousy that will keep the priests from choosing Jesus. Sensing danger in Pilate's offer, the priests outwit him by inciting the crowd to request Barabbas. Pilate's efforts to save Jesus are feebler here than in other gospels. Though sincere in asking, "What crime has he committed?", he quickly yields to pressure and surrenders Jesus. Instead of clear lines drawn between supportive Romans and a hostile crowd, Mark presents a Jesus who receives support from no one.

(15) Mockery by the Soldiers. You feel Christ's pain and shame as he becomes the soldiers' cruel and unexpected entertainment. You can't help but cringe as you speak of the rough and mocking treatment he received. Words like "striking," "spitting,"

A leading question.

Like a whispered aside.

"Incited" sounds like it means.

Seeking a second chance.

Pilate seems pitiful and indecisive.

Angrily complying: "All right, have it your way."

to *press* their demand that he *honor* the custom, ▪ *Pilate* rejoined, ▪▪ "Do you want me to release the *king* of the *Jews* for you?" ▪▪ He was *aware,* of course, ▪ that it was out of *jealousy* that the chief priests had handed him over. ▪▪ Meanwhile, ▪ the chief priests *incited* the crowd to have him release *Barabbas* instead. ▪▪ Pilate *again* asked them, ▪▪ "What am I to *do* with the man you call the *king* of the *Jews?*" ▪▪ They *shouted* back, ▪▪ *"Crucify* him!" ▪▪ Pilate *protested,* ▪▪ *"Why?* ▪ What *crime* has he committed?" ▪▪ They only shouted the *louder,* ▪▪ *"Crucify* him!" ▪▪ So Pilate, ▪ who wished to *satisfy* the crowd, ▪ released *Barabbas* to them, ▪ and after he had had Jesus *scourged,* ▪ he *handed* him over ▪ to be *crucified.* ▪▪▪

Christ's pain is yours.

Your empathy is evident.

"Striking," "spitting," "mocking" sound like they mean.

(15) The *soldiers* now led Jesus away into the hall known as the *praetorium;* ▪▪ at the same time they assembled the *whole* cohort. ▪▪ They *dressed* him in *royal* purple, ▪ then wove a *crown* of *thorns* ▪ and *put* it on him, ▪ and began to *salute* him, ▪▪ "All *hail!* ▪ *King* of the *Jews!*" ▪▪ Continually *striking* Jesus on the head with a *reed* ▪ and *spitting* at him, ▪ they *genuflected* before him and pretended to pay him *homage.* ▪▪ When they had *finished* mocking him, ▪ they *stripped* him of the purple, ▪ dressed him in his *own* clothes, ▪ and led him out to *crucify* him. ▪▪▪

Slowly. Proud of his resolve and stamina.

Contrast "crucified him" with "rolling dice."

Speak with mocking voice of soldiers.

(16) A man named *Simon* of *Cyrene,* ▪ the father of *Alexander* and *Rufus,* ▪ was coming in from the fields ▪ and they pressed him into *service* ▪ to *carry* the *cross.* ▪▪ When they *brought* Jesus to the site of *Golgotha* ▪ (which means *"Skull Place"*), ▪ they tried to give him wine *drugged* with *myrrh,* ▪ but he would not *take* it. ▪▪ Then they *crucified* him ▪ and *divided* up his *garments* ▪ by rolling *dice* for them to see what each should take. ▪▪ It was about *nine* in the morning ▪ when they *crucified* him. ▪▪ The *inscription* proclaiming his *offense* read, ▪▪ "The *King* of the *Jews.*" ▪▪▪

Another insult.

"Ha, Ha": Make a single laughing sound. Different voices for "bystanders" and "priests." Both groups feel vindicated, thinking that Christ is an obvious fraud.

Narrator = sad and discouraged.

With him ▪ they crucified two *insurgents,* ▪ one at his *right* and one at his *left.* ▪▪ People going by kept *insulting* him, ▪ *tossing* their heads and saying, ▪▪ "Ha, ha! ▪▪ So *you* were going to *destroy* the temple and *rebuild* it in *three* days! ▪▪ *Save* yourself now by *coming down* from that cross!" ▪▪ The chief priests and the scribes *also* joined in and *jeered:* ▪▪ "He saved *others* but he *cannot* save *himself!* ▪▪ Let the *'Messiah,'* ▪ the *'king* of *Israel,'* ▪ *come down* from that cross ▪ *here* and *now* ▪ so that we can *see* it and *believe* in him!" ▪▪ The men who had been *crucified* with him ▪ *likewise* kept taunting him. ▪▪▪

Much emotion on the Hebrew, not on the translation.

In hushed tones.

Hushed and derisive.

(17) When *noon* came, ▪ *darkness* fell on the *whole* countryside ▪ and lasted until *midafternoon.* ▪▪ At that time Jesus *cried* in a *loud* voice, ▪▪ *"Eloi,* ▪ *Eloi,* ▪ *lama sabachthani?"* ▪▪ which means, ▪▪ "My *God,* ▪ my *God,* ▪ *why* have you *forsaken* me?" ▪▪▪ A few of the bystanders who *heard* it remarked, ▪▪ *"Listen!* ▪ He is calling on *Elijah!"* ▪▪▪ Someone *ran* off, ▪ and soaking a sponge in *sour wine,* ▪ stuck it on a *reed* to try to make him *drink.* ▪▪ The man said, ▪▪ "Now let's *see* whether Elijah *comes* to take him down." ▪▪▪

Climax of the passion. Slowly. Pause.

Suggest deeper significance of tearing. All people now have access to the presence of God.

Sincere and understated.

Speak like you know and love these women.

Then *Jesus,* ▪ uttering a *loud* cry, ▪ *breathed* his *last.* ▪▪▪ At that *moment* ▪ the *curtain* in the *sanctuary* was *torn* in two from *top* to *bottom.* ▪▪ The *centurion* who stood *guard* over him, ▪ on *seeing* the manner of his death, ▪ declared, ▪▪ *"Clearly* ▪ this man *was* the *Son* of *God!"* ▪▪ There were also *women* present looking on from a *distance.* ▪▪ Among them were *Mary Magdalene,* ▪ *Mary* the mother of James the *younger* ▪ and *Joses,* and *Salome.* ▪▪ These women had *followed* Jesus when he was in *Galilee* ▪ and attended to his *needs.* ▪▪ There were also many *others* who had come up with him to Jerusalem. ▪▪▪

With respect and love for Joseph.

Admiring his courage.

Only Mark mentions this.

Let your words caress him.

Your tone hints at hope and resurrection.

(18) As it grew *dark* ▪ (it was *Preparation* Day, ▪ that is, ▪ the eve of the *sabbath*), *Joseph* from *Arimathea* arrived— ▪ a *distinguished* member of the *Sanhedrin.* ▪▪ He was *another* who looked forward to the *reign* of *God.* ▪▪ He was *bold* enough to seek an *audience* with Pilate, ▪ and *urgently* requested the *body* of Jesus. ▪▪ Pilate was *surprised* that Jesus should have *died* so *soon.* ▪▪ He *summoned* the centurion ▪ and *inquired* whether Jesus was *already* dead. ▪▪ Learning from him that he *was* dead, ▪ Pilate *released* the corpse to *Joseph.* ▪▪ Then, ▪ having bought a *linen shroud,* ▪ Joseph took him *down,* ▪ *wrapped* him in the linen, ▪ and *laid* him in a *tomb* which had been cut out of *rock.* ▪▪ Finally ▪ he rolled a *stone* across the *entrance* of the tomb. ▪▪ Meanwhile, ▪ *Mary Magdalene* and *Mary* the mother of *Joses* ▪ *observed* where he had been laid. ▪▪▪

[Shorter: Mark 15:1–39]

"mocking" and "stripped" lend onomatopoeic sound to the soldiers' violent scorn.

(16) The Way of the Cross. Speak of Simon as of someone known and respected (tradition says he became a bishop); his sons, at least, are apparently known to the community Mark addresses. In that light, Simon's "pressed" service seems more like a privilege. Refusing anything to dull his pain, Jesus is nailed to the cross. Mark lumps into one sentence Jesus' crucifixion and the callous behavior of the soldiers who roll dice at the foot of his cross. Mark's brevity and sparse details amplify the sadness of the scene and Jesus' total abandonment.

Three groups of detractors taunt Jesus: the bystanders, the priests and the insurgents. Their taunts are hurled at Jesus as if by children suddenly emboldened by his helplessness. There's more than insult in their jibes; there's a sense of vindication, and Christ's scandalous circumstance only serves to affirm that *this* could not possibly be the great Messiah.

(17) The Death of Jesus. Narrate the death from the perspective of one of the women disciples who looked on "from a distance." "Darkness" has come bringing gloom, hushed tones, the need to look and listen carefully and a jumpiness not known in daylight. Don't soften Jesus' cry of abandonment. The Hebrew line rings with pathos and intensity, but the English translation is whispered, as if by someone in the crowd repeating the outcry to those nearby. The onlookers break the mood with hushed jeers. Even a presumed act of kindness ("soaking a sponge in sour wine") is just an excuse for another taunt ("Now let's see whether Elijah comes").

Hear the "loud cry" echoing in your being before you announce Jesus' death. The pace quickens as you narrate events that vindicate the claims Jesus made about himself: The temple curtain is mysteriously and symbolically torn, a pagan soldier proclaims his faith in Jesus and faithful disciples are watching from a distance. Pain over Jesus' death yields to hope as you list the pious women.

(18) The Burial. With affection, perhaps wishing you could have done it yourself, you narrate Joseph's courageous efforts to recover and bury Jesus' body. Pilate is surprised, or maybe disappointed, that Jesus is so soon dead; his effort to verify this will only make more striking the reversal of the third day. The final moments with a deceased loved one are the hardest. All in us that clings to life resists the closing of the casket or the rolling of the stone. Read with care, caressing Jesus with your words as you speak of "linen," "tomb" and "entrance."

MARCH 28, 1991

HOLY THURSDAY: EVENING MASS OF THE LORD'S SUPPER

READING I The Easter Triduum, from Holy Thursday evening until Easter Sunday, constitutes a single act of worship. As the people of God we begin that prayer tonight with this reading—a reading that puts us in touch with our roots as a community of faith. Though the passage consists of a lot of details, seemingly mundane, about how, where and when one is to prepare and eat a certain meal, a lofty tone should characterize your proclamation. This night is like no other night and this meal is like no other meal. Your voice needs to tell us that. Imagine yourself chosen to proclaim the history of the royal line just prior to the coronation of a new monarch. No matter what details were included in that narrative, your dignified tone would say: This is significant, listen well!

Remembering that it is God who is giving these instructions, begin with a strong, authoritative voice that can also be tender and compassionate. The first two sentences establish the authority. God is in control and speaks slowly and deliberately. "If a family . . ." introduces the compassion. God cares about family budgets and finances. This observance is not to place undue strain on any family. Take care to avoid a dull, shopping-list delivery. Use the short sentences to convey God's attention to detail, varying your energy and pace.

Don't shy away from the graphic description. "Slaughtered" is a powerful word that sounds like it means. "Blood" applied to "doorposts" and "lintel," "roasted flesh," "unleavened" and "bitter" all are graphic details that add to the seriousness of the events for which God prepares the people.

"Loins girt," "sandals on the feet" and "staff in hand" lead to one of the key announcements of the passage: "You shall eat *like those who are in flight.*" Pause, then make the second key announcement: "It is the Passover . . ." God's tone becomes terrifyingly serious in the description of the "striking down [of] every firstborn." The people should sense they are in the hands of a powerful God—but a God in whose hands they, at least, are safe. "Seeing the blood, I will pass over you . . . no destructive blow will come upon you" requires strong, reassuring emphasis. The final sentence is a summary that tells us *why* we are here throughout the next three days: to "feast," to "celebrate" this "perpetual institution."

LECTIONARY #40

READING I Exodus 12:1–8, 11–14

A reading from the book of *Exodus* ▪ ▪ ▪

Your lofty tone will help put us in touch with our tradition: Easter is our New Year.

Note the time references: "this month," "first month," "tenth of this month."

God's concern for human needs.

The Lord said to *Moses* and *Aaron* in the land of *Egypt,* ▪ ▪ "*This* month shall stand at the *head* of your calendar; ▪ ▪ you shall *reckon* it the *first* month of the year. ▪ ▪ Tell the *whole* community of Israel: ▪ ▪ On the *tenth* of this month ▪ every one of your families must *procure* for itself a *lamb,* ▪ one apiece for *each* household. ▪ ▪ If a family is too *small* for a whole lamb, ▪ it shall *join* the nearest household in procuring one ▪ and shall *share* in the lamb in *proportion* to the number of persons who *partake* of it. ▪ ▪ The lamb must be a *year-old male* and *without blemish.* ▪ ▪ You may *take* it from either the *sheep* or the *goats.* ▪ ▪ You shall *keep* it until the *fourteenth* day of this month, ▪ and then, ▪ with the whole *assembly* of Israel present, ▪ it shall be *slaughtered* during the evening *twilight.* ▪ ▪ They shall take some of its *blood* ▪ and apply it to the two *doorposts* and the *lintel* of *every* house in which they partake of the lamb. ▪ ▪ That *same* night ▪ they shall *eat* its roasted flesh with *unleavened* bread ▪ and *bitter* herbs. ▪ ▪ ▪

Your tone says this is important, not a dull set of directions.

"Slaughtered" sounds like it means. Use the graphic imagery.

"This is *how* you are to eat it: ▪ ▪ with your loins *girt,* ▪ *sandals* on your feet ▪ and your *staff* in hand, ▪ you shall eat like those who are in *flight.* ▪ ▪ It is the *Passover* of the Lord. ▪ ▪ For on this *same* night ▪ I will go through *Egypt,* ▪ *striking* down every *first-born* of the land, ▪ both *man* and *beast,* ▪ and executing *judgment* on all the *gods* of Egypt— ▪ *I,* ▪ the *Lord!* ▪ ▪ But the *blood* will *mark* the houses where *you* are. ▪ ▪ *Seeing* the blood, ▪ I will *pass* over you; ▪ ▪ thus, ▪ when I *strike* the land of Egypt, ▪ *no* destructive blow will come upon *you.* ▪ ▪ ▪

"You shall eat . . .": a key line. Pause. Then another key line.

Don't minimize the severity of God's judgment. "Human" is more inclusive.

Note: "I" used four times in two sentences.

"This day shall be a *memorial feast* for you, ▪ which *all* your generations shall *celebrate* with *pilgrimage* to the Lord, ▪ as a *perpetual* institution." ▪ ▪ ▪

Your listeners are one of those "generations." Speak to them.

READING II 1 Corinthians 11:23–26

A reading from the first letter of *Paul* ▪ to the Corinthians ▪▪▪

Speak with gratitude.

"He was betrayed": Don't gloss over that.

Speak as Jesus—intimately, among friends.

"Remembrance" is the key concept. Simply; with quiet joy.

I received from the *Lord* what I handed on to *you,* ▪▪ namely, ▪ that the Lord Jesus ▪ on the night in which he was *betrayed* ▪▪ took *bread,* ▪ and after he had given *thanks,* ▪ *broke* it and said, ▪▪ "This is my *body,* ▪ which is for *you.* ▪▪ Do this in *remembrance* of me." ▪▪ In the same way, ▪ after the supper, ▪ he took the *cup,* ▪ saying, ▪▪ "This cup is the *new covenant* in my *blood.* ▪▪ *Do* this, ▪ whenever you drink it, ▪ in remembrance of *me.*" ▪▪ *Every* time, then, ▪ you *eat* this bread ▪ and *drink* this cup, ▪▪ you proclaim the *death* of the Lord ▪ until he *comes!* ▪▪▪

GOSPEL John 13:1–15

A reading from the holy *gospel* according to *John* ▪▪▪

Emphasis on Jesus' awareness and the lateness of the "hour."

Stress the love.

Contrast "Judas" who handed over Jesus with "the Father" who handed everything over to Jesus.

Your tone suggests how unexpected this was.

"Come on, Lord, you don't have to do that for me."

Insistent. (Peter obviously missed the point.)

Teaching, not reproaching, Peter.

Almost too much enthusiasm.

Communicate Jesus' love for Peter.

Before the feast of *Passover,* ▪ Jesus *realized* that the hour had *come* for him to *pass* from *this* world to the *Father.* ▪▪ He had *loved* his *own* in this world, ▪ and would *show* his love for them to the *end.* ▪▪ The devil had *already* induced *Judas,* ▪ son of Simon Iscariot, ▪ to *hand* Jesus over; ▪▪ and so, ▪ during the *supper,* ▪ Jesus— ▪ fully *aware* that he had *come* from God ▪ and was *going* to God, the *Father* who had handed *everything* over to him— ▪ *rose* from the meal and *took* off his cloak. ▪▪ He picked up a *towel* and *tied* it around himself. ▪▪ Then he poured *water* into a basin ▪ and began to *wash* his disciples' *feet* ▪ and *dry* them with the towel he had around him. ▪▪ Thus he came to *Simon Peter,* ▪ who *said* to him, ▪▪ "Lord, ▪ are *you* going to wash my *feet?*" ▪▪ Jesus answered, ▪▪ "You may not realize *now* what I am doing, ▪ but *later* you will *understand.*" ▪▪ Peter replied, ▪▪ "You shall *never* wash my feet!" ▪▪ "If I do *not* wash you," ▪ Jesus answered, ▪▪ "you will have *no share* in my *heritage.*" ▪▪ "Lord," ▪ Simon Peter said to him, ▪▪ "then not *only* my feet, ▪ but my *hands* and *head* as well." ▪▪▪ Jesus *told* him, ▪▪ "The man who has *bathed* has no *need* to wash [*except* for his feet]; ▪▪ he is *entirely* cleansed, ▪ just as *you* are; ▪▪ though not *all.*" ▪▪ (The reason he said, ▪ "Not *all* are washed clean," ▪ was that he *knew* his *betrayer.*) ▪▪▪

READING II You are privileged to remember for us a pivotal moment in our story as God's people. There is much emotion here: gratitude ("I received from the Lord what I handed on . . ."), regret ("on the night in which he was betrayed . . ."), selfless giving ("This is my body, which is for you"), the pain of parting ("Do this in remembrance of me"), pride-filled and hope-filled gratitude ("Every time . . . you proclaim the death . . . until he comes!").

The first lines are spoken in Paul's voice, emphasizing the origin of the mystery we celebrate this night. The words of institution ("This is my body. . . . This cup. . . .") can be spoken in the voice of Jesus—Jesus, who is sharing a final, intimate moment with his closest friends; Jesus, who knows (though his friends do not) how and how soon his body and blood will be offered up; Jesus, who wants those intimate words also spoken to each of his friends gathered in your church tonight. These are all too familiar words that should be spoken and heard as if for the first time tonight. You can achieve that by speaking slowly and thinking of how a loved one, lying on a deathbed, would speak final words to family and friends.

Paul returns in the last sentence. He must speak quietly, tenderly and with deep conviction. Simplicity is the key. Don't stress every word trying to convince your listeners. Your own belief in the truth spoken here, stated with a simple and quiet joy, will be powerfully persuasive.

GOSPEL What an amazing event, made even more amazing by the fact that only John records it! John's unique perspective is highlighted here as he talks of aprons, towels and dirty feet. John's Jesus wants to be remembered for rolling up his sleeves.

Jesus' awareness that his "hour" has come is very important to this passage. John says "Jesus realized" and was "fully aware" and contrasts that with Peter and the apostles who did "not realize" what Jesus was doing and would "understand" only "later." Knowing his time is short, Jesus is driven by an urgency to make sure that the followers who survive him will remember his style as well as his words. Founders of religious communities have doubtless wished the same thing. Jesus guarantees his style won't be forgotten—by pouring water into a basin.

Jesus' desire to model tender and loving humility should infect your reading. Stress the phrases: "loved his own . . . would show his love. . . ." Let your voice suggest that what Jesus freely did was something that would not have been required of even the lowliest slave. Peter thinks he is outdoing his friends by being unwilling to let Jesus so demean himself. But Jesus insists that this kind of humility typifies his whole life and ministry and that if Peter is to have a share in that ministry he must be comfortable with this symbol. In characteristic overstatement, Peter invites a fuller cleansing. This is a touching, human exchange. Jesus tolerates Peter's naiveté and even admires his zeal: "The man . . . is entirely cleansed, just as *you* are. . . ."

Direct Jesus' question to your own listeners. Then, with as much care and respect as he had for his followers, explain Jesus' meaning to your assembly, calling them (and yourself) to remembrance of the Lord not by remembering what he did but by *doing* what he did.

Ask your listeners, too.

Jesus speaks with affection for his friends.

After he had washed their feet, ▪ he *put* his cloak back on and *reclined* at table once more. ▪▪ He *said* to them: ▪▪

"Do you *understand* what I just *did* for you? ▪▪
You address me as *'Teacher'* and *'Lord,'* ▪
and *fittingly* enough, ▪
for that is what I *am.* ▪▪
But if *I* washed your feet— ▪
I who *am* Teacher and Lord— ▪
then *you* must wash each *other's* feet. ▪▪
What I just did was to give you an *example:* ▪▪
as *I* have done, ▪ so *you* must do." ▪▪▪

FROM THE KEY

Units of thought. Many sentences contain more than one idea. Running too many words together blurs meaning and fails to distinguish ideas. Punctuation—meant for the eye, not the ear—does not always indicate clearly which words to group together or where to pause. You must identify the units of thought and use your voice to distinguish one from another. The listener is totally dependent on you for this organization of ideas.

The pause marks (▪ , ▪▪ , ▪▪▪) in the scripture texts serve two purposes: to divide the text into units that communicate a single image or thought and to indicate the lengths of pauses between these units.

Pace. What's too fast and what's too slow? That depends on what you're reading, where and for whom. The larger the church, the larger the assembly and the more complex the text, the slower you must read. If you're going to make a mistake, better to be too slow than too fast. Your listeners have not spent time with this reading as you have. For them it's new. They need time to absorb it. They need time to catch your words and comprehend what you've said.

You'll read more slowly if you read ideas rather than words, if you share images rather than sentences. "Think" the ideas (as if for the first time) and "see" the images in your own mind before sharing them with the assembly. In real conversation you don't recite lists of ideas or arguments supporting a certain position. Your mind "thinks them up" one at a time. And it takes time for that to happen. Give yourself that time.

Dialogue, however, often moves at a faster pace than the rest of the passage—this helps the assembly hear the give-and-take going on between the speakers.

MARCH 29, 1991

GOOD FRIDAY

LECTIONARY #41

READING I Isaiah 52:13—53:12

A reading from the book of the prophet ▪ *Isaiah* ▪▪▪

Voice of God; proud and strong.

See, ▪ my servant shall *prosper,* ▪
he shall be *raised high* and *greatly* exalted. ▪▪

"Man" can be "a human being."

Even as many were *amazed* at him— ▪
so *marred* was his look beyond that of man, ▪
and his *appearance* beyond that of *mortals*— ▪▪

The sense of the verse is: In the way that many were amazed at him (because he was so disfigured that he didn't look human), in the same way many will be astonished by him.

So shall he *startle* many *nations,* ▪
because of *him* ▪ *kings* shall stand *speechless;* ▪▪
For those who have not been *told* ▪ shall *see,* ▪▪
those who have not *heard* ▪ shall *ponder* it. ▪▪

New voice (of the gentile nations or a grieving disciple).

Who would *believe* what we have heard? ▪▪
To *whom* has the arm of the Lord
been *revealed?* ▪▪
He grew up like a *sapling* before him, ▪
like a *shoot* from the *parched* earth; ▪▪
There was in him no *stately bearing* to make us
look at him, ▪
nor *appearance* that would *attract* us to him. ▪▪

Emphasis on the sound of lament. "Men" can be "people." "Man" can be "a person."

He was *spurned* and *avoided* by men, ▪
a man of *suffering,* ▪ accustomed to *infirmity,* ▪
One of those from whom men *hide* their faces, ▪
spurned, ▪ and *we* held him ▪ in *no esteem.* ▪▪▪

Stress is on his bearing our *guilt.*

Yet it was *our* infirmities that he bore, ▪
our *sufferings* that he *endured,* ▪
While we thought of him as *stricken,* ▪
as one *smitten* by God and *afflicted.* ▪▪

The words "smitten," "pierced," "crushed" sound like they mean.

But he was *pierced* for our offenses, ▪
crushed for our *sins;* ▪▪
Upon him was the *chastisement* that
makes us whole, ▪
by his *stripes* we were *healed.* ▪▪

"Stripes": marks on the back left by a whipping.

We had all gone *astray* like *sheep,* ▪
each following his *own* way; ▪▪

"His" could be "his or her."

But the Lord *laid* upon *him*
the *guilt* of us all. ▪▪

Quieter.

Though he was *harshly* treated, ▪ he *submitted* ▪
and opened *not* his mouth; ▪▪

Image of Jesus as Lamb of God.

Like a *lamb* led to the *slaughter* ▪
or a *sheep* before the *shearers,* ▪

READING I This Song of the Suffering Servant is indeed a song—a dirge, in fact. It is a long, sobbing and repetitive look at the bruised and bleeding face of God's sinless servant. Though Isaiah was describing the purpose of God's people, Israel, and their role in God's plan of salvation, the inclusion of this sublime text in our Good Friday liturgy focuses us on Jesus as the perfect fulfillment of this prophecy.

So it is of Jesus that we sing this day and, though a dirge usually speaks of past glory and future sorrow, this song reverses that pattern and proclaims a glory born of sorrow. It is God's voice that begins the song, proudly offering the Servant as one to be admired and praised. Soon, however ("Who would believe . . . ?"), the voice shifts to that of the gentile nations who recognize the Servant (Israel) as God's instrument and confess their guilt for causing his enormous suffering.

To prepare to proclaim this extraordinarily powerful passage, think of a tragedy you have witnessed—an auto accident, the burning of a home. Recall the reactions of those most directly affected by the tragedy: their alternating inability to look at the scene *and* to turn away from it; their tendency to look back again and again while uttering the same words of grief and disbelief. Such is your tone here. And instead of the gentile nations looking upon the "pierced" and "crushed" Servant, imagine yourself as Mary, the mother of Jesus, looking at the crucified Lord. The aptness of the imagery is striking. As with all poetry, the sound of the passage becomes an important part of the meaning it communicates, so use the words and mournful sound to achieve a powerful proclamation.

The second paragraph begins with disbelief; with the terrible regret of looking back and realizing a great opportunity was missed: "He grew up in our midst. There was nothing extraordinary about him. So we all shunned him and paid him no attention."

Next comes the painful realization that his suffering was for our sake. We stupidly thought he was "smitten by God" for his own failings, "But he was pierced for our offenses . . . our sins." We went astray and he paid the price. Use the strong "sound-like-they-mean" words like "spurned . . . smitten . . . pierced . . . crushed" to add to the weight of injustice thrown at God's servant.

The injustice is further enunciated in the next paragraph. Unlike ourselves, when we experience trouble, this man of sorrow "was silent and opened not his mouth." Speak this section with great intensity, feeling his pain, aware of his innocence, angry yet grateful that this "lamb" went willingly "to the slaughter." Rage and grieve at the final humiliation of being buried "with evildoers . . . though he had done no wrong." There's an acceptance that somehow all this was within the will of God as you say "But the Lord was pleased . . ."

God's voice returns in the final paragraphs with another oracle of future glory for the humble servant and of hope for the "many" for whom his voluntary suffering has won "pardon." Again, fill God's voice with pride, with an urgency to convince us that this suffering has not been wasted but was instead expiatory—"an offering for sin" that justifies and heals. End the reading with the tone of a eulogist speaking at the funeral of some great leader who has been assassinated. You know that the work of the one you mourn will continue to make a difference, so your voice is strong. This Jesus who suffered is now the Lord who reconciles.

READING II There's a marvelous harmony between these words of Hebrews and those we just heard from Isaiah. The author reminds us that in Christ we have a brother with whom we all have something in common: a humanity that experiences suffering. We can "confidently approach" this "high priest" because he became one with all who suffer and are tempted—being set apart only by his innocence and total commitment to God's will. In Isaiah we heard that "Through his suffering my servant will justify many." Here we are told that Jesus has been made a "great high priest," our perfect representative before God.

Your goal is twofold: to convince and to celebrate. These are words spoken to troubled, despairing hearts that need encouragement. Think of someone who's lost a job or a loved one, or someone who's just gone through a divorce. Convince them that Jesus understands their pain, experienced pain himself and can be expected to give "mercy and favor and . . . help in time of need."

The celebration is muted but it's hidden in all your words. The second paragraph presents Jesus at Gethsemani, and perhaps elsewhere—weeping over Lazarus, mourning Judas' betrayal—pleading to be spared the fate that awaited him. "And he was heard." That's the celebration. Though he was "Son," he obeyed, and through his suffering makes "eternal salvation" available to all. That our own suffering can also bring perfection is a great mystery and a hope that you are called to share convincingly.

he was *silent* ▪▪ and opened *not* his *mouth.* ▪▪

More words that sound like they mean: "oppressed," "condemned."

Oppressed and *condemned,* ▪ he was
taken away, ▪▪
and who would have thought any *more*
of his *destiny?* ▪▪
When he was *cut* off from the land of the living, ▪
and *smitten* for the *sin* of his people, ▪

With anger and regret at this indignity.

A *grave* was assigned him among the *wicked* ▪
and a *burial* place with *evildoers,* ▪▪
Though he had done *no wrong* ▪
nor *spoken* any *falsehood.* ▪▪

Tone of acceptance.

[But the Lord was *pleased*
to *crush* him in *infirmity.*] ▪▪▪

God's voice. Again proud and proclaiming.

If he *gives* his *life* as an *offering* for sin, ▪
he shall *see* his descendants in a *long* life, ▪
and the *will* of the *Lord* shall be *accomplished*
through him. ▪▪▪

A quieter voice: persuasive and intense.

Because of his *affliction* ▪
he shall see the *light* in *fullness* of days; ▪▪
Through his suffering, ▪ my servant shall
justify many, ▪
and their *guilt* he shall *bear.* ▪▪▪

Climax! Proclaim!

Therefore I will *give* him his *portion*
among the *great,* ▪
and he shall *divide* the *spoils* with the *mighty,* ▪

A hope-filled summary. End with upward inflection. Ritardando: "for their offenses."

Because he *surrendered* himself to *death* ▪
and was *counted* among the *wicked;* ▪▪
And he shall *take* away the *sins* of *many,* ▪
and win *pardon* for their offenses. ▪▪▪

READING II Hebrews 4:14–16; 5:7–9

A reading from the letter to the *Hebrews* ▪▪▪

With great confidence; rejoicing.

We have a *great* high priest who has *passed* through the *heavens,* ▪ *Jesus,* ▪ the *Son of God;* ▪▪ let us *hold fast* to our profession of faith. ▪▪ For we do *not* have a high priest who is *unable* to *sympathize* with our *weakness,* ▪ but one who was *tempted* in every way that *we* are, ▪ yet *never sinned.* ▪▪ So let us *confidently* approach the *throne* of *grace* ▪ to receive *mercy* and *favor* ▪ and to find *help* in time of *need.* ▪▪▪

He can sympathize. He knows our pain.

Persuade. Again, confidence.

Stress Christ's own pain. This is why he understands ours.

In the days when he was in the *flesh,* ▪ Christ offered *prayers* and *supplications* with loud *cries* and *tears* to God, ▪ who was able to *save* him from death, ▪ and he was *heard* because of his *reverence.* ▪▪ *Son* though he *was,* ▪ he learned *obedience* from what he suffered; ▪▪ and when *perfected,* ▪ he became the *source* of eternal salvation for *all* who *obey* him. ▪▪▪

Ritardando: "because . . . reverence." Note Jesus "learned" obedience.

Jesus modeled obedience, now we follow him! Ritardando: "for . . . him."

The *Passion* of our *Lord Jesus Christ* according to *John* ▪ ▪ ▪

(1) *Jesus* went out with his *disciples* across the Kidron *valley.* ▪ ▪ There was a *garden* there, ▪ and he and his disciples *entered* it. ▪ ▪ The place was familiar to *Judas* as well ▪ (the *one* who was to *hand* him over) ▪ because Jesus had often *met* there with his *disciples.* ▪ ▪ Judas took the *cohort* as well as *police* ▪ supplied by the chief *priests* and the *Pharisees,* ▪ and came there with *lanterns,* ▪ *torches* ▪ and *weapons.* ▪ ▪ Jesus, ▪ *aware* of all that would *happen* to him, ▪ stepped *forward* and *said* to them, ▪ ▪ *"Who* is it you want?" ▪ ▪ *"Jesus* the *Nazorean,"* ▪ they replied. ▪ ▪ "I am *he,"* ▪ he answered. ▪ ▪ (Now *Judas,* ▪ the one who was to hand him over, ▪ was *right there* with them.) ▪ ▪ As Jesus said to them, ▪ "I am *he,"* ▪ they *retreated* slightly and *fell* to the ground. ▪ ▪ Jesus put the question to them *again,* ▪ ▪ "Who is it you *want?"* ▪ ▪ *"Jesus* the *Nazorean,"* ▪ they repeated. ▪ ▪ "I have *told* you, ▪ *I* am *he,"* ▪ Jesus said. ▪ ▪ "If I am the one you *want,* ▪ let *these* men *go."* ▪ ▪ (This was to *fulfill* what he had *said,* ▪ ▪ "I have not lost *one* of those you *gave* me.") ▪ ▪

Then ▪ Simon *Peter,* ▪ who had a *sword,* ▪ *drew* it and *struck* the slave of the high priest, ▪ *severing* his right *ear.* ▪ ▪ (The slave's name was *Malchus.*) ▪ ▪ At *that* Jesus said to Peter, ▪ ▪ *"Put* your sword back in its *sheath.* ▪ ▪ Am I not to *drink* the cup the Father has *given* me?" ▪ ▪ ▪

(2) Then the *soldiers* of the cohort, ▪ their *tribune,* ▪ and the Jewish police ▪ *arrested* Jesus and *bound* him. ▪ ▪ They led him first to *Annas,* ▪ the father-in-law of *Caiaphas* who was *high priest* that year. ▪ ▪ (It was *Caiaphas* who had proposed to the Jews the *advantage* of having *one* man *die* for the people.) ▪ ▪ ▪

Simon Peter, ▪ in company with *another* disciple, ▪ kept *following* Jesus *closely.* ▪ ▪ This disciple, ▪ who was *known* to the high priest, ▪ *stayed* with Jesus as far as the high priest's *courtyard,* ▪ while *Peter* was left standing at the *gate.* ▪ ▪ The disciple *known* to the high priest *came* out and *spoke* to the *woman* at the gate, ▪ and then *brought* Peter in. ▪ ▪ This *servant girl* who kept the gate ▪ *said* to Peter, ▪ ▪ "Aren't *you* one of this man's *followers?"* ▪ ▪ *"Not I,"* ▪ he replied. ▪ ▪ ▪

Now the night was *cold,* ▪ and the *servants* and the *guards* who were *standing* around ▪ had made a

Garden is familiar, peaceful place.

Shadow of Judas changes garden mood.

"Lanterns . . .": symbolic of hour of darkness.

Jesus speaks with authority.

Crowd not self-assured.

Jesus' concern for his friends. "Men" can be "people."

Violence. "Struck" and "sever" sound like they mean.

Jesus confronts Peter.

Romans as well as Jews.

An aside. Spoken quietly.

Suggest Peter's frustration at being left out.

Quick, but softly. Not wanting to be overheard.

PASSION John's Passion is a story of Christ's irrevocable movement toward glory. Everything in the narrative is subordinated to this. Episodes mentioned by the synoptics that detract from the image of a Christ fully in control of his destiny are excised. The garden agony, the help of Simon, the mourning women, the ridicule hurled at the crucified Jesus: All are missing from this account so that the appearance of a Jesus who is in charge might not be compromised.

Roman complicity with the Jewish authorities is introduced here earlier than in the synoptic versions, yet John's persistent use of the term "the Jews" suggests a hostility toward the Jewish people that holds them responsible for Christ's death—a responsibility inherited by each successive generation. Of course, that is not the case. Papal and episcopal statements have made it clear that when these texts are used, listeners should be made aware that the church does not hold the Jewish people guilty. To counter potential misinterpretations you might substitute "the Jewish authorities" or "the religious leaders" wherever "the Jews" occurs, and that is obviously the author's intention, since the phrase "the Jews" is consistently used to describe those in power.

(1) The peaceful mood of the familiar garden is immediately shattered by the shadow of Judas who arrives with a noisy crowd of soldiers bearing lanterns, torches and weapons. A double irony: Those who bring on the "hour of darkness" come bearing light, and so large a cohort comes against the unarmed Jesus. Remember John's Jesus has not just emerged from the garden agony. He speaks with authority, aware of what will unfold. And he takes the initiative, challenging them with his question. Their response is less self-assured. They are bowled over, in fact, by Jesus' "I am he." John paints a mob made brave only by their numbers. Jesus is still playing shepherd. "Let these men go" reveals his willingness to accept the crowd's designs against him but not against his friends. Peter's response is violent. "Struck" and "sever" (words that sound like they mean) help suggest his rage. Jesus matches Peter's energy. "Put your sword back" echoes "Get behind me, Satan." Stress again Jesus' *choice* to "drink the cup."

(2) Note it's the Roman soldiers and their tribune, as well as the Jewish guards who arrest Jesus. Don't gloss over this reference to Roman complicity. Speak "the advantage . . . for the people" in Caiaphas' voice. Peter's first denial can be underplayed. He does not carry with him a memory of his grandiose Last Supper protestations of loyalty. That will come later. Now your narration

suggests his frustration at being unable to get close to the action. When the "other disciple" gets him through the gate he makes an over-the-shoulder response to the girl's question (probably trying to keep "the disciple" from hearing him). Jesus' composure before the high priest is remarkable. He is not intimidated. His confidence is taken for disrespect, earning him a slap. The anger and violence of the guard should be in your tone when you *narrate* as well as when you speak his line. Jesus is recovering from the "sharp blow" as he begins his answer. His second clause then is spoken more strongly than the first. Surely Peter cringed at the sight of Jesus being slapped. Then suddenly *he* is slapped with a question, "Are you not a disciple . . . ?" His answer is quick. The persistent "relative of the man whose ear Peter had severed" asks again. Speak the narration "Peter denied it again" with the intensity that would have filled Peter's angry response. You report the crowing of the cock with the regret that must have flooded Peter's heart.

The scene before Pilate is a drama cast between good and evil. John gives us a picture of Jewish authorities among whom were both men of sincerity (Nicodemus and Joseph of Arimathea) and men who became chief instigators of the death of Jesus. In proclaiming this Passion we are left with the characters John has created, and it cannot be denied that, in their tug-of-war, Pilate comes off looking better than the religious authorities. That pulling back and forth gives life and excitement to this part of the narrative. John spends more time with this scene than the synoptics, and it is here that we might hope against hope that the story will end differently.

(3) "At daybreak" and "demanded" are both clues suggesting that Pilate was annoyed at being dragged from his bed to hear a "religious" case. Their exchange indicates no love lost between Pilate and the Jewish leaders. Pilate questions Jesus and is annoyed at being questioned back by this Jew who has disturbed his sleep. Slowly Pilate seems to be drawn over to Jesus, but he does not take him seriously yet: "So . . . , you *are* a king?" "Truth! What does that mean?"

The exchange about Barabbas could be played as Pilate's effort to resolve the problem quickly. It doesn't work. His effort intensifies. Your few words of narration must suggest the awful violence of the scourging and the crowning with thorns.

Suggest that he approached cautiously . . . fearfully.

charcoal *fire* to warm themselves by. ▪▪ Peter *joined* them and stood there ▪ *warming* himself. ▪▪

The high priest *questioned* Jesus, ▪ *first* about his *disciples,* ▪ then about his *teaching.* ▪▪ Jesus *answered* by saying: ▪▪

Jesus does not hold back.

"I have spoken *publicly* to any who
would *listen.* ▪▪
I always taught in a *synagogue*
or in the *temple* area
where all the Jews *come together.* ▪▪
There was nothing *secret* about
anything I said. ▪▪

Tone of frustration, not disrespect.

"Why do you question *me?* ▪▪ Question those who *heard* me when I spoke. ▪▪ It should be *obvious* they will *know* what I said." ▪▪ At this *reply,* ▪ one of the guards who was standing nearby gave Jesus a *sharp blow* on the *face.* ▪▪ "Is *that* any way to answer the *high priest?*" he said. ▪▪ Jesus replied, ▪▪ "If I said anything *wrong* produce the *evidence,* ▪ but if I spoke the *truth* ▪ why *hit* me?" ▪▪ *Annas* next sent him, ▪ *bound,* ▪ to the high priest *Caiaphas.* ▪▪▪

Deliver line like a slap: fast and hard.

All through this, ▪ Simon *Peter* had been *standing* there warming himself. ▪▪ They *said* to him, ▪ "Are you not a *disciple* of his?" ▪▪ *He denied:* ▪ "I am *not!*" ▪▪ "But did I not *see* you with him in the *garden?*" ▪ *insisted* one of the high priest's slaves— ▪ as it happened, ▪ a *relative* of the man whose *ear* Peter had *severed.* ▪▪ Peter *denied* it *again.* ▪▪ At that *moment* ▪ a *cock* began to *crow.* ▪▪

Her motivation may be revenge. Peter's voice: angry.

"Peter . . . again." Speak with his anger.

(3) At *daybreak* they brought Jesus from *Caiaphas* to the *praetorium.* ▪▪ They did not *enter* the praetorium *themselves,* ▪ for they had to avoid *ritual impurity* ▪ if they were to eat the *Passover supper.* ▪▪ *Pilate* came out to them. ▪▪ "What *accusation* do you *bring* against this man?" ▪ he demanded. ▪▪ "If he were not a *criminal,*" ▪ they retorted, ▪ "we would certainly *not* have *handed* him over to you." ▪▪ At *this* Pilate said, ▪▪ "Why do you not *take* him and pass *judgment* on him according to *your* law?" ▪▪ *"We* may not put anyone to *death,"* ▪ the Jews answered. ▪▪ (This was to *fulfill* what Jesus had said, ▪ indicating the *sort* of death he would die.) ▪▪▪

It's daybreak. Pilate is annoyed. They woke him up.

Demanding.

Each annoyed with the other.

Pilate went back into the *praetorium* and *summoned* Jesus. ▪▪ "Are you the *King* of the *Jews?*" ▪ he asked him. ▪▪ Jesus *answered,* ▪▪ "Are you saying this on your *own,* ▪ or have *others* been *telling* you about me?" ▪▪ *"I* am no *Jew!"* ▪ Pilate retorted. ▪▪ "It is your *own people* and the *chief priests* who have handed you over to me. ▪▪ What have you *done?*" ▪▪ Jesus answered: ▪

Irritated by Jesus' impudence.

Peaceful and sincere.

"My *kingdom* does not *belong* to *this* world. ▪▪
If my kingdom *were* of this world, ▪
my subjects would be *fighting*
to *save* me from being handed over to the Jews. ▪▪
As it is, ▪ *my* kingdom is not *here.*" ▪▪▪

At this Pilate *said* to him, ▪▪ *"So,* then, ▪ you *are* a king?" ▪▪ Jesus replied: ▪

"It is *you* who say I am a king. ▪▪
The reason I was *born,* ▪
the reason why I *came* into the world, ▪
is to *testify* to the *truth.* ▪▪
Anyone *committed* to the truth *hears*
my voice." ▪▪▪

"Truth!" ▪ said Pilate, ▪▪ "What does *that* mean?" ▪▪

Trying to offer a quick resolution. May be trying to put words in their mouths.

After *this* remark, ▪ Pilate went out *again* to the Jews and *told* them: ▪▪ "Speaking for *myself,* ▪ I find *no case* against this man. ▪▪ *Recall* your custom ▪ whereby I *release* to you someone at *Passover* time. ▪▪ Do you *want* me to release to you the *king* of the *Jews?*" ▪▪ They shouted back, ▪▪ "We want *Barabbas,* ▪ not *this* one!" ▪▪ *(Barabbas* was an *insurrectionist.)* ▪▪▪

Suggest the horrific pain.

Soldiers mocking . . . making sport.

Pilate's *next* move ▪ was to *take* Jesus and have him *scourged.* ▪▪ The soldiers then wove a *crown* of *thorns* and *fixed* it on his head, ▪ throwing around his shoulders a cloak of *royal purple.* ▪▪ *Repeatedly* they came up to him and said, ▪▪ "All *hail, King* of the *Jews!"* ▪▪ *slapping* his face as they did so. ▪▪▪

Underlying pity. Rev. NAB restores the more familiar "Behold the man."

They can't let Pilate weaken.

(4) Pilate went out a *second* time and *said* to the crowd: ▪▪ *"Observe* what I do. ▪▪ I am going to bring him out to you to make you *realize* that I find *no* case against him." ▪▪ When Jesus *came* out *wearing* the crown of thorns and the purple *cloak,* ▪ Pilate *said* to them, ▪▪ *"Look* at the man!" ▪▪ As *soon* as the chief priests and the temple police *saw* him they *shouted,* ▪ *"Crucify* him! ▪ *Crucify* him!" ▪▪ *Pilate* said, ▪▪ *"Take* him and crucify him *yourselves;* ▪▪ *I* find no *case* against him." ▪▪ "We have our *law,"* ▪ the Jews responded, ▪▪ "and *according* to that law he must *die* ▪ because he made himself *God's Son."* ▪▪ When Pilate *heard* this kind of talk, ▪ he was more *afraid* than ever. ▪▪▪

Pilate's frustration now turns on Jesus.

Jesus' composure is persuasive.

Going back into the praetorium, ▪ he said to *Jesus,* ▪ "Where do you *come* from?" ▪▪ Jesus would not give him *any* answer. ▪▪ "Do you *refuse* to speak to me?" ▪ Pilate asked him. ▪ "Do you not *know* that I have the power to *release* you ▪ and the power to *crucify* you?" ▪▪ Jesus answered: ▪

"You would have *no* power over me *whatever* ▪
unless it were *given* you from above. ▪▪

(4) Pilate's tone after the scourging sounds like: "Look, I've listened to you, I've punished him for you, that's all I'm going to do." The cries of "Crucify him" both anger and frighten Pilate. He didn't expect that. He's not done with this mess after all. His frustration and growing anger at the religious leaders are now directed at Jesus: "Where do you come from? Do you refuse . . . ? Do you not know . . . ?" Jesus' composure is disconcerting but persuasive. The intensity builds. Sensing that Pilate is weakening, the religious men pressure and threaten him. Pilate, who "heard" the veiled threats to report him to Caesar, makes a final effort to win pity for Jesus ("What! Shall I crucify your king?") and then relents.

(5) John does not describe the crucifixion. Take time with the short narration, stressing that Jesus carried the cross "by himself." Your tone speaks of sorrow and the great horror of crucifixion. Proclaim the inscription as might a herald reading from a scroll. The dialogue between Pilate and the priests is animated and angry. The soldiers are greedy and insensitive; the narration and their dialogue should suggest that.

The tone changes dramatically when you speak of "his mother." Speak of each of the women as if you know her. Remember, Jesus is dying as he speaks. No despair characterizes Jesus' voice on "I am thirsty." John has him muster his last strength to fulfill scripture. Strength and full awareness also distinguish his last statement. Pause after it. Imagine Jesus dropping his head in death, then quietly, firmly, read the awesome narration: "he . . . delivered over his spirit." This is the climax of John's gospel, the most glorious moment of Jesus' "hour of glory."

The implied threat is not well veiled. "Friend of Caesar": a title of honor bestowed by Rome on high-ranking officials.

Last effort to forestall.

Ritardando: "Pilate . . . crucified."

As narrator you are grieved by this. Slowly, to convey horror of crucifixion.

Proclaimed.

Anger through clenched teeth. They want to persuade him.

Ritardando: second "I have written."

"His tunic . . . no seam": as if spoken by soldiers.

Greed.

Change mood. Convey grief of the women.

That is *why* ▪ he who *handed* me over to you ▪
is guilty of the *greater* sin." ▪▪

After this, ▪ Pilate was *eager* to release him, ▪ but the Jews *shouted,* ▪▪ "If you *free* this man you are no *'Friend* of *Caesar.'* ▪▪ Anyone who makes himself a *king* ▪ becomes Caesar's *rival."* ▪▪ Pilate *heard* what they were saying, ▪ then brought Jesus *outside* and took a seat on a *judge's* bench at the place called the *Stone Pavement—* ▪ *Gabbatha* in Hebrew. ▪▪ (It was the *Preparation* Day for *Passover,* ▪ and the hour was about noon.) ▪▪ He *said* to the Jews, ▪▪ *"Look* at your *king!"* ▪▪ At this they shouted, ▪▪ *"Away* with him! ▪▪ *Away* with him! ▪▪ *Crucify* him!" ▪▪ *"What!"* ▪ Pilate exclaimed. ▪▪ "Shall I *crucify* your *king?"* ▪▪ The chief priests *replied,* ▪▪ "We *have* no king but *Caesar."* ▪▪ In the *end,* ▪ Pilate *handed* Jesus over to be *crucified.* ▪▪▪

(5) Jesus was *led* away, ▪ and *carrying* the cross by *himself,* ▪ went out to what is called the *Place* of the *Skull* (in Hebrew, *Golgotha*). ▪▪ There they *crucified* him, ▪ and *two others* with him: ▪ one on either *side,* ▪ *Jesus* in the middle. ▪▪ Pilate had an *inscription* placed on the cross which *read,* ▪▪
JESUS THE *NAZOREAN,* ▪
THE *KING* OF THE *JEWS.*

This inscription, ▪ in *Hebrew, Latin* and *Greek,* ▪ was read by *many* of the Jews, ▪ since the *place* where Jesus was crucified was near the *city.* ▪▪ The *chief priests* of the Jews tried to *tell* Pilate, ▪▪ "You should *not* have written, ▪ 'The *King* of the Jews.' ▪▪ Write instead, ▪▪ 'This man *claimed* to be king of the Jews.'" ▪▪ Pilate *answered,* ▪▪ "What I have *written,* ▪ *I have written."* ▪▪▪

After the soldiers had *crucified* Jesus they took his *garments* and divided them *four* ways, ▪ *one* for *each* soldier. ▪▪ There was also his *tunic,* ▪ but this tunic was woven in *one piece* from top to bottom and had no *seam.* ▪▪ They *said* to each other, ▪▪ "We shouldn't *tear* it. ▪▪ Let's throw *dice* to see who *gets* it." ▪▪ (The *purpose* of this was to have the Scripture *fulfilled:* ▪▪
"They *divided* my garments among them; ▪▪
for my *clothing* they *cast lots.*") ▪▪
And this was what the soldiers *did.* ▪▪▪

Near the *cross* of Jesus ▪ there stood his *mother,* ▪ his mother's *sister, Mary* the wife of *Clopas,* ▪ and Mary *Magdalene.* ▪▪ *Seeing* his mother there with the disciple whom he *loved,* ▪ Jesus *said* to his

Quietly . . . haltingly. Speaking through pain. Mary becomes an adopted mother.

Jesus' voice stronger.

All remaining strength mustered to speak this. Jesus' "spirit" is the Holy Spirit, the spirit of the new creation. Jesus' death is the giving of the Spirit.

mother, ▪▪ *"Woman,* ▪ there is your *son."* ▪▪ In turn he said to the *disciple,* ▪▪ *"There* is your *mother."* ▪▪ From that hour onward, ▪ the disciple *took* her into his *care.* ▪▪▪ After that, ▪ *Jesus,* ▪ realizing that *everything* was now *finished,* ▪ to bring the Scripture to *fulfillment* ▪ said, ▪ "I am *thirsty."* ▪▪ There was a *jar* there, ▪ full of *common wine.* ▪▪ They stuck a sponge *soaked* in this wine on some *hyssop* ▪ and *raised* it to his lips. ▪▪ When Jesus *took* the wine, ▪ he said, ▪▪ *"Now* ▪ it is *finished."* ▪▪ Then he *bowed* his head, ▪▪ and *delivered* over his *spirit.* ▪▪▪

Hold listeners' attention.

Slowly. An important symbol.

Be persuasive.

(6) Since it was the *Preparation Day* ▪ the Jews did not want to have the bodies *left* on the cross during the *sabbath,* ▪ for that sabbath was a solemn *feast* day. ▪▪ They asked Pilate that the *legs* be *broken* ▪ and the bodies be *taken* away. ▪▪ Accordingly, ▪ the *soldiers* came and *broke* the legs of the men crucified with Jesus, ▪ first of *one,* ▪ then of the *other.* ▪▪ When they came to *Jesus* and saw that he was *already* dead, ▪ they did *not* break his legs. ▪▪ One of the soldiers ran a *lance* into his *side,* ▪ and *immediately blood* and *water* flowed out. ▪▪ (This *testimony* has been given by an *eyewitness,* ▪ and his testimony is *true.* ▪▪ He tells what he *knows* is true, ▪ so that you may *believe.*) ▪▪ These events took place for the *fulfillment* of *Scripture:* ▪▪

"Break *none* of his bones." ▪▪

There is still *another* Scripture passage which says: ▪▪

"They shall *look* on him
whom they have *pierced."* ▪▪▪

With tenderness.

The burial of a king!

This garden is a new Eden.

Pause. Then hint the hope with "This is the gospel. . . ."

Afterward, ▪ *Joseph* of *Arimathea,* ▪ a *disciple* of Jesus ▪ (although a *secret* one for *fear* of the Jews), ▪ asked Pilate's permission to *remove* Jesus' body. ▪▪ Pilate *granted* it, ▪ so they came and took the body away. ▪▪ *Nicodemus* ▪ (the man who had first come to Jesus at *night*) ▪ *likewise* came, ▪ bringing a mixture of *myrrh* and *aloes* which weighed about a *hundred pounds.* ▪▪ They *took* Jesus' body, ▪ and in accordance with Jewish *burial* custom ▪ *bound* it up in wrappings of cloth with perfumed oils. ▪▪ In the place where he had been crucified there was a *garden,* ▪ and in the garden a new *tomb* ▪ in which *no* one had ever been laid. ▪▪ Because of the Jewish Preparation Day ▪ they laid Jesus *there,* ▪ for the tomb was *close* at hand. ▪▪▪

(6) What remains is denouement, but with a few peaks. Though the predominant tone is subdued, increase your intensity when speaking of the soldiers who "broke the legs" and "ran a lance." "Blood and water" is both a sure biological sign of death and a powerful theological symbol. And don't be strident when asserting the veracity of "this testimony." A quiet voice filled with confidence will serve better.

The closing paragraph is spoken with reverence and tenderness, the grief held mostly in check. Imagine yourself telling a woman about how her husband was killed saving your life on the battlefield. You try to avoid overwhelming her with sorrow, but you state the facts with an obvious love for the one who gave his life for you. "They buried him there," you say, "because that was the best they could do." This "battlefield" tomb was the best they could do for Jesus but, *mirabile dictu!*, it didn't have to do for long. It was in a garden, after all, the garden of the new creation.

READING I This night is a beginning. And so we begin at the beginning and tell the story of God's creation.

Many have encountered James Weldon Johnson's compelling rendering of the creation story. Johnson speaks of a God who "spits out" the seven seas, hollows out the valleys and bulges up the mountains with the soles of his feet and, "like a mammy bending over her baby," molds clay into human life. One leaves the poem with a clear image of a God who deeply cares for and is intimately involved with all creation. God looks at "his moon and his sun and his little stars" and says "That's good!" Our story presents more a God of power than a "mammy." But this God also works with a mother's love to fashion a beautiful home for the man and woman who will be birthed into it. So you, too, must leave your listeners with an image of a caring God. That can best be done by your use of two of the refrains in this passage: "God saw how good it was" and "Evening came and morning followed. . . ." The affirmation of goodness should suggest the smile that fills a mother's face when she kisses her child. The identification of each day does not sound like a tired worker checking off the day's accomplishments but like a woman counting off the months of her pregnancy, aware of the growth within her and of her movement toward the full ripening of the life she carries.

Three other refrains complete the repeated pattern found in each of the days of creation. 1. Introduction: "Then God said. . . ." 2. God's command: "Let there be. . . ." 3. The accomplishment of the command: "And so it happened. . . ." Then the two refrains discussed above follow: 4. Affirmation of goodness and 5. Identification of the day. Avoid a rote delivery and use these refrains to help you draw your listeners deeper and deeper into the pattern of God's creative work.

Before the "beginning" there was chaos. Dark, terrifying chaos. If you've seen a large lake or the ocean at night you know the kind of water "swept" by that "mighty [and thunderous] wind."

Remember the God who creates, and find an appropriate voice. God *enjoys* this work. Be enthusiastic! But remember, too, that it's God's voice, not God's hand, that creates. So speak with enthusiastic *power.*

MARCH 30–31, 1991

EASTER VIGIL

LECTIONARY #42

READING I Genesis 1:1—2:2

A reading from the book of *Genesis* ▪▪▪

Speak the first three words with all that is in you.

In the beginning, ▪▪ when God created the *heavens* and the *earth,* ▪ the earth was a *formless wasteland,* ▪ and *darkness* covered the abyss, ▪▪ while a mighty *wind* swept over the *waters.* ▪▪▪

"Mighty wind" sounds like it means.

Light breaks the darkness. Joyfully, and very slowly.

Then God *said,* ▪▪ "Let there be *light,"* ▪▪▪ and there *was* light. ▪▪ God *saw* how *good* the light was. ▪▪ God then *separated* the light from the darkness. ▪▪ God called the light ▪ *"day,"* ▪ and the darkness he called ▪ *"night."* ▪▪ Thus *evening* came, ▪ and *morning* followed— ▪ the *first* day. ▪▪▪

Watch it happening, then speak what you see.

Then God said, ▪▪ "Let there be a *dome* in the middle of the *waters,* ▪ to *separate* one body of water from the other." ▪▪▪ And so it *happened:* ▪▪ God *made* the dome, ▪ and it separated the water *above* the dome ▪ from the water *below* it. ▪▪ God *called* the dome ▪ "the *sky."* ▪▪▪ *Evening* came, ▪ and morning *followed*— ▪ the *second* day. ▪▪▪

Tenderly.

Then God said, ▪▪ "Let the water *under* the sky be *gathered* into a *single basin,* ▪ so that the *dry land* may appear." ▪▪▪ And so it *happened:* ▪▪ the water under the sky *was* gathered into its basin, ▪ and the dry land *appeared.* ▪▪ God *called* the dry land ▪ "the *earth,"* ▪▪ and the basin of the water he called ▪ "the *sea."* ▪▪ God saw how *good* it was. ▪▪▪ *Then* God said, ▪▪ "Let the *earth* bring forth *vegetation:* ▪ every kind of *plant* that bears *seed* ▪ and every kind of *fruit* tree on earth that bears *fruit* with its seed *in* it." ▪▪▪ And so it *happened:* ▪▪ the earth *brought* forth *every* kind of plant that bears seed ▪ and *every* kind of fruit tree on earth that bears fruit with its *seed* in it. ▪▪ God saw how *good* it was. ▪▪▪ *Evening* came, ▪ and *morning* followed— ▪ the *third* day. ▪▪▪

Faster pace.

With emotion.

Faster pace.

Rejoice in all the manifestations of light.

Then God said: ▪▪ "Let there be *lights* in the dome of the sky, ▪ to separate *day* from *night.* ▪▪ Let them *mark* the fixed times, ▪ the *days* and the *years,* ▪ and serve as *luminaries* in the dome of the sky, ▪ to shed *light* upon the earth." ▪▪▪ And so it *happened:* ▪▪ God *made* the two *great* lights, ▪ the *greater* one to govern the *day,* ▪ and the *lesser* one to govern the

It was a beautiful day.

night; ▪ and he made the *stars.* ▪ God *set* them in the dome of the sky, ▪ to *shed* light upon the *earth,* ▪ to *govern* the day and the night, ▪ and to *separate* the light from the darkness. ▪▪ God saw how *good* it was. ▪▪▪ Evening *came,* ▪ and morning *followed*— ▪ the *fourth* day. ▪▪▪

Then God said, ▪▪ "Let the *water teem* with an *abundance* of living creatures, ▪ and on the *earth* ▪ let *birds fly* beneath the dome of the sky." ▪▪▪ And so it *happened:* ▪▪ God created the great *sea monsters* ▪ and *all kinds* of swimming creatures with which the water *teems,* ▪ and all kinds of *winged birds.* ▪▪ God saw how *good* it was, ▪▪ and God *blessed* them, ▪ saying, ▪▪ "Be *fertile,* ▪ *multiply,* ▪ and *fill* the water of the seas; ▪▪ and let the *birds* multiply on the *earth.*" ▪▪▪ *Evening* came, ▪ and *morning* followed— ▪ the *fifth* day. ▪▪▪

More variety and more delight. Distinguish between "wild" and "creeping."

"Creeping" sounds like it means.

"Man and woman" is also true to the spirit of this text.

Then God said, ▪▪ "Let the *earth* bring forth *all kinds* of living creatures: ▪ *cattle,* ▪ *creeping* things, ▪ and *wild* animals of *all* kinds." ▪▪▪ And so it *happened:* ▪▪ God made *all kinds* of wild animals, ▪ all kinds of *cattle,* ▪ and *all* kinds of *creeping* things of the earth. ▪▪ God *saw* how *good* it was. ▪▪▪ Then God *said:* ▪▪ "Let us make *man* in our *image,* ▪ after *our* likeness. ▪▪ Let them have *dominion* over the *fish* of the *sea,* ▪ the *birds* of the *air,* ▪ and the *cattle,* ▪ and over *all* the wild *animals* ▪ and all *creatures* that *crawl* on the ground." ▪▪

An Inclusive Language Lectionary *says: "So God created humankind in the divine image; in the image of God humankind was created; male and female God created them."*

God created *man* in his *image;* ▪▪
in the *divine* image he created him; ▪▪
male and *female* he created them. ▪▪

As a blessing!

God can't give enough.

God *blessed* them, ▪ saying: ▪▪ "Be *fertile* and *multiply;* ▪▪ *fill* the earth and *subdue* it. ▪▪ Have *dominion* over the *fish* of the sea, ▪ the *birds* of the air, ▪ and all the *living things* that *move* on the earth." ▪▪ God *also* said: ▪▪ *"See,* ▪ I give you every *seed*-bearing plant *all* over the earth ▪ and every *tree* that has seed-bearing *fruit* on it ▪ to be your *food;* ▪▪ and to all the *animals* of the land, ▪ all the *birds* of the air, ▪ and all the *living creatures* that *crawl* on the *ground,* ▪ I give all the *green plants* for food." ▪▪▪ And so it *happened.* ▪▪▪ God *looked* at *everything* he had made, ▪▪ and he *found* it *very good.* ▪▪▪ *Evening* came, ▪ and *morning* followed— ▪ the *sixth* day. ▪▪▪

Slower.

All put together, it's very good!

With pride.

Ritardando: "from . . . undertaken." And the resting was also good.

Thus the *heavens* and the *earth* and all their *array* were *completed.* ▪▪▪ Since on the *seventh* day God was *finished* with the *work* he had been doing, ▪ he *rested* on the seventh day ▪ from *all* the work he had undertaken. ▪▪▪

[Shorter: Genesis 1:1, 26–31]

"Then God said" moves us through the sequence of events, and each repetition of the phrase requires a new build and fresh energy. Pause before each "And so it happened" and then, with wide-eyed wonder, describe what you've just *seen.*

Those who love the earth and wish to protect its resources do so, in part, because they realize this planet was entrusted to us by the God who designed every detail—from the "plant that bears seed" to the "fruit tree . . . that bears fruit with its seed in it." And it was good, and evening came and morning followed.

Rejoice in the gift of light. The sun that makes things grow. The romantic moon that makes dark places less fearful. And the stars! Many, magnificent and mysterious. And it was good, and evening came and morning followed.

"Winged birds . . . sea monsters . . . swimming creatures!" The waters teem and the skies are filled with fluttering wings. "And God blessed them." And evening came and morning followed.

A zoo of living creatures "wild" and "creeping." God is as excited as a child watching a parade of circus animals of "all kinds . . . all kinds . . . all kinds." And they're really good.

Out of the goodness of what went before comes God's greatest good: a creature made "in our image, after our likeness." The voice slows and takes on a tender and solemn quality, in the way parents bequeath all their worldly goods to their children. So God bestows all the world's riches on man and woman. Theirs is "dominion" and blessing: "Be fertile . . . multiply." God looked and it was "very good." Evening came and morning followed.

Pride fills your announcement that the work was completed. Let your voice convey awe as you finish this creation story: God created *everything,* and it was *very good.*

READING II What kind of a God would put any person through such a trial? What kind of person would take seriously such a request from such a God? Our culture shouts "Bravo!" to those objections. Not true for the culture from which the Genesis author comes. It was not uncommon to offer human sacrifice to the gods of various ancient cults. So for Abraham to take God's brutal request seriously is quite believable. Now you must make it believable to your listeners.

The horror of this story lies not in Isaac's close call. The horrifying part of the story is the turmoil experienced by Abraham as he prepares to carry out this gruesome mission. Focus your efforts on coming to grips with the emotions of a man preparing to murder his own son. Abraham's naiveté ("Ready!") quickly turns to anguish as God's powerful voice surprises him with the request for a human holocaust. Don't give away the shock by making God's voice too angry or threatening.

Obviously Abraham has not hinted to his son or family the true nature of his mission. The objective tone of the narration, as he saddles the donkey and takes servants, paints for us his stoic face. The dialogue, in particular, both with the servants and with Isaac, shows Abraham's determination to avoid alarming his son. The boy's question is genuine. He's confused and says so. Abraham covers his pain as he answers, ironically, that God will provide the sheep. We know a ram waits in the brambles. Abraham thinks only of Isaac.

The narration continues to describe Abraham preparing, like a robot, for the sacrifice. Your voice must suggest the immense (but unseen) effort it took to force his arms and hands to prepare the altar and arrange the wood. The emotional strain becomes more apparent as you describe him placing the boy "on top of the wood." As you relate how Abraham took the knife "to slaughter his son" remember that he thought he was really going to do it. That should send a shiver down everyone's spine. Pause before God's voice intervenes so the shiver can do its work. "But" is like a heavenly hand reaching out and catching Abraham's wrist just in time. God's voice is at first urgent and authoritative. Then it mellows into tenderness and compassion. Relate quickly, and with relief, the incident with the ram. "Yahweh-yireh" means "The Lord will see [to it]." You might want to say this translation immediately after the Hebrew words.

The tender, compassionate voice of God is back to promise blessings. Abraham's obedience brought great reward for him and for all of us, his "descendants" in faith.

READING II Genesis 22:1–18

"God . . . test" is the introduction and summary of the entire story. Narrator knows it's only a test. God calls loudly. "Ready" is hard word to read convincingly. Practice.

Shock us with this command.

Abraham feigns composure, but you must hint at his inner turmoil.

A reading from the book of *Genesis* ▪ ▪ ▪

God put Abraham to the *test.* ▪ ▪ He *called* to him, ▪ ▪ *"Abraham!"* ▪ ▪ *"Ready!"* ▪ he replied. ▪ ▪ Then God said: ▪ ▪ "Take your son *Isaac,* ▪ your *only* one, whom you *love,* ▪ and *go* to the land of Moriah. ▪ ▪ There you shall *offer* him up as a *holocaust* ▪ on a height that I will *point* out to you." ▪ ▪ Early the next morning ▪ Abraham *saddled* his donkey, ▪ *took* with him his *son* Isaac, ▪ and two of his *servants* as well, ▪ and with the *wood* that he had cut for the holocaust, ▪ *set* out for the place of which God had *told* him. ▪ ▪ ▪

Abraham working hard to hide his pain.

Isaac is confused.

Abraham makes quick response to avoid giving real answer.

On the *third* day Abraham got *sight* of the place from afar. ▪ ▪ Then he said to his *servants:* ▪ ▪ "Both of you *stay* here with the donkey, ▪ while the *boy* and *I* go on over yonder. ▪ ▪ We will *worship* ▪ and then *come back* to you." ▪ ▪ Thereupon Abraham *took* the wood for the holocaust ▪ and *laid* it on his son Isaac's shoulders, ▪ while he himself carried the *fire* and the *knife.* ▪ ▪ As the two walked on *together,* ▪ Isaac *spoke* to his father Abraham. ▪ ▪ *"Father!"* ▪ he said. ▪ ▪ *"Yes,* son," ▪ he replied. ▪ ▪ Isaac continued, ▪ ▪ *"Here* are the fire and the wood, ▪ but where is the *sheep* for the holocaust?" ▪ ▪ *"Son,"* ▪ Abraham answered, ▪ ▪ "God *himself* will *provide* the sheep for the holocaust." ▪ ▪ Then the two *continued* going forward. ▪ ▪

Abraham's emotional turmoil is in your voice.

Second "Abraham" more intense, not louder, than the first. Authoritative and tender. Pause and look up before responding as Abraham.

Suggest Abraham's relief and joy.

When they *came* to the place of which God had *told* him, ▪ Abraham built an *altar* there ▪ and arranged the *wood* on it. ▪ ▪ Next he *tied up* his son Isaac, ▪ and *put* him on *top* of the wood on the *altar.* ▪ ▪ Then he *reached* out and took the *knife* ▪ to *slaughter* his son. ▪ ▪ But the Lord's *messenger called* to him from heaven, ▪ ▪ *"Abraham,* ▪ *Abraham!"* ▪ ▪ ▪ *"Yes,* Lord," ▪ he answered. ▪ ▪ "Do *not* lay your hand on the boy," ▪ said the messenger. ▪ ▪ "Do not do the *least* thing to him. ▪ ▪ I *know* now how *devoted* you are to God, ▪ since you did not *withhold* from me your own *beloved* son." ▪ ▪ As Abraham *looked* about, ▪ he spied a *ram* caught by its horns in the thicket. ▪ ▪ So he went and *took* the ram ▪ and offered it up as a *holocaust* ▪ in *place* of his son. ▪ ▪ ▪ Abraham *named* the site *Yahweh-yireh;* ▪ ▪ hence people now say, ▪ ▪ "On the *mountain* the *Lord* will *see."* ▪ ▪ ▪

God's voice is full of pride, compassion and generosity.

Again the Lord's messenger called to Abraham from heaven and said: ▪ ▪ "I *swear* by myself, ▪ declares the Lord, ▪ that because you *acted* as you *did* in not *withholding* from me your beloved *son,* ▪ I will *bless* you *abundantly* ▪ and make your *descendants* as *countless* as the *stars* of the sky and the *sands* of the seashore; ▪▪ your descendants shall take *possession* of the gates of their *enemies,* ▪ and *in* your descendants ▪ *all* the *nations* of the earth shall find *blessing*— ▪ all *this* ▪ because you *obeyed* my *command."* ▪▪▪

[Shorter: Genesis 22:1–2, 9, 10–13, 15–18]

READING III Exodus 14:15—15:1

You're telling this story to people eager to hear it again. Be eager to tell it.

A reading from the book of *Exodus* ▪▪▪

God; powerful and commanding.

The Lord said to *Moses,* ▪▪ "Why are you *crying out* to me? ▪▪ Tell the Israelites to *go forward.* ▪▪ And *you,* ▪ lift up your *staff* ▪ and, with hand *outstretched* over the sea, ▪ *split* the sea in two, ▪ that the Israelites may *pass* through it on *dry* land. ▪▪ But I will make the Egyptians *so obstinate* ▪ that they will go in *after* them. ▪▪ Then I will receive *glory* through *Pharaoh* and all his *army,* ▪ his *chariots* and *charioteers.* ▪▪ The Egyptians shall *know* that *I* am the *Lord,* ▪ when I *receive* glory through Pharaoh and his chariots and charioteers." ▪▪▪

Take time with "Pharoah," "army," "chariots" and "charioteers." This refrain will be repeated over and over.

Faster pace: "through . . . charioteers."

Much activity. Build suspense.

The *angel* of God, ▪ who had been *leading* Israel's camp, ▪ now *moved* and went around *behind* them. ▪▪ The column of *cloud* also, ▪ *leaving* the front, ▪ took up its place *behind* them, ▪ so that it came *between* the camp of the Egyptians and that of *Israel.* ▪▪ But the cloud now became *dark,* ▪ and thus the night *passed* without the *rival* camps coming any *closer* together *all night long.* ▪▪▪ Then Moses *stretched* out his hand over the sea, ▪ and the Lord *swept* the sea with a *strong east wind* throughout the night ▪ and so *turned* it into *dry* land. ▪▪ When the water was thus *divided,* ▪ the Israelites *marched* into the *midst* of the sea on dry land, ▪ with the water like a *wall* to their *right* and to their *left.* ▪▪

Activity stops. Waiting. What will happen?

The answer. Sound like the powerful wind!

A marvelous sight!

Such fools!

Quietly.

Sudden agitation. "Panic" and "clogged" sound like they mean.

The Egyptians *followed* in *pursuit;* ▪ all Pharaoh's *horses* and *chariots* and *charioteers* went after them ▪ *right* into the *midst* of the sea. ▪▪ In the night watch just before *dawn* ▪ the Lord *cast* through the column of the fiery cloud upon the Egyptian force ▪ a *glance* that threw it into a *panic;* ▪ and he so *clogged* their chariot wheels that they could *hardly* drive. ▪▪ With that ▪ the Egyptians sounded the *retreat* before Israel, ▪ because the *Lord* was fighting for them *against* the Egyptians. ▪▪

READING III This is a story best told around a campfire where eager young faces ask: Tell us again about Moses and how he made the waters part so our people could get through safely but our enemies didn't. Then an equally eager face begins, "The Lord said to Moses . . ." Knowing this is *our* story, not simply that of a people who lived long ago, and telling it with enthusiasm will add life and variety to a story that could possibly be boring. Think of Moses, years later, retelling these events in the first person. "The Lord said to *me,* 'Moses, why are you crying out . . . tell the Israelites . . . lift up your staff . . . split the sea'!" As narrator you must be as involved in the story as Moses was.

God's voice speaks the opening lines, stating facts and promises, not persuading Moses. [Imagine a real estate tycoon gazing at a model of a development he plans to build and stating with absolute confidence, "The road will wind through here, the lake will be dug out there, homes will dot the hills and the golf course will be the finest in the state."] Now narrate the events that led to the fulfillment of God's promise. First there's activity ("The angel . . . moved . . . The column of cloud . . . took up its place behind them") then darkness and waiting "all night long." (And this waiting is precisely what the Easter Vigil is all about!) Suddenly Moses takes action. Your voice must convey the sound of the wind that sweeps the sea. Stretch the "s" sounds in "swept," "sea," "strong" and "east" and the "n" of "wind" to create the sound of the storm. The power of God's command is followed by your marveling at the walls of water through which the people march "on *dry* land."

Your tone is almost mocking as you describe the Egyptians foolishly pursuing the Israelites "right into the midst of the sea." Become hushed as you speak of the "night watch just before dawn," then build volume and intensity as the Egyptians panic and sound the retreat.

God's powerful voice returns to order the sealing of the Egyptians' fate. It's a serious and sober voice, not angry or vindictive. God's justice is uncompromising. Not a single Egyptian is spared. Again, no vindictiveness but no apologies either.

In amazement you recall seeing the Israelites march on dry land through the miraculous corridor of water. You speak with pride that it was to your people that God showed such favor and such wonders. A reverential awe fills your voice as you tell of how they "feared . . . and believed."

At the conclusion of a particularly moving performance the audience sometimes responds with momentary silence before their appreciation erupts into applause. The same happens here. Awe at seeing God's great power turns into jubilant song. The joyous gratitude of those who sang must be your joy, too, as you invite *all* to rejoice over God's saving power.

READING IV Love is a place of excess. Our most convincing displays of affection are reserved for those we love, but often so is our greatest anger. God is transcendent, a spirit whose ways are so different from ours. Yet over and over scripture portrays a God who thinks and acts much as we do. Like the tiles of a mosaic, we piece together scripture's many images of God and discover that, though each is incomplete, together they comprise a striking portrait. On this "tile" God is a husband. Not a newlywed in the thrall of first love but a middle-aged lover old enough to know betrayal but young enough to forgive and love with renewed passion. And God's passion does not steer clear of excess.

The entire passage is an elaboration of the analogy of God as husband and Israel (us) as estranged wife. Your first task is to be convincing. Persuade us that God can love us, long for us, like a husband loves a wife; that God can forgive like some rare spouses forgive their partner's infidelity. All the emotions are here. First the initial anger: "For a brief moment I abandoned you. . . . In an outburst of wrath . . . I hid my face." Then a forgiveness that's nothing short of miraculous: "but with great tenderness I will take you back . . . with enduring love I take pity on you."

God is crazy in love with us and wants to say so. And you're the messenger chosen to speak the words. God's compassion overflows on "O afflicted . . . and unconsoled." Speak as if you were drawing a person you've forgiven into your embrace. God promises to restore us like a worker rebuilds a city. Only, in place of bricks, God will use precious stones glowing blue as the sky and red as the burning sun. God further promises that all needs will be met, all fears removed.

We could easily introduce this passage saying: A reading from the book of the *poet* Isaiah. This is a reading that is all imagery and tone. Let your proclamation capture the fire in the heart of a God who offers precious stones as a sign of love, a love more solid and enduring than the mountains from which the stones were mined.

God's powerful voice.

Then the Lord told Moses, ▪▪ *"Stretch* out your *hand* over the sea, ▪ that the *water* may flow *back* upon the Egyptians, ▪ upon their *chariots* and their *charioteers."* ▪▪ So Moses *stretched* out his hand over the sea, ▪ and at *dawn* the sea *flowed* back to its *normal* depth. ▪▪ The Egyptians were *fleeing* head on *toward* the sea, ▪ when the Lord *hurled* them into its midst. ▪▪ As the water *flowed* back, ▪ it *covered* the chariots and the charioteers of Pharaoh's *whole* army which had *followed* the Israelites into the sea. ▪▪ Not a *single one* of them *escaped.* ▪▪ But the Israelites had marched on *dry* land through the *midst* of the sea, ▪ with the water like a *wall* to their *right* and to their *left.* ▪▪ Thus the Lord *saved* Israel on that day from the *power* of the Egyptians. ▪▪ When Israel *saw* the Egyptians lying *dead* on the seashore ▪ and beheld the *great power* that the Lord had shown *against* the Egyptians, ▪ they *feared* the Lord and *believed* in him ▪ and in his servant *Moses.* ▪▪▪

"Dawn" is the moment of liberation.

Uncompromising justice.

Climax.

As if you can hardly believe it. Slowly.

Awe and reverence. Hushed.

Pause.

Then Moses and the Israelites sang this *song* to the Lord: ▪▪

The song is in your voice and on your face!

I will *sing* to the *Lord,* ▪
for he is *gloriously triumphant;* ▪▪
horse and *chariot* he has *cast* into the *sea.* ▪▪▪

READING IV Isaiah 54:5–14

A reading from the book of the prophet ▪ ***Isaiah*** ▪▪▪

Persuade us this is true. Strive for loving, tender quality.

He who has become your *husband* ▪
is your *Maker;* ▪▪
his *name* is the *Lord* of *hosts;* ▪▪
Your *redeemer* is the *Holy One* of Israel, ▪
called *God* of all the earth. ▪▪
The Lord *calls* you *back,* ▪
like a *wife forsaken* ▪ and *grieved* in spirit, ▪
A wife married in *youth* ▪ and then *cast* off, ▪
says your God. ▪▪

Husband-wife imagery. Conflict is over, reconciliation begins.

For a brief moment I *abandoned* you, ▪
but with great *tenderness* I will
take you *back.* ▪▪
In an *outburst* of wrath, ▪ for a *moment*
I *hid* my *face* from you; ▪▪
But with *enduring love* I take *pity* on you, ▪
says the Lord, your *redeemer.* ▪▪

God wants desperately to convince us of this.

This is for me like the days of *Noah,* ▪
when I *swore* that the *waters* of Noah
should *never* again *deluge* the earth; ▪▪

Israel's exile is compared to Noah's flood.

So I have sworn *not* to be *angry* with you, ▪
  or to *rebuke* you. ▪▪

Excessive language. Don't hold back.

Though the mountains *leave* their place ▪
  and the hills be *shaken,* ▪

Climax of reading.

My *love* shall *never* leave you ▪
  nor my *covenant* of *peace* be shaken, ▪
  says the *Lord,* ▪ who has *mercy* on you. ▪▪▪

As if embracing the one with whom you're reconciling.

O *afflicted* one, ▪ *storm*-battered and *unconsoled,* ▪
  I lay your *pavements* in carnelians, ▪

"Carnelians" = reddish quartz.

  and your foundations in *sapphires;* ▪▪
I will make your battlements of *rubies,* ▪

"Carbuncles" = smooth, round, deep-red garnets.

  your *gates* of carbuncles, ▪
  and all your *walls* of *precious stones.* ▪▪

"Sons and daughters" is more inclusive.

All your sons shall be taught by the *Lord,* ▪
  and *great* shall be the *peace* of your children. ▪▪

Comforting and reassuring.

In *justice* shall you be established, ▪
  far from the fear of oppression, ▪
  where destruction *cannot* come *near* you. ▪▪▪

READING V Isaiah 55:1–11

A reading from the book of the prophet ▪ *Isaiah* ▪▪▪

Thus says the *Lord:* ▪▪
All you who are *thirsty,* ▪

Note the imperatives. You are God calling all who are in need. See them in your assembly.

  come to the *water!* ▪▪
You who have no *money,* ▪
  come, ▪ receive *grain* and *eat;* ▪▪
Come, ▪ without *paying* and without *cost,* ▪
  drink *wine* and *milk!* ▪▪

Ask the questions sincerely. Expect an answer.

Why spend your money for what is *not bread;* ▪
  your *wages* for what *fails* to satisfy? ▪▪
Heed me, ▪ and you shall eat *well,* ▪
  you shall *delight* in rich fare. ▪▪
Come to me *heedfully,* ▪

The heart of God's promise. Pace is slow.

  listen, ▪ that you may have *life.* ▪▪
I will *renew* with you the *everlasting* covenant, ▪
  the *benefits* assured to *David.* ▪▪

Promises made to David won't be forgotten but will be renewed.

As I made him a *witness* to the peoples, ▪
  a *leader* and commander of *nations,* ▪
So shall *you* summon a nation you *knew* not, ▪
  and *nations* that knew *you* not ▪ shall *run*
    to you, ▪
Because of the *Lord,* your *God,* ▪
  the *Holy One* of Israel, ▪ who has
    glorified you. ▪▪▪

Urgency. Act before it's too late! Faster pace.

Seek the Lord while he may be *found,* ▪
  call him while he is *near.* ▪▪

READING V You sometimes hear of a philanthropic restaurant owner who throws open the doors on a holiday to all in need of a good meal. On this greatest of holidays, God reminds us that the doors of God's own place of rest and nourishment are always open. And admission is free. God addresses us directly in this passage. "You who are thirsty . . . come! You who have no money, come . . . come, without paying . . . drink wine and . . . delight in rich fare"! Imagine God, apron tied around the waist, rounding up those who've spent "wages" (and their lives) "for what fails to satisfy."

God's promise is new life with all the "benefits assured to David." Shift imagery, now, from restaurateur to insurance salesperson. God is urgent and insistent about selling us a "benefits" package. What had been promised to David will now be renewed. But the customer seems uninterested and rises to leave. A final effort is heard in "Seek the Lord. . . ." God is working hard to persuade the listener of the urgency of this situation. Do it now, God says, while there is time, before it's too late! No one is unworthy, no one will be turned away. Not the "scoundrel" nor the "wicked"; for ours is a God "generous in forgiving" and as different from us as earth is from sky.

The final section might best be understood by children. A father once marveled at how his two-year-old daughter covered her eyes and cringed each time he said, "I'm a monster; I'm going to get you." Without benefit of mask or costume the father became a frightening monster by simply saying so. God's words also actualize what they represent. God says it and it is! (Remember tonight's first reading?) Speak with confidence, knowing the truth of what you say. That truth is a comfort for your listeners, for God says, "My word . . . shall do my will." God's promise, after all, is about much more than good food and drink. It is about life.

READING VI The prophet speaks from a basic premise: Wisdom is the source of all prosperity. Without wisdom one finds only disaster. No one discovers wisdom alone for it is a gift only God can give. That conviction supports your entire proclamation.

Now imagine yourself a teacher confronting a student who has somehow run afoul of the system. Motivated by love, you begin your exhortation: "Hear . . . listen, and know prudence!" (Note the exclamation point.) How did you get into this mess, you ask, living "in the land of your foes, grown old . . . defiled . . . accounted with those destined for the nether world?" As if leaning over the offender, your whole presence asks: Do you know why? You don't wait for the answer, but give it yourself: "You have forsaken the fountain of wisdom!" If you "walked in the way of God" you wouldn't have these troubles. So *"learn* where prudence is" that you may also find peace!

The best disciplinarians do this. After scolding us for wrong behavior, they point out the advantages of right behavior. They give us hope that we can change, that help is available. After exhorting us to "learn," Baruch breaks into song praising the God who is our only hope of finding the wisdom we need. Ask the questions "Who has found . . . ? Who has entered . . . ?" with an energy that says you can't wait to give the answer yourself. The God "who knows all things" has found her. With joy and a quickened tempo describe this God who "established the earth . . . and filled it," whom the sun and the stars obey gladly. Let the twinkling stars tell you how you should sound and look as you proclaim: "shining with joy for [your] maker."

Note the personification of Wisdom. She has been given to Jacob, she has appeared on earth, "she is the book of the precepts of God." Speak with tenderness and love. Israel believed that the Law was God's gift, so they loved the Law that could teach them and save them from self-destruction. Our society usually views the law negatively, but Baruch knew clinging to the law would yield life. So he pleads (and so must you) that, for our own good, we must "receive her [and] walk by her light." Sing the last lines with Baruch. We *know* what pleases God. So our hearts shout, "Blessed are we!"

Plurals are more inclusive. Emphasis on God's mercy.

Let the scoundrel *forsake* his way, ▪
and the *wicked* man his *thoughts;* ▪▪
Let him *turn* to the Lord for *mercy;* ▪▪
to our *God,* ▪ who is *generous* in forgiving. ▪▪
For *my* thoughts are not *your* thoughts, ▪

God's plans are not our plans, God's methods not our methods.

nor are *your* ways *my* ways, says the Lord. ▪▪
As high as the *heavens* are above the *earth,* ▪
so high are *my* ways above *your* ways
and *my* thoughts above *your* thoughts. ▪▪▪

Balance "just as . . ." with "so shall. . . ." Watch the pauses.

For just as from the *heavens*
the rain and snow *come down* ▪
And do not *return* there
till they have *watered* the earth, ▪
making it *fertile* and *fruitful,* ▪

"To the one" is more inclusive.

Giving *seed* to him who *sows*
and *bread* to him who *eats,* ▪▪

Pause—then complete the comparison.

So shall my *word* be
that *goes forth* from my *mouth;* ▪▪
It shall not return to me *void,* ▪

God's "will" is eternal life for all.

but shall *do my will,* ▪
achieving the *end* ▪ for which I *sent* it. ▪▪▪

READING VI Baruch 3:9–15, 32—4:4

A reading from the book of the prophet ▪ *Baruch* ▪▪▪

You begin with exhortation motivated by love.

Hear, O Israel, ▪ the *commandments* of *life:* ▪▪
listen, ▪ and know *prudence!* ▪▪

Ask: Do you know why?

How *is* it, Israel, ▪
that you are in the land of your *foes,* ▪
grown *old* in a *foreign* land, ▪
Defiled with the *dead,* ▪▪
accounted with those ▪ *destined* for the *nether* world? ▪▪

Answer: Here's why!

You have *forsaken* the fountain of *wisdom!* ▪▪
Had you *walked* in the way of *God,* ▪
you would have *dwelt* in enduring *peace.* ▪▪

Here's the better way; follow it and find peace!

Learn where prudence is, ▪
where *strength,* ▪ where *understanding;* ▪▪
That you may know *also*
where are the *length* of *days,* ▪ and *life,* ▪
where *light* of the *eyes,* ▪ and *peace.* ▪▪▪

Dramatic shift in mood. A song of praise.

Who has *found* the place of wisdom, ▪
who has *entered* into her *treasuries?* ▪▪

"He who knows" = God. "Her" = wisdom. Faster tempo. Joyous.

He who knows *all things* knows *her;* ▪▪
he has *probed* her by his *knowledge*— ▪▪
He who *established* the earth for all time, ▪
and *filled* it with four-footed beasts; ▪▪

"Dismisses light" = sundown.

He who *dismisses* the light, ▪ and it *departs,* ▪

"Calls it" = sunrise. High energy.

calls it, ▪ and it *obeys* him *trembling;* ▪ ▪
Before whom the *stars* at their posts
shine and *rejoice;* ▪ ▪
When he *calls* them, ▪ they answer, ▪ ▪

Shout! This is wonderfully gleeful!

"Here we are!" ▪
shining with *joy* for their Maker. ▪ ▪
Such is our *God;* ▪ ▪
no *other* is to be *compared* to him: ▪ ▪
He has *traced* out all the way of *understanding,* ▪

"Her" = understanding.

and has *given* her to *Jacob,* ▪ his servant, ▪ ▪
to *Israel,* ▪ his *beloved son.* ▪ ▪

"She" = wisdom, now personified as the Book of the Law. "Mortals" is more inclusive.

Since then she has *appeared* on earth, ▪
and *moved* among men. ▪ ▪
She is the *book* of the *precepts* of *God,* ▪
the *law* that endures *forever;* ▪ ▪
All who *cling* to her will *live,* ▪
but those will *die* who *forsake* her. ▪ ▪

Stretch (sustain) the word "Turn."

Turn, O Jacob, ▪ and *receive* her: ▪ ▪
walk by her light toward *splendor.* ▪ ▪

"Glory" = the law.

Give not your glory to *another,* ▪

"Privileges" = knowing and observing the law.

your *privileges* to an *alien* race. ▪ ▪
Blessed are we, ▪ O *Israel;* ▪ ▪

Shout (or whisper!) but with joy.

for what *pleases God* ▪ is *known* to us! ▪ ▪ ▪

READING VII Ezekiel 36:16–28

From prophet's voice, shift immediately into God's angry voice.

A reading from the book of the prophet ▪ *Ezekiel* ▪ ▪ ▪

"Their land" = their own land.

Some lectionaries delete this line.

Emphasize the strong words to convey the anger.

This is why God is angry: idolatry.

Thus the *word* of the Lord *came* to me: ▪ ▪ Son of man, ▪ when the house of Israel *lived* in their land, ▪ they *defiled* it by their *conduct* and *deeds.* ▪ ▪ In my sight ▪ their conduct was like the *defilement* of a menstruous woman. ▪ ▪ Therefore I *poured* out my *fury* upon them ▪ [because of the *blood* which they poured out on the ground, ▪ and because they *defiled* it with *idols*]. ▪ ▪ I *scattered* them among the nations, ▪ dispersing them over *foreign* lands; ▪ ▪ according to their conduct and deeds I *judged* them. ▪ ▪ But when they *came* among the nations ▪ [*wherever* they came], ▪ they served to *profane* my *holy name,* ▪ because it was *said* of them: ▪ ▪ "These are the people of the *Lord,* ▪ yet they had to *leave* their land." ▪ ▪ So I have *relented* because of my holy name ▪ which the house of Israel *profaned* among the nations where they came. ▪ ▪ Therefore *say* to the house of Israel: ▪ ▪ Thus says the Lord *God:* ▪ ▪ Not for *your* sakes do I act, ▪ house of Israel, ▪ but for the sake of my *holy name,* ▪ which you profaned

Speak with the voice of the foreigners.

The change of attitude begins.

Faster pace on the repetitions.

READING VII The foreigners among whom Israel was dispersed are questioning God's fidelity to the covenant. "These are the people of the Lord," they say, "yet they had to *leave* their land." Such talk is an embarrassment to God who decides, for the sake "of my holy name," to relent and start anew with these stubborn children.

Except for the first line, it is exclusively God's voice heard throughout the reading. But, unlike Reading V where God beckons tenderly, here God's voice is full of anger. The anger may feel out of place after the readings that preceded, but it is a part of the mosaic we are forming this night. And the anger is righteous, for the people have "defiled" their land with conduct. "Like the defilement of a menstruous woman" is a culturally conditioned image that suggests becoming unclean through disregard for the law. Because we no longer understand menstruation as a sign of defilement, it's best to drop this image. "Fury," "scattered," "dispersing," "judged," "profane" are all strong words that convey God's wrath.

A transition begins midway through when God orders the prophet to announce a shift in policy. "I have relented," says God. But we sense a pulling in two directions. Three times God repeats that the holy name was "profaned among the nations." Let the repetitions suggest a frustrated God who reluctantly adopts a new approach. Though God insists that "Not for your sakes do I act," like a loving parent scolding a child, God's mercy and love soon overwhelm the call of justice. The dialogue becomes more intense and personal: From "I will prove the holiness of *my* great name," God moves to "I will take you away . . . I will sprinkle clean water upon you . . . I will give you *a new heart* . . . I will put *my spirit* within *you."* Love triumphs. By the time we hear the tender "you shall be my people, and I will be your God," we know God has not only saved a "name," but also a people who are being empowered "to live by [God's] statutes . . . [to] live in the land of [their] fathers [ancestors]." Our baptism does the same for each of us. It empowers us "to live."

EPISTLE The catechumens among us hear Paul's words with special clarity. They die and are buried in the waters of baptism and rise in the "glory" of "new life." Yet, with earnest concern, Paul speaks to each of us who are called to renew our baptismal promises this night. "Are you not aware . . . ?" he asks. Our old self died and was buried with Christ. But that's not bad news, for now we also rise with him. Words such as "death" and "buried" do not contrast with words such as "raised" and "new life" as strikingly as one might expect, for Paul's point is that death is the way to life. So your tone is upbeat throughout the balance of ideas. "If we have been united with him through . . . death, so shall we be [united with him] through . . . resurrection." Paul is excited about what "we *know*": Freedom and life are now available to all who believe. The sentences are declarative: "This we know . . ."! "Christ . . . will never die again . . ."! "Death has no more power . . ."! Without racing, the pace moves rather quickly, then slows dramatically on lines such as "death has no more power over him" and "his life is life for God."

The last line must be spoken with enthusiasm and tenderness and faith. Do that by thinking first of your own spiritual death and resurrection and then sharing your joy with all the assembly. It's Easter. The world is alive as never before!

The anger slowly yields to mercy and love.

Gradually becoming more personal, intense and tender.

Great intensity.

"Ancestors" is more inclusive.

Ritardando: "and I . . . God." Resurrection joy is in your voice.

among the *nations* to which you came. ▪▪ I will *prove* the holiness of my great name, ▪ profaned among the nations, ▪ in whose *midst* you have profaned it. ▪▪ Thus the nations shall *know* that *I* am the *Lord,* ▪ says the Lord God, ▪ when in their *sight* I prove my *holiness* through *you.* ▪▪ For I will *take* you *away* from among the nations, ▪ *gather* you from *all* the foreign lands, ▪ and bring you back to your *own* land. ▪▪ I will sprinkle *clean water* upon you to *cleanse* you from all your *impurities,* ▪ and from all your *idols* I will cleanse you. ▪▪ I will give you a *new heart* ▪ and place a *new spirit* within you, ▪ *taking* from your bodies your *stony* hearts ▪ and *giving* you *natural* hearts. ▪▪ I will put my *spirit* within you ▪ and make you *live* by my *statutes,* ▪ careful to *observe* my decrees. ▪▪ You shall live in the land I gave your *fathers;* ▪▪ *you* shall be my *people,* ▪ and *I* will be your *God.* ▪▪▪

EPISTLE Romans 6:3–11

A reading from the letter of *Paul* ▪ to the *Romans* ▪▪▪

Paul's style is personal and direct.

Use the balances. Rev. NAB says: "For if we have grown into union with him through a death like his, we shall also be united with him in the resurrection."

Be persuasive.

"Someone" is more inclusive.

Pace quickens a bit.

"Death . . . him.": slower.

"His life . . . God.": slowly.

Speak to those who need this good news!

Are you not *aware* that we who were *baptized* into Christ Jesus ▪ were baptized into his *death?* ▪▪▪ Through baptism into his *death* ▪ we were *buried* with him, ▪ so that, just as Christ was *raised* from the dead by the *glory* of the *Father,* ▪ we *too* might live a *new* life. ▪▪ If we have been *united* with him through likeness to his *death,* ▪ so shall we be through a like *resurrection.* ▪▪ This we *know:* ▪▪ our *old* self was *crucified* with him ▪ so that the *sinful* body might be *destroyed* ▪ and we might be *slaves* to sin *no longer.* ▪▪ A man who is *dead* has been *freed* from sin. ▪▪ If we have *died* with Christ, ▪ we believe that we are also to *live* with him. ▪▪ We know that *Christ,* ▪ once *raised* from the dead, ▪ will *never* die again; ▪▪ death has no more *power* over him. ▪▪ His death was death to *sin,* ▪ *once* for *all;* ▪▪ his *life* ▪ is life for *God.* ▪▪▪ In the *same* way, ▪ *you* must consider yourselves *dead* to *sin* ▪ but *alive* for *God* in Christ *Jesus.* ▪▪▪

GOSPEL Mark 16:1–8

A reading from the holy *gospel* according to *Mark* ▪ ▪ ▪

When the sabbath was *over,* ▪ *Mary Magdalene,* ▪ *Mary* the mother of *James,* ▪ and *Salome* ▪ bought perfumed *oils* ▪ with which they *intended* to go and *anoint* Jesus. ▪ ▪ Very *early,* ▪ just after *sunrise,* ▪ on the *first* day of the week ▪ they came to the *tomb.* ▪ ▪ They were *saying* to one another, ▪ ▪ "Who will *roll* back the *stone* for us ▪ from the *entrance* to the tomb?" ▪ ▪ When they *looked,* ▪ ▪ they found that the stone *had* been rolled back. ▪ ▪ (It was a *huge* one.) ▪ ▪ On *entering* the tomb ▪ they saw a *young man* sitting at the right, ▪ dressed in a *white robe.* ▪ ▪ This *frightened* them *thoroughly,* ▪ but he *reassured* them: ▪ ▪ "You need not be *amazed!* ▪ ▪ You are looking for *Jesus* of *Nazareth,* ▪ the one who was *crucified.* ▪ ▪ He has been *raised* up; ▪ ▪ he is not *here.* ▪ ▪ *See* the place where they *laid* him. ▪ ▪ *Go* now ▪ and tell his *disciples* and *Peter,* ▪ ▪ 'He is going *ahead* of you to *Galilee,* ▪ where you will *see* him ▪ just as he *told* you.'" ▪ ▪ ▪ They made their way out and *fled* from the tomb *bewildered* and *trembling;* ▪ ▪ and because of their *great* fear, ▪ ▪ they said *nothing* to *anyone.* ▪ ▪ ▪

GOSPEL All of this night's readings, and the centuries of history they represent, lead to this silent Sunday morning when the sun shone brightly into an empty tomb. The God of surprises who parted seas and stopped a dagger's plunge has saved the best surprise for last: A dead man walks among the living.

Three tired, frightened women, whose names you speak as reverently as you can, are making a sad journey. Mark spends much time setting the scene and the mood of heaviness that surrounds it. The women are loaded down with "perfumed oils" and with their heavy hearts. The hour is early, barely light, and fears and sorrow loom largest in that twilight. They ponder the heaviness of the stone and wonder who, if anyone, can roll it back for them. And then without fanfare, or even Matthew's "earthquake," they look and see that the stone has been rolled back. Mark brings in heaviness one more time by telling us ingenuously "it was a huge one."

The women quickly enter and find the "young man"; your tone suggests the surprise and shock that so thoroughly frightened them. His exclamation, "You need not be amazed," must either shake them from their frozen fear or stop them from rushing out the door. That done, he immediately begins to soothe with his knowledge of who they are looking for and why he's not there. For final assurance he points out the "place where they laid him," a place the women would consider sacred and for which he shows great respect.

Then the young man commissions them for a ministry of evangelization: "Go now and tell. . . ." He gives the message the insistent tone and emphasis he hopes the women will use when they relay it to the disciples.

The young man, it seems, got poor marks for persuasion. This is the greatest event in human history and the women go off and say "nothing to anyone." Scholars tell us Mark's gospel originally ended with those words. And perhaps his is the truest rendering: How many of us, given the shock of Easter morning, could race down a hill singing about a dead man coming back to life? But maybe Mark's is also the most provocative ending, because for us believers who already know the song of resurrection, this ending becomes a challenge to recall the melody, to sing it boldly and to invite others into that jubilant Alleluia.

READING I Except for the first seven words, this entire reading is spoken in the persona of Peter. Impetuous, fumbling, foot-in-the-mouth Peter speaks with uncharacteristic self-confidence and understanding. His conviction comes from the fact (which he states bluntly) that he has *seen* everything he describes.

Speak to your assembly with a quiet assumption that all are acquainted with Jesus, your voice gradually building in intensity in anticipation of the "anointed . . . good works . . . and healing" (lines 4–8) you are about to enumerate. Your enthusiasm perceptibly grows as you speak "of the way God anointed him. . . ."

"We are witnesses" is both an expression of Peter's fervor and his assertion of credibility: I was there, I saw it! Subordinate the negative images of the first half of the next sentence to the Easter good news that completes the sentence. Achieve this by speaking "they killed him . . . on a tree" softly and at a slightly faster rate than normal, then slowing considerably and increasing your volume for "only to have. . . ." Avoid any hint of arrogance while saying "by us who ate" but, filled with a sense of how *blessed* you are, humbly identify yourself as one of those who "ate and drank with him." Let that grateful humility carry you to the end of the reading, making it clear that the good fortune you shared can now be shared by "everyone who believes in him."

READING II *(Colossians 3:1–4)* Five short sentences means five sentences read *slowly*. Paul is excited. He is exhorting the Colossians. You will need to concentrate in order to exhort, convey his enthusiasm and still speak slowly!

The first sentence presents an if-then proposition. *If* "you have been raised . . . with Christ" *then* you should "set your heart on . . . higher realms." "After all, you have died!" Say that as if you were reminding someone they had won a big prize! The consequences for Paul are patently obvious. "Your life is now hidden [buried] with Christ" (through this new focus on spiritual rather than material things). When Christ appears then you shall appear (rise) with him in glory. It's that simple. And it's that wonderful.

MARCH 31, 1991

EASTER SUNDAY

LECTIONARY #43

READING I Acts 10:34, 37–43

A reading from the *Acts* of the *Apostles* ▪ ▪ ▪

Emphasize "Peter."

Peter ▪ *addressed* the people in these words: ▪ ▪ "I take it you *know* what has been reported all over Judea about *Jesus* of Nazareth, ▪ beginning in Galilee with the *baptism* John preached; ▪ ▪ of the way God *anointed* him with the *Holy Spirit* and *power.* ▪ ▪

Gradually building intensity.

A shift: greater enthusiasm.

He went about doing *good works* and *healing* all who were in the *grip* of the devil, ▪ ▪ and *God* was with him. ▪ ▪

I was there!

We are witnesses ▪ to *all* that he did in the land of the Jews ▪ and in Jerusalem. ▪ ▪ They *killed* him finally, ▪ *'hanging* him on a tree,' ▪

Emphasis on resurrection.

only to have God *raise him up* on the third day ▪ and grant that he be *seen,* ▪ not by *all,* ▪ but only by such *witnesses* as had been *chosen* beforehand by God— ▪ ▪

With humility.

by *us* ▪ who *ate* and *drank* with him ▪ after he *rose* from the dead. ▪ ▪

Build from "preach" to "bear witness."

He *commissioned* us to preach to the people ▪ and to *bear witness* that he is the one *set apart* by God ▪ as *judge* of the living and the dead. ▪ ▪

"Testify" echoes "witness." Stress "prophets."

To him all the *prophets* testify, ▪ saying that everyone who *believes* in him ▪ has

Ritardando: "through his name."

forgiveness of *sins* through his name." ▪ ▪ ▪

READING II Colossians 3:1–4

A reading from the letter of *Paul* ▪
to the *Colossians* ▪ ▪ ▪

Slowly.

Since you have been *raised up* in company with *Christ,* ▪ set your *heart* on what pertains to *higher* realms ▪ where Christ is seated at God's *right hand.* ▪ ▪

Exhorting.

Be intent on things *above* ▪ rather than on things of *earth.* ▪ ▪

"You have died!": This is good news!

After all, ▪ you have *died!* ▪ ▪ Your life is *hidden* now with Christ in God. ▪ ▪ When Christ our life *appears,* ▪ then *you* shall appear *with* him ▪ in *glory.* ▪ ▪ ▪

Or:

READING II   1 Corinthians 5:6–8

A reading from the first letter of *Paul* ▪ to the *Corinthians* ▪ ▪ ▪

Slowly.

Good-natured chiding.

No stress on "old yeast."

Emphasis is on celebration.

Do you not *know* ▪ that a little *yeast* ▪ has its effect *all* through the dough? ▪ ▪ Get *rid* of the old yeast to make of yourselves *fresh* dough, ▪ ▪ *unleavened* loaves, ▪ as it were; ▪ ▪ Christ our Passover has been *sacrificed.* ▪ ▪ Let us *celebrate* the feast not with the *old yeast,* ▪ that of *corruption* and *wickedness,* ▪ but with the *unleavened bread* ▪ of *sincerity* and *truth.* ▪ ▪ ▪

GOSPEL   John 20:1–9

A reading from the holy *gospel* according to *John* ▪ ▪ ▪

Create the suspense.

Mary's mood: weary and mournful.

Great distress!

Slow down.

Realization dawning.

Climax. Pause first.

Early in the morning ▪ on the *first* day of the week, ▪ while it was still *dark,* ▪ *Mary Magdalene* came to the *tomb.* ▪ ▪ She saw that the *stone* had been *moved* away, ▪ ▪ so she *ran* off to *Simon Peter* and the *other* disciple ▪ (the one Jesus *loved*) ▪ *and told* them, ▪ ▪ "The Lord has been *taken* from the tomb! ▪ We don't know *where* they have *put* him!" ▪ ▪ At that, ▪ Peter and the other disciple *started out* on their way toward the tomb. ▪ ▪ They were running *side* by *side,* ▪ but then the *other* disciple *outran* Peter ▪ and reached the tomb *first.* ▪ ▪ He did not *enter* ▪ but bent down to *peer* in, ▪ and saw the *wrappings* lying on the ground. ▪ ▪ Presently, ▪ Simon Peter came along behind him and *entered* the tomb. ▪ ▪ He *observed* the wrappings on the ground ▪ and saw the piece of cloth which had covered the *head* ▪ not *lying* with the wrappings, ▪ but *rolled* up in a place by *itself.* ▪ ▪ Then the disciple who had arrived *first* at the tomb *went* in. ▪ ▪ ▪ He *saw* ▪ ▪ and *believed.* ▪ ▪ ▪ (*Remember,* ▪ as yet they did not *understand* the Scripture ▪ that Jesus had to *rise* from the dead.) ▪ ▪ ▪

READING II *(1 Corinthians 5:6–8)* You're throwing a party and come in to find the cook using stale ingredients when the cupboards are brimming with fresh items. "The little bit of old yeast you use will affect the whole loaf," you say, "so use the good stuff! It would be foolish not to use the best." Christ victorious over death is our cause for celebration. Dare we bring out anything less than the best (sincerity and truth) for such a celebration? Don't become overbearing or angry in your delivery. You're in too good a mood to be mad at the cook. And, by the way, three short sentences mean three sentences read *slowly.*

GOSPEL The images are still of death and darkness. Speak of Mary in a way that conveys the mood with which she approached the tomb: weary and greatly saddened. Upon seeing that the stone had been moved she *ran off.* Communicate her obvious distress both as you narrate her seeking out Peter and in her dialogue.

Peter and John immediately catch her contagious anxiety and run off to investigate. Again, let your narration convey their frantic and impulsive response; but let *them* do the racing, not you. Because much is made of John's waiting for Peter to first enter the tomb as being a sign of Peter's preeminence among the apostles, you could give focus to that line by slowing down and speaking "He did not enter" in hushed tones. John's response to the empty tomb is an awed silence of faith.

Peter's arrival brings action back into the scene. He "entered," "observed the wrappings" and "saw the . . . cloth." Suddenly the tempo slows again as the realization dawns on Peter that the carefully rolled up cloth negates the possibility of the body being stolen. John's entry into the tomb reintroduces the mystery and awe. "He saw and believed" is John's climactic statement of faith.

The closing parenthetical statement has no trace of self-admonishment. It is filled with joy for it is spoken not so much with an emphasis on the disciples' previous lack of understanding but on their present level of awareness and exultation.

READING I Honeymoons. Married or not, we all have them now and then—in new jobs, new friendships or romantic relationships. Even presidents have them during their initial days in office. Mistakes are more easily excused, hurts are more easily forgotten and anything seems possible during those times of beginnings and new life. Luke describes the honeymoon of the new "community of believers" formed after the ascension of Jesus. The apostles were among them then, the very ones who had eaten and laughed and walked and slept under the stars with Jesus. What exciting times, we think now; how exciting to be a believer then, when miracles were commonplace and when your faith might cost your life.

This passage is not a history lesson, it's a beacon shining through the ages illuminating the possibilities of the Christian life. Heroism, idealism, selflessness are all possible in that beacon's light. Yes, it proclaims boldly, the same Spirit who empowered our ancestors can make of ours a community that is "of one heart and one mind." Speak with energy, enthusiasm and joy of these ancestors; speak as if you knew them and now want to brag about them. Speak not just to brag but to call us to that same radical and joyous living of our faith that enabled them to lay their goods (and their lives) at the feet of the apostles (and their Lord). Their life-style was a miracle; on this Sunday of Eastertime can we hope for anything less than miracles?

READING II Imagine you're scaling a building with a sectional ladder just long enough to reach the first-floor landing. There you find the next section of the ladder that, after you attach it, takes you to the second landing where another ladder section is waiting to advance you to the next landing and so on. Today's letter from John works the same way. Each sentence relies on the one before it and sets up the one after it. Like the ladder sections that must overlap to achieve strength, these sentences repeat information from the previous sentence before advancing the thought with new information.

The ladder analogy should tell you two things: Build carefully and proceed slowly. The opening sentence is the first ladder section. It's the most important idea and it ought to be stated boldly. Next comes a more softly spoken explanation that builds in intensity until you reach a new peak: "that we keep his commandments." A brief downhill slide ("his commandments are not burdensome") and then another peak: "Everyone begotten . . . is this faith of ours."

You achieve more emphasis by asking "Who?" and telling us, than by simply telling

APRIL 7, 1991

SECOND SUNDAY OF EASTER

LECTIONARY #45

READING I Acts 4:32–35

Short reading = slow reading.

A reading from the *Acts* of the *Apostles* ▪ ▪ ▪

You're happy to recall this.

"His": "Their" is more inclusive, here and below. Your tone says: "Hard as it may be to believe."

"Even harder *to believe, but true."*

The community of *believers* were of *one heart* and one *mind.* ▪ ▪ *None* of them ever claimed *anything* as his own; ▪ ▪ rather ▪ *everything* was held in *common.* ▪ ▪ With *power* ▪ the apostles bore *witness* to the resurrection of the Lord Jesus, ▪ and great *respect* was paid to them *all;* ▪ ▪ nor was there anyone *needy* among them, ▪ for all who owned *property* or *houses* ▪ *sold* them ▪ and *donated* the proceeds. ▪ ▪ They used to *lay* them at the *feet* of the apostles ▪ to be *distributed* to everyone according to his *need.* ▪ ▪ ▪

Again joy and admiration.

READING II 1 John 5:1–6

First of six consecutive weeks we read from 1 John.

A reading from the first letter of *John* ▪ ▪ ▪

Central idea. Boldly.

Everyone who *believes* that Jesus is the *Christ* ▪
has been begotten by *God.* ▪ ▪ ▪

Softer. Almost an aside.

Now, ▪ everyone who *loves* the *father* ▪
loves the *child* he has begotten. ▪ ▪ ▪

Growing stronger.

We can be *sure* that we love God's *children* ▪
when we love *God* ▪
and *do* what he has *commanded.* ▪ ▪ ▪
The *love* of God consists in *this:* ▪ ▪

A new peak of energy.

that we *keep* his *commandments*— ▪ ▪
and his commandments are not *burdensome.* ▪ ▪

Strong again. With pride in "this faith of ours."

Everyone begotten of God *conquers* the *world,* ▪
and the *power* that has conquered the world ▪
is this *faith* of ours. ▪ ▪ ▪

Like a politician. Emphatically.

Who, then, ▪ is conqueror of the world? ▪ ▪
The one who *believes* that Jesus is the

Slowly and deliberately.

Son of *God.* ▪ ▪
Jesus Christ it is ▪ who came through *water*

Allusion to Christ's baptism and his death and resurrection.

and *blood*— ▪ ▪
not in water *only,* ▪
but in water *and* in blood. ▪ ▪ ▪

You testify, too!

It is the *Spirit* who *testifies* to this, ▪ ▪
and the *Spirit* is *truth.* ▪ ▪ ▪

GOSPEL John 20:19–31

A reading from the holy *gospel* according to *John* ▪ ▪ ▪

Fear turns into joy.

On the *evening* of that *first* day of the week, ▪ even though the disciples had *locked* the doors of the place where they were ▪ for *fear* of the *Jews,* ▪ ▪ *Jesus* came and *stood* before them. ▪ ▪ ▪ *"Peace* be with you," ▪ he said. ▪ ▪ When he had *said* this, ▪ he showed them his *hands* and his *side.* ▪ ▪ At the *sight* of the Lord the disciples *rejoiced.* ▪ ▪ ▪ *"Peace* be with you," ▪ he said again. ▪ ▪

Stress "Jesus," whose entrance surprises them.

Joyous tone.

"As the *Father* has sent *me,* ▪
so *I* send *you."* ▪ ▪ ▪

"Breathed" sounds like it means.

Then he *breathed* on them and said: ▪ ▪

With authority. "Men's" can be dropped or you could substitute "others."

"Receive the *Holy Spirit.* ▪ ▪
If you *forgive* men's *sins,* ▪
they are *forgiven* them; ▪ ▪
if you hold them *bound,* ▪
they are *held* bound." ▪ ▪ ▪

Shift in mood.

It happened that *one* of the Twelve, ▪ *Thomas* ▪ (the name means *"Twin"*), ▪ was *absent* when Jesus came. ▪ ▪ The other disciples kept *telling* him: ▪ ▪ "We have *seen* the Lord!" ▪ ▪ His *answer* was, ▪ ▪ "I'll *never* believe it ▪ without *probing* the *nail-prints* in his hands, ▪ without putting my *finger* in the nail-marks ▪ and my *hand* into his *side."* ▪ ▪ ▪

Disciples are ecstatic. Thomas is almost argumentative.

Faster pace.

A *week* later, ▪ the disciples were once *more* in the room, ▪ and *this* time Thomas *was* with them. ▪ ▪ *Despite* the locked doors, ▪ Jesus *came* and stood before them. ▪ ▪ *"Peace* be with you" ▪ he said; ▪ ▪ then, ▪ to Thomas: ▪ ▪ "Take your *finger* and *examine* my hands. ▪ ▪ Put your *hand* into my *side.* ▪ ▪ Do not *persist* in your unbelief, ▪ but *believe!"* ▪ ▪ Thomas said in *response,* ▪ ▪ "My *Lord* and my *God!"* ▪ ▪ Jesus *then* said to him: ▪ ▪

"Then, to Thomas": Emphasize the shift.

Not angry, but firm.

"My Lord . . . God": Build.

"You became a believer because you *saw* me. ▪ ▪
Blest are they who have *not* seen and
have believed." ▪ ▪ ▪

Climax. Look at assembly.

Narrator is believer.

Jesus performed many *other* signs as well— ▪ ▪ signs not *recorded* here— ▪ in the presence of his *disciples.* ▪ ▪ But *these* have been recorded to help you *believe* that Jesus *is* the Messiah, ▪ the *Son* of *God,* ▪ so that through this *faith* ▪ you may have *life* in his name. ▪ ▪ ▪

Ritardando: "Jesus is . . . God." Then a little faster to the end.

us (e.g., "Who's going to be the next President of the United States? Why, the senator from . . ."). John uses this device to say who is "conqueror of the world." The last sentence is a statement of faith in Jesus who was baptized by John ("water") and gave his life ("blood"). The "Spirit" *testifies* to that. Today with your words, as each day with your life, you must also.

GOSPEL This rich gospel story requires several rapid mood shifts as well as character definition and strong emotional involvement. The narrator is a concerned and proselytizing teacher whose purpose in sharing this story is the building-up of the listeners' faith. Carry that awareness throughout the reading. The historical reality of the resurrection is another goal of this passage; that's obvious from the start. The opening sentence embodies two distinct moods: "Though the disciples had locked their doors" (fear rules their hearts) "on the first day . . . Jesus came" (Amazing thing! Cause for rejoicing!). Start with joy, interject the fear, and finish with the amazing news.

What Jesus says and does addresses the apostles' anxiety and their eroded faith. He speaks "Peace" and shows his "hands and side." Repeat the peace greeting, stretching the word "Peace" and pausing briefly after it. Stretching the word means you bridge the pause by holding the "s" sound at the end of peace and then fall onto the "be with you." Move slowly through Jesus' dialogue. He does three things: commissions them to go in his name, imparts the Holy Spirit and empowers them to forgive sins. Give each action its own tone and coloring.

A major shift in mood occurs, beginning with "it happened that one of the Twelve. . . ." The sacred moment is shattered as Thomas and the others argue about the Lord's appearance. Make the disciples as insistently firm as Thomas is skeptical. As you narrate Jesus' second appearance, take on the persona of a disciple who is glad to be vindicated before Thomas. Jesus' peace greeting takes less time here. Keep the momentum going between Thomas and Jesus. "Thomas said in response" should be spoken very slowly as if Thomas were slowly bending, then suddenly falling to his knees. Thomas's words come from his deepest being. He addresses Jesus with two different titles. Build your intensity from the first to the second. For Thomas and for us, Jesus' reply constitutes the climax of the reading.

The last paragraph is a denouement that lets you express concern for the condition of *our* faith while confessing who Jesus is in *your* life.

READING I Peter pulls no punches about the past: "You handed over" God's servant Jesus even though "Pilate was ready to release him"; you "disowned the Holy and Just one" and preferred a murderer. You killed the "Author of life." He says all that and somehow he still has an audience. The overtones of forgiveness are evident long before Peter mentions the possibility of sins being wiped away.

In the second paragraph he presents mitigating factors: "ignorance" and "fulfillment" of prophecy. We're past that now, we hear him saying, so here's the next step: "Reform your lives!" There's urgency and paternal love in that exhortation. "Turn to God," he urges (is he remembering now the courtyard and the crowing cock?), "that your sins may be wiped away." So joyous an offer of generous forgiveness could only come from someone who experienced it firsthand. Like Peter—or, perhaps, *yourself.*

READING II "Ladies and gentlemen . . ." "My fellow Americans . . ." "My little ones . . ." Three salutations, and each could be addressed to the same audience. Yet how different the mood each one establishes, how distinctive the speaker-audience relationship each implies! John expresses clearly how he feels about those to whom he pens his letter: they are his spiritual children, children for whom he cares with pastoral love and great devotion.

The hard thing about which John writes is sin. I am trying to keep you from sinning, he says. But we do sin, and Jesus is the remedy for our sins and "those of the whole world." John takes another step. When we accept Christ's gift of forgiveness, we enter relationship with him that is validated by the way we live our lives. To say we "know" Christ, that is, to claim we are "intimate" with him, without living the way he asks us, is a charade. In fact it's a lie. You're not afraid to use such a strong word because you're speaking out of love and trying to steer us clear of danger. Speak with total confidence trusting the truth of everything you say. The last sentence reassures us you are not judging or condemning but calling us to an ideal you think we can attain.

APRIL 14, 1991

THIRD SUNDAY OF EASTER

LECTIONARY #48

READING I Acts 3:13–15, 17–19

Become Peter: bold and authoritive.

A reading from the *Acts* of the *Apostles* ▪ ▪ ▪

"Ancestors" is more inclusive.

Titles usually reserved for God.

Pained regret.

Leave no room for doubt.

Peter said to the people: ▪ ▪ "The 'God of *Abraham,* ▪ of *Isaac,* ▪ and of *Jacob,* ▪ ▪ the God of our *fathers,*' ▪ has *glorified* his Servant *Jesus,* ▪ whom *you* handed over and *disowned* in Pilate's presence ▪ when Pilate was ready to *release* him. ▪ ▪ You disowned the *Holy* and *Just One* ▪ and preferred *instead* ▪ to be granted the release of a *murderer.* ▪ ▪ You put to *death* ▪ the *Author* of *life.* ▪ ▪ But God *raised* him from the dead, ▪ and *we* are his *witnesses.* ▪ ▪ ▪

"Brothers and sisters" is more inclusive. Not a whining excuse, just a fact.

Speak out of his experience.

"Yet I *know,* my brothers, ▪ that you acted out of *ignorance,* ▪ just as your *leaders* did. ▪ ▪ God has brought to *fulfillment* by this means ▪ what he *announced* long ago through all the *prophets:* ▪ ▪ that his Messiah would *suffer.* ▪ ▪ Therefore, ▪ *reform* your lives! ▪ ▪ *Turn* to *God,* ▪ that your *sins* may be *wiped* away!" ▪ ▪ ▪

READING II 1 John 2:1–5

Second of six consecutive weeks we read from 1 John.

A reading from the first letter of *John* ▪ ▪ ▪

Your greeting sets the tone. Use eye contact.

Offer hope and forgiveness.

My *little* ones, ▪
I am writing this to keep you from *sin.* ▪ ▪
But if anyone *should* sin, ▪
we have, ▪ in the presence of the *Father,* ▪
Jesus Christ, ▪ an *intercessor* who is *just.* ▪ ▪
He is an *offering* for our sins, ▪
and not for *our* sins *only,* ▪
but for those of the *whole world.* ▪ ▪ ▪

Present this as logical.

"One" is more inclusive.

"Is a liar": eye contact.

Plurals are more inclusive: "But those who keep. . . have . . . in them." Ritardando: "made perfect in [them.]"

The way we can be *sure* of our knowledge of him ▪
is to *keep* his *commandments.* ▪ ▪
The man who *claims,* ▪ ▪ "I have *known* him," ▪
without keeping his commandments, ▪
is a *liar;* ▪ ▪ in such a one there is *no* truth. ▪ ▪
But whoever *keeps* his word ▪
truly has the *love* of *God* made *perfect* in him. ▪ ▪ ▪

GOSPEL Luke 24:35–48

A reading from the holy *gospel* according to *Luke* ▪ ▪ ▪

With hearts still burning from Emmaus.

The *disciples* recounted what had *happened* on the *road* to *Emmaus* ▪ and how they had come to know *Jesus* ▪ in the *breaking* of *bread.* ▪ ▪ ▪

"Peace": Calm and gentle.

Panic contrasts with Jesus' greeting.

Frustration.

While they were still *speaking* about all this, ▪ he *himself* stood in their midst [and *said* to them, "*Peace* to you."] ▪ ▪ In their *panic* and *fright* ▪ they thought they were seeing a *ghost.* ▪ ▪ He *said* to them, ▪ ▪ "Why are you *disturbed?* ▪ ▪ *Why* do such *ideas* cross your mind? ▪ ▪ Look at my *hands* and my *feet;* ▪ ▪ it is really *I.* ▪ ▪ *Touch* me, ▪ and see that a *ghost* does not have *flesh* and *bones* as *I* do." ▪ ▪ [As he *said* this ▪ he *showed* them his hands and feet.] ▪ ▪ They were still *incredulous* for sheer *joy* and *wonder,* ▪ so he said to them, ▪ ▪ "Have you anything here to *eat?*" ▪ ▪ They gave him a piece of cooked *fish,* ▪ which he *took* and *ate* in their presence. ▪ ▪ Then he *said* to them, ▪ ▪ "*Recall* those words I spoke to you when I was *still* with you: ▪ ▪ everything *written* about me in the *law* of *Moses* and the *prophets* and *psalms* ▪ had to be *fulfilled.*" ▪ ▪ Then he *opened* their minds to the *understanding* of the Scriptures. ▪ ▪ ▪

Their "joy" keeps them from seeing clearly.

A final "proof."

Urging them to remember, but he must still explain.

Teaching tone.

Eye contact. Commissioning the disciples, and your assembly.

He *said* to them: ▪ ▪ "Thus it is *likewise* written that the Messiah must *suffer* ▪ and *rise* from the dead on the *third* day. ▪ ▪ In *his* name, ▪ *penance* for the *remission* of sins is to be *preached* to all the *nations,* ▪ beginning at *Jerusalem.* ▪ ▪ *You* are *witnesses* of this." ▪ ▪ ▪

GOSPEL Sometimes a person expresses the need to see miracles, some unmistakable sign, in order to believe. Then, when you point to one, no matter what the kind, he or she may say, "Oh, that's not a miracle!" Hearing claims of the resurrection, most of the disciples insisted on proof—seeing Jesus, touching his hands and side—so Jesus appears and what happens? Panic, fright, doubts, troubled hearts and talk of seeing a ghost. Even when they touch his hands and feet they remain "incredulous," and Jesus consumes a fish to convince them he's real.

The reading opens with the excitement of the two disciples who recognized Jesus in the "breaking of the bread." Immediately, the energy doubles as all the disciples panic. Imagine any group thinking they're seeing a ghost and you'll know the intensity with which to color the scene. Jesus tries to reason, needing to speak loudly to be heard over their panicked outcries. There must be the same frustration in his voice now that he earlier expressed on the road to Emmaus: "What little sense you have! How slow you are to believe." Is there reluctance in his offer to eat the fish, to play the magician forced to say, "Look. Nothing up my sleeve! See? No tricks, it's really me." When he says "recall those words . . . ," he's not asking them *if* they remember, he's *ordering* them to remember what he had spoken to them before. Then, as with Cleopas and friend, he opens up "the Scriptures."

Jesus lectures at the end reminding them his death and resurrection fulfilled scripture. Now the evidence they've *seen* must enable them to become witnesses to the resurrection for those of us who believe but have *not* seen.

READING I Keep two things in mind: One, Peter and John are under arrest for healing a cripple and teaching about Jesus; two, Luke tells us Peter is "filled with the Holy Spirit" as he launches into this speech. Imagine *yourself* under arrest for doing a "good deed," a good deed that manifested the *power* of God working in *you*. Suddenly the fire of the Spirit starts burning within you as you begin to explain your actions. Would you not become a volcano, bold and fearless, proudly admitting what you've done and in whose name you were proud to do it? Peter, remember, has a history of his own: abandoning Jesus in the garden, his threefold denial, the fearful waiting in the upper room. What a relief to be done with all that! What freedom comes from a willingness to risk everything for Jesus!

Peter stands before hostile leaders and elders but uses the opportunity to defend and proselytize. This amazing miracle of healing has occurred precisely because of the man they crucified, he insists. His confidence is growing, boldness replacing all earlier fears, and though he speaks of "power," he refers to "that name" with great and gentle reverence. Convince the leaders that "the stone rejected" by them has been thrown back into their lives. Then, without malice, with direct eye contact and with real desire to share even with them the good news of Jesus, tell them "*no* other name in the *whole world*" can save.

READING II This passage is read on All Saints Day. Read that commentary for further discussion. On that day when we celebrate the heroes of our past, John's words fill us with the hope that we can *all* be saints. In light of today's first reading and of the tenuous situation in which the disciples found themselves in the early days after the resurrection, we sense a more sober message: "The world does not recognize us"! Yet John's message makes it possible to live in a hostile world. Forget what the world sees or doesn't see, he tells us. The greater danger is *our* not seeing "what we are" and what God has done for us.

Note the "Dearly beloved" greeting in the middle. It signals intimate and *intense* communication. John is working hard to communicate his message. Right now, in the midst

APRIL 21, 1991

FOURTH SUNDAY OF EASTER

LECTIONARY #51

READING I Acts 4:8–12

A reading from the *Acts* of the *Apostles* ▪▪▪

A spirit of boldness. "If we have to explain, then, by gosh, we will!"

Peter, ▪ *filled* with the *Holy Spirit,* ▪ spoke up: ▪▪ *"Leaders* of the people! ▪▪ *Elders!* ▪▪ If we must *answer* today ▪ for a *good deed* done to a *cripple* ▪ and explain *how* he was restored to health, ▪▪ then *you* and all the people of Israel must *realize* ▪ that it was done in the *name* of *Jesus Christ* ▪ the *Nazorean*

No malice. Less stress on "whom you crucified" than on "whom God raised."

whom you *crucified* ▪ and whom God *raised* from the *dead.* ▪▪ In the *power* of that name ▪ this man *stands* before you *perfectly* sound. ▪▪ This *Jesus* ▪ is 'the stone *rejected* by *you* the *builders* ▪ which has

Total conviction.

become the *cornerstone.'* ▪▪ There is no *salvation* in *anyone* else, ▪ for there is no other *name* in the *whole*

"Men" can be "humanity" or "all people."

world given to men ▪ by which we are to be *saved."* ▪▪▪

READING II 1 John 3:1–2

Third of six consecutive weeks we read from 1 John. Short reading = slow reading.

A reading from the first letter of *John* ▪▪▪

See what *love* the Father has *bestowed* on us ▪

With genuine delight.

in letting us be called *children* of *God!* ▪▪▪

Insistent.

Yet *that* is what we *are.* ▪▪
The *reason* the world does not *recognize* us ▪

An explanation.

is that it *never* recognized the *Son.* ▪▪▪
Dearly *beloved,* ▪
we *are* God's children *now;* ▪▪

Offering hope in the face of trial.

what we shall *later* be ▪ has not *yet*
come to light. ▪▪

Don't relax; maintain insistent tone.

We know that when it *comes* to light ▪
we shall be like *him,* ▪

Look at the asssembly with joy.

for we shall *see* him ▪ as he *is.* ▪▪▪

GOSPEL John 10:11–18

Eye contact is essential in this passage.

A reading from the holy *gospel* according to *John* ▪ ▪ ▪

Jesus said: ▪ ▪
"I am the *good shepherd;* ▪ ▪
the good shepherd lays down his *life*
for the sheep. ▪ ▪

Look at individual faces.

The *hired hand,* ▪ who is *no* shepherd ▪
nor *owner* of the sheep, ▪
catches sight of the *wolf* coming ▪

Discrediting the hired hand.

and *runs* away, ▪ *leaving* the sheep
to be *snatched* and *scattered* by the wolf. ▪ ▪
That is because he works for *pay;* ▪ ▪

Pause.

he has no *concern* for the sheep. ▪ ▪ ▪

Earnest and intense.

"I am the *good* shepherd. ▪ ▪
I *know* my sheep ▪

Knowing is loving.

and my sheep know *me* ▪
in the *same* way that the *Father* knows *me* ▪
and *I* know the *Father;* ▪ ▪
for *these* sheep I will give my *life.* ▪ ▪

Still intense but less personal.

I have *other* sheep
that do not *belong* to this fold. ▪ ▪

"Them" = gentiles.

I must lead *them,* too, ▪
and they shall *hear* my voice. ▪ ▪

A sense that it must be so.

There shall be *one* flock then, ▪ *one* shepherd. ▪ ▪ ▪
The Father *loves* me for this: ▪ ▪

Not boasting or argumentative.

that I *lay* down my life ▪
to take it *up* again. ▪ ▪
No one *takes* it from me; ▪ ▪

Create a sense that he's saying more about his love for us than anything about himself.

I lay it down *freely.* ▪ ▪
I have *power* to lay it down, ▪
and I have *power* to take it *up* again. ▪ ▪
This *command* ▪ I received from my *Father.*" ▪ ▪ ▪

of whatever trials or fears or setbacks we experience, right now we belong to God. That's great news! And later, even better news: We shall see God and we shall be *like* God. You don't have a lot of words with which to make an impact; so today, more than ever, your face, intensity and desire to communicate will be the medium that is also the message.

GOSPEL A play or film director staging this scene for a production of the life of Jesus would need to work closely with the actor playing Christ. If he were having difficulty speaking these words with convincing sincerity, the director might utilize a rehearsal technique to put the actor in touch with the intimate relationship between Jesus and his friends that this scene exhibits. Drawing the actors playing the apostles into a tight circle and placing Jesus in the center, the director might ask that actor to speak Jesus' lines while moving from person to person, looking into the eyes of one, grasping the shoulder of another, cradling the face of a third in his hands as he spoke with his own face only inches away. The hushed tones such physical proximity would elicit might appropriately convey the laying-down-his-life kind of love Jesus professes for his friends.

Your task is to persuade us that Jesus desires with us the same closeness he had with his disciples. This discourse could easily sound like courtroom-style progressive reasoning: I do this, the hired hand does that; my motives are these, his are those, etc. Clearly, that's not the spirit of his words. There's a rhythm here that builds to and climaxes in Christ's assertion that "for these sheep I will give my life." See him in that circle of friends above, longing to enlarge it with the sheep "that do not belong to this fold." There's an urgency in his voice regarding them; "I *must* lead them, too."

In the closing lines he expresses the freedom with which he sacrifices himself for them. They've never seen such radical love, and he knows he must help them understand it. Jesus is who he is, the Good Shepherd, precisely because he *freely* lays down his life. Why must they understand this? Because if they don't, they won't understand how loved they are.

READING I A former enemy can't become a trusted friend overnight; fear and disbelief are sooner served than the bread of hospitality. Saul needs introductions and explanations. Barnabas knows Saul's history and understands the fears it generates, and he lobbies hard on Saul's behalf and persuades the apostles of Saul's conversion. From "on his journey" to "at Damascus" can be spoken as an indirect quote in Barnabas's voice.

Once accepted, Saul wastes no time proving his sincerity, "expressing himself quite openly" about Jesus. The response of the "Greek-speaking Jews" is stated so matter-of-factly it creates a comic effect. The tone (filled with tension) you employ in speaking of how he "debated with them" will alert us that their response was hostile. Your tone shifts to concern as you tell of the efforts of "the brothers" to escort him quickly and safely out of town.

Though we've just heard of efforts to kill Saul, everywhere, we're told, "the church was at peace." Luke is writing of an internal peace, the kind that prevails despite external circumstances. It was a peace of the heart, the place where "fear of the Lord" is born and where the "consolation" of the Spirit is experienced.

READING II John XXIII said, "The heart follows the mind almost as often as the mind follows the heart." Sometimes our hearts don't *feel* what our minds know; sometimes, if we cling to what we know, the feeling *will* follow. The author of the First Letter of John tells us, with profound intimacy, that we can be sure, "no matter what our consciences [hearts] charge us with," that we abide in God. God has the knowledge ("all is known to him") that can overwhelm our doubting hearts.

The word "beloved" continues John's tone of encouragement. Sometimes it's those among us who try the hardest that question most our goodness and God's closeness. John leaves no room for doubt: "We can be *sure* that God is with us." And in case you're wondering why, I'll be glad to tell you, he says. List the reasons ("keeping his commandments . . . doing what is pleasing") as a way of bolstering the confidence of your listeners.

Don't suddenly change your tone for the last two sentences. True, John is teaching, but he speaks as if to only one beloved

APRIL 28, 1991

FIFTH SUNDAY OF EASTER

LECTIONARY #54

READING I Acts 9:26–31

A reading from the *Acts* of the *Apostles* ▪ ▪ ▪

Speak with understanding of situation and motives.

When *Saul* arrived back in *Jerusalem* ▪ he *tried* to join the *disciples* there; ▪ ▪ but it turned out ▪ that they were all *afraid* of him. ▪ ▪ They even *refused* to believe that he *was* a disciple. ▪ ▪ Then *Barnabas*

Barnabas taking charge, lobbying for Saul.

took him in charge ▪ and *introduced* him to the *apostles.* ▪ ▪ He *explained* to them how on his

"On his journey . . . Damascus" = indirect quote (see Key).

journey ▪ Saul had *seen* the Lord, ▪ who had *conversed* with him, ▪ and how Saul had been speaking out *fearlessly* in the name of Jesus ▪ at *Damascus.* ▪ ▪ Saul *stayed on* with them, ▪ moving

Suggest Saul's confidence.

freely about Jerusalem ▪ and *expressing* himself quite *openly* in the name of the Lord. ▪ ▪ He *even*

Signal that the debate was not friendly.

addressed the *Greek*-speaking Jews and *debated* with them. ▪ ▪ They ▪ for *their* part ▪ responded by trying to *kill* him. ▪ ▪ When the brothers *learned* of this, ▪ some of them took him down to *Caesarea* ▪ and sent

For his safety.

him off to *Tarsus.* ▪ ▪ ▪

With pride and gratitude.

Meanwhile ▪ throughout all *Judea,* ▪ *Galilee* and *Samaria* ▪ the church was at *peace.* ▪ ▪ It was being *built* up ▪ and was making steady *progress* in the *fear* of the Lord; ▪ ▪ at the *same* time ▪ it enjoyed the

Ritardando.

increased *consolation* of the *Holy Spirit.* ▪ ▪ ▪

READING II 1 John 3:18–24

Fourth of six consecutive weeks we read from 1 John
Eye contact. Very sincere.

A reading from the first letter of *John* ▪ ▪ ▪

Little *children,* ▪
let us love in *deed* and in *truth* ▪

Honest and direct.

and not merely *talk* about it. ▪ ▪
This is our way of knowing we are *committed*
to the truth ▪
and are at *peace* before him ▪
no matter what our *consciences* may
charge us with; ▪ ▪
for God is *greater* than our hearts ▪
and *all* is known to him. ▪ ▪ ▪

Eye contact.

Beloved, ▪
if our consciences have *nothing*
to charge us with, ▪

Persuasive. Assuring.

we can be *sure* that God is with us ▪
and that we will *receive* at his hands ▪
whatever we ask. ▪▪

Answer the "Why" with new energy.

Why? ▪▪ Because we are keeping
his *commandments* ▪
and doing what is *pleasing* in his sight. ▪▪
His commandment is *this:* ▪▪

Speak to each person.

we are to *believe* in the name of his *Son,* ▪
Jesus Christ, ▪▪
and are to *love* one another as he
commanded us. ▪▪
Those who *keep* his commandments *remain*
in him ▪
and he in *them.* ▪▪

The Spirit is a great gift.

and this is how we *know* that he remains in us: ▪▪
from the *Spirit* that he gave us. ▪▪▪

GOSPEL John 15:1–8

A reading from the holy *gospel* according to *John* ▪▪▪

Focus on Jesus and Father as vine and vinegrower.

Jesus said to his *disciples:* ▪▪
"I am the *true vine* ▪
and my Father is the *vinegrower.* ▪▪

Negative image.

He *prunes* away
every *barren* branch, ▪
but the *fruitful* ones

Positive image.

he trims *clean* ▪
to *increase* their *yield.* ▪▪▪

Praise and encouragement.

You are clean *already,* ▪
thanks to the *word* I have spoken to you. ▪▪
Live on in *me,* ▪ as *I* do in *you.* ▪▪

"You need me."

No more than a *branch* can bear fruit of itself
apart from the *vine,* ▪
can *you* bear fruit
apart from *me.* ▪▪

Focus is on Jesus and disciples as vine and branches. "He" and "him" can be "those" and "them."

I am the *vine,* ▪ *you* are the *branches.* ▪▪
He who lives in *me* ▪ and *I* in *him,* ▪
will produce *abundantly,* ▪

Insistent yet loving.

for *apart* from me ▪ you can do *nothing.* ▪▪

"A man" can be "A person."

A man who does *not* live in me ▪
is like a *withered,* ▪ *rejected* branch, ▪

A painful image even for Jesus.

picked up to be thrown in the *fire* ▪
and *burnt.* ▪▪▪
If you *live* in me, ▪
and my *words* stay *part* of you, ▪

Inspire confidence.

you may ask what you *will*— ▪▪
it will be *done* for you. ▪▪

Pride and joy.

My Father has been *glorified*
in your bearing *much* fruit ▪

Ritardando.

and becoming my *disciples."* ▪▪▪

person. He wants us to know that the Christian life is not always lonely or fraught with fear. When we keep the commandments God *is* with us, and we know that truth "from the Spirit that he gave us." Now just make sure the assembly knows that the message was meant for them.

GOSPEL When do we resort to poetry? When the mind alone can't apprehend a thought or feeling, and our *senses* are required to help us see and hear and smell the slippery concept that eludes our reason. Jesus knows that images give shape and sound and fragrance to the radical ideas he has come to share. And so he wraps his thoughts in images of vines and branches, fruit and fire and decay.

Writers write in thought units, and readers must share one unit at a time. Frequently sentences contain more than one thought, so a reader must use his or her voice to distinguish one from another. The layout of today's text can help you with that. Almost every line introduces a new thought unit; this does not mean you pause at the end of each line, but it does mean you look for and *lift out* the new information each line offers.

This poetry characterizes the union between Jesus and his disciples: They are one plant, each living in and through the other. Branches can't yield fruit "apart from the vine," yet a vine has no fruit without its branches. There is here both praise ("You are clean already") and caution ("every barren branch" will be pruned, "a withered branch" will be "thrown in the fire and burnt"). These images require a tone of warning.

In the final sentences Jesus reinforces the theme of oneness, informing his disciples of the blessings and benefits that union will yield. There are bells ringing in his final exclamation of joy and praise. We share this joy as disciples when we bear "much fruit."

READING I (See the commentary for the second reading on January 13 for additional material on this text, as well as LTP's book, *When Christians Speak About Jews.*)

Look at the personalities: Peter—elder, apostle, Jew; Cornelius—centurion, devout and God-fearing, gentile. These unlikely companions have been brought together by divine intervention (each has had a vision) and neither knows exactly why. Cornelius greets Peter as if he were an angel who has just stepped out of his vision. Peter responds with warm humility, sensing immediately something is different about this Roman.

The meaning of his vision suddenly dawns on Peter; as he "begins to see," he can't help feeling foolish for his earlier prejudice that denied membership in the church to non-Jews. In his voice we hear acknowledgment that he has made a mistake.

In the midst of his realization fireworks go off; the Spirit descends "upon all who were listening," much to the surprise of everyone in the room. This sort of thing wasn't supposed to happen to gentiles, hence the surprise of the "circumcised believers" who look around them in amazement.

The slowness with which Peter perceived the truth is not evidence that there's molasses in his veins. He plucks the opportunity offered by this moment. Turning to his companions, he asks a rhetorical question, whose answer these events have made too plain. Then, in his rightful role as leader, he gives the "orders that they be baptized." And then, quite naturally, he stays with them to celebrate.

READING II If there's a difficulty with John's simple poetry, it's with the earnestness and directness of his style. "Beloved . . ." —even in our families we sometimes find it hard to speak so lovingly, looking at a person squarely in the eye. Now we have to speak that way to a large group of people. Choose the person in your life you could most comfortably address so openly and fix that person's face in your mind's eye as you begin.

"Let us love . . . because love is of God." Whoever has no love has never known God, for God *is* love. This is a mild imperative followed by uncomplicated statements. Then an explanation: "God's love was revealed . . . *this* way." God took the initiative, you insist, by sending "his only Son." The closing summary is not the summation of a logical argument, it's the last verse of a love song, sung with joy and gratitude that can't be faked and that becomes contagious.

MAY 5, 1991

SIXTH SUNDAY OF EASTER

LECTIONARY #57

READING I Acts 10:25–26, 34–35, 44–48

A reading from the *Acts* of the *Apostles* ▪▪▪

Cornelius is awed by Peter.

Peter entered the house of *Cornelius* ▪ who *met* him, ▪ dropped to his *knees* before Peter ▪ and bowed *low.* ▪▪ Peter said as he *helped* him to his feet, ▪▪ *"Get* up! ▪▪ I am *only* a man *myself."* ▪▪▪

No reproach. Warm humility.

Almost embarrassed by how wrong he has been.

"The Man" can be "the person."

Peter proceeded to *address* ▪ [the *relatives* and *friends* of Cornelius] in *these* words: ▪▪ "I begin to see how *true* it is ▪ that *God* shows *no partiality.* ▪▪ Rather, ▪ the man of *any* nation who *fears* God ▪ and acts *uprightly* ▪▪ is *acceptable* to him." ▪▪▪

Faster pace. Excitement and awe.

They can hardly believe it.

Answer is obvious, but pause to wait for it.

Suggest the lingering joy.

Peter had not *finished* these words when the *Holy* Spirit descended upon *all* who were listening to Peter's message. ▪▪ The *circumcised* believers who had *accompanied* Peter ▪ were *surprised* that the *gift* of the Holy Spirit should have been poured out on the *Gentiles* also, ▪ whom they could hear *speaking* in *tongues* and *glorifying God.* ▪▪ Peter put the *question* at that point: ▪▪ "What can *stop* these people who have *received* the Holy Spirit, ▪ even as *we* have, ▪ from being *baptized* with *water?*" ▪▪ So he gave *orders* ▪ that they be *baptized* in the name of *Jesus Christ.* ▪▪ After this was *done,* ▪ they asked him to *stay* with them for a few days. ▪▪▪

READING II 1 John 4:7–10

Fifth of six consecutive weeks we read from 1 John.

A reading from the first letter of *John* ▪▪▪

Look at the whole assembly as the beloved.

Beloved, ▪
let us *love* one another ▪
because love is of *God;* ▪▪
everyone who *loves* is *begotten* of God ▪
and has *knowledge* of God. ▪▪

"The man" can be "the one" or "anyone."

The man *without* love has known *nothing* of God, ▪
for God *is* love. ▪▪▪

Slowly. Stress each word.

God's love was *revealed* in our midst in *this* way: ▪▪

God is the initiator.

he sent his only *Son* to the world ▪
that we might have *life* through him. ▪▪

Slowly. Contrast "we" and "God" and "God" and "us."

Love, then, ▪ consists in *this:* ▪▪
not that *we* have loved *God,* ▪
but that *he* has loved *us* ▪▪

End of a love song, not a courtroom argument. Ritardando: "as an offering for our sins."

and has sent his *Son* ▪ as an *offering*
for our *sins.* ▪▪▪

GOSPEL John 15:9–17

A reading from the holy *gospel* according to *John* ▪▪▪

Eye contact.

Jesus said to his *disciples:* ▪▪
"As the *Father* has loved *me,* ▪
so *I* have loved *you.* ▪▪
Live on in my love. ▪▪

The challenge starts.

You *will* live in my love
if you *keep* my *commandments,* ▪
even as *I* have kept my *Father's* commandments, ▪
and live in *his* love. ▪▪
All this I *tell* you

Sincere concern.

that my *joy* may be *yours* ▪
and *your* joy may be *complete.* ▪▪▪

The challenge continues.

This is my commandment: ▪▪
love *one another*
as *I* have loved *you.* ▪▪

Slowly, aware of what you're asking.

There is no *greater* love than *this:* ▪▪
to lay down one's *life* for one's *friends.* ▪▪
You are my friends
if you do what I *command* you. ▪▪

Contrast "slaves" and "friends." Suggest what "friends" implies.

I no longer speak of you as *slaves,* ▪
for a slave does not *know* what his
master is about. ▪▪
Instead, ▪ I call you *friends* ▪
since I have made *known* to you *all*
that I heard from my *Father.* ▪▪

Stress Christ's initiative.

It was not *you* who chose *me,* ▪
it was *I* who chose *you*

Another challenge.

to go forth and bear *fruit.* ▪▪
Your fruit must *endure,*
so that *all* you ask the Father in *my name* ▪
he will *give* you. ▪▪▪

A command to love.

The *command* I give you is *this:* ▪▪

Ritardando: "that you love one another."

that you *love* one another." ▪▪▪

GOSPEL If Hallmark were to make a greeting card of this gospel they'd bring in an editor with sharp scissors. Into the wastebasket would go all references to commandments, laying down one's life and bearing fruit. Remaining would be Jesus' references to love, joy and friendship. As you can see, the wastebasket would get more than the card.

Jesus mixes challenge with his protestations of love that are divinely earnest: "As the Father has loved me, so I have loved you. . . . All this I tell you that my joy may be yours and your joy may be complete. . . . I no longer speak of you as slaves, . . . I call you friends." Don't dilute the intimacy. Speak with emphasis. Reveal Christ's great love for his friends as if he were speaking to one disciple at a time. In scripture, Moses, Joshua and David were called "servants" or "slaves of God"; only Abraham was called a "friend of God." Jesus gives the apostles a title reserved until then for just one person. It's a special moment for this group that your tone should reverence and reflect.

But with the love, Jesus offers the challenge: Keep my commandments. Love one another. Lay down your life. Go forth and bear fruit. Your fruit must endure. *Love one another.* He can demand so much because he loves so much. He asks no more than he's already given or is about to give: This is a discourse that John situates at the Last Supper, remember, and Jesus knows what lies ahead.

As in the second reading where we heard of God's initiative, Jesus speaks of *choosing* us and, he says, it's a choice with a purpose. Through the ages Jesus' voice comes to your church (and through *you*) today to encourage his "friends" *there* to bear much fruit, to speak assurances of his love and to request —no—to "command" that they "love *one another.*"

READING I Luke addresses the Book of Acts to a person of some apparent political importance. Consequently his attitude is subdued, polished and professional in the style of a news commentator. He becomes more storyteller than newscaster when he relates one of Jesus' post-resurrection appearances. Pause after "he told them" and speak *all* that follows with the voice of Jesus trying to fill the apostles with hope.

The apostles respond with a sincere question that betrays their lack of understanding. Ask it with energy, expecting a "yes" from Jesus. Jesus responds patiently, still the teacher, making yet another earnest attempt to help them understand.

Follow Jesus' exhortation with a fast-paced narration: "No sooner had he said this. . . ." Stop abruptly and become an apostle watching the scene. Then, slowly, tell us how he was "lifted up."

Maintain the hushed mood of wide-eyed awe as you start the third paragraph: "they were still . . . heavens." Raise your volume and tempo on "when two men . . . white" as if their sudden appearance jolted the apostles out of their reverie. Make the angels strong and energetic, not saccharine or scolding. "This Jesus . . . *will return,*" they say. There's work to do in the meantime. So let's get to it! They said it to the apostles; you say it to the rest of us.

READING II There is tremendous energy here and a flow that builds and crescendos steadily and rhythmically to a climactic finish. One could get carried away by the rhythm and create a powerful effect just with the sound of the reading. But the author's ideas are complex and important. Therefore you must go slow to do the job right. Slow does not mean without energy, without enthusiasm. Without those elements the reading has no meaning. Move through the reading phrase-by-phrase, paying close attention to the pauses and giving the stresses extra punch. Build one thought upon another, like blocks, to create the structure of the author's thesis. Note how in this last sentence each phrase is like a stone in a stream. You must skip from one to another to get across. But remember, skipping is fun and requires both energy and care.

Let your intensity increase in line nine as you compare what God can do for us with what God has done for Christ. As you describe the glory that was given to Christ, make us feel that we, too, can receive that glory.

The last sentence is the climax of the reading. We can almost hear trumpets in

MAY 9, 1991

THE ASCENSION OF THE LORD

LECTIONARY #59

READING I Acts 1:1–11

The beginning of the *Acts* of the *Apostles* ▪ ▪ ▪

As a news commentator: smooth and straightforward.

In my *first* account, ▪ Theophilus, ▪ I dealt with all that Jesus *did* and *taught* until the day he was *taken* up to heaven, ▪ having first *instructed* the apostles he had chosen through the Holy Spirit. ▪ ▪ In the time *after* his suffering ▪ he *showed* them in many *convincing* ways that he was *alive,* ▪ *appearing* to them over the course of *forty days* ▪ and *speaking* to them about the *reign* of *God.* ▪ ▪ On *one* occasion when he *met* with them, ▪ he told them ▪ *not* to *leave* Jerusalem: ▪ ▪ *"Wait,* rather, ▪ for the *fulfillment* of my Father's promise, ▪ of which you have *heard* me speak. ▪ ▪ *John* baptized with *water,* ▪ but within a few days ▪ *you* will be baptized with the *Holy Spirit."* ▪ ▪

Now, tell a story.

"Not . . . Jerusalem": Spoken as Jesus.

Contrast "now" and "exact."

While they were with him they *asked,* ▪ ▪ "Lord, ▪ are you going to *restore* the rule to Israel *now?"* ▪ ▪ His answer was: ▪ ▪ "The *exact* time it is not *yours* to know. ▪ ▪ The Father has *reserved* that to *himself.* ▪ ▪ You will receive *power* when the *Holy Spirit* comes down on you; ▪ ▪ then you are to be my *witnesses* in Jerusalem, ▪ throughout *Judea* ▪ and *Samaria,* ▪ yes, ▪ even to the *ends* of the *earth."* ▪ ▪ No *sooner* had he said this ▪ ▪ than he was *lifted* up before their eyes in a *cloud* ▪ which *took* him from their sight. ▪ ▪

Inspire them and build from "Jerusalem" to "ends of the earth."

"No sooner . . . their sight": Fast . . . pause . . . then slow.

Entrance of "two men" breaks the mood. Use pauses to convey their mystification at this sudden appearance.

They were still *gazing* up into the heavens ▪ when two men ▪ dressed in white ▪ stood beside them. ▪ ▪ "Men of Galilee," ▪ they said, ▪ ▪ *"why* do you stand here looking up at the *skies?* ▪ ▪ This *Jesus* who has been *taken* from you ▪ *will return,* ▪ just as you saw him go up into the heavens." ▪ ▪ ▪

READING II Ephesians 1:17–23

A reading from the letter of *Paul* ▪ to the *Ephesians* ▪ ▪ ▪

Remember, you're praying.

May the *God* of our Lord Jesus Christ, ▪ the *Father* of *glory,* ▪ grant you a spirit of *wisdom* and *insight* to know him *clearly.* ▪ ▪ May he *enlighten* your innermost vision ▪ that you may know the *great hope* to which he has called you, ▪ the *wealth* of his glorious *heritage* to be distributed among the members of the church, ▪ ▪ and the immeasurable *scope* of his *power* ▪ in *us* who *believe.* ▪ ▪ It is like the *strength* he showed in *raising* Christ from the *dead* ▪ and *seating* him at his right hand in heaven, ▪ *high* above every *principality,* ▪ *power,* ▪ *virtue,* ▪ and *domination,* ▪ and every *name* that can be given ▪ in *this* age ▪ or the age to *come.* ▪ ▪

Skip, with energy, from one phrase to another.

Visualize and paint four different images. Don't speed up.

Joyous climax.

He has put *all things* under Christ's feet ▪ and has made him ▪ thus *exalted,* ▪ *head* of the *church,* ▪ which is his *body:* ▪ ▪ the *fullness* of him who *fills* the universe in *all its parts.* ▪ ▪ ▪

Ritardando: "in . . . parts."

GOSPEL Mark 16:15–20

The *conclusion* of the holy *gospel* according to *Mark* ▪ ▪ ▪

"Eleven" reminds us of Judas's betrayal.

[*Jesus* appeared to the *Eleven* and] said to them: ▪ ▪ "Go into the *whole* world ▪ and proclaim the *good news* to all creation. ▪ ▪ The man who *believes* in it and accepts *baptism* ▪ will be *saved;* ▪ ▪ the man who *refuses* to believe in it ▪ will be *condemned.* ▪ ▪ *Signs* like these will *accompany* those who have professed their *faith:* ▪ ▪ they will use my *name* to expel *demons,* ▪ they will speak entirely *new* languages, ▪ they will be able to handle *serpents,* ▪ they will be able to drink *deadly* poison without *harm,* ▪ ▪ and the *sick* upon whom they *lay* their *hands* will *recover."* ▪ ▪ ▪ Then, ▪ *after* speaking to them, ▪ the Lord Jesus was taken up into *heaven* ▪ and took his seat at God's *right* hand. ▪ ▪ The Eleven went *forth* and preached *everywhere.* ▪ ▪ The Lord *continued* to work with them throughout ▪ and *confirm* the message through the *signs* which accompanied them. ▪ ▪ ▪

Encouraging them. Giving them confidence. "The one" is more inclusive. Contrasting attitudes on "saved" and "condemned."

Moderately fast. Build intensity on each "they will . . ."

"And the sick . . .": slower. Look at assembly, not up to heaven.

Slowly.

those lines. Look to all parts of your assembly as you earnestly proclaim that we, the church, are Christ's body filled at every moment with his presence and love.

GOSPEL Jesus appears to "the Eleven," is then "taken up into heaven," but somehow still continues "to work with them." This is not really the story of a farewell but of an unbroken relationship that transcends time and space. Jesus is as present at the end of this episode as at the beginning—and in equally marvelous ways. His sudden and miraculous appearance among the disciples is matched by the "signs" that Jesus works *with* them after the ascension. There is no sense of sadness or of letting go. Instead there is hope and promise.

But not immediately. The opening is subtly bittersweet. The reference to "the Eleven" reminds us that though the good news will be proclaimed to "all creation," some "will be saved" and, sadly, some will not. The memory of Judas can teach us how to speak Jesus' prophecy: with a longing for all to share the life of the kingdom and great regret over those who "refuse" and "will be condemned." The momentary sadness is brushed aside by consideration of the "signs" that will accompany those who believe. "And the sick upon whom they lay their hands . . ." breaks the pattern of the four-fold "They will . . ." That break appropriately throws the focus to that final promise, because it is the most important. Build your intensity through the first four assertions, then slow down and visualize the hand of a caring minister on the head of an ailing believer.

"Then" breaks the bedside mood, not to shift our focus up where Jesus is taken "into heaven" but to focus us *out* where Jesus goes forth disguised, as on the Emmaus road, to continue the "work" of the kingdom and to "confirm" the message of salvation—only now his disguise has him looking remarkably like you and me.

READING I They must have been exciting times—and scary, too. Jesus is gone and this band of twelve, reduced to eleven, must now direct the course of the movement born in the wake of his resurrection and ascension. What to do? Where to start? Because Jesus initiated a new Israel and because Israel had twelve tribes, what's needed first is to return the number of elders to a full complement of twelve.

Peter rises in the assembly, his role as leader readily acknowledged, reviews the events that led Judas to be deleted from their number and suggests what the next step might be. Give Peter a confident voice, the kind that would inspire a small band of believers to feel they've been left in good hands. He quotes scripture with authority, then stipulates the criteria by which a replacement for Judas should be sought. Stress the importance of his being someone who knew and walked with the Lord from the beginning of his ministry, and someone who was witness to the resurrection.

Name the nominees respecting the upright, holy men they must have been (note, the "loser" gets the bigger mention). "Then they prayed." Pause to let that simple sentence sink in. Their prayer was not simple lip service. Pray the prayer slowly; you might even memorize it and pray with your eyes closed.

Their radical trust in God is demonstrated by their drawing "lots." Use the prayer and this narration to create suspense about the outcome, then speak the name "Matthias," suggesting a good man was chosen to be the new apostle.

MAY 12, 1991

SEVENTH SUNDAY OF EASTER

LECTIONARY #61

READING I Acts 1:15–17, 20–26

A reading from the *Acts* of the *Apostles* ▪ ▪ ▪

Speak of Peter with reverence.

"Brothers and sisters" is more inclusive.

Don't rush. Show Peter is in charge.

In those days *Peter* stood up in the midst of the brothers— ▪ there must have been a *hundred* and twenty gathered together. ▪ ▪ *"Brothers,"* ▪ he said, ▪ ▪ "the saying in *Scripture* ▪ uttered *long* ago by the Holy Spirit through the mouth of *David* ▪ ▪ was destined to be *fulfilled* ▪ in *Judas,* ▪ the one that *guided* those who *arrested* Jesus. ▪ ▪ He was one of our *number* ▪ and he had been given a *share* in this ministry of ours. ▪ ▪ ▪

He's setting up his suggestion.

"It is written in the Book of *Psalms,* ▪ ▪
'May *another* take his office.' ▪ ▪

From when Jesus was baptized till he ascended.

"It is entirely *fitting,* therefore, ▪ that one of those who was of our *company* while the Lord Jesus moved *among* us, ▪ from the *baptism* of John until the day he was *taken up* from us, ▪ should be named as *witness* with us to his *resurrection."* ▪ ▪ At that they nominated *two,* ▪ *Joseph* ▪ (called *Barsabbas,* ▪ also known as *Justus*) ▪ and *Matthias.* ▪ ▪ Then they *prayed:* ▪ ▪ "O *Lord,* ▪ you read the *hearts* of men. ▪ ▪ Make *known* to us *which* of these two you *choose* for this *apostolic* ministry, ▪ replacing *Judas,* ▪ who *deserted* the cause ▪ and went the way he was *destined* to go." ▪ ▪ They then drew *lots* between the two men. ▪ ▪ The choice fell to *Matthias,* ▪ who was *added* to the eleven *apostles.* ▪ ▪ ▪

Both are good candidates.

"All people" is more inclusive.

Create suspense.

Your tone says: "A great choice."

READING II 1 John 4:11–16

A reading from the first letter of *John* ▪ ▪ ▪

Eye contact. Sincere.

Beloved, ▪ ▪
if God has *loved* us so, ▪
we must have the *same* love for *one another.* ▪ ▪
No one has ever *seen* God. ▪ ▪
Yet if we *love* one another ▪
God *dwells* in us, ▪
and his love is brought to *perfection* in us. ▪ ▪
The way we *know* we remain in him ▪
and he in *us* ▪
is that he has given us of his *Spirit.* ▪ ▪

Show the assembly you believe this.

We have seen for *ourselves,* ▪ and can *testify,* ▪
that the Father has sent the Son as *savior*
of the world. ▪ ▪

Speak for yourself as well.

Ask us to acknowledge Jesus. "God dwells . . . " can be: "God dwells in that person, and that person dwells in God."

When anyone *acknowledges* that Jesus is
the *Son* of *God,* ▪
God *dwells* in him ▪
and *he* in *God.* ▪ ▪
We have come to *know* and to *believe* ▪
in the *love* God has for us. ▪ ▪

Use plurals to be more inclusive: i.e., "those" and "them."

God *is* love, ▪
and he who *abides* in love ▪
abides in *God,* ▪
and *God* in *him.* ▪ ▪ ▪

Quietly, let your face announce this is joyous news. Ritardando: "and God in [them]."

READING II The best popular songs contain a "hook"—a line or phrase so catchy that it hooks you because you can't forget it. We wait for the hook in a song because it's our favorite part, and we can always tell where the hook is because it's usually the only part of a song people remember well enough to sing. John's hook is the last sentence of this passage: "God is love. . . ." How we love those words! Most of us can quote them verbatim because we have heard them many, many times. But have we really heard the rest of the passage? Probably not as well and not as often. Today let's make sure the entire passage gets heard, not just the hook.

To generate the appeal of the first sentence you'll need sustained eye contact. Energetically make the point that when we "love one another" God is present among us. Share directly and simply that the Spirit is our assurance of remaining one with God.

Notice that throughout you speak as "we," including yourself in everything you say. Have you seen for *your*self and can *you* testify that God sent Jesus to be our savior? The conviction in your voice must clearly say, "Yes." Speak "When anyone acknowledges . . ." not as a statement but as a request for that acknowledgment in the hearts of all your listeners.

Now the hook: It's best to speak it simply and softly. When something is absolutely, undeniably true we don't need to shout it. Like deep waters, deep truths are still and make little noise. It's essential, however, that your face broadcasts clearly that "love" is a place *worth* abiding because there will God be found.

GOSPEL This is a unique passage in that it consists entirely of a prayer of Jesus, and the entire prayer is for his disciples—and for us. Don't tell us *about* Jesus' prayer; *become* Jesus at prayer and let the assembly be the disciples in whose presence you pray. Because you're speaking to God rather than teaching the disciples, there's no need to sound preachy or didactic, not even on statements like "they do not belong to the world. . . ." Your voice is soft and sincere and full of intense concern for these friends from whom you'll soon be parted. You don't want eye contact with your assembly today; instead you want to look upward or outward over their heads.

Jesus prays that the disciples be protected by the "name" of God, a semitism representing the divine life itself. He also prays that their unity duplicate the unity between Father and Son, and he recalls the solicitous care he lavished on them so that "not one of them was lost." Now, however, he will be leaving these friends, and he worries that they will suffer at the hands of "the world" and "the evil one." While he longs for them to share his "joy," he knows and fears that hardships are inevitable.

A rush of thoughts and feelings seems to flood Jesus' mind and heart as he prays. Allow yourself to feel each one, then share them one at a time as you would in your own prayers to God.

GOSPEL John 17:11–19

A reading from the holy *gospel* according to *John* ▪ ▪ ▪

Raise your eyes to heaven.

Jesus looked up to *heaven* and prayed: ▪ ▪
"O Father most *holy,* ▪ ▪
protect them with your *name* which you have *given* me, ▪ ▪
[that they may be *one,* ▪ even as *we* are one.] ▪ ▪
As *long* as I was *with* them, ▪

Stating the fact that he cared for them.

I *guarded* them with your name which you gave me. ▪ ▪
I kept careful *watch,* ▪
and not *one* of them was *lost,* ▪

With regret, remember Judas.

none but him who was *destined* to be lost— ▪
in fulfillment of *Scripture.* ▪ ▪

Urgency because of his imminent departure.

Now, however, ▪ I come to *you;* ▪ ▪
I say all this while I am *still* in the world ▪
that they may share my *joy* ▪ *completely.* ▪ ▪
I gave them your *word,* ▪
and the world has *hated* them for it; ▪ ▪
they do not *belong* to the world, ▪
[any more than *I* belong to the world.] ▪ ▪
I do not ask you to take them *out* of the world, ▪

Jesus prays protection from the devil.

but to *guard* them from the *evil* one. ▪ ▪
They are not *of* the world, ▪
any more than *I* am of the world. ▪ ▪

"Consecrate them" means "make them holy."

Consecrate them by means of *truth*— ▪ ▪
'Your *word* is truth.' ▪ ▪
As you have sent *me* into the world, ▪

Reference to his voluntary death.

so I have sent *them* into the world; ▪ ▪
I consecrate myself for *their* sakes now, ▪

Slowly.

that *they* may be consecrated in *truth.*" ▪ ▪ ▪

MAY 18, 1991

PENTECOST VIGIL

LECTIONARY #63

READING I Genesis 11:1–9

A reading from the book of *Genesis* ▪ ▪ ▪

As narrator you know this innocent age is lost. "People" is more inclusive.

At that time ▪ the *whole world* spoke the *same* language, ▪ using the *same words.* ▪ ▪ While men were *migrating* in the east, ▪ they came upon a *valley* in the land of Shinar and *settled* there. ▪ ▪ They *said* to one another, ▪ ▪ *"Come,* ▪ let us mold *bricks* and *harden* them with *fire."* ▪ ▪ They used *bricks* for *stone,* ▪ and *bitumen* for *mortar.* ▪ ▪ *Then* they said, ▪ ▪ *"Come,* ▪ let us *build* ourselves a *city* ▪ and a *tower* with its top in the *sky,* ▪ and so make a *name* for ourselves; ▪ ▪ *otherwise* ▪ we shall be *scattered all* over the *earth."* ▪ ▪ ▪

"Bitumen" = a mineral that burns like asphalt.

"A tower": a stepped, pyramid-like structure whose top was seen as a meeting place between gods and people. "Make a name": arrogance.

The *Lord* came down to *see* the city and the tower that the men had *built.* ▪ ▪ Then the Lord *said:* ▪ ▪ "If *now,* ▪ while they are *one* people, ▪ all speaking the *same language,* ▪ they have *started* to do *this,* ▪ *nothing* will *later stop* them from doing *whatever* they *presume* to do. ▪ ▪ Let us then *go* down ▪ and there *confuse* their language, ▪ so that one will *not understand* what another *says."* ▪ ▪ Thus the Lord *scattered* them ▪ from there ▪ *all* over the *earth,* ▪ and they *stopped* building the city. ▪ ▪ That is why it was called *Babel,* ▪ because *there* ▪ the Lord *confused* the speech of *all* the *world.* ▪ ▪ It was from *that* place that he *scattered* them *all over the* earth. ▪ ▪ ▪

"People" is more inclusive.

Narrator is aware these are consequences of human choices. With regret.

Ritardando: "all . . . earth."

Or:

READING I Exodus 19:3–8, 16–20

A reading from the book of *Exodus* ▪ ▪ ▪

No ordinary climb!

Moses ▪ went up the mountain to *God.* ▪ ▪ Then the Lord *called* to him and said, ▪ ▪ *"Thus* shall you say to the house of Jacob; ▪ *tell* the Israelites: ▪ ▪ You have seen for *yourselves* how I treated the Egyptians ▪ and how I *bore* you up on *eagle wings* ▪ and brought you *here* to *myself.* ▪ ▪ Therefore, ▪ if you *hearken* to my voice ▪ and *keep* my covenant, ▪ ▪ you shall be

God is awesome, proud yet tender.

READING I *(Genesis 11:1–9)* The feast of Pentecost celebrates the undoing of what we see in this passage: the alienation of nation from nation.

You must lay the groundwork for the Pentecost marvel by building clear images of a human pride seeking to "make a name" for itself, of human efforts to be like the gods. Create a tension between the narrator reporting this event of final alienation and the Babel builders who dive arrogantly into their project, blind to the potential consequences. The narrator speaks with nostalgia of "that [good] time" when all spoke the *"same* language, using the *same words."* But a haughty tone infects lines like "a tower . . . in the sky" and "make a name for ourselves," reflecting the intent of the speakers to thwart God's designs. The Lord responds to this affront with human reasoning and emotions. The narrator returns, summarizing what happened to the world as a result of pride. The final sentence is delivered slowly and with a tone of regret.

READING I *(Exodus 19:3–8, 16–20)* Pentecost is a many-layered celebration. Part of our cause for celebrating this day is the covenant of Sinai. All Eastertime has been a trek up the slopes of Sinai in anticipation of this event.

As narrator, suggest that Moses' trip up the mountain was no ordinary hike, but an encounter of great consequence. God speaks with awesome authority, not holding back but taking pride in the way divine solicitude delivered Israel from slavery. Take time with the "kingdom of priests" and "holy nation" images, somewhat softening your volume without losing the grandeur of the delivery. The narration that precedes the people's response should create a sense of excitement and urgency. The people answer simply and soberly. Speak slowly and with conviction: "Everything . . . *we will do."*

Now the fireworks! The "But" that begins the second sentence of paragraph two should tell you how impressive a show it must have been. Despite "peals of thunder" (build) "and lightning" and (another build) "a very loud trumpet blast" (probably a metaphor for the howling wind), despite all that, Moses led the people to the mountain anyway. Paint those images slowly, one brushstroke at a time.

READING I *(Ezekiel 37:1–14)* Your two major challenges are: to bring these fantastic images to life and to use the repetitions that border on refrains to lead us deeper into the ideas and intensify our experience of the images. The temptation will be strong to say "I will *open* your graves and you shall *rise* from them" with energy and conviction, but then to repeat the promise just two lines later in a flat and lifeless way as if the words were a nuisance to be gotten around as quickly as possible. Earlier in the reading the same temptation occurs when the voice of God repeats "I will bring spirit into you, that you may come to life." To treat these lines as redundancies is to miss the style, indeed the power, of this literature. When a musical phrase is repeated, the familiarity brings pleasure and etches the song into our memories. Let these repetitions do the same.

Pay close attention to the stresses, noting how it is possible to achieve variety through the stressing of different words in the repeated phrases. The voice of God, urgent and strong, tells Ezekiel what to prophesy. After heeding that insistent voice he watches in fear-filled wonder as the amazing events take shape.

Remember, there is no narrator in this scripture. It is spoken entirely by Ezekiel. It must be told with his voice and his emotional involvement using every word of the text to achieve the necessary effect. To do any less would be a disservice to the prophet.

my *special possession,* ▪ *dearer* to me than all other people, ▪ though *all* the earth is mine. ▪▪ You shall be to me a kingdom of *priests,* ▪ a *holy* nation. ▪▪ *That* ▪ is what you must *tell* the Israelites." ▪▪

Excitement and urgency.

So Moses went and summoned the *elders* of the people. ▪▪ When he set before them *all* that the Lord had *ordered* him to tell them, ▪ the people all *answered* together, ▪ *"Everything* the Lord has said, ▪ *we will do."* ▪▪▪

The theophany begins.

On the morning of the *third* day there were peals of *thunder* ▪ and *lightning,* ▪ and a *heavy cloud* over the mountain, ▪▪ and a very loud *trumpet* blast, ▪ so that all the people in the camp *trembled.* ▪▪ But

Moses and people overcome fear and go out.

Moses ▪ *led* the people out of the camp ▪ to *meet* God, ▪ and they stationed themselves at the *foot* of the mountain. ▪▪

Slowly.

"Smoke" and "fire" are manifestations of God.

Mount Sinai was all wrapped in *smoke,* ▪ for the Lord came down upon it in *fire.* ▪▪ The smoke *rose* from it as though from a *furnace,* ▪

"Trembled" and "violently" sound like they mean.

and the whole mountain *trembled violently.* ▪▪ The trumpet blast grew *louder* and *louder,* while Moses

Experience the excitement yourself.

was *speaking* ▪ and God answering him with *thunder.* ▪▪▪

When the Lord *came down* to the top of Mount Sinai, ▪ he *summoned* Moses to the *top* of the *mountain.* ▪▪▪

Or:

READING I Ezekiel 37:1–14

A reading from the book of the prophet ▪ *Ezekiel* ▪▪▪

This does not happen every day.

The hand of the *Lord* came upon me, ▪▪ and he *led* me out in the *spirit* of the Lord ▪ and *set* me in the *center* of the plain ▪ which was now *filled* with

See the "bones" before you speak.

bones. ▪▪ He made me *walk* among them in *every* direction ▪ so that I saw how *many* they were on the

Marvel at what you see.

surface of the plain. ▪▪ How *dry* they were! ▪▪ He asked me: ▪▪ Son of man, ▪▪ can these bones *come* to *life?* ▪▪ "Lord God," I answered, ▪▪ "you *alone*

"Prophesy" = "prŏf-e-sigh."

know that." ▪▪ Then he said to me: ▪▪ *Prophesy* over these bones, ▪ and *say* to them: ▪▪ Dry bones, ▪▪ *hear* the word of the Lord! ▪▪ *Thus* says the Lord God to

God is promising *these things.*

these bones: ▪▪ *See!* ▪▪ I will bring *spirit* into you, ▪ that you may *come* to *life.* ▪▪ I will put *sinews* upon you, ▪ make *flesh* grow over you, ▪ cover you with *skin,* ▪ and put *spirit* in *you* ▪ so that you may come to life ▪ and *know* that I am the Lord. ▪▪▪ I

Stress "as . . . told" *to emphasize prophet's compliance.*

prophesied *as* I had been *told,* ▪▪ and even as I was prophesying ▪ I heard a *noise;* ▪▪ it was a *rattling* ▪

An incredible sight!

Stress "prophesy" both times, building the second.

Voice of God.

He sees but he can't believe it!

Voice of God.

God speaking as Israel.

God's voice: making promises.

God wants promises taken seriously.

Final, emphatic assurance.

as the bones *came together,* ▪ *bone* joining *bone.* ▪ ▪ I *saw* the sinews and the flesh come upon them, ▪ and the skin *cover* them, ▪ but there was *no spirit* in them. ▪ ▪ Then he said to me: ▪ ▪ *Prophesy* to the spirit, ▪ *prophesy,* son of man, ▪ and *say* to the spirit: ▪ ▪ Thus says the *Lord God:* ▪ ▪ From the four winds *come,* O spirit, ▪ and *breathe* into these slain ▪ that they may *come* to *life.* ▪ ▪ I prophesied *as he told me,* ▪ ▪ and the spirit *came* into them; ▪ ▪ they came *alive* ▪ and *stood* upright ▪ a *vast* army. ▪ ▪ *Then* he said to me: ▪ ▪ Son of man, ▪ ▪ these bones are the *whole house* of *Israel.* ▪ ▪ They have been saying, ▪ "Our bones are *dried* up, ▪ our hope is *lost,* ▪ and we are *cut* off." ▪ ▪ Therefore, ▪ *prophesy* ▪ and *say* to them: ▪ ▪ Thus *says* the Lord God: ▪ ▪ O my *people,* ▪ ▪ I will *open* your graves ▪ and have you *rise* from them, ▪ ▪ and bring you *back* to the land of Israel. ▪ ▪ Then you shall *know* that I am the Lord, ▪ ▪ when I open your *graves* and have you *rise* from them, ▪ O my people! ▪ ▪ I *will* put my spirit in you ▪ that you may *live,* ▪ ▪ and I *will* settle you upon your land; ▪ ▪ thus you shall know that *I am* the Lord. ▪ ▪ I have *promised,* ▪ ▪ and I *will do it,* ▪ says the Lord. ▪ ▪ ▪

Or:

READING I Joel 3:1–5

This reading requires that you expend much energy.

"People" is more inclusive.

Get excited about all this!

Dropping "men" is more inclusive: "your old shall dream . . ."

Awesome and foreboding.

See the images. Make each distinct.

Comforting. You must believe this to convince others.

A reading from the book of the prophet ▪ *Joel* ▪ ▪ ▪

Thus says the Lord: ▪ ▪
I will *pour* out
my *spirit* upon *all* mankind. ▪ ▪
Your *sons* and *daughters* shall *prophesy,* ▪ ▪
your *old* men shall *dream dreams,* ▪
your *young* men shall see *visions;* ▪ ▪
Even upon the *servants* and the *handmaids,* ▪
in those days, ▪ I will *pour* out my *spirit.* ▪ ▪
And I will work *wonders* in the *heavens* and
on the *earth,* ▪ ▪
blood, ▪ ▪ *fire,* ▪ ▪ and *columns* of *smoke;* ▪ ▪
The *sun* will be turned to *darkness,* ▪
and the *moon* to *blood,* ▪
At the *coming* of the *Day* of the *Lord,* ▪
the *great* ▪ and *terrible* day. ▪ ▪ ▪
Then *everyone* shall be *rescued*
who *calls* on the name of the *Lord;* ▪ ▪
For on Mount Zion there shall be a *remnant,* ▪
as the Lord has *said,* ▪
And in *Jerusalem* ▪ *survivors* ▪
whom the *Lord* shall *call.* ▪ ▪ ▪

READING I *(Joel 3:1–5)* Joel is a prophet and prophets work hard. So do those who proclaim their words. Note the number of words marked for stress in the passage. You may wish to vary the words to emphasize, but you'll not be able to avoid use of great energy to communicate Joel's message. Except for the first line, the entire passage is spoken in the person of "the Lord." You are speaking for Joel who is speaking for God. There is tremendous urgency in these lines, as if the message must be shared before it's too late. There are vivid and powerful images of youngsters prophesying, old people dreaming, young people seeing visions; of "blood, fire, and columns of smoke"; of a darkened sun and a bloody moon; all on that "great and terrible day." Those last two adjectives describe the mood of the entire reading. You are speaking of great, remarkable events. But they are also "terrible": not awful as much as awesome, like an eclipse—too fascinating not to look at, but blinding if you linger too long.

A significant pause after "terrible day" allows a transition to the message of comfort that follows. After alarming your audience with the reality of the threat, you must console them with reassurance that some "shall be rescued," that a remnant of survivors will hear the call of the Lord and find in God's arms a place of refuge.

READING II Sometimes Paul theologizes; other times he teaches, chides, exhorts or argues. And then there are times when he, like Jesus, shares the word of life. For many, the eighth chapter of Romans is such a time. That is why this passage must be proclaimed from the depth of our own experience of patient endurance and expectant hope. Find your own inward groaning, the part of you that awaits "redemption." You have known what it means to hope for what cannot be seen. Drawing on that experience will make convincing your declaration that "hope is *not* hope if its object is seen."

If you have experienced the Spirit's help and found your helplessness and wordlessness turned to prayer, then you can convincingly speak these words of solace and encouragement. The last sentence must be spoken directly to the assembly. Become the searcher of hearts and speak comfort, speak assurance to individual eyes and faces who may need to hear that the Spirit understands their inner pain and groanings.

GOSPEL The "last . . . day of the festival" is used here by the designers of the lectionary as a reference to Pentecost, the last day of our 50-day Easter festival. However, in the gospel, this "last day" refers to the final day of *Sukkot*, the Jewish Feast of Booths or Tabernacles. Besides commemorating Israel's wanderings in the desert, the Feast of Tabernacles also celebrates with much thanksgiving the gathering of the harvest. For seven days of the feast, water was brought into the city from the Pool of Siloam where it was diverted from the Spring of Gihon. Prayers were then offered for plentiful rain. In the midst of this prayer and rejoicing Jesus "cried out." "If anyone thirsts, let him [that one] come to *me,*" he says. Picture him speaking in the midst of the celebrating crowds and needing to speak boldly if he is to be heard.

As always with a short reading, you must read slowly and carefully or it will be over before your listeners have tuned in. Because of grammatical ambiguity as to whether Christ or the believer is the source of the "living water" (this translation chooses Christ, the Revised NAB opts for the believer), let your stress in the final line of Christ's address go to *"rivers* of *living* water," the central image of the passage. The parenthetical statement that ends the passage will sound anticlimactic coming after Christ's prophetic words. You can mitigate that effect. Read as though taking the assembly into your confidence, sharing special information with them in a hushed tone that is not flat, but charged with intensity.

READING II Romans 8:22–27

A reading from the letter of *Paul* ▪
to the *Romans* ▪ ▪ ▪

"Groans" and "agony" sound like they mean.

Build. Invest yourself.

A straightforward declaration, then urgent, insistent! "He" can be changed to "one."

Slowly.

We know that all creation *groans* ▪ and is in *agony* even until *now.* ▪ ▪ Not only *that,* ▪ but we ourselves, ▪ although we have the *Spirit* as first fruits, ▪ groan *inwardly* while we await the *redemption* of our *bodies.* ▪ ▪ In *hope* we were saved. ▪ ▪ But hope is *not* hope if its object is *seen;* ▪ ▪ how is it possible for one to *hope* for what he *sees?* ▪ ▪ And hoping for what we *cannot* see ▪ means *awaiting* it with *patient* endurance. ▪ ▪

Understanding and compassion. No reproach.

Rev. NAB uses "itself" rather than "himself."

Great sincerity.

The Spirit too ▪ *helps* us in our weakness, ▪ ▪ for we do not know how to *pray* as we *ought;* ▪ ▪ but the Spirit *himself* makes *intercession* for us ▪ with groanings which *cannot* be expressed in *speech.* ▪ ▪ He who *searches hearts* ▪ *knows* what the Spirit means, ▪ ▪ for the Spirit *intercedes* for the saints ▪ ▪ as God himself *wills.* ▪ ▪ ▪

GOSPEL John 7:37–39

A reading from the holy *gospel* according
to *John* ▪ ▪ ▪

"On . . . festival" = slowly and quietly. Then increase volume and pace. Remember: Jesus "cried out."

"That one" is more inclusive.

On the *last* and *greatest* day of the festival, ▪ Jesus *stood* up and *cried* out: ▪ ▪

"If anyone *thirsts,* ▪ let him come to *me;* ▪ ▪
Let him *drink* ▪ who *believes* in me. ▪ ▪
Scripture has it: ▪ ▪
'From within him *rivers* of *living* water
shall flow.'" ▪ ▪

Hushed but intense. Don't throw it away.

(Here he was referring to the *Spirit,* ▪ whom those that came to believe in him were to *receive.* ▪ ▪ There was, of course, ▪ ▪ *no* Spirit as *yet,* ▪ ▪ since Jesus had not yet been *glorified.)* ▪ ▪ ▪

MAY 19, 1991

PENTECOST

LECTIONARY #64

READING I Acts 2:1–11

A reading from the *Acts* of the *Apostles* ▪ ▪ ▪

Calm before the storm. Slowly.

When the day of Pentecost *came* ▪ it found the brethren *gathered* in one place. ▪ ▪ *Suddenly* ▪ from up in the *sky* ▪ there came a *noise* like a *strong,* ▪ *driving wind* ▪ which was heard *all* through the house where they were seated. ▪ ▪ *Tongues* ▪ as of *fire* appeared ▪ which *parted* ▪ and came to rest on *each* of them. ▪ ▪ All were *filled* with the *Holy Spirit.* ▪ ▪ They began to *express* themselves in *foreign* tongues ▪ and make *bold* proclamation as the Spirit *prompted* them. ▪ ▪ ▪

Louder. Create excitement but don't rush.

Stretch "filled." Reverently and slowly, then faster on "They began . . ."

Staying in Jerusalem at the time ▪ were devout Jews of *every nation* under heaven. ▪ ▪ These *heard* the sound, ▪ and *assembled* in a *large* crowd. ▪ ▪ They were much *confused* ▪ because *each* one *heard* these men speaking his *own* language. ▪ ▪ The whole occurrence *astonished* them. ▪ ▪ They asked in *utter amazement,* ▪ ▪ "Are not *all* of these men who are speaking *Galileans?* ▪ ▪ *How* is it ▪ that each of us hears them in his *native tongue?* ▪ ▪ We are *Parthians,* ▪ *Medes,* ▪ and *Elamites.* ▪ ▪ We *live* in Mesopotamia, Judea, and Cappadocia, ▪ ▪ *Pontus,* ▪ the province of Asia, Phrygia and Pamphylia, ▪ ▪ *Egypt,* ▪ and the regions of Libya around Cyrene. ▪ ▪ There are even visitors from *Rome—* ▪ all *Jews,* ▪ or those who have come *over* to Judaism; ▪ ▪ Cretans and Arabs *too.* ▪ ▪ Yet *each* of us hears them speaking in his *own* tongue ▪ about the *marvels* God has *accomplished."* ▪ ▪ ▪

Questions and confusion.

This is unbelievable! "People" and "their" are more inclusive.

"Are not all . . .": looking around. "People" is more inclusive than "men." "Our own" is more inclusive than "his."

"Pontus": new build.

"Egypt": new build.

"Our" is more inclusive than "his." Ritardando: "marvels . . . accomplished."

READING I A hotel full of vacationers is awakened suddenly by a clanging bell, a howling alarm or voices frantic and shrill. The confused guests gather at a central area where all fearfully inquire about the origin of the strange noises that roused them.

The second paragraph of this reading describes just such a scene—huddled visitors to Jerusalem being pulled into the streets by some thunderous phenomenon. The thunder, however, occurs in the previous paragraph. It is there that you will need to create enough excitement to make the second paragraph plausible.

Start setting the scene with the opening narration. Let your tone color and slow your pace from "Pentecost came" to the end of the sentence. Alert your listeners that the storm is coming. "Suddenly" sounds like it means. Take a pause to create suspense and then create the "noise" of the "strong, driving wind." Note the "s" and "n" sounds that, when held and stretched, can produce the very sound you are describing. Picture each scene before you speak and describe it with all its attendant emotions.

Now you're ready to describe the effects of all this excitement on the populace of Jerusalem. Let the words "confused," "astonished" and "utter amazement" suggest the feeling you want to create. The phenomenon of tongues multiplies both the confusion and the questions. The listing of the places of origin should add to the overall animation if you vary the pacing and start new builds (renewing your energy) on "Pontus" and on "Egypt." Confusion turns to awe-filled joy in the last sentence as the speaker shifts from observer to believer and makes a statement of faith about the *"marvels* God has accomplished."

READING II Crises are the times when differences melt and our oneness, intensified by the predicament we share, is spotlighted. Think of a time when neighbors were forced by some natural calamity into the same boat. Whether the cause was flood, fire, snowfall or earthquake, seeing people ignore differences and respond instead to a common need is not easily forgotten. Draw on such a memory in preparing to proclaim Paul's message. The only difference here is that what opens our eyes to the oneness and shuts them to the differences is not a disaster but the fountain of the Spirit.

The opening proclamation is strong, uncompromising and full of authority. Then retain the authority but soften the boldness and address a community that has splintered into factions, reminding them that the one who sends the gift of the Spirit is the same Lord who insists on their oneness in that Spirit.

The passage is so beautifully balanced and logical that you could easily forget to undergird it with emotional intensity. If you remember that Paul cares passionately for the Corinthians and greatly desires harmony among them, and if you recall the need for harmony among the factions that arise within your own parish, you'll communicate both the logic and the passion of this intense passage.

GOSPEL The first line of this passage tells us much. We're not immediately told the disciples' reaction to Jesus' sudden appearance. We might imagine them standing frozen, mouths agape. Jesus speaks first: "Peace. . . ."

Still no reaction from the disciples. Jesus initiates again. Let your narration of Jesus showing his hands and side reflect concern and the desire of Jesus' heart that his friends be calmed and reassured.

Finally the disciples respond. "At the sight of the Lord . . . the disciples rejoiced." (Note: Stress "Lord" rather than "sight," for the disciples rejoiced not at the sight but at the *certainty* that it was the Lord.) Then Jesus quietly repeats his greeting. His next line might be more comfort than commission: As the Father made possible for me to do what I had to do, so I will make possible for you to do what you must do.

The next line is critical. Make "breathed" sound like it means, stretching the word, then pausing before "and said." The "breathing" should mark a transition. Reassured by the Lord's presence, the disciples can receive their commission to go forth binding and loosing in the name of Jesus and the power of the Holy Spirit.

READING II 1 Corinthians 12:3–7, 12–13

A reading from the first letter of *Paul* ▪ to the *Corinthians* ▪ ▪ ▪

Slowly. Bold and with authority.

No one can say: ▪ *"Jesus is Lord,"* ▪ ▪ *except* in the *Holy Spirit.* ▪ ▪

Reasoned yet impassioned!

There are *different* gifts, ▪ but the *same* Spirit; ▪ ▪ there are different *ministries* ▪ but the same *Lord;* ▪ ▪ there are different *works* ▪ but the same *God* who accomplishes *all* of them in *every* one. ▪ ▪ To *each* person ▪ the manifestation of the Spirit is given for the *common* good. ▪ ▪ ▪

Insistent.

Let your eyes sweep assembly.

Start a new build.

The body is *one* and has many *members,* ▪ ▪ but *all* the members, ▪ *many* though they are, ▪ are *one body;* ▪ ▪ and so it is with *Christ.* ▪ ▪ It was in *one Spirit* that all of us, ▪ whether Jew or Greek, ▪ slave or free, ▪ were *baptized* into *one body.* ▪ ▪ All of us have been given to *drink* of the *one Spirit.* ▪ ▪ ▪

Ritardando: "of . . . Spirit."

GOSPEL John 20:19–23

A reading from the holy *gospel* according to *John* ▪ ▪ ▪

Slowly. Suggest the disciples' fear. (It's Easter evening.)

On the evening of that *first* day of the week, ▪ even though the disciples had *locked* the doors of the place where they were ▪ for *fear* of the Jews, ▪ ▪ *Jesus* came ▪ and *stood* before them. ▪ ▪ ▪ *"Peace* ▪ be with you," he said. ▪ ▪ When he had said this, ▪ he *showed* them his *hands* and his *side.* ▪ ▪ At the sight of the *Lord* ▪ the disciples *rejoiced.* ▪ ▪ *"Peace* ▪ be with you," ▪ he said again. ▪ ▪

"Peace . . . you": quietly.

To reassure them.

Stress "Lord," not "sight."

"The disciples rejoiced": sudden exclamation.

Comforting.

"As the *Father* has sent *me,* ▪
so *I* send *you."* ▪ ▪

Transition. "Breathed" sounds like it means.

Then he *breathed* on them and said: ▪ ▪

Commission them. "People's" is more inclusive.

"Receive the *Holy Spirit.* ▪ ▪
If you *forgive* men's sins, ▪ ▪
they *are* forgiven them; ▪ ▪
if you hold them *bound,* ▪ ▪
they are *held* bound." ▪ ▪ ▪

MAY 26, 1991

TRINITY SUNDAY

LECTIONARY #166

READING I Deuteronomy 4:32–34, 39–40

A reading from the book of *Deuteronomy* ▪ ▪ ▪

Insistent and energetic, but not argumentative.

"People" is more inclusive.

With a sense of awe. Address different parts of assembly.

Slowly, using each phrase to build intensity.

Images of Exodus: the plagues, the parted Red Sea, the escape from Pharaoh.

New energy.

Urgency, as if to say: "This is not an option."

Final reminder of God's love.

Moses said to the *people:* ▪ ▪ *"Ask* now of the days of old, ▪ before your *time,* ▪ ever since God *created* man upon the *earth:* ▪ ▪ ask from one *end* of the sky to the *other:* ▪ ▪ Did anything so *great* ever happen *before?* ▪ ▪ Was it ever *heard* of? ▪ ▪ Did a people *ever* hear the voice of *God* speaking from the midst of *fire,* ▪ as *you* did, ▪ ▪ and *live?* ▪ ▪ Or did *any* god venture to go and take a *nation* for himself from the midst of *another* nation, ▪ by *testings,* ▪ by *signs* and *wonders,* ▪ by *war,* ▪ with his *strong* hand and *outstretched* arm, ▪ and by great *terrors,* ▪ *all* of which the Lord, your God, ▪ did for *you* in *Egypt* before your very *eyes?* ▪ ▪ This is why you must now *know,* ▪ and *fix* in your *heart,* ▪ ▪ that the *Lord* is *God* ▪ in the *heavens* above ▪ and on *earth* below, ▪ and that there is *no* other. ▪ ▪ You must keep his *statutes* and *commandments* which I *enjoin* on you today ▪ that *you* and your *children* after you may *prosper,* ▪ and that you may have *long life* on the land which the *Lord,* your *God,* ▪ is giving you *forever."* ▪ ▪ ▪

READING II Romans 8:14–17

A reading from the letter of *Paul* ▪
to the *Romans* ▪ ▪ ▪

Read slowly, with authority and conviction.

"Children" is more inclusive.

"Abba" is said with familiarity and trust.

Dropping "himself" is more inclusive..

Convince us our God-given rights.

"Suffer" contrasts with "glorified."

All who are *led* by the *Spirit* of God ▪ are *sons* of God. ▪ ▪ You did not receive a spirit of *slavery* ▪ leading you back into *fear,* ▪ but a spirit of *adoption* ▪ through which we *cry* out, ▪ ▪ *"Abba!"* ▪ (that is, ▪ *"Father"*). ▪ ▪ The Spirit *himself* gives witness with *our* spirit ▪ that we *are* children of God. ▪ ▪ But *if* we are children, ▪ we are *heirs* as well: ▪ ▪ heirs of *God,* ▪ heirs with *Christ,* ▪ if only we *suffer* with him ▪ so as to be *glorified* with him. ▪ ▪ ▪

READING I A true orator is someone with a good memory who knows a people's history and evokes it with passion and vivid detail. Recall the events that have swept over Eastern Europe. Would not an orator do well to imitate Moses in speaking of them? "Did anything so great ever happen before? Was it ever heard of?" Events that boggle the mind fill it with questions that express the magic and miracle of what we see unfolding before us: "Can you believe? Who would have thought?" But human memory is short; excitement wanes, and the recently impossible soon becomes taken for granted.

Moses fights that human tendency to forget. With great oratorical skill he shares his profound awareness of the marvels that God worked for Israel. His purpose is to awaken the drowsy memories of his people, to fuel in them the sense of awe that burns in him.

You can do the same by remembering *why* you are reading: to inspire, to awaken, to fill your listeners with awe. Moses is being pushy: "Ask," he says, "I dare you, ask! Survey all of history and see if anything like what our God has done was ever done before."

Once rolling, his train is hard to stop. Question after question demands a response. Let your tone say, "Well, I'm waiting." The last and longest question can be a trap unless you allow yourself to slow down while simultaneously building intensity, making each phrase another finger jab in the face of your forgetful neighbors.

Suddenly Moses' homily shifts. He withdraws his finger and extends his arms instead in an impassioned plea for fidelity to the God who has shown such love. Awareness of that love makes the injunction to "keep his statutes" more an appeal than a command. Next, Moses establishes a cause-and-effect relationship: Keep the commandments and your children will prosper. So much depends on our fidelity—prosperity, long life, land—that living our commitment is hardly an option. With urgency motivated by love, call us to that faithfulness.

READING II Don't let this brief and fluid passage lull you into an emotionless reading. It joyfully proclaims great news: We are children of God. Your tone and sustained eye contact tell us to live like we believe that! You haven't been called to timidity and shyness, you say; no, you've been given permission to call the great God "Abba . . . Father."

Imagine a friend who has been promoted to a position of increased authority that he or she seems unable or unwilling to exercise. How would you encourage that person to appropriate their rightful authority? With how much energy and with what tone would you insist that the ability to hire and fire, to reproach and approve, was given to him or her by the boss for a good reason?

Speak to us the same way: "The Spirit himself gives witness. . . ." Give us a sense of the new status bestowed on us through God's goodness. "If we are children, we are *heirs.*" Do you know what that means? Your tone both asks and answers that question: I'll tell you what it means: We are "heirs of *God*" (can you believe that?) *and* "heirs with *Christ*" (honest, it's true!).

And only one thing is needed: a willingness to suffer with Christ, for if we do (now here's why we speak with a smile instead of a frown), we will be glorified with him.

GOSPEL Writers often say much more than they seem to. Eleven disciples made their way to a mountain in Galilee. This seems simple enough until we look more closely. "Eleven" immediately conjures the painful memory of Judas's desertion; Galilee and the mountain site in particular evoke the expectation that these will be places of revelation—as they have been so often in scripture. The implications are obvious. Read slowly, allowing the nuances to surface. What you narrate is a moment of awe in the lives of the eleven: So recently fearful and plagued with doubts, these men now fall on their faces to worship.

Immediately Jesus responds by offering assurance and final instructions. His tone is all strength and confidence—qualities he'd like to bestow on this timid group. Having declared his authority, he shifts focus to their responsibilities: "Go . . . make . . . baptize . . . teach . . . know." This is not the CEO at a board of directors meeting; this is Jesus, their friend and counselor, who encourages with each word of command, inviting them into closer intimacy through the living out of the ministry he entrusts to them. Remembering that baptizing "in the name" of someone signifies belonging to that person should tell us how to speak the baptismal formula: as the offer of life and love that it is.

Jesus has an advantage over every friend who has ever left loved ones; he can assure them of his abiding presence after he's gone. Doubtless that would be done while clasping hands, embracing or looking deeply into the other's eyes. Because your hands can't touch your listeners, let your words reach out to them instead.

GOSPEL Matthew 28:16–20

A reading from the holy *gospel* according to *Matthew* ▪ ▪ ▪

Slowly. Nuance "eleven," "Galilee" and "mountain."

The *eleven disciples* made their way to *Galilee,* ▪ to the *mountain* to which *Jesus* had summoned them. ▪ ▪

Suggest their strong emotions.

At the *sight* of him, ▪ those who had entertained *doubts* ▪ *fell* down in *homage.* ▪ ▪ ▪ Jesus came forward and *addressed* them in these words: ▪ ▪

Confidence and strength.

"Full *authority* has been given to me ▪
both in *heaven* and on *earth;* ▪ ▪

Appeals to share his ministry.

go, therefore, ▪ and make *disciples*
of *all* the nations. ▪ ▪
Baptize them in the name
'of the *Father* ▪
and of the *Son,* ▪
and of the *Holy Spirit.*' ▪ ▪

"Everything" = asking them to give their lives.

Teach them to carry out *everything*
I have commanded you. ▪ ▪

Final assurance. Eye contact.

And know that I am with you *always,* ▪
until the *end* of the *world!"* ▪ ▪ ▪

JUNE 2, 1991

THE BODY AND BLOOD OF CHRIST

LECTIONARY #169

READING I Exodus 24:3–8

A reading from the book of *Exodus* ▪ ▪ ▪

Don't rush. These "words and ordinances" affect their entire lives.

"We will do . . .": strong and dignified.

Urgency and mounting expectancy.

Altar symbolized God. Sprinkling symbolized union.

Slower. Humbly and gratefully.

Sealing the union between God and people.

When *Moses* came to the people ▪ and related all the *words* and *ordinances* of the Lord, ▪ they all answered with *one* voice, ▪ ▪ "We will do *everything* that the Lord has told us." ▪ ▪ Moses then *wrote* down all the words of the Lord ▪ and, ▪ rising *early* the next day, ▪ he *erected* at the foot of the mountain ▪ an *altar* and *twelve pillars* ▪ for the twelve *tribes* of Israel. ▪ ▪ Then, having sent certain young men of the Israelites to offer *holocausts* ▪ and *sacrifice* young bulls as *peace* offerings to the Lord, ▪ ▪ Moses took *half* of the *blood* and put it in the *large bowls;* ▪ ▪ the *other* half he splashed on the *altar.* ▪ ▪ Taking the book of the *covenant,* ▪ he read it *aloud* to the people, ▪ who *answered,* ▪ ▪ "All that the Lord has *said,* ▪ we will *heed* and *do.*" ▪ ▪ Then he took the *blood* and sprinkled it on the *people,* ▪ saying, ▪ ▪ "This is the *blood* of the *covenant* ▪ which the Lord has *made* with you ▪ in accordance with all these *words* of his." ▪ ▪ ▪

READING II Hebrews 9:11–15

A reading from the letter to the *Hebrews* ▪ ▪ ▪

Slowly. Use the pauses. Understand what you are saying.

Contrasting heaven ("perfect tabernacle") with the human-built Jerusalem temple.

This is our faith: Jesus suffered and died to earn our redemption.

Insistent. Convincing.

When Christ came as *high priest* of the *good* things which came to be, ▪ he entered *once* for *all* ▪ into the *sanctuary,* ▪ passing through the *greater* and more *perfect* tabernacle not made by *hands,* ▪ that is, ▪ not belonging to *this* creation. ▪ ▪ He *entered* ▪ *not* with the blood of *goats* and *calves* ▪ but with his *own* blood, ▪ and achieved *eternal* redemption. ▪ ▪ For if the blood of *goats* and *bulls* ▪ and the sprinkling of a *heifer's* ashes can *sanctify* those who are defiled ▪ so that their *flesh* is cleansed, ▪ how much *more* will the blood of *Christ,* ▪ who through the *eternal* spirit

READING I A momentous event in the life of Israel: At Sinai, with Moses as mediator, God fashions a covenant with these former slaves who begin to glimpse the meaning of being God's chosen people. A sense of expectancy fuses with the solemnity of a sacred ritual, creating a profound experience of the intimate bond between God and the people.

Suggest the expectancy by the way you narrate the interaction between Moses and the people. "All the words and ordinances" refers not only to the ten commandments but also to laws regarding every aspect of the social and religious life of the people. The Israelites respond with unanimous assent and await the next step in the process. Moses then writes, erects an altar and sends young men to offer holocausts. The expectancy and urgency rise throughout these events and peak in the graphic outpouring of blood.

Don't shy from this trenchant image. Blood is a source and sign of life, and here it becomes a symbol of the union between God and the people. Embrace that word with vigor each time it occurs. Make sure it is heard, for it is a link to the gospel. Let it suggest new life, hope and reconciliation, as well as the unbreakable bond God seeks with the people.

With sincerity and love, speak the words of the people now more slowly than in the first sentence. They are humbled by God's initiative and generous love, and their words reflect that. Moses' final comment is the seal placed on this newly formed union, and the blood is the enduring sign that God and people will belong to each other forever.

READING II The first sentence might make us wince as we look at this passage. A firm grasp of its meaning should ease our fears: Christ is high priest of spiritual blessings ("the good things which came to be"); he has not entered into the Temple of Jerusalem but into the "greater and more perfect tabernacle" of heaven that is not of human origin.

The rest of the paragraph is clearer: Christ entered with a blood sacrifice, but not the annually repeated sacrifice of "goats and calves." No, he entered with the once-for-always sacrifice of himself, which has achieved "eternal [not temporary] redemption." The author proceeds with logic: "If the blood of goats . . . can sanctify . . . , how much more will the blood of Christ!" Though there is the reasoning of a lawyer here, there is also the passion of a believer. That passion is best communicated with eye contact and a tone that says you are already convinced of everything you say.

The second paragraph gets tough again. Verses 16 and 17 that follow the end of this passage clarify the legal point the author is making: One only receives an "inheritance" *after* the writer of a will has died. "Since his [Jesus'] death *has* taken place for [to enable] deliverance from transgressions committed under the first covenant, those who are called may [now] receive the promised eternal inheritance." Jesus had to die in order for us to receive the inheritance he willed us. He did die. Now we can claim the inheritance of forgiveness and eternal life!

GOSPEL (Refer also to commentary on this passage contained in the Palm Sunday passion reading.) The first paragraph looks like a long staircase that stands between us and our destination. From the bottom looking up, the stairs seem such wasted effort: Why can't we vault them or take the elevator? But look again. Though the "body and blood" content is in the second paragraph, the first is more than wasted effort. In response to the disciples' inquiry, Jesus reveals that he has thought about and carefully prepared for this event, and his forethought surrounds the affair with mystery and majesty. There are clear implications: This is to be no ordinary meal; this meal merits our full attention, respect and reverence. Something extraordinary is likely to happen here. Surely the disciples left with a sense of all of that, and surely all of that was powerfully reinforced by the accurate fulfillment of Christ's prophecy. Doubtless these disciples entered the upper room with heightened expectancy and excitement.

Suddenly we're in the midst of the meal, and immediately we know it is no ordinary dinner. "This is my body . . . my blood." Shocking words. Revolutionary words. Intimate words of a dear friend spoken as a last will and testament to those dearest and closest to him. The way you speak the action words "took," "blessed," "broke" and "gave" will establish that intimacy. Jesus' focus is on his friends, giving them a means of remaining connected with him after he's gone, a means they don't yet know they need. Speak simply, slowly and softly. Even the intensity of his solemn assurance is best underplayed, letting the emotional fervor be spoken by your eyes rather than your lips.

The afterthought of the last sentence is significant, for it reveals the attitude that should characterize our lives: thanksgiving and praise.

offered himself up *unblemished* to God, ▪ cleanse our *consciences* ▪ from *dead* works ▪ to worship the *living God!* ▪ ▪ ▪

Slower. Less fiery.

This is why he is *mediator* of a *new* covenant: ▪ ▪ since his death *has* taken place ▪ for deliverance from transgressions committed under the *first* covenant, ▪ those who are *called* ▪ may *receive* the promised eternal *inheritance.* ▪ ▪ ▪

Eye contact and a smile.

GOSPEL Mark 14:12–16, 22–26

A reading from the holy *gospel* according to *Mark* ▪ ▪ ▪

Start calmly but at a good pace.

On the first day of *Unleavened Bread,* ▪ when it was customary to sacrifice the *paschal lamb,* ▪ the *disciples* said to Jesus, ▪ ▪ "*Where* do you wish us to go to prepare the Passover *supper* for you?" ▪ ▪ He sent *two* of his disciples with these *instructions:* ▪ ▪ "Go into the *city* ▪ and you will come upon a man carrying a *water* jar. ▪ ▪ *Follow* him. ▪ ▪ Whatever *house* he enters, ▪ say to the *owner,* ▪ ▪ 'The *Teacher* asks, ▪ ▪ Where is my *guestroom* where I may eat the Passover with my *disciples?*' ▪ ▪ Then he will show you an *upstairs* room, ▪ *spacious,* ▪ *furnished,* ▪ and all in *order.* ▪ ▪ *That* is the place you are to get *ready* for us. ▪ ▪ The disciples *went* off. ▪ ▪ When they *reached* the city ▪ they found it *just* as he had told them, ▪ and they *prepared* the Passover supper. ▪ ▪ ▪

Jesus: as if he were watching these events on a screen in his mind. Slowly showing he's in control.

Your tone reveals their incredulity.

Slowly, gently and simply.

During the meal ▪ he took *bread,* ▪ *blessed* and *broke* it, ▪ and *gave* it to them. ▪ ▪ "*Take* this," ▪ he said, ▪ ▪ "this is my *body.*" ▪ ▪ He likewise took a *cup,* ▪ gave *thanks* ▪ and *passed* it to them, ▪ ▪ and they all *drank* from it. ▪ ▪ He said to them: ▪ ▪ "This is my *blood* ▪ the blood of the *covenant,* ▪ to be *poured out* on behalf of *many.* ▪ ▪ I solemnly *assure* you, ▪ I will *never* again drink of the *fruit* of the *vine* ▪ until the day when I drink it *new* ▪ in the *reign* of *God.*" ▪ ▪ ▪

Eye contact.

Contrast "never again" with "when I drink it new."

They gave thanks.

After singing *songs* of *praise* ▪ they walked out to the Mount of *Olives.* ▪ ▪ ▪

JUNE 9, 1991

TENTH SUNDAY IN ORDINARY TIME

LECTIONARY #90

READING I Genesis 3:9–15

A reading from the book of *Genesis* ▪ ▪ ▪

Slowly, then a bit faster.

[After *Adam* had *eaten* of the tree] ▪ the Lord God *called* him and *asked* him, ▪ ▪ "Where *are* you?" ▪ ▪ He answered, ▪ ▪ "I *heard* you in the garden; ▪ but I was *afraid,* ▪ because I was *naked,* ▪ so I *hid* myself." ▪ ▪ Then he asked, ▪ ▪ "Who *told* you that you were naked? ▪ ▪ You have *eaten,* then, ▪ from the tree of which I had *forbidden* you to eat!" ▪ ▪ The man replied, ▪ ▪ "The *woman* whom you put here with me— ▪ *she* gave me *fruit* from the tree, ▪ and so I *ate* it." ▪ ▪ The Lord God then *asked* the woman, ▪ ▪ "*Why* did you *do* such a thing?" ▪ ▪ The woman answered, ▪ ▪ "The serpent *tricked* me into it, ▪ so I *ate* it." ▪ ▪ ▪

"He" = God. Slight pause before shifting back to narrator.

"And so . . ." = "What else could I do?"

Eve shows greater awareness of responsibility.

Then the Lord God said to the *serpent:* ▪ ▪
"Because you have *done* this, ▪
you shall be *banned*
from *all* the animals ▪
and from all the wild creatures; ▪ ▪
On your *belly* shall you crawl, ▪
and *dirt* shall you eat
all the days of your *life.* ▪ ▪
I will put *enmity* between you and the woman, ▪ ▪
and between *your* offspring and *hers;* ▪ ▪
He will strike at your *head,* ▪
while *you* strike at his *heel.*" ▪ ▪ ▪

God's anger is fully released.

Stress serpent's debased condition. "Crawl" sounds like it means.

Gospel dramatizes this "enmity."

Contrast "head" and "heel."

READING I This passage, where the snake shares the spotlight with Adam and Eve, is read on the feast of the Immaculate Conception (please read that commentary). Today, however, because of the gospel that follows, the snake commands center stage. Remember that the snake appears within the context of a *story.* Don't overlook the requirements of storytelling: creating the characters, animating the dialogue, using the narration to establish mood and pace.

Following the finger-pointing and blame-shifting of the two humans, vividly illustrating the "divided house" of which Jesus speaks in the gospel, the snake appears and receives the full brunt of God's fury. Take time with the curse of banishment and the promise of "enmity." Probably the last sentence is the most important. The woman's offspring will strike at the serpent's head, where great harm can be done, while the serpent will be allowed only to impotently strike at the heel, where little damage can be done.

READING II Paul utters here what ought to be every lector's creed: "We believe and so we speak." The kind of personal faith of which Paul speaks ought to animate all our proclamation.

Paul has no trouble being very personal, speaking of and through his experience. The most personal of Paul's letters, Second Corinthians, reveals a great deal about this often enigmatic figure. Here we learn of Paul's expectation to be raised by God at the second coming and of being presented to Christ. Paul also expects that the "grace bestowed in abundance," through his fruitful ministry among the Corinthians, will result in "greater glory to God" because of the ever growing number of those "who give thanks." A straightforward and confident delivery laced with honest emotion will be most effective.

In the next paragraph Paul reflects on the reality of suffering in his and our lives: "Though our body is being destroyed," do not lose heart because our "inner being is renewed each day." Paul does not look at our transitory existence with its attendant pain; instead he focuses on "what is unseen," the life to come that lasts forever. Such reflections should be spoken simply, not without emotion but without fanfare, without a soapbox. The simplicity, if sincere, will be powerful.

Finally he uses the image of a tent (Paul was a tentmaker) to speak of the human body that, when destroyed in death, we will trade in for a "dwelling . . . not made by hands," that is, a glorious resurrected body that will "last forever." These are words of hope offered in the face of pain to all who suffer.

GOSPEL The gospel opens on a scene of confusion and great activity. No sooner is Jesus indoors than a large crowd swells around him, making impossible even the simple task of eating. His family reacts to this mad scene by assuming Jesus himself is mad, just as scribes arrive to accuse him of working his miracles through the power of "the prince of demons." Assume the posture of a solicitous narrator, with definite feelings about the details you enumerate and the characters you introduce. Allow your attitude to color our perception of the crowd (insensitive and greedy), the family (confused and concerned) and the scribes (angry and jealous of his popularity).

Jesus takes control of the turmoil, calling everyone together to answer the charges of the scribes. The second charge he answers in a parable: "How can Satan expel Satan?" He doesn't have much patience for the poor logic and malice of his accusers. He is

READING II 2 Corinthians 4:13—15:1

First of five consecutive weeks we read 2 Corinthians.

A reading from the second letter of *Paul* ▪ to the *Corinthians* ▪ ▪ ▪

Start upbeat.

We have that spirit of *faith* of which the Scripture says, ▪ ▪ "Because I *believed,* ▪ I *spoke* out." ▪ ▪ We believe ▪ and so *we speak,* ▪ knowing that he who raised up the Lord *Jesus* ▪ will raise *us* up *along* with Jesus ▪ and place both *us* and *you* in his *presence.* ▪ ▪ Indeed, ▪ everything is ordered to your *benefit,* ▪ so that the *grace* bestowed in *abundance* ▪ may bring greater *glory* to God ▪ because they who give *thanks* ▪ are *many.* ▪ ▪ ▪

Expectant hope of resurrection.

Rev. NAB says: "so that the grace bestowed in abundance on more and more people may cause the thanksgiving to overflow for the glory of God."

We do not lose *heart* ▪ because our *inner* being is *renewed* each day, ▪ even though our *body* is being *destroyed* at the same time. ▪ ▪ The present *burden* of our trial is *light* enough ▪ and *earns* for us an eternal weight of *glory* beyond *all* comparison. ▪ ▪ We do not fix our gaze on what is *seen* ▪ but on what is *unseen.* ▪ ▪ What is seen is *transitory;* ▪ ▪ what is *not* seen lasts *forever.* ▪ ▪ ▪

Contrast "seen" with "unseen" and "transitory" with "lasts."

"Tent" = our bodies. Give hope to those who suffer now.

Indeed, ▪ we know that when the *earthly* tent in which we dwell is *destroyed* ▪ we have a dwelling provided for us by *God,* ▪ a dwelling in the *heavens,* ▪ not made by *hands,* ▪ ▪ but to last *forever.* ▪ ▪ ▪

GOSPEL Mark 3:20–35

A reading from the holy *gospel* according to *Mark* ▪ ▪ ▪

Narrator is interested observer with a definite point of view.

Jesus came to the house with his *disciples* ▪ and *again* the *crowd* assembled, ▪ making it *impossible* for them to get any *food* whatever. ▪ ▪ When his family *heard* of this ▪ they came to take *charge* of him, ▪ saying, ▪ ▪ "He is *out* of his *mind*"; ▪ ▪ while the *scribes* who arrived from Jerusalem asserted, ▪ ▪ "He is *possessed* by *Beelzebul,*" ▪ and "He *expels* demons ▪ with the help of the *prince* of demons." ▪ ▪ *Summoning* them, ▪ he then began to speak to them by way of *examples:* ▪ ▪ "How can *Satan* expel Satan? ▪ ▪ If a kingdom is torn by *civil strife,* ▪ that kingdom cannot *last.* ▪ ▪ If a household is *divided* according to loyalties, ▪ that household will *not* survive. ▪ ▪ *Similarly,* if Satan has suffered *mutiny* in his ranks ▪ and is torn by *dissension,* ▪ he cannot *endure;* ▪ ▪ he is *finished.* ▪ ▪ No one can enter a strong man's *house*

They're convinced.

Jealousy and judgment.

Taking charge.

Impatience and anger just below the surface.

He's saying: Your argument is ludicrous.

Insistent and thorough.

and despoil his *property* ▪ unless he has *first* put him under *restraint.* ▪▪ Only *then* can he *plunder* his house. ▪▪▪

Slower and softer.

"Humankind" and "people" are more inclusive.

"That person" is more inclusive; so is dropping "his."

Narrator rushes to explain.

"I give you my *word,* ▪ *every* sin will be *forgiven* mankind ▪ and all the *blasphemies* men utter, ▪ but whoever blasphemes against the *Holy Spirit* ▪ will *never* be forgiven. ▪▪ He carries the *guilt* of his sin without *end."* ▪▪ He spoke *thus* because they had *said,* ▪▪ "He is *possessed* by an *unclean* spirit." ▪▪▪

Shouted by the crowd.

Shouted back to the crowd.

Softer, with gratitude and love.

Look at the assembly.

His *mother* and his *brothers* arrived, ▪ and as they stood *outside* ▪ they sent word to him to *come out.* ▪▪ The crowd seated around him *told* him, ▪▪ "Your *mother* and your *brothers* and *sisters* are outside *asking* for you." ▪▪ He said in reply, ▪▪ "*Who* are my mother and my brothers?" ▪▪ And gazing around him at those seated in the *circle* he continued, ▪▪ "*These* are my mother and my brothers. ▪▪ Whoever does the *will* of *God* ▪ is brother and sister and mother to me." ▪▪▪

insistent and thorough in his rebuttal, and his tone reveals his contempt for their arrogance and self-righteousness.

Read this text in a fiery manner. This is a stern judge speaking, not the gentle Jesus of sentimental portraits. He is uncompromising in his judgment. His affirmation of God's universal pardon contrasts sharply with his assertion that blasphemy against the Holy Spirit is not forgiven. The narrator justifies that harsh sentence by reminding us of what they had said.

Even the narrator is surprised at the uncompromising nature of the discipleship Jesus demands of his followers. He keeps his family standing outside and doesn't allow their message to win them entry into his presence. Instead, Jesus asks out loud, "Who are my mother and my brothers?" Answer the question while doing what Jesus did: Gaze around at those seated before you, and tell us, with genuine affection and gratitude, that those who do the will of God are "brother and sister and mother" to the Lord.

FROM THE KEY

Inclusive Language. What is inclusive language and why is it so important? Archbishop Raymond Hunthausen in a 1990 pastoral letter offered the following comments:

"Inclusive language, with respect to the liturgy, is a way of speaking and writing that does not give the impression of needlessly excluding certain persons. I urge each of us to be especially sensitive to the use of language that may be sexist, racist, clericalist or anticlericalist, anti-Semitic, as well as being offensive to the disabled.

Most of our liturgical books were translated immediately after Vatican Council II, at a time when sensitivity to language that excludes or offends had not yet become part of our consciousness. Unfortunately, exclusive langauge is liberally scattered throughout our liturgical books. Though the issue of inclusive language is complex, we must try to be sensitive about how we address or speak of one another in the faith community and the way we refer to God. Care must be taken in choice of texts and in other pastoral adaptations, for often the integrity of the word of God or the very meaning of the rite may be at stake.

Appropriate adaptation, in accord with liturgical guidelines, demands knowledge, time, energy and thought. Official changes in texts and translations may seem slow in coming, so our understanding and our patience are essential. There are instances when the language of impatience and protest can do more harm to the unity of the assembly than the use of exclusive langauge."

The readings throughout this workbook are from the New American Bible. Though the revised New Testament of the New American Bible is not yet approved for lectionary use, often citations from that version (designated "Rev. NAB") are given in the margin notes in an attempt to provide language that is less exclusive. These variations may be of use in settings where the scriptures are read or studied apart from the liturgy. The Revised NAB is undergoing further work, both to ensure inclusive language as much as possible and to present the texts in a way that will enable good proclamation. These revisions should be completed in the next few years.

READING I You've probably seen the bumper sticker that admonishes: "Let go and let God." Today God reminds us of who is in charge through Ezekiel's beautiful poetry. The tone of the closing line "As I . . . have spoken, so will I do" pervades the entire passage. God, author of life, sovereign Lord of the universe, says: "Watch what I will do; see the life I will generate; wait for the wonders I will work!"

God's confidence rings in your voice as you announce the decision to take from "the crest of the cedar" (a symbol of the house of David) "a tender shoot" that will be nursed into a majestic tree. This promise of restoration for the exiled nation, this pledge of utopian renewal under God's nurturing care, must be spoken with gentle confidence, suggesting how God handles the fragile shoot with care and love.

The lines describing the growth and fruitfulness of the tree that accommodates "birds of every kind" are a song of joyous celebration. Ezekiel paints vivid images of the paradise God is readying for the people.

Having seen the marvels God has accomplished, "All the trees" (the nations of the earth) shall know that God is Lord. God announces this, as a statement of fact, not as a boast. Know that I can "bring low" or "lift high" and even "make the withered tree bloom," says the Lord. The regal power of these lines prepares us for the final assertion that as God says, so will God do.

READING II If you've ever watched a blind person walking self-assuredly down a street, then you've seen the kind of "confidence" Paul cites here. The blind person seems to walk with a sixth sense unknown to the rest of us. Paul tells us that in spiritual terms that sense is "faith." And faith is what it takes to walk through a life that feels like an exile. Our home is "with the Lord"; anything this side of heaven is less than ideal and often painful. Yet we endure this life and strive to please God by all we do, for one day our lives "are to be revealed before the tribunal of Christ" where we will all be judged according to how we lived while "in the body."

Like Paul, be confident as you read, reassuring us that, though this life we *see* is often fraught with distress, there is a homeland in Christ in which we confidently believe though it remains *unseen*. The words "I repeat" clearly signal the need for a "build" (see Key), so increase the intensity as you express the desire to be "at home with the Lord."

As for the reality of earthly existence, Paul says: Make the best of it, for you'll be judged

JUNE 16, 1991

ELEVENTH SUNDAY IN ORDINARY TIME

LECTIONARY #93

READING I Ezekiel 17:22–24

A reading from the book of the prophet ▪ *Ezekiel* ▪▪▪

Bright energy and strength.

Thus says the *Lord God:* ▪▪

"Crest of the cedar" = house of David; "tender shoot" = new leader.

I, *too,* ▪ will take from the *crest* of the cedar, ▪
from its topmost branches tear off ▪
a *tender* shoot, ▪

Repetition of mountain image requires "build" (see Key).

And *plant* it on a high and *lofty* mountain; ▪▪
on the mountain heights of *Israel* I will plant it. ▪▪

Like a song of celebration.

It shall put forth *branches* and bear *fruit,* ▪
and become a *majestic* cedar. ▪▪

Images of shelter and protection.

Birds of every kind shall *dwell* beneath it, ▪
every winged thing in the *shade* of its boughs. ▪▪

A regal pronouncement.

And *all* the trees of the field shall *know* ▪

No pause after "Lord."

that *I,* ▪ the *Lord,*

Contrast "bring low" with "lift high" and "wither up" with "make . . . bloom."

Bring *low* the *high* tree, ▪
lift *high* the *lowly* tree, ▪
Wither up the *green* tree, ▪
and make the *withered* tree ▪ *bloom.* ▪▪

"So will I do": equal emphasis on each word.

As I, ▪ the *Lord,* ▪ have *spoken,* ▪ *so will I do.* ▪▪▪

READING II 2 Corinthians 5:6–10

Second of five consecutive weeks we read 2 Corinthians.

A reading from the second letter of *Paul* ▪ to the *Corinthians* ▪▪▪

"Confident" sets the tone.

Boldly.

Contrast "away" with "at home" and "body" with "Lord."

More inclusive: "so that all may receive their recompense . . . according to their lives . . ."

We continue to be *confident.* ▪▪ We know that while we *dwell* in the *body* ▪ we are *away* from the *Lord.* ▪▪ We walk by *faith,* ▪ not by *sight.* ▪▪ I *repeat,* ▪▪ we are *full* of confidence, ▪ and would *much* rather be *away* from the *body* ▪ and at *home* with the *Lord.* ▪▪ This being so, ▪ we make it our *aim* to *please* him ▪ whether we are *with* him ▪ or *away* from him. ▪▪ The lives of *all* of us are to be revealed before the *tribunal* of Christ ▪ so that *each* one may receive his *recompense,* ▪ *good* or *bad,* ▪ according to his *life* in the *body.* ▪▪▪

GOSPEL Mark 4:26–34

A reading from the holy *gospel* according to *Mark* ▪ ▪ ▪

Engagingly, like a storyteller instead of a teacher.

Jesus said to the *crowd:* ▪ ▪ "This is how it is with the *reign* of *God.* ▪ ▪ A man scatters *seed* on the ground. ▪ ▪

Suggest the passage of time.

He goes to *bed* and gets up ▪ *day* after *day.* ▪ ▪ Through it all ▪ the seed *sprouts* and *grows* ▪ without his knowing *how* it happens. ▪ ▪ The soil produces of

Farmer can do nothing but trust.

itself ▪ first the *blade,* ▪ then the *ear,* ▪ *finally* the ripe *wheat* in the ear. ▪ ▪ When the crop is *ready* ▪

Faster pace; joyful.

he 'wields the *sickle,* ▪ ▪ for the time is *ripe* for harvest.'" ▪ ▪ ▪

Trying to find another image.

He went on to *say:* ▪ ▪ "What *comparison* shall we use for the reign of God? ▪ ▪ What *image* will help to

"I have it!"

present it? ▪ ▪ It is like a *mustard* seed ▪ which, ▪ when *planted* in the soil, ▪ is the *smallest* of *all* the earth's seeds, ▪ yet once it is *sown,* ▪ *springs* up to become the *largest* of shrubs, ▪ with branches *big*

Warmth and security.

enough for the *birds* of the sky to build *nests* in its

Narrator approves of methodology.

shade." ▪ ▪ ▪ By means of *many* such parables ▪ he *taught* them the message in a way they could *understand.* ▪ ▪ To *them* he spoke *only* by way of parable, ▪

As if you don't understand why he didn't explain things to the crowd.

while he kept explaining things *privately* ▪ to his *disciples.* ▪ ▪ ▪

on how you lived this life. Stress "please him," and contrast "with him" and "away from him" as you argue your point. "Good or bad," our recompense, Paul suggests, will be based not on the gifts with which we entered the world but on what we've accomplished with them by the time we leave it.

GOSPEL If parables didn't exist, we'd have to invent them. They do so much work and save so much effort; no wonder Jesus made recourse to them on so many occasions. Because they are cast in everyday language and utilize everyday symbols, they open windows into mysteries and cut doors into the unknown.

In the first parable stress the details that make the point that the harvest develops on its own, independent of the farmer's efforts. It's a story that can comfort those who fear that they are not doing enough to further the kingdom, so give it an encouraging tone.

Suggest the passage of time as you describe the development of the seed into ripe wheat, for it is a key component of the analogy Jesus draws. "Day after day" spans several months, and by the time the sprouting seed meets the sickle, a season has passed. Your tone throughout speaks of trust and of confident knowledge that the crop is developing as it should.

Jesus looks around and spots question marks on people's faces. So, like any good teacher, he reaches for another image to erase the questions. Doubtless, on occasion, Jesus improvised; this seems to be one of those times. Pause briefly after "What image . . ." as if to think. Then let your face announce, "I have it!" and continue at a faster pace with the mustard seed parable. Because it's short (one sentence!) and so familiar, try a simple trick. Speak each phrase with excited energy, but pause between the phrases as if you were truly thinking up what you will say next. Vary the pause lengths as you discover, with excitement, the details of the analogy.

Now it's your turn to put question marks on faces. Tell your listeners that Jesus explained the parables only to the disciples in ways that made them wonder, "Why?" Perhaps you can use the homily to explain.

READING I Let's play a game. What's wrong with this sentence: "The Lord addressed Job out of the window." Right, you got it. The scripture says "storm," not "window." Make a difference? You bet it makes a difference! But why will so many lectors speak that sentence as if they would have *said* "window?" It's too big a mystery to delve into now; what matters is that *you* don't make that mistake. You must understand that a divine voice thundering out of a storm is a thing of wonder, a thing of majesty, and you are the instrument through which that magnificent sound will be heard. God help you if you turn the storm into a window.

Through poetic imagery God is claiming control over all the forces of the universe. The sea is an infant emerging from the womb, clothed with "clouds" and covered with blankets of "darkness." As vast as it is, says the Lord, the sea is nothing compared with me, for I was able to "shut [it] within doors . . . [and] set limits for it." Though not angry, God's question is bold and immodest. It's a reminder to Job that God's greatness goes unquestioned.

The last three lines are half question and half exclamation, so how do we proclaim? A suggestion: Make it an exclamation by dropping the "When" in "When I set . . ." and read instead "I set limits for it . . . And said . . . here shall your proud waves be stilled!" From out of the storm comes the voice of a God who knows how to quiet an ocean and the trembling of a human heart.

READING II An unusual word in a text can become the focal point of a reading. If the word is a strong action word, the opportunity is all the richer for the word to set the tone and direction of the proclamation. Paul offers us the word "impels" with all the energy and conviction it suggests.

What a powerful opening statement: "The love of Christ *impels* us"! It motivates, persuades, urges and obliges us to enter the new creation that comes to birth as a result of Christ's death. When Christ died, we all died with him. Now it is possible for each of us to live, not for ourselves, but for him who died for our sake. The really good news is that living for Christ is better than living for ourselves. Therefore we announce that truth with urgent joy!

Christ's death and resurrection changed everything. We can't judge with the same criteria anymore. Recall the last time you wrongly judged someone, and let the sting of

JUNE 23, 1991

TWELFTH SUNDAY IN ORDINARY TIME

LECTIONARY #96

READING I Job 38:1, 8–11

Short reading means: Go slowly!

A reading from the book of *Job* ▪ ▪ ▪

The *Lord* addressed Job out of the *storm* ▪ and said: ▪
Who shut within doors the *sea,* ▪

"Who did?" "I did!"

when it *burst* forth from the *womb;* ▪
When I made the clouds its *garment* ▪
and thick *darkness* its *swaddling* bands? ▪
When I set *limits* for it ▪
and *fastened* the bar of its door, ▪
And said: ▪ ▪ *Thus* far shall you come ▪
but *no* farther, ▪

A powerful, not angry, God speaks.

and *here* shall your *proud* waves be *stilled!* ▪ ▪ ▪

READING II 2 Corinthians 5:14–17

Third of five consecutive weeks we read 2 Corinthians.

A reading from the second letter of *Paul* ▪
to the *Corinthians* ▪ ▪ ▪

Start with a strong and urgent voice.

Gratitude.

Recall your own tendency to judge.

The love of Christ *impels us* ▪ who have reached the *conviction* ▪ that since *one* died for *all,* ▪ *all* died. ▪ ▪ He *died* for all so that those who *live* ▪ might live no longer for *themselves,* ▪ but for *him* who for their sakes *died* ▪ and was *raised* up. ▪ ▪ ▪

More inclusive: "if any are in Christ, they are . . ."

Climax.

Because of this ▪ we no longer look on *anyone* in terms of mere *human* judgment. ▪ ▪ If at *one* time we so regarded *Christ,* ▪ we no *longer* know him by this standard. ▪ ▪ This means that if *anyone* is in *Christ,* ▪ he is a *new creation.* ▪ ▪ The *old* order has passed *away;* ▪ ▪ now ▪ *all* is *new!* ▪ ▪ ▪

GOSPEL Mark 4:35–41

A reading from the holy *gospel* according to *Mark* ▪ ▪ ▪

End of a long day. All is calm for now.

One day as *evening* drew on ▪ *Jesus* said to his *disciples,* ▪ ▪ "Let us cross over to the *farther* shore." ▪ ▪ *Leaving* the crowd, ▪ they *took* him away in the *boat* in which he was *sitting,* ▪ while the *other* boats *accompanied* him. ▪ ▪ It happened that a bad *squall* blew up. ▪ ▪ The waves were *breaking* over the boat ▪ and it began to ship water *badly.* ▪ ▪ Jesus was in the *stern* through it all, ▪ sound *asleep* on a *cushion.* ▪ ▪ They finally *woke* him and *said* to him, ▪ ▪ "*Teacher,* ▪ doesn't it *matter* to you that we are going to *drown?*" ▪ ▪ He *awoke* ▪ and *rebuked* the wind ▪ and said to the *sea:* ▪ ▪ "*Quiet!* ▪ ▪ *Be still!*" ▪ ▪ ▪ The wind *fell* off ▪ and everything grew *calm.* ▪ ▪ Then he *said* to them, ▪ ▪ "Why are you so *terrified?* ▪ ▪ Why are you *lacking* in *faith?*" ▪ ▪ ▪ A great *awe* overcame them at this. ▪ ▪ They kept *saying* to one another, ▪ ▪ "*Who* can this *be* ▪ that the wind and the sea *obey* him?" ▪ ▪ ▪

Faster tempo. Louder.

Incredulous.

Afraid to disturb him.

"Quiet! Be still.": An intense whisper. "The wind . . . grew calm": in voice of the apostles.

Disappointment.

A little frightened, but also fascinated.

that memory color your declaration that "we no longer look on anyone in terms of mere human judgment."

The last two sentences of this passage could be scripture enough for today. What a profound and joyous revelation! Announce the news slowly, a phrase at a time, as if you'd just made the discovery of what this means.

GOSPEL It's been a long day and Jesus is tired. He asks for a respite from the crowd by requesting a ride across the lake. Clouds are gathering, but the disciples comply. So far you've given us the calm before the storm. Suddenly you change the mood by changing the tempo. Louder and faster you announce the arrival of the squall. Hint at the disciples' mounting fear as you describe the breaking waves and the tossing boat.

Disbelief colors your voice when you tell us Jesus was sound asleep through all this, for it must have been one terrible storm to panic these experienced fishermen. Imagine the disciples hesitating about whether or not to awaken Jesus, nudging each other perhaps, as they work up the courage to do the inevitable. Finally they wake him with what is perhaps one of the funniest lines in the gospels. Can you picture one of the disciples confronting the Lord as a worried friend asking: "Doesn't it matter to you that we are going to drown?" Because they've repressed the question for so long, it nearly bursts from them.

Jesus responds slowly; he is in no hurry to quiet the storm. After allowing the wind and the rain to momentarily assault his face, he utters his command in an intense whisper. Speak with the relieved voice of the disciples when you narrate that everything grew calm.

Jesus is genuinely surprised and disappointed by the disciples' fear. They frequently have witnessed Jesus' miraculous power and often experienced his radical commitment to serving others' needs. But none of that experience is remembered here. Although he is not angry, Jesus asks questions that are pointed and embarrassing. It would seem the disciples are more awestricken by Jesus' expectation of unquestioning faith than by his miraculous control of the storm. Their closing question is a mix of excitement, fear and awe. They know they stand in the presence of a terrifying and enthralling mystery, so they say the only thing they (and we) can say, "Who can this be . . . ?"

READING I In today's gospel Jesus overcomes sickness and death, healing a woman's hemorrhage on his way to raising a child from the dead. Before that, however, we hear in this passage from Wisdom that death and sickness are not of God's making; indeed, they are the antithesis of what God is.

The presence and experience of suffering raise hard questions for people. Be aware that these questions may be rumbling through the minds of some of your listeners. Approach the ambo with a quiet serenity. You might think of a pastoral care minister in a hospital who must comfort a grieving family. Survey the group, take a breath, then gently launch into your explanation.

A slow pace will help your effectiveness. While striving to absolve God of guilt for the "destruction" that surrounds us, realize that you may be addressing many who are struggling with the issue of whether or not to blame God for the pain that has invaded their lives. Some of these people you may know personally, so speak in a persuasive but nonthreatening manner. Reverence and delight characterize your attitude toward the "creatures of the world" fashioned by God in the beginning and among which "there is not a destructive drug" (the physical world cannot cause our spiritual death).

The second paragraph reiterates the opening theme: God is not the author of death but of life. The reading pivots on the word "but" and becomes suddenly foreboding. Speaking of death in *spiritual* as well as physical terms, the narrator attests that Satan's "envy" concocted the bitter pill of death and those who belong to Satan must swallow it.

READING II Paul comes on like a teacher, coach or parent: You are rich in "every respect, in faith and discourse, in knowledge, in total concern"; now be that way in "your work of charity" as well! It's a very human response: We're doing great. Let's do better.

Whether you picture Paul in a locker room or classroom, the motivational pitch goes on. Jesus was your model; what he does for you, you must do for others. The literary device called *chiasmus,* which reverses the order of words in two otherwise parallel phrases, makes your point: Jesus made himself *poor* though he was *rich* so that you might become *rich* by his *poverty.*

Paul persuasively continues his appeal: Helping others should not "impoverish you," for there is a balance in God's plans. Your surplus can relieve their need now, but later

JUNE 30, 1991

THIRTEENTH SUNDAY IN ORDINARY TIME

LECTIONARY #99

READING I Wisdom 1:13–15; 2:23–24

A reading from the book of *Wisdom* ▪ ▪ ▪

With firm conviction.

God did *not make death,* ▪
not does he *rejoice* in the *destruction*
of the living. ▪ ▪

Recalling the perfection of God's creation in the beginning.

For he fashioned *all* things that they might
have being; ▪ ▪
and the *creatures* of the world are *wholesome,* ▪

"Destructive drug": the physical world around us does not have the capacity to cause spiritual death.

And there is not a *destructive* drug *among* them ▪
nor any domain of the *nether* world ▪ on *earth,* ▪ ▪
For *justice* is *undying.* ▪ ▪ ▪

This repeats idea above, so build. "Humanity" is more inclusive than "man" and "him."

For *God* formed man to be *imperishable;* ▪ ▪
the image of his *own* nature he made him. ▪ ▪
But by the *envy* of the *devil,* ▪ *death* entered
the world, ▪
and they who are in *his possession* ▪
experience it. ▪ ▪ ▪

READING II 2 Corinthians 8:7, 9, 13–15

Fourth of five consecutive weeks we read 2 Corinthians.

A reading from the second letter of *Paul* ▪
to the *Corinthians* ▪ ▪ ▪

Affirming.

Just as you are *rich* in *every* respect, ▪ in *faith* and *discourse,* ▪ in *knowledge,* ▪ in total *concern,* ▪ and in our *love* for you, ▪ you may also *abound* in your work of *charity.* ▪ ▪ ▪

Here's why you should be generous: Jesus was generous with you.

Generosity is not to be feared. Equality is the goal, not bankruptcy.

First contrast "plenty" and "need," then "their" and "your."

"The one" is more inclusive.

You are well *acquainted* with the *favor* shown you by our *Lord* Jesus Christ: ▪ ▪ how for *your* sake he made himself *poor* ▪ though he was *rich,* ▪ so that *you* might *become* rich ▪ by his *poverty.* ▪ ▪ The *relief* of others ought not to *impoverish* you; ▪ ▪ there should be a certain *equality.* ▪ ▪ *Your plenty* at the present time should supply *their need* ▪ so that *their* surplus may in turn one day supply *your* need, ▪ with *equality* as the result. ▪ ▪ It is written, ▪ ▪ "He who *gathered* much ▪ had no *excess* ▪ and he who gathered *little* ▪ had no *lack.*" ▪ ▪ ▪

GOSPEL Mark 5:21–43

A reading from the holy *gospel* according to *Mark* ▪ ▪ ▪

Reluctant to enter the crowd.

"Jairus" = Jeye-rŭs. "Seeing Jesus": pause for decision to approach, then whisper request.

Crowd is demanding and obnoxious.

When *Jesus* had crossed back to the *other* side of the *Sea* of *Galilee* in the boat, ▪ a large *crowd* gathered around him ▪ and he stayed *close* to the lake. ▪ ▪ One of the *officials* of the *synagogue,* ▪ a man name *Jairus,* ▪ came *near.* ▪ ▪ *Seeing* Jesus, ▪ he *fell* at his *feet* ▪ and made this *earnest* appeal: ▪ ▪ "My little *daughter* is *critically* ill. ▪ ▪ *Please* come and *lay* your *hands* on her ▪ so that she may get *well* ▪ and *live."* ▪ ▪ The two *went* off together ▪ and a large crowd *followed,* ▪ *pushing* against Jesus. ▪ ▪ ▪

Emphasize the hopelessness of her condition.

She's fearful, but filled with faith.

Faster pace. Excited joy.

Rejoicing stops abruptly.

He's serious; he wants to know.

They can't believe him.

Her fear is poignant.

Great tenderness.

There was a *woman* in the area who had been afflicted with a *hemorrhage* for a *dozen* years. ▪ ▪ She has received *treatment* at the hands of doctors of *every* sort ▪ and *exhausted* her *savings* in the process, ▪ yet she got *no relief;* ▪ ▪ on the *contrary,* ▪ she only grew *worse.* ▪ ▪ She had *heard* about Jesus ▪ and came up *behind* him in the crowd ▪ and put her *hand* to his *cloak.* ▪ ▪ "If I just *touch* his clothing," ▪ she thought, ▪ ▪ "I shall get *well."* ▪ ▪ ▪ *Immediately* her flow of blood *dried* up ▪ and the feeling that she was *cured* of her affliction ran through her *whole* body. ▪ ▪ Jesus was immediately *conscious* that *healing power* had gone out from him. ▪ ▪ *Wheeling* about in the crowd, ▪ he began to ask, ▪ ▪ *"Who* touched my clothing?" ▪ ▪ His *disciples* said to him, ▪ ▪ "You can *see* how this crowd *hems* you in, ▪ yet you *ask,* ▪ ▪ 'Who *touched* me?'" ▪ ▪ *Despite* this, ▪ he kept *looking* around to *see* the woman who had *done* it. ▪ ▪ *Fearful* ▪ and beginning to *tremble* ▪ now as she *realized* what had happened, ▪ the woman came and *fell* in front of him ▪ and *told* him the *whole* truth. ▪ ▪ He *said* to her, ▪ ▪ *"Daughter,* ▪ it is your *faith* that has cured you. ▪ ▪ Go in *peace* ▪ and be free of this illness." ▪ ▪ ▪

Their blunt announcement shatters previous mood.

Comforting. A call to faith.

A man of great authority!

"Wailing" and "loudly" sound like what they mean.

He had not *finished* speaking ▪ when people from the official's *house* arrived saying, ▪ ▪ "Your daughter is dead. ▪ ▪ Why *bother* the Teacher *further?"* ▪ ▪ Jesus *disregarded* the report that had been brought ▪ and *said* to the official: ▪ ▪ *"Fear* is *useless.* ▪ ▪ What is *needed* is *trust."* ▪ ▪ He would not permit *anyone* to follow him ▪ except *Peter,* ▪ *James,* ▪ and James's brother *John.* ▪ ▪ As they *approached* the house of the synagogue leader, ▪ Jesus was struck by the *noise* of people *wailing* and crying *loudly* on all sides. ▪ ▪ He entered and *said* to them: ▪ ▪ "Why do you make this

perhaps their surplus will relieve yours. Paul's grammatical constructions are the kindling for his argument; it remains for you to provide the spark that sets it blazing.

Referring to the Israelites' gathering of manna in the desert, the last sentence presents the futility of greed. In the desert God assured equality by seeing to it that all had only enough for their needs. Thus those who "gathered much had no excess" while those who "gathered little had no lack."

GOSPEL It's a scene right out of the tabloids: A prominent official driven by concern for his moribund child falls at the feet of a notorious faith healer who, at best, is viewed with skepticism by the rest of the establishment. What courageous love compelled this father to risk everything for the sake of his little daughter! Imagine Jairus finally breaching the crowd that surrounds Jesus, pausing for a last moment of decision, then collapsing to his knees. His "earnest appeal" might be a fervent whisper instead of a shout, with the words "and live" betraying the fear that his child teeters at the edge of death. Jesus joins him, and the crowd envelops them.

The opening of the second paragraph sounds like a promo for the next Oprah Winfrey or Phil Donahue show. Describe the woman's predicament with the same energy that one of the TV personalities would employ: "a dozen years . . . exhausted her savings . . . no relief . . . she only grew worse"! Imagine the woman, grateful for the camouflage of the crowd, as she gingerly reaches out her hand to touch Jesus' clothing. Her one sentence of (indirect) dialogue must reveal the impossible faith of a woman who, despite years of dead ends, tries one more time.

The narration of the healing echoes with the joy that raced through the woman as she sensed she was cured of her affliction. Jesus interrupts the joy when he wheels around, challenging the crowd with his question. If the disciples needed a good laugh, Jesus just gave them an opportunity. What do you mean, they protest, *everybody's* touching you! The rest of the scene exudes a tear-jerking poignancy. Sensing Jesus' penetrating gaze and "beginning to tremble," perhaps even fearing punishment or a reversal of the healing, the woman, like Jairus, falls at his feet. With surprising tenderness Jesus leans down and confirms the good news of her healing.

Just as we're drying our tears for the woman, an avalanche of bad news comes rumbling toward us. And could it have been delivered more bluntly? The child is dead. Don't bother the man anymore. Imagine Jesus waving off those insensitive messengers as he advises Jairus of the necessity of trust. As if needing to focus his energies for the task at hand, Jesus first forbids anyone but his closest disciples to follow him, then later dismisses the entourage of mourners that he discovers at the girl's home. Use the words "wailing and crying loudly" to suggest the distasteful din the mourners were creating. Jesus is undiplomatic and almost harsh in his reaction to them, so the mourners respond with ridicule. But Jesus doesn't put up with it for long; he throws them out.

The final scene is powerfully moving. See the parents enter timidly, clutching each other for support. Observe the disciples, confused yet expectant. And watch Jesus, confident and tender, taking the child's hand and whispering to her softly to "get up." The mood changes quickly. Jesus is not into passing out boxes of tissues. "Immediately" the girl rises and walks around. Jesus' only response to the family's astonishment is an admonition to silence and an order to get on to more important matters: giving her something to eat.

"The child is not dead": boldly, then softer for "She is asleep."

"Put them all out": Indirect quote, spoken by Jesus.

din with your wailing? ▪▪ The child is not *dead.* ▪▪ She is *asleep."* ▪▪ At this they began to ridicule him. ▪▪ Then he *put* them all *out.* ▪▪▪

Slowly. Visualize what you describe.

"Talitha, koum": a gentle whisper.

Mood changes.

"Not to let anyone know about it" and "Give her . . . eat": indirect quotes, spoken as Jesus (see Key).

Jesus took the child's *father* and *mother* and his own *companions* ▪ and *entered* the room where the child *lay.* ▪▪ Taking her *hand* ▪ he *said* to her, ▪▪ *'Talitha, koum,'* ▪▪ which means, ▪▪ "Little *girl,* ▪ *get* up." ▪▪▪ The girl, ▪ a child of *twelve,* ▪ stood up *immediately* ▪ and began to *walk* around. ▪▪ At *this* the family's *astonishment* was *complete.* ▪▪▪ He enjoined them *strictly* not to let anyone *know* about it, ▪ and *told* them to give her something to *eat.* ▪▪▪

[Shorter: Mark 5:21–24, 35–43]

FROM THE KEY

Stress (italics). The italics attempt to identify the operative words in a sentence, the ones that convey the meaning. Verbs do that best. They speak of action and intention. Next come nouns. Nouns are the people, places and things of a text—obviously important. Then there are color words like adverbs and adjectives. Stress these for variety or when they clarify the author's meaning.

The verb is generally more important in most verb-adverb combinations. In "He *looked* out at the people" ("looked" is the verb; "out" is the adverb), habit would have us stress *out.* To correct this, repeat the sentence several times without the adverb ("He looked at the people"), then reinsert the adverb and you should find yourself stressing the verb.

Context and variety determine whether a noun or adjective will be stressed. For example, "You shall be a glorious *crown* . . . a *royal* diadem." Prepositions are rarely stressed (unless you're saying: "He ran toward the wall and then *through* it!"). Don't hesitate to alter the stresses. But if you do, know why you're doing it.

If when reading a sentence it seems there are too many stresses, you're probably right. Italics do not always indicate the same degree of stress. When several words are italicized in a sentence, one or more may be subordinate. The passage "With their *hands* they will *support* you, that you may never *stumble* on a *stone"* contains four italicized words, but "support" and "stumble" receive the greater stress. No one way is the best way to accent a passage. When you combine the author's intent and the needs of your assembly—making the author's words as alive today as when they were first written—then you've found the best way to proclaim.

In any case, do not feel obligated to memorize all the stresses. The stress marks in this workbook are only suggestions. Feel free to disagree with them.

JULY 7, 1991

FOURTEENTH SUNDAY IN ORDINARY TIME

LECTIONARY #102

READING I Ezekiel 2:2–5

A reading from the book of the prophet ▪ *Ezekiel* ▪▪▪

Intensity from the start.

Spirit entered into me ▪ and *set* me on my *feet,* ▪▪ and I *heard* the one who was speaking *say* to me: ▪▪

Shift to God's voice. Uncompromising tone.

Son of *man,* ▪ I am *sending* you to the *Israelites,* ▪ *rebels* who have rebelled against *me;* ▪▪ they and

"Ancestors" is more inclusive.

their fathers have *revolted* against me to this *very* day. ▪▪ *Hard* of face and *obstinate* of heart are they to

Slowly, with renewed energy. Use pauses and eye contact.

whom I am *sending* you. ▪▪ But *you* shall *say* to them: ▪▪ Thus says the *Lord God!* ▪▪ And whether they *heed* or *resist*— ▪ for they are a *rebellious* house— ▪ they shall know that a *prophet* has been among them. ▪▪▪

READING II 2 Corinthians 12:7–10

Last of five consecutive weeks we read 2 Corinthians.

A reading from the second letter of *Paul* ▪ to the *Corinthians* ▪▪▪

Paul is unimpressed with his mystical visions.

As to the extraordinary *revelations,* ▪ in order that I might not become *conceited* ▪ I was given a *thorn* in

"Thorn in the flesh . . . (build) an angel of satan . . ."

the *flesh,* ▪ an angel of *Satan* to *beat* me ▪ and keep me from getting *proud.* ▪▪ *Three* times I *begged* the

Insistent. "Begged" sounds like it means.

Lord that this might *leave* me. ▪▪ He said to me, ▪▪ "My *grace* is *enough* for you, ▪ for in *weakness* ▪

Like a soothing balm.

power reaches *perfection."* ▪▪ And so I willingly *boast* of my weaknesses instead, ▪ that the *power* of

Fresh energy.

Christ may rest upon me. ▪▪▪

Therefore I am *content* with weakness, ▪ with

A proud litany.

mistreatment, ▪ with *distress,* ▪ with *persecutions* and *difficulties* ▪ for the sake of *Christ;* ▪▪ for when I

Rejoicing: "It doesn't all depend on me!"

am *powerless,* ▪ it is *then* ▪ that I am *strong.* ▪▪▪

READING I Some scriptures contain a single line that, because of its message and the power of its language, echoes in your spirit long after you've heard it. Such lines of singular power dominate the passage that contains them and are both a challenge and a joy for any proclaimer. The climactic sentence that concludes this reading is such a line; read it and see if you don't breathe out a "wow" in the silence that follows it.

God speaks strongly in this passage. All the language is of "rebels" who have "revolted" and become "hard of face and obstinate of heart." To these God sends Ezekiel, Israel's most unusual prophet, who speaks as if he's possessed by God's spirit. God places a hard message within him and orders him to proclaim it boldly to the rebellious house of Israel. Prophets never were welcome figures; they shook things up, they demanded change, they spoke God's truth—a message seldom appreciated by those who have strayed. They also proved God's fairness for they always warned of the consequences of infidelity to the covenant. That's Ezekiel's purpose here.

Stubborn and rebellious as the Israelites are, says God to Ezekiel, warn them anyway. Then, "whether they heed or resist," at least they will know that a *prophet*—my spokesperson, my *living* appeal for reform, my visible sign of love and fidelity, my *self* in human guise—yes, then they'll know "that a prophet has been among them"! The way you speak that line should make us look around to see if we've recognized the prophets among *us*.

READING II The opposition of his enemies prompted Paul to walk a road he was loathe to travel. If they needed "extraordinary revelations" to accept the validity of his ministry, Paul reasons, then boast he would. And boast he did in the section just prior to the present passage. Now he qualifies: Regarding these revelations, he says, let me tell you that God didn't allow my head to swell over them. No, indeed, God made sure there was an aspect to my experience that kept me humble!

No one knows if Paul's "thorn in the flesh" was a physical affliction, a persistent temptation or possibly some human opponent. Regardless, Paul beseeched the Lord "three times" (a shadow of Christ's threefold prayer in the garden) to let this cup pass, but he (like the Lord) was obliged to drink it.

Jesus' words to Paul are like a soothing balm applied to his wounded "flesh." "My grace," he says, "is enough for you." Then, applying the topsy-turvy logic of the kingdom, he adds, "in weakness power reaches perfection." Jesus' words not only soothe but they teach, and Paul is a willing student. He readily masters the perverse wisdom of the God of reversals: "I . . . boast of my *weaknesses,"* he says proudly, delighting in the divine power that is thus manifested through him.

Paul concludes by chanting a litany of the afflictions he gladly endures. These are his merit badges, the stripes on his sleeve; for the weaker he is, the more powerfully God can work through him. Paul's realization that everything doesn't all depend on him is comforting news for everyone (maybe even for those of us who proclaim the word)!

GOSPEL What a sad and tragic story! What an indictment of human nature: "No prophet is without honor except in his native place, among his own kindred, and in his own house." Imagine the profound sadness in Jesus as he spoke these words. Perhaps we more readily connect anger with this scene, imagining Jesus kicking the dust from his feet as he storms out of town. But look closely: "He could work no miracle there . . . so much did their lack of faith *distress* him." Would it not grieve any heart to find that those least receptive to one's gifts are the very people whose lives had been the playground and classrooms of one's youth?

Begin with a festive tone. Jesus is going home, and his arrival brings an unusually "large audience" to the synagogue. But the mood quickly turns sinister, for we immediately sense why they came: to discredit, to ridicule, to laugh at this "son of Mary." First the spectators question the authenticity of Jesus' ministry (Just where does he get his wisdom? How does he stage those miracles?), and then they speculate on his family origins. Let the energy build throughout the series of questions, as if the questioners feed off of each other's boldness. The narrator sums it up by saying Jesus was just "too much for them." (Speak that as an indirect quote.)

To the "kindred" who recently had tried to spirit him away because they thought he was crazy (Mark 3:21), Jesus quotes a familiar proverb about prophets. The words themselves are powerful, so Jesus can speak them with wistful resignation rather than with overdramatized emotion. As narrator, be aware of Jesus' pain in the final sentences and suggest he "made [his] rounds" not only to teach but, perhaps, also to forget.

GOSPEL Mark 6:1–6

A reading from the holy *gospel* according to *Mark* ▪ ▪ ▪

Expectant homecoming mood.

Jesus went to his *own* part of the country ▪ followed by his *disciples.* ▪ ▪ When the *sabbath* came ▪ he began to *teach* in the synagogue ▪ in a way that kept his *large* audience *amazed.* ▪ ▪ They said: ▪ ▪ "Where did he *get* all this? ▪ ▪ What kind of *wisdom* is he *endowed* with? ▪ ▪ How is it such *miraculous* deeds are accomplished by *his* hands? ▪ ▪ Isn't this the *carpenter,* ▪ the son of *Mary,* ▪ a brother of *James* and *Joses* and *Judas* and *Simon?* ▪ ▪ Aren't his *sisters* our *neighbors* here?" ▪ ▪ They found him *too much* for them. ▪ ▪ ▪ Jesus' *response* to all this was: ▪ ▪ "No *prophet* is without *honor* ▪ *except* in his *native* place, ▪ among his own *kindred,* ▪ and in his *own house."* ▪ ▪ ▪ He could work no *miracle* there, ▪ apart from *curing* a few who were *sick* by laying *hands* on them, ▪ so *much* did their *lack* of faith *distress* him. ▪ ▪ He made the rounds of the *neighboring* villages *instead,* ▪ and spent his time *teaching.* ▪ ▪ ▪

Questions grow bolder and angrier.

Disbelief.

"Too much for them": Speak as an indirect quote.

Sadly resigned.

Narrator is defensive and solicitous for Jesus.

Making the best of a painful situation.

JULY 14, 1991

FIFTEENTH SUNDAY IN ORDINARY TIME

LECTIONARY #105

READING I Amos 7:12–15

A reading from the book of the prophet ▪ *Amos* ▪▪▪

"Amaziah" = Ă-mah-zeye-āh. Like he's talking to a despised underling.

Amaziah ▪ (priest of Bethel) ▪ said to *Amos,* ▪▪ *"Off* with you, ▪ *visionary,* ▪ *flee* to the land of *Judah!* ▪▪ *There* earn your bread by *prophesying,* ▪ but *never* again prophesy in *Bethel;* ▪▪ for it is the *king's* sanctuary and a *royal* temple." ▪▪ Amos *answered* Amaziah, ▪▪ *"I* was no prophet, ▪ nor have I belonged to a *company* of prophets; ▪▪ I was a *shepherd* and a dresser of *sycamores.* ▪▪ The *Lord* took me from following the flock, ▪ and *said* to me, ▪▪ *Go,* ▪ *prophesy* to my people *Israel."* ▪▪▪

He acts so superior.

"What makes you think I'd want to be known as a prophet?"

"This was God's idea." "Prophesy" = prŏ-fe-sigh.

READING II Ephesians 1:3–14

First of seven consecutive weeks we read from Ephesians.

A reading from the letter of *Paul* ▪ to the *Ephesians* ▪▪▪

Let eye contact invite assembly to praise with you.

Praised by the *God* and *Father* of our *Lord* Jesus Christ, ▪ who has *bestowed* on us in Christ ▪ every spiritual *blessing* in the heavens! ▪▪ God *chose* us in him ▪ before the world *began,* ▪ to be *holy* and *blameless* in his sight, ▪▪ to be *full* of *love:* ▪▪ he likewise *predestined* us through Christ Jesus ▪ to be his adopted *sons*— ▪ such was his *will* and *pleasure*— ▪ that all might *praise* the divine *favor* he has bestowed on us ▪ in his *beloved.* ▪▪▪

You can hardly believe God could do so much!

"Sons and daughters" is more inclusive.

Christ's role is exalted.

It is in Christ and through his *blood* that we have been *redeemed* ▪ and our sins *forgiven,* ▪ so immeasurably *generous* is God's *favor* to us. ▪▪ God has given us the *wisdom* to understand *fully* the mystery, ▪ the *plan* he was pleased to decree in Christ, ▪ to be carried out in the *fullness* of time: ▪▪ namely, ▪ to bring *all* things in the heavens and on earth into *one* ▪ under *Christ's* headship. ▪▪▪

One phrase at a time.

"We" (the Jews) contrasts with "you" (the Gentiles).

In him we were *chosen:* ▪ for in the *decree* of God, ▪ who administers *everything* according to his will and

READING I What was the line from last week's gospel: "No prophet is without honor except in his native place"? Amos was far from home shaking up the local establishment when Amaziah, the high priest of Bethel, who should have valued and heeded Amos's warnings, turns on him, ordering him to flee. Political rivalry and personal jealousy color Amaziah's words of banishment. Bethel is the *"king's* sanctuary and a *royal* temple," and he is its designated guardian. What right does this self-appointed, uneducated country bumpkin have to come stirring things up? "Off with you," he demands scornfully, practically spitting out the word "visionary." Next he insinuates Amos's prophesying is his occupation instead of his ministry: "There," he sneers with mounting hostility, "earn your bread by prophesying."

Because true prophets never *volunteer,* Amos defends his ministry by insisting God grabbed him by the collar and ordered, "Go, prophesy." Because the prophets of Bethel were such a disreputable group, Amos vehemently dissociates himself from their number: "I was no prophet." His lowly origins, however, as "shepherd" and "dresser of sycamores," he wears as a badge of honor. Though not eager to be a prophet, when God said prophesy, Amos did.

READING II Remember the opening scene from *The Sound of Music*? On a hilltop a girl surveys the countryside, skips about appreciating the flowers, spins in an ecstatic embrace of earth and sky, then throws open her arms in a burst of joyous song. Bring to your proclamation an enthusiasm like Maria's for God's goodness revealed in the manifold gifts bestowed on us: "every spiritual blessing . . . sins forgiven . . . wisdom." Use these words as you would the lyrics of a song, listening to the cadences, stretching the syllables, hitting high and low notes, varying your tempo. The first sentence explodes like Maria's "The hills are alive." Filled with gratitude, God's praise issues from your lips. "God *chose* us," you say, *predestined* us, in fact, to be adopted children. Caring for us is God's great "pleasure" that evokes our response of praise.

The second paragraph enumerates God's good deeds at a slower pace. Because it consists of two long sentences comprised of many phrases, read it slowly, identify the thought in each phrase and use your inflection to distinguish one thought from another. For example: "God has given us the wisdom to understand *fully* the mystery, [that is] the *plan* he was pleased to decree in Christ, [which is] to be *carried out* in the fullness of time."

The last paragraph presents Paul's

expanded vision of "church." "Church" no longer means "local community" but "global community," where everyone is incorporated into Christ's body. The "we" of the first sentence and the "you" of the second refer respectively to Jews and Gentiles. What was first extended to God's chosen people now is extended to "you too" because you've accepted the gospel ("glad tidings") that was preached to you. That acceptance, Paul says, "sealed [you] with the Holy Spirit" and put your name, as it were, on the will. For now, like the Jews, you share in the inheritance of which the Spirit is the "first payment." All this has a tone of reassurance, as if you were taking aside the black sheep of the family to convince the person that he or she has not been left out of the family's benefits or affection.

GOSPEL "Tell me what to do and I'll do it. Give me the materials and I'll build it. Point me in the right direction and I'll go there." For some of us, willingness to serve the reign of God might be expressed in such terms. "Don't make me think or plan, just give me the tools and let me work."

Jesus says "No" to that simplistic approach. Working for the kingdom is not simply a matter of work hours; it's essentially a matter of radical trust in God. Kingdom builders receive no blueprints and few tools except their native gifts and God's providence. That may not seem like much to go on, but, apparently, that's the way Jesus wants it.

Be ready to act at a moment's notice, says Jesus. Don't be weighed down by the tools of your trade and don't be limited by what you think are essentials. Entrust yourself to the mercy of God. Such advice (or is it survival training?) must be shared with tender compassion. Jesus is no drill sergeant enumerating the do's and don'ts of boot camp; he is teaching the apostles to be his representatives, to model what living in the reign of God entails.

Note, Jesus sends "the Twelve," not "the seventy-two." His tone necessarily is more intimate and solicitous with these privileged friends. Jesus can be frank: "Whatever house you find . . . stay there"—in other words, don't shop around for the most luxurious home and don't insult your host by leaving for better accommodations. And Jesus can be fiercely loyal: "If any place will not receive you . . . shake its dust from your feet."

The going off is joyous and the ministry, nothing short of amazing!

Speak to your assembly like you would to a beloved relative who needs reassurance.

Ritardando: "To praise his glory."

counsel, ▪ *we* were predestined to *praise* his *glory* ▪ by being the *first* to *hope* in *Christ.* ▪▪ In him you *too* were chosen; ▪▪ when you *heard* the glad tidings of salvation, ▪ the word of *truth,* ▪ and *believed* in it, ▪ you were sealed with the *Holy Spirit* who had been *promised.* ▪▪ He is the *pledge* of our inheritance, ▪ the first *payment* against the full redemption of a people God has made his *own* ▪ to *praise* his *glory.* ▪▪▪

[Shorter: Ephesians 1:3–10]

GOSPEL Mark 6:7–13

A reading from the holy *gospel* according to *Mark* ▪▪▪

Speak of "the Twelve" with affection.

Gives them "authority" over death and evil.

Speak in Jesus' voice, giving his friends survival training.

Be prudent and courteous.

Don't tolerate abuse.

Joyous departure.

Amazing, incredible results.

Jesus summoned the *Twelve* ▪ and began to *send* them out *two* by *two,* ▪ giving them *authority* over *unclean spirits.* ▪▪ He instructed them to take *nothing* on the journey but a *walking stick*— ▪▪ no *food,* ▪ no *traveling* bag, ▪ not a *coin* in the purses in their belts. ▪▪ They were, ▪ however, ▪ to wear *sandals.* ▪▪ "Do not bring a *second* tunic," ▪ he said, ▪▪ and added: ▪▪ "Whatever *house* you find yourself in, ▪ *stay* there until you *leave* the locality. ▪▪ If any place will not *receive* you or *hear* you, ▪ shake its *dust* from your *feet* in testimony *against* them as you leave." ▪▪ With that they *went* off, ▪ preaching the need of *repentance.* ▪▪ They *expelled* many *demons,* ▪ *anointed* the sick with *oil,* ▪ and worked *many* cures. ▪▪▪

JULY 21, 1991

SIXTEENTH SUNDAY IN ORDINARY TIME

LECTIONARY #108

READING I Jeremiah 23:1–6

A reading from the book of the prophet ▪ *Jeremiah* ▪▪▪

Anger and threat. Stretch the word "Woe."

Woe to the *shepherds* ▪ who *mislead* and *scatter* the flock of my pasture, ▪ says the Lord. ▪▪ Therefore, ▪ thus says the *Lord,* ▪ the *God* of Israel, ▪ against the *shepherds* who shepherd my *people:* ▪▪ You have *scattered* my sheep and *driven* them away. ▪▪ You have not *cared* for them, ▪▪ but *I* will take care to *punish* your evil deeds. ▪▪ I myself will *gather* the *remnant* of my flock from all the *lands* to which I have *driven* them ▪ and *bring* them back to their *meadow;* ▪▪ there they shall *increase* and *multiply.* ▪▪ I will appoint *shepherds* for them ▪ who will shepherd them so that they need no longer *fear* and *tremble;* ▪▪ and *none* shall be *missing,* ▪ says the Lord. ▪▪▪

Look about. Demand attention.

Great disappointment. Contrast "not cared" with "take care."

God's voice is still strong and assertive.

Starting to soften.

Poetic prophecy announcing great news.

Behold, ▪ the days are *coming,* ▪ says the Lord, ▪
when I will raise up a *righteous* shoot to David; ▪▪
As *king* he shall reign and govern *wisely,* ▪
he shall do what is *just* and *right* in the land. ▪▪
In *his* days ▪ Judah shall be *saved,* ▪
Israel shall dwell in *security.* ▪▪
This is the *name* they give him: ▪▪
"The *Lord* ▪ our *justice.*" ▪▪▪

Let the words reach out and comfort.

Slowly, with expectant hope.

READING II Ephesians 2:13–18

Second of seven consecutive weeks we read from Ephesians.

A reading from the letter of *Paul* ▪ to the *Ephesians* ▪▪▪

Be sure to go slow.

"Blood" suggests Christ's great sacrificial love for us.

In *Christ Jesus* ▪ you who once were *far* off ▪ have been brought *near* through the *blood* of *Christ.* ▪▪ It is he who is our *peace,* ▪ and who made the two of us *one* ▪ by breaking down the barrier of *hostility* that kept us *apart.* ▪▪ In his own *flesh* ▪ he *abolished* the

READING I Too often the evening news brings reports of people in authority who through some abuse have harmed those entrusted to their care. Politicians, religious leaders and businesspeople have disappointed us by failing to live up to their responsibilities. Jeremiah accuses the "shepherds" of doing precisely the opposite of what they have been charged to do. Shepherds should gather and protect; these shepherds have "scattered [God's] sheep and driven them away."

There is disappointment in God's accusation, a tone that asks: How could you have squandered the responsibility I entrusted you with? Imagine the rage of parents who come home to find their children missing because the babysitter left them alone to attend a nearby party.

The shepherds have permitted chaos, so God asserts control. "You have not cared . . . but *I* will take care . . ." expresses God's angry determination to reestablish order while doling out just punishment to those who disturbed the order. The double use of the word "care" cleverly contrasts notions of nurturance and threat. Though God now speaks of restoration, your tone carries the determination of a mighty monarch proclaiming boldly. Only the last phrase, "and none shall be missing . . . ," softens into the more pastoral tone that will characterize the poetic oracle of paragraph two.

Here God describes how differently the ideal future king will rule. Let the words reach out to embrace and comfort the weary "sheep"; and speak the closing title as if it were the name of one whose reign will set all things right.

READING II Sometimes a little package can be laden with so much tape and wrapping that it seems impossible to get at what's inside. In such cases the best way to proceed is slowly and carefully. Tearing hard and fast can make you break the contents.

Paul has given us a tightly wrapped package that contains a simple message: By shedding his blood for us, Christ made all people one. The core message is embellished with other peripheral ideas: Jesus broke down the religious barrier that kept apart Jews (who were near) and Gentiles (who were far off) by abolishing the Mosaic law with its commands and precepts. He thereby made us "one new [people]," and we have "access . . . to the Father."

The complex sentence structure makes it difficult to get at the gift that Paul has packaged. The solution: Go slow. Speak with an awareness that you share news worth hearing and in a way that tells your listeners that *they* have been transformed from those who "were far off" to those who are near!

In the last sentence Paul wants to make sure that his point is understood. It's all been said already, so now say it as if you were Jesus, trying to draw your people to your bosom where they will find the Spirit who opens the door to the Father.

GOSPEL Open the passage with the disciples' jubilant enthusiasm as they gather around Jesus competing to disclose the exciting and surprising events they've experienced. Jesus wants to hear it all and invites them to come by themselves to "an out-of-the-way place" where they can rest and converse without interruption. Jesus' eagerness to hear of his friends' success should be evident in the way you speak his summons.

The narrator's unsympathetic response to the crowd's efforts to be near Jesus sets up the poignancy of Jesus' contrasting response when his attempt to escape them fails. Speak, therefore, of how the crowd "hastened on foot to the place," not with the agitated and expectant mood of the people but with the disapproval of one who thinks they are being unfeeling.

Picture Jesus disembarking and scrutinizing the crowd with a gentle and resigned shake of the head. "He pitied them" conveys all that we know of Jesus' love for us. Jesus does not disappoint. Seeing that they (and we) "were like sheep without a shepherd," he begins to do what he did best—pour himself out for them.

"New person" is more inclusive. "Two" = Jews and Gentiles.

"Cross" = a reminder of the price of reconciliation.

Eye contact. Convince us.

law with its *commands* and *precepts,* ▪ to create in himself *one new* man ▪ from us who had been *two,* ▪ and to make *peace,* ▪ reconciling *both* of us to God in *one* body ▪ through his *cross* ▪ which put that *enmity* to *death.* ▪▪ He came and *"announced* the good news of peace to you who were *far* off, ▪ *and* to those who were *near";* ▪▪ through *him* ▪ we *both* have access in *one Spirit* to the *Father.* ▪▪▪

GOSPEL Mark 6:30–34

A reading from the holy *gospel* according to *Mark* ▪▪▪

Joyous. "All that they . . . had taught" = indirect quote as if spoken by apostles.

Jesus is also jubilant.

Narrator is irritated with crowd.

They wouldn't leave him alone.

The apostles *returned* to Jesus ▪ and *reported* to him all that they had *done* ▪ and what they had *taught.* ▪▪ He *said* to them, ▪▪ "Come by *yourselves* to an out-of-the-way place and *rest* a little." ▪▪ People were coming and going in *great* numbers, ▪ making it *impossible* for them to so much as *eat.* ▪▪ So Jesus and the apostles went off in the *boat* ▪ by *themselves* ▪ to a deserted place. ▪▪ People *saw* them leaving, ▪ and many got to *know* about it. ▪▪ People from all the towns *hastened* on *foot* to the place, ▪ arriving *ahead* of them. ▪▪▪

With Jesus' compassionate resignation. Then pause.

Suggest that "teach" is an act of great love.

Upon disembarking ▪ Jesus saw a *vast* crowd. ▪▪▪ He *pitied* them, ▪ for they were like *sheep* without a *shepherd;* ▪▪ and he began to *teach* them at *great length.* ▪▪▪

JULY 28, 1991

SEVENTEENTH SUNDAY IN ORDINARY TIME

LECTIONARY #111

READING I 2 Kings 4:42–44

Short reading = slow reading.

A reading from the second book of *Kings* ▪ ▪ ▪

"Baal-shalishah": Check pronunciation key.

A man came from *Baal-shalishah* ▪ bringing to *Elisha,* ▪ the man of *God,* ▪ *twenty* barley loaves made from the *firstfruits,* ▪ and fresh *grain* in the ear. ▪ ▪

Sounds like a reasonable request.

"Give it to the *people* to *eat,*" Elisha said. ▪ ▪ But his servant *objected,* ▪ ▪ "How can I set *this* before a *hundred* men?" ▪ ▪

Shocked and disbelieving. "People" is more inclusive.

"Give it to the people to *eat,*" ▪ Elisha *insisted.* ▪ ▪ "For thus says the *Lord,* ▪ ▪ 'They shall *eat* and there shall be some *left over.*'" ▪ ▪ ▪

Confident trust.

And when they *had* eaten, ▪ there *was* some left over, ▪ as the Lord has *said.* ▪ ▪ ▪

Amazed at the fulfillment.

READING II Ephesians 4:1–6

Third of seven consecutive weeks we read from Ephesians.

A reading from the first letter of *Paul* ▪ to the *Ephesians* ▪ ▪ ▪

"Plead" is what you say and plead is what you do.

I *plead* with you ▪ as a *prisoner* for the *Lord,* ▪ to live a life *worthy* of the *calling* you have received, ▪ ▪ with perfect *humility,* ▪ *meekness,* ▪ and *patience,* ▪ ▪ *bearing* with one another *lovingly.* ▪ ▪

Renewed energy. Tell us: "Don't give up."

Make every *effort* to preserve the *unity* ▪ which has the *Spirit* as its *origin* ▪ and *peace* as its *binding* force. ▪ ▪

Still pleading for unity, not reading a list. Don't stress "ones" but the nouns instead.

There is but *one* body and *one* Spirit, ▪ just as there is but one *hope* ▪ given *all* of you by your *call.* ▪ ▪ There is one *Lord,* ▪ one *faith,* ▪ one *baptism;* ▪ ▪ one *God* and *Father* of *all,* ▪ who is *over* all, ▪ and works *through* all, ▪ and is *in* all. ▪ ▪ ▪

Stress prepositions.

READING I In this passage the man "from Baal-shalishah" finds himself in a predicament. He's being required to do something that defies logic by a reasonable and reliable "man of God." When a voice of authority contradicts logic, instinct tells us to trust logic (particularly if it's our own). So to Elisha's confident admonition that he "Give it to the people," the man responds with a disbelieving, "How can I set *this* before a *hundred men [people]*?"

Elisha is *calmly* insistent. His confidence in God's power to multiply is heard in the prophecy that "there shall be some left over." His trust lets him insist with kindness. The last sentence is spoken with amazement of one whose expectations have been overturned.

READING II Though seldom shy about telling people what to do, Paul's imprisonment at the time of this writing adds urgency to his plea that the Ephesians live a worthy life. Paul coaches our reading through his choice of the second word of the passage. "Plead" is a powerful word that suggests both psychological attitude and bodily expression. You can't plead without a certain physical intensity, without reaching out to your listeners, without caring about what you say *and* to whom you say it.

If a woman visiting her daughter and son-in-law were to hear the couple threatening to divorce each other, she might intercede with the same intensity as Paul that they should "live a life worthy of the calling [they] have received . . . [and] with perfect humility, meekness, and patience [bear] with one another lovingly." She might remind them that they are not alone in their struggle to reconcile, for the "God and Father of all" works *in* and *through* them to keep them one.

That kind of zeal must propel you through the reading as you urge us to preserve the gift of unity that emanates from the Spirit. The litany of "ones" ("Lord," "faith," "baptism," etc.) will not become redundant if you remember that each noun is unique and needs individual emphasis. Stressing the prepositions at the end reminds us that God's presence is not separate from but is woven into the very fabric of our lives.

GOSPEL Typical of John's narrative, it is Jesus in this gospel, not the disciples, who shows concern for feeding the people. That initiative makes possible a reading that suggests perhaps a playful motive behind Jesus' question to Philip.

Jesus plays a game when he coyly asks his question and awaits the alarmed response of Philip and the others. Until that question the narrator paints a scene of large proportions: "A vast crowd" follows this miracle worker to a mountaintop, having seen the signs he was performing. It is nearly Passover, the holiest time of the year, and against this stately backdrop Jesus asks his mock-serious question, which the narrator seems to enjoy labeling a ruse. It doesn't fail to elicit a colorful response from Philip.

Sometimes our words reveal a deeper faith than we ever expected to find within ourselves. Andrew's noting the presence of the lad with the five fish suggests an incipient awareness that Jesus might indeed be able to do some good with so little. The pretense over, Jesus takes charge and gives orders for the people to sit on the spring grass, creating a festive atmosphere and rejoicing as he gives thanks and distributes "as much [food] as they wanted." The narrator marvels at the number of baskets filled by the leftovers.

The only miracle that all four evangelists record,this "sign" has a profound effect on the people who allow their awe to well up into coronation frenzy. The ending, however, is melancholy, suggesting the inevitable loneliness of one who gives people not what they want but what they need.

GOSPEL John 6:1–15

First of five weeks we read from John's gospel instead of Mark's.

A reading from the holy *gospel* according to *John* ▪ ▪ ▪

Emphasize magnitude of crowd and astounding nature of Jesus' signs.

It's spring time.

He begins to anticipate their need.

Enjoying the put-on.

As if that was the craziest question you've ever heard.

Jesus crossed the *Sea* of *Galilee* ▪ [to the shore] of *Tiberias;* ▪ ▪ a *vast* crowd kept *following* him ▪ because they saw the *signs* he was performing for the *sick.* ▪ ▪ Jesus then went up the *mountain* ▪ and sat down there with his *disciples.* ▪ ▪ The Jewish feast of *Passover* was near; ▪ ▪ when Jesus *looked* up and caught sight of a vast *crowd* coming toward him, ▪ he said to *Philip,* ▪ ▪ "Where shall we buy *bread* for these people to *eat?*" ▪ ▪ (He knew *well* what he intended to *do* ▪ but he asked this to *test* Philip's *response.)* ▪ ▪ Philip replied, "Not even with *two hundred* days' wages could we buy *loaves* enough to give each of them a *mouthful!*" ▪ ▪ ▪

Half-hoping the suggestion might prove helpful.

Jesus taking charge.

Here "men" means adult males.

Pause.

They're amazed.

One of Jesus' *disciples,* ▪ *Andrew,* ▪ Simon Peter's *brother,* ▪ remarked to him, ▪ ▪ "There is a *lad* here who has five *barley* loaves and a couple of dried *fish,* ▪ but what good is *that* for so *many?*" ▪ ▪ Jesus said, ▪ ▪ "Get the people to *recline.*" ▪ ▪ Even though the men numbered about *five thousand,* ▪ there was *plenty* of grass for them to find a *place* on the ground. ▪ ▪ Jesus then took the *loaves* of *bread,* ▪ gave *thanks,* ▪ and *passed* them around to those *reclining* there; ▪ ▪ he did the *same* with the dried *fish,* ▪ as *much* as they *wanted.* ▪ ▪ When they had had *enough,* ▪ he *told* his disciples, ▪ ▪ "Gather up the *crusts* that are left over ▪ so that *nothing* will go to *waste.*" ▪ ▪ At this, ▪ they gathered *twelve* baskets full of pieces ▪ *left over* by those who had been fed with the *five* barley loaves. ▪ ▪ ▪

Growing excitement.

Recognizing the danger and his responsibility.

When the people *saw* the sign he had performed ▪ they began to say, ▪ ▪ "This is *undoubtedly* the *Prophet* who is to come into the world." ▪ ▪ At that, ▪ Jesus *realized* that they would come and *carry* him off to make him *king,* ▪ so he *fled* back to the mountain ▪ *alone.* ▪ ▪ ▪

AUGUST 4, 1991

EIGHTEENTH SUNDAY IN ORDINARY TIME

LECTIONARY #114

READING I Exodus 16:2–4, 12–15

A reading from the book of *Exodus* ▪ ▪ ▪

As if speaking of yourself and your community.

Like an angry teenager to a parent.

The whole Israelite community *grumbled* against *Moses* and *Aaron.* ▪ ▪ The Israelites *said* to them, ▪ ▪ "Would that we had *died* at the Lord's hand in the land of *Egypt,* ▪ as we sat by our *fleshpots* and ate our *fill* of bread! ▪ ▪ But *you* had to lead us into this *desert* ▪ to make the *whole* community die of *famine!*" ▪ ▪ ▪

God responds to their hunger.

"Daily" portions to prevent hoarding.

Then the *Lord* said to Moses, ▪ ▪ "I will now rain down *bread* from *heaven* for you. ▪ ▪ *Each* day ▪ the people are to go out and *gather* their *daily* portion; ▪ ▪ thus will I *test* them, ▪ to see whether they *follow* my instructions or *not.* ▪ ▪ ▪

God asserting dominion.

"I have *heard* the grumbling of the Israelites. ▪ ▪ *Tell* them: ▪ ▪ In the evening *twilight* you shall eat *flesh,* ▪ and in the *morning* ▪ you shall have your fill of *bread,* ▪ so that you may know that I, the *Lord,* ▪ am your *God.*" ▪ ▪ ▪

Slowly.

Making a wonderful discovery. Amazed.

A pun here: "manna" means "what is this?" in Hebrew.

Not just information, but a reminder to be grateful.

In the *evening* ▪ *quail* came up and *covered* the camp. ▪ ▪ In the *morning* ▪ a *dew* lay all about the camp, ▪ and when the dew *evaporated,* ▪ there on the *surface* of the desert ▪ were fine *flakes* like *hoarfrost* on the ground. ▪ ▪ On *seeing* it, ▪ the Israelites *asked* one another, ▪ ▪ "What *is* this?" ▪ ▪ for they did not *know* what it was. ▪ ▪ But *Moses* told them, ▪ ▪ "This is the *bread* ▪ which the *Lord* has given you to eat." ▪ ▪ ▪

READING II Ephesians 4:17, 20–24

Fourth of seven consecutive weeks we read from Ephesians.

A reading from the letter of *Paul* ▪ to the *Ephesians* ▪ ▪ ▪

Slowly; with authority.

"Don't live like mindless people."

Less passion now; reasoning.

Your tone says: "Forget the way you were before."

I *declare* ▪ and *solemnly* attest in the Lord ▪ that you must *no* longer live as the *pagans* do— ▪ their minds *empty.* ▪ ▪ That is *not* what you learned when you learned *Christ!* ▪ ▪ I am *supposing,* ▪ of course, ▪ that he has been *preached* and *taught* to you in accord with the *truth* that is in Jesus: ▪ ▪ *namely,* ▪ that you must lay *aside* your *former* way of life ▪ and the *old* self which *deteriorates* through *illusion* and *desire,* ▪ ▪

READING I No sooner have the Israelites tasted freedom than they get a taste for the bounty they knew in Egypt. You should have let us die there with our bellies full, instead of leading us to starve in the desert. Let your voice mimic their moaning to Moses. Such gratitude for the gift of freedom that God just purchased for them! God's response is restrained, but there can be an edge and somewhat of a grudging quality in the announcement that "I will test them" by raining "bread from heaven."

God decides to demonstrate, yet again, the constancy of divine love for this unruly people. "I have heard the grumbling of the Israelites," God says, but will prove to them they have nothing to grumble about. God's response is both gracious and powerful; though mindful of the people's needs, God is determined to assert authority through that act of graciousness.

The last paragraph is wonderful: Sadness turns to joy, want turns to plenty, and the impossible becomes reality. Read slowly and be as amazed as the Israelite grumblers when you narrate the discovery of the "quail" and the "fine flakes." In Moses' response we hear the resignation of one who has been vindicated almost against his will. We almost could applaud his anger if we ourselves were not such frequent recipients of undeserved mercy.

READING II No matter what they're trying to correct—overeating, overdrinking, overworking—people who make changes in their life-styles need reminders to observe their commitments. Married couples know fidelity is not as easy as saying, "I do"; and Paul knows that becoming a Christian doesn't end on the day one is baptized. So he writes to the Ephesians with reminders that their commitment to Christ entails a whole new way of life and becoming in fact a *new person.*

Paul opens his letter with a solemn declaration. Start slowly, allowing his authority to be heard in your tone. There is an uncompromising urgency in Paul's address as he insists that their initiation into Christ abolished the possibility of living the old way: "That is *not* what you learned when you learned Christ!"

Strive for balance as you name "the truth that is in Jesus." Contrast what we must lay aside ("former way of life"), with what we must acquire ("spiritual way of thinking") and put on ("that new [person] created in God's image"). Your tone is negative and disapproving as you describe what we should take off, but positive and hopeful when you tell us what to put on. Speak throughout as someone who's yearning, even cheering, for our success.

GOSPEL When someone is working miracles, any person of sense stays abreast of the latest events. This crowd, however, was caught unaware—they turned their heads and Jesus slipped away. When you start, narrate with the crowd's sense of urgency and confusion, which only increases when they finally find Jesus. Jesus arrived where he is by walking on water. The crowd knows he didn't take a boat, so they wonder how he got there. In their inquiry about when he came we can almost hear the question: Did we miss a miracle?

Jesus doesn't speak of his miraculous crossing; instead he tells them that they misunderstand the importance of the signs they have seen. They are focused totally on the "perishable food" that filled their bellies, rather than on the "food that remains unto *life eternal*" (given only by the Son of Man). Yearning for them to recognize him for who he truly is, Jesus' tone invites their dialogue.

The people eagerly follow his lead: "What must we do?" they ask. It's simple, answers Jesus, have faith in me. But the group again becomes myopic and insists on miracles and proofs. They are not evil, only human in their desire to see Jesus conjure manna from the air in a miraculous display that would top anything their ancestors witnessed.

Calmly, Jesus begins to teach them what is "the real heavenly bread." Like the woman at the well, these people are literalists who think Jesus will satisfy their here-and-now hunger. Their request, sincere and energetic, is so much wasted effort.

Finally, because nothing else will do it, Jesus speaks bluntly. Like the thirst of the Samaritan woman, their hunger will be sated only when they find their home in Jesus.

Your tone says: "Do this instead!" "New person" is more inclusive.

and acquire a *fresh,* ▪ *spiritual* way of thinking. ▪▪
You must *put on* that *new* man ▪ created in *God's image,* ▪ whose *justice* and *holiness* ▪ are born of *truth.* ▪▪▪

GOSPEL John 6:24–35

A reading from the holy *gospel* according to *John* ▪▪▪

Narrate with crowd's agitation and confusion.

When the crowd *saw* that neither *Jesus* nor his *disciples* were at the *place* where they had eaten the *bread,* ▪ they *too* embarked in the boats ▪ and went to *Capernaum* ▪ *looking* for Jesus. ▪▪▪

Even more confused now.

When they *found* him on the *other* side of the lake, ▪ they said to him, ▪▪ *"Rabbi,* ▪ when did you *come* here?" ▪▪ Jesus *answered* them: ▪▪

Chiding at first.

"I *assure* you, ▪
you are not *looking* for me because
you have seen *signs* ▪
but because you have eaten your *fill*
of the *loaves.* ▪▪

Pleading with them to see clearly.

You should not be working for *perishable* food ▪
but for food that *remains* unto *life eternal,* ▪
food which the *Son* of *Man* will give you; ▪▪
it is on *him* that God the Father has set
his *seal."* ▪▪

An honest question.

At this ▪ they said to him, ▪▪ "What must we *do* to perform the *works* of *God?"* ▪▪ Jesus replied: ▪▪

An honest answer.

"This is the work of God: ▪▪
have *faith* in the One he *sent."* ▪▪

"So that we *can* put faith in you," ▪ they asked him, ▪▪

A dishonest question. All they want are miracles.

"what *sign* are you going to perform for us to *see?* ▪▪
What is the 'work' *you* do? ▪▪ Our *ancestors* had

Their tone implies: "Can you do better?"

manna to eat in the desert; ▪▪ according to *Scripture,* ▪▪
'He gave them *bread* from the *heavens* to eat.'" ▪▪
Jesus said to them: ▪▪

Patient and earnest.

"I solemnly *assure* you, ▪▪
it was not *Moses* who gave you bread
from the heavens; ▪▪
it is my *Father* who gives you the *real*
heavenly bread. ▪▪
God's bread comes down from *heaven* ▪
and gives *life* to the world." ▪▪

Much energy. They mean it, but they missed the boat.

"Sir, ▪ *give* us this bread *always,"* they besought him. ▪▪

Jesus *explained* to them: ▪▪
"I *myself* am the bread of *life.* ▪▪

Tender, gentle and loving.

No one who comes to *me* ▪ shall ever be *hungry,* ▪
no one who *believes* in me ▪ shall *thirst*
again." ▪▪▪

AUGUST 11, 1991

NINETEENTH SUNDAY IN ORDINARY TIME

LECTIONARY #117

READING I 1 Kings 19:4–8

A reading from the first book of *Kings* ▪ ▪ ▪

Slowly. His every step is an effort.

No melodrama; he means it.

As narrator you care about Elijah.

Elijah can't believe his eyes.

The angel means business!

Your tone grows stronger and more determined. Say "Horeb" with reverence.

Elijah went a day's journey into the *desert,* ▪ until he came to a *broom* tree and *sat* beneath it. ▪ ▪ He *prayed* for *death:* ▪ ▪ "This is *enough,* ▪ O Lord! ▪ ▪ *Take* my life, ▪ for I am no better than my *fathers."* ▪ ▪ He *lay* down and fell *asleep* under the broom tree, ▪ ▪ but then an *angel* touched him ▪ and *ordered* him to *get* up and *eat.* ▪ ▪ He *looked* ▪ and there at his head was a *hearth* cake and a jug of *water.* ▪ ▪ After he *ate* and *drank,* ▪ he lay down *again,* ▪ but the angel of the Lord came back a *second* time, ▪ *touched* him, ▪ and *ordered,* ▪ ▪ "Get up and *eat,* ▪ else the *journey* will be too *long* for you!" ▪ ▪ He *got* up, ▪ ▪ *ate* and *drank;* ▪ ▪ then *strengthened* by that food, ▪ he walked *forty days* and *forty nights* ▪ to the *mountain* of God, ▪ *Horeb.* ▪ ▪ ▪

READING II Ephesians 4:30—5:2

A reading from the letter of *Paul* ▪ to the *Ephesians* ▪ ▪ ▪

Fifth of seven consecutive weeks we read from Ephesians.

Don't waste this poignant image.

You know how hard this is—let your voice confess it.

We must because Christ did.

Eye contact.

Ritardando: "a gift of pleasing fragrance."

Do nothing to *sadden* the *Holy Spirit* ▪ with whom you were *sealed* against the day of *redemption.* ▪ ▪ Get *rid* of all *bitterness,* ▪ all *passion* and *anger,* ▪ *harsh* words, ▪ *slander,* ▪ and malice of *every* kind. ▪ ▪ In *place* of these, ▪ ▪ be *kind* to one another, ▪ *compassionate,* ▪ and mutually *forgiving,* ▪ ▪ just as God has forgiven *you* in *Christ.* ▪ ▪ ▪

Be *imitators* of God as his dear *children.* ▪ ▪ Follow the way of *love,* ▪ even as *Christ* loved *you.* ▪ ▪ He *gave* himself for us as an *offering* to God, ▪ a gift of *pleasing* fragrance. ▪ ▪ ▪

READING I Who would imagine a great prophet of Israel pleading for death, or his biographer admitting it? Yet here are both. So make your listeners sit up and notice this trenchant honesty.

Thwarted in his efforts to turn Israel away from paganism and pursued by the minions of Queen Jezebel who seek to kill him, Elijah is pushed into despair. Read the opening line suggesting that each step through the desert intensified the fear and exhaustion weighing on Elijah. "He prayed for death" is like saying "He could take no more." Elijah's earnest prayer is spoken with averted eyes.

Speak as a sympathetic narrator when you describe Elijah's rest under the broom tree and the surprise of the angel's visit. Then speak with the same disbelief with which the sleepy-eyed Elijah would have squinted at the cake and jug of water.

Elijah is prepared to succumb to his exhaustion, but the angel will have none of it. The second angelic order is spoken with discipline ("Get up and eat"), then develops into concern ("else the journey will be too long for you"). The narration of the journey to Horeb should mirror Elijah's gradually returning strength. By the time you say "he walked forty days," your voice is full of the determination that propelled Elijah to his unforgettable encounter with God.

READING II Writers strive to compose compelling opening lines and memorable closings. Here Paul has achieved both. You can't ignore his opening line. Use it well, speaking slowly as you scan the entire assembly. It's a powerful metaphor that can't help but sadden us a little. Connect the second sentence to the first, making it clear that "bitterness, all passion and anger, [etc.]" are the very things that "sadden the Holy Spirit." Take care not to read flippantly, as if you were asking us to remember to put our dirty socks in the hamper. Read with the painful awareness that "bitterness" often dies a slow death, that you are asking us to reverse the bad habits of many years. Urge the alternative behaviors on us, arguing that kindness and compassion are the example given us by Christ.

We learn Christianity by imitating Christ, says Paul. Encourage us to "follow the way of love" in hushed tones, as if you were giving confidential advice. A TV ad of a few years back counseled, "If you want to get someone's attention, whisper." Try that tactic with the last line where we find Paul's memorable closing. Jesus' self-sacrifice remains forever the perfume that sweetens our lives.

GOSPEL The predicament is an ancient one: A familiar face can't be the bearer of divine truth. No, we look for fantastic, spectral entities to be the true messengers of God. It's a wonder God still speaks at all.

Begin narrating with the caged energy with which a tiger paces its cell. The people "murmur" because they are not bold enough to challenge Jesus directly. Their direct quotes are spoken in a hushed, gossipy tone; they talk among themselves, not directing their remarks to Jesus.

Jesus would hear their murmuring even if he were wearing earplugs for it invades his entire being, so he repels it with a loud command to "stop." Recovering his patience, he then states the theme of the passage: "No one can come to me unless the Father . . . draws [them]. I will raise . . ." Anyone who is open to God's promptings will be drawn to me, says Jesus. These strong, self-disclosing statements reveal Jesus' confidence and inner strength, and these statements should be spoken with those qualities.

Jesus quickly inserts an aside lest the crowd misunderstand. Let me remind you, he says, that "only the one who is from God . . . has seen the Father." And if you believe that, he adds, you'll live forever.

His tone softens as he asserts his readiness to be food for them. He knows that they don't want to hear this, yet he presses the point, invoking the ghosts of their ancestors who "ate" yet "died." Picture him pointing to himself in a gesture of humble surrender and ultimate generosity when he offers himself as bread "for a person to eat and never die."

Jesus does not beg in the last sentence. He offers an option, fully aware that his listeners can as easily respond "no" as "yes." Speak slowly and with authority.

GOSPEL John 6:41–51

A reading from the holy *gospel* according to *John* ▪ ▪ ▪

Repressed energy waiting for release.

The *Jews* started to murmur in *protest* ▪ because *Jesus* claimed, ▪ ▪ "I am the *bread* that came down from *heaven.*" ▪ ▪ They kept *saying:* ▪ ▪ "Is this not *Jesus,* ▪ the son of *Joseph?* ▪ ▪ Do we not *know* his father and mother? ▪ ▪ How can *he* claim to have come down from *heaven?*" ▪ ▪ ▪

Indignant and judgmental.

Erupting; then cooling off.

"*Stop* your murmuring," ▪ Jesus told them. ▪ ▪
"*No* one can come to me
unless the *Father* who *sent* me ▪ *draws* him; ▪ ▪
I will *raise* him up on the *last* day. ▪ ▪
It is *written* in the prophets: ▪ ▪
'They shall all be *taught* by *God.*' ▪ ▪
Everyone who has *heard* the Father
and *learned* from him ▪
comes to *me.* ▪ ▪
Not that anyone has *seen* the Father— ▪
only the *one* who is from *God*
has seen the Father. ▪ ▪
Let me *firmly* assure you, ▪ ▪
he who *believes* has *eternal* life. ▪ ▪
I am the *bread* of life. ▪ ▪
Your *ancestors* ate *manna* in the desert, ▪
but they *died.* ▪ ▪
This is the bread that comes down from *heaven,*
for a man to *eat* and *never* die. ▪ ▪
I *myself* am the living bread
come down from heaven. ▪ ▪
If anyone *eats* this bread ▪
he shall live *forever;* ▪ ▪
the bread I will *give* ▪
is my *flesh,* ▪ for the life of the *world.*" ▪ ▪ ▪

"Them" is more inclusive.

Jesus speaks of himself with great self-confidence.

Faster pace; an aside.

"The one" is more inclusive.

Sincerely.

"One" is more inclusive than "a man."

Rev. NAB *says: "whoever eats this bread lives forever."*

"I can give no more."

AUGUST 14, 1991

ASSUMPTION VIGIL

LECTIONARY #621

READING I 1 Chronicles 15:3–4, 15; 16:1–2

A reading from the first book of *Chronicles* ▪ ▪ ▪

Stir up excitement.

Stress "ark of the Lord."

David assembled *all* Israel in *Jerusalem* ▪ to bring the *ark* of the *Lord* to the place which he had *prepared* for it. ▪ ▪ David *also* called together the *sons* of *Aaron* and the *Levites.* ▪ ▪

The Levites *bore* the ark of God on their *shoulders* with *poles,* ▪ as Moses had *ordained* according to the word of the *Lord.* ▪ ▪ ▪

David *commanded* the chiefs of the Levites to *appoint* their brethren as *chanters,* ▪ to *play* on musical instruments, ▪ ▪ *harps,* ▪ *lyres,* ▪ and *cymbals,* ▪ ▪ to make a *loud* sound of *rejoicing.* ▪ ▪ ▪

Watch it happening as you describe.

They *brought* in the ark of God ▪ and set it within the *tent* which David had *pitched* for it. ▪ ▪ Then they offered up *holocausts* and *peace* offerings to God. ▪ ▪ When David had *finished* offering up the holocausts and peace offerings, ▪ he *blessed* the people in the name of the Lord. ▪ ▪ ▪

Make it sound like a blessing.

Ritardando: "in the name of the Lord."

READING I After several efforts and setbacks (including being captured by the Philistines), the ark of the covenant, the most sacred object of the Israelites, is to be enshrined in the City of David. Cause for rejoicing! We have no counterpart, but someone bringing to your town the Declaration of Independence, Liberty Bell and Statue of Liberty might cause a similar stir.

Though the ark doesn't arrive until the last paragraph, narrate the description of David's preparations with a tone of expectant joy, the way you might describe your preparations for the biggest party you've ever given. Take time naming those musical instruments to suggest that no expense was spared!

Describe the actual enshrinement slowly and reverently, as if speaking of a powerful and awe-inspiring person rather than an object. Climax the anticipation and joy of arrival in the last line, especially by lifting out the word "blessed." Speak slowly and deliberately as if *you* were blessing the people. That word will connect us with the message of the gospel. Mary is the "Ark of the New Covenant," who bore within her body not words etched in stone but the living Word of God.

READING II This brief passage presents Paul in a familiar mode: progressive reasoning. If this, then that; when that, then this. It's simple enough for the eye but not for the ear. So you have two reasons to read slowly: because a short reading always means a slow reading and because progressive reasoning will be progressive mumbling if rushed.

When corruptible becomes incorruptible and mortal becomes immortal, then scripture will be fulfilled. And here's *what* will be fulfilled: "Death is swallowed up . . . !"

Death is like a scorpion whose "sting" is "sin" (which gets its power from the law). But (and that's a big "but") Jesus conquers sin, which is the poison that causes death. And so no sin means no death. (Be careful not to mispronounce the word "immortality.")

GOSPEL You'll never read a shorter gospel than this, so you'll have to work hard to make sure you have everyone's attention before you begin. Do that by surveying the assembly. Begin the narration quietly, and let the words "a woman called out" break the silence of the listening crowd. Obviously the woman must shout to be heard from the midst of the throng, and her exclamation about the mother of Jesus is full of the kind of envy that says: Oh, if only I could have been that mother!

Among those who "hear the word of God and keep it" Mary is first and foremost. The line is spoken with joy, not reproof. (Picture Mary in the crowd and speak right to her.) Jesus does not deny her blessedness. He only clarifies the reason why: not because she bore and fed him, but because she trusted that the promise of the Lord to her would be fulfilled.

READING II 1 Corinthians 15:54–57

A reading from the first letter of *Paul* ▪ to the *Corinthians* ▪ ▪ ▪

Proclaim the fulfilled scripture.

First "O death" loudly. Second, whispered.

Give thanks as you read.

When the *corruptible* frame takes on *incorruptibility* ▪ ▪ and the *mortal* ▪ *immortality,* ▪ ▪ *then* will the saying of Scripture be *fulfilled:* ▪ ▪ *"Death* is *swallowed* up in *victory."* ▪ ▪ "O *death,* ▪ where is *your* victory? ▪ ▪ O death, ▪ where is your *sting?"* ▪ ▪ The sting of death is *sin,* ▪ and sin gets its *power* from the *law.* ▪ ▪ But *thanks* be to *God* ▪ who has given *us* the victory through our Lord *Jesus Christ.* ▪ ▪ ▪

GOSPEL Luke 11:27–28

Establish eye contact before you start.

A reading from the holy *gospel* according to *Luke* ▪ ▪ ▪

Picture Mary, your mother, standing right before you.

Ritardando: "who . . . it." "Keep it": almost whispered, but intense.

While Jesus was *speaking* to the *crowd,* ▪ a woman *called* out, ▪ ▪ *"Blest* is the womb that *bore* you ▪ and the breasts that *nursed* you!" ▪ ▪ "Rather," ▪ he replied, ▪ ▪ *"blest* are they who *hear* the *word* of *God* ▪ ▪ and *keep* it." ▪ ▪ ▪

AUGUST 15, 1991

ASSUMPTION

LECTIONARY #622

READING I Revelation 11:19; 12:1–6, 10

A reading from the book of *Revelation* ▪▪▪

Calm before the storm.

God's temple in heaven ▪ *opened* ▪ and *in* the temple could be seen the *ark* of his *covenant.* ▪▪

Sudden excitement.

Ritardando: "a crown . . . stars."

Use the words to emphasize pain.

Let the terror show on your face.

Slowly. Emphasize menace.

Contrast "shepherd" and "iron rod."

Calm returning. "Desert" = traditional place of refuge for God's people.

A great *sign* appeared in the sky, ▪ a *woman* ▪ *clothed* with the sun, ▪ with the *moon* under her *feet,* ▪ and on her *head* a crown of twelve stars. ▪▪ Because she was with *child,* ▪ she *wailed* aloud in *pain* as she *labored* to give birth. ▪▪ Then *another* sign appeared in the sky: ▪▪ it was a huge *dragon,* ▪ *flaming* red, ▪ with seven *heads* and ten *horns;* ▪▪ on his head were seven *diadems.* ▪▪ His tail swept a *third* of the *stars* from the sky ▪ and *hurled* them down to the *earth.* ▪▪ Then the dragon *stood* before the woman about to give birth, ▪ ready to *devour* her child when it should be *born.* ▪▪▪ She gave birth to a *son*— ▪ a boy who is destined to *shepherd* all the nations with an *iron rod.* ▪▪ Her child was *snatched* up to God and to his *throne.* ▪▪ The woman herself *fled* into the *desert,* ▪ where a *special* place had been *prepared* for her by God. ▪▪▪

Balance ideas in first line with their counterparts in second: "salvation" = "reign" and "power" = "authority."

Then ▪ I heard a *loud voice* in *heaven* say: ▪▪
"Now have *salvation* and *power* come, ▪
the *reign* of our God and the *authority*
of his *Anointed* One." ▪▪▪

READING II 1 Corinthians 15:20–26

A reading from the first letter of *Paul* ▪ to the *Corinthians* ▪▪▪

Start strong.

Reason well and slowly, but still animated. "Human being" is more inclusive than "man."

Stress the balance of ideas.

Christ has been *raised* from the dead, ▪ the *first fruits* of those who have fallen *asleep.* ▪▪ Death came through a *man;* ▪▪ hence the *resurrection* of the dead comes through a man *also.* ▪▪ Just as in *Adam* ▪ all *die,* ▪ so in *Christ* ▪ all will come to *life* again, ▪ but *each* one in proper *order:* ▪▪ *Christ* the first fruits ▪ and *then,* ▪ at his coming, ▪ *all* those who *belong* to him. ▪▪ After that will come the *end,* ▪

READING I The passage reads like a storm: first the quiet that precedes the violent display of wind, thunder and lightning flash; then, again a peaceful calm.

The opening presents a vision of the heavenly temple opening its doors, revealing the "ark of [the] covenant," a symbol of God's presence in the midst of people. Because this is a vision, and a cosmic one at that, your voice must be expansive, intense, charged with emotion.

Now work through the reading (yes, work; remember, good reading requires much energy). "Sun" and "moon" are words that can be expanded and sustained. Paint the image one brushstroke at a time and see it yourself as you tell it. "Wailed" sounds like it means, as does "labored."

Another sign! It's "flaming red" (suggesting murder) and it "swept," "hurled" and was "ready to devour." Use these words to sustain the overriding mood of menace, particularly on the image of the dragon waiting to devour the newborn child. Pause. Then announce the birth of a boy who would "shepherd" (a gentle word) but with an *"iron* rod." Immediately some benevolent force snatched the child (see the woman cowering, the beast about to strike; then—just in time—the rescue), while the woman flees to the desert.

The last sentence proudly announces that such daring rescues can and will be repeated through the "power . . . of his Anointed One."

READING II Some readings are wired to a rheostat—starting out low and dim, gradually building intensity. Then there are those wired to switches. A flick and they're on! This is one of the latter. Start with a strong and joyous announcement of Christ's resurrection. "First fruits" implies not only that Christ was first, but first of many to follow.

Paul is a great juggler; his writing balances ideas gracefully as it moves us along the path of his argument. Death came through a man [human being], so resurrection comes through a man [human being]. In "Adam all die"; in "Christ all . . . come to life." But "in proper order. . . ." First "Christ," "then . . . all." "After that . . . the end." This is joyous good news, because we "who belong to him" will share new life.

When speaking about "the end" and Christ's ultimate victory, let your voice become expansive, filled with the regal power it describes. Read the last sentence slowly, majestically and with conviction that in Christ's victory we all are victors.

GOSPEL (See the gospel of the Fourth Sunday of Advent for additional commentary on this passage.) Today we celebrate a great and ancient feast of Mary and the first line of her prayer-song sets the tone: "My being proclaims the greatness of the Lord." From the yes that set her on the road to the "hill country" to the moment of her death, Mary's life was a proclamation of God's goodness. She goes in haste to Elizabeth. Mary and Elizabeth are kin by more than blood, and that awareness should pervade the opening paragraph. Fill it with the excitement of babies leaping (any woman who has borne a child knows the profound joy of feeling its movement), relatives reuniting, arms embracing and promises being fulfilled.

Whatever her reason for visiting Elizabeth, the encounter is life-giving. If there has been any fear in Mary's mind that the angel's words would be fulfilled, Elizabeth's "Blessed is she . . ." dispels it, for Mary responds with song. Speak Elizabeth's line, then, as more of a promise than an observation, with extra emphasis on those last three words.

The canticle is an outpouring of joy celebrating a God of contradiction and surprises, a God responsible for great reversals like raising up the lowly and deposing the mighty, feeding the hungry while sending the rich away empty. We see here a God of the *Anawim,* of whom Mary is foremost, those "poor ones" who rejoice in their neediness. Mary's awareness of this fills her song and is the source of her joy. Let your voice be joyous as it proclaims those reversals. The song ends with a double repetition of the word "promised." Mary's whole life was promise and fulfillment. So, in fact, are ours. Don't let those words go unnoticed.

Pause before the last sentence; then announce that Mary returned home, revitalized and prepared to face what lay ahead.

Slow and majestic.

when, ▪ after having *destroyed* every *sovereignty,* ▪ *authority,* ▪ and *power,* ▪ he will *hand* over the kingdom ▪ to *God* the *Father.* ▪▪ Christ must *reign* ▪ until God has put all *enemies* under his *feet.* ▪▪▪

GOSPEL Luke 1:39–56

A reading from the holy *gospel* according to *Luke* ▪▪▪

"In haste": In Greek can also mean "very thoughtfully."

Mary *set* out, ▪ proceeding in *haste* ▪ into the hill country to a town of Judah, ▪ where she entered *Zechariah's* house ▪ and greeted *Elizabeth.* ▪▪ When Elizabeth *heard* Mary's greeting, ▪ the baby *stirred* in her womb. ▪▪ Elizabeth was *filled* with the *Holy Spirit* ▪ and *cried* out in a *loud* voice: ▪▪ *"Blessed* are you among women ▪ and *blessed* is the fruit of your womb. ▪▪ But who am *I* ▪ that the mother of my *Lord* should come to *me?* ▪▪ The *moment* your greeting *sounded* in my ears, ▪ the baby *stirred* in my womb for *joy.* ▪▪ *Blessed* is she who *trusted* ▪ that the Lord's *words* to her ▪ would be *fulfilled."* ▪▪▪

Note: "cried out in a loud voice."

Climax of first half and theme of entire reading.

Joy-filled proclamation.

Then *Mary* said: ▪▪
"My *being* proclaims the *greatness* of the *Lord,* ▪
my *spirit* finds *joy* in God my savior, ▪
For he has *looked* upon his servant in
her *lowliness;* ▪
all *ages* to come shall call me *blessed.* ▪▪
God ▪ who is *mighty* ▪ has done *great* things
for me, ▪
holy is his name; ▪▪
His *mercy* is from *age* to *age*
on those who *fear* him. ▪▪

Extol a powerful God who cares for needy and lowly.

Continue a build to "high places."

"He has shown *might* with his arm; ▪▪
he has *confused* the *proud* in their
inmost thoughts. ▪▪
He has *deposed* the *mighty* from their thrones ▪
and *raised* the *lowly* to high places. ▪▪

More softly and gently.

The *hungry* he has given every *good* thing, ▪
while the *rich* he has sent *empty* away. ▪▪
He has *upheld* Israel his *servant,* ▪
ever *mindful* of his *mercy;* ▪▪
Even as he *promised* our fathers, ▪
promised *Abraham* and his *descendants*
forever." ▪▪▪

"Promised" is echo of "Lord's words to her" above. "Ancestors" is more inclusive than "fathers." Ritardando: "promised Abraham . . . forever."

Mary *remained* with Elizabeth about three months ▪▪ and then returned home. ▪▪▪

Returned strengthened to face what was ahead.

AUGUST 18, 1991

TWENTIETH SUNDAY IN ORDINARY TIME

LECTIONARY #120

READING I Proverbs 9:1–6

Use the pauses. Each statement builds the sense of joy.

She's willing to do the work herself for her guests.

Gentle and solicitous. "Those" is more inclusive than "him."

A hostess wanting to please.

Contrast "forsake" and "advance." Ritardando: "in the way of understanding."

A reading from the book of *Proverbs* ▪ ▪ ▪

Wisdom has built her *house,* ▪
she has *set* up her *seven columns;* ▪ ▪
She has *dressed* her *meat,* ▪ *mixed* her *wine,* ▪
yes, ▪ she has *spread* her table. ▪ ▪
She has *sent out* her maidens; ▪ ▪ she calls
from the *heights* out over the city: ▪ ▪
"Let whoever is *simple* turn in *here;* ▪ ▪
to him who lacks *understanding,* ▪ I say, ▪
Come, ▪ *eat* of my food, ▪
and drink of the *wine* I have mixed! ▪ ▪
Forsake foolishness ▪ that you may *live;* ▪ ▪
advance in the way of *understanding.* ▪ ▪ ▪

READING II Ephesians 5:15–20

Sixth of seven consecutive weeks we read from Ephesians.

Urgently, like you're racing the clock, but don't run thoughts together. "People" is more inclusive.

Contrast "ignorance" and "will of the Lord."

Last negative thought, then transition: Here's what you should do!

Look at assembly and be grateful for them.

Ritardando: "In the name . . . Christ."

A reading from the letter of *Paul* ▪
to the *Ephesians* ▪ ▪ ▪

Keep *careful watch* over your *conduct.* ▪ ▪ Do not act like *fools,* ▪ but like *thoughtful* men. ▪ ▪ Make the *most* of the *present* opportunity, ▪ for these are *evil* days. ▪ ▪ Do not continue in *ignorance,* ▪ but try to discern the *will* of the *Lord.* ▪ ▪ Avoid getting *drunk* on wine; ▪ ▪ that leads to *debauchery.* ▪ ▪ Be *filled* with the *Spirit,* ▪ addressing one another in *psalms* and *hymns* and *inspired* songs. ▪ ▪ Sing *praise* to the Lord with all your *hearts.* ▪ ▪ Give *thanks* to God the Father *always* and for *everything* ▪ in the name of our *Lord Jesus Christ.* ▪ ▪ ▪

READING I Where would we be without the mind of the poet? How could we speak of intangible realities like life, truth, God? Fortunately we don't need to answer those questions because the poetic mind has forged tools which let us speak about slippery realities.

The author of Proverbs first personifies God as Lady Wisdom then, through an extended metaphor, informs us that she "has built her house" (the world) and set up "seven columns" (an ancient concept of how the earth and sky were supported). She has prepared the festive foods of meat and wine mixed with spices. Her table is beautifully adorned. Her maidens she has "sent out," for Lady Wisdom is doing the housework today and herself inviting guests to her supper. A joyous tone pervades these opening lines as Wisdom anticipates the excitement of the feast she is preparing.

Her call (like that of her antagonist, Madam Folly) goes out to the "simple," that is, whoever is unlearned and pure of heart. Persons guileless and sincere are welcome to eat and drink in Wisdom's home. Speak her invitation as if to orphans on the street whom you are eager to bring in from the cold.

Because Madam Folly also stands in her doorway inviting the simple to taste her poisonous, death-dealing sweets, Lady Wisdom must entreat earnestly that those passing by not be seduced by "foolishness" and seek instead her "way of understanding. Ask us, then, to "forsake" and "advance" in a way that suggests our lives depend on heeding your advice.

READING II This is not the kind of pep talk a coach would give a team at the start of the season. It would come at halftime during the championship game after a miserable first half where the team played their worst and looked as if they'd never worn uniforms before. Without racing, strive for a pace that suggests you don't have long to speak. They'll soon be back on the field, and you won't send them back until you've had your say.

All the sentences are short and contain simple ideas. Though the pace is fast, pause slightly between sentences as if you were thinking of each new idea on the spot. First you caution ("keep careful watch"); then you're angry ("do not act like fools"); next you motivate ("make the most of the present opportunity") and so on.

Then Paul catches his breath and tries a new tack. Now that you know what *not* to do, he says, here's what you *ought* to do. List the admonitions with a slower pace and a gentler tone. As you look out and speak to the assembly, remember that your smile and joyous attitude remind the people of Christ's own love for them.

GOSPEL Imagine yourself facing an international assembly of scripture scholars to whom you will present a paper that critiques much of the accepted wisdom on biblical scholarship. If you're shaking, stop imagining; you've gotten the point.

Next week's gospel states that many of Jesus' disciples abandoned him for making the very claims we hear in today's gospel and that he "knew from the start . . . the ones who refused to believe." We have to expect, then, that before he uttered these declarations Jesus knew many would consider them "hard to endure." Yet he risks the contempt of the crowd for the sake of the truth. Throughout the passage be mindful of the people's skepticism and downright scorn and speak as if you've gritted your teeth and dug in your heels against their ridicule.

After Jesus' initial assertions the crowd voices their confusion. Apparently they're not all nonbelievers, or there would be no argument. Let the question be spoken by one who really wants to believe and who seeks an answer.

Imagine Jesus overhearing and responding directly to the questioner. His pace is quick, his energy is high as he grasps the moment: "Let me solemnly assure you . . . if you do not eat . . . you have no life in you." More slowly, but still with great intensity, he presents the alternatives to death: They have "life *eternal* . . . and I will *raise* him [them] up." Then, in an almost intimate whisper, he attests his flesh and blood are *real* food and drink.

Jesus now addresses the crowd again with renewed hope of convincing them: "The one who *feeds* on my flesh . . . *remains* in me." The imagery is intimate—Father begetting Son, friend giving life to friend. Jesus vows his willingness to give his life that we might live.

The intimate moment is over. Jesus contrasts himself with the manna of their ancestors. Speak the ending as a summation, as if Jesus is stating: I've said all I can say; the evidence is clear; the rest is up to you.

GOSPEL John 6:51–58

A reading from the holy *gospel* according to *John* ▪ ▪ ▪

Knowing you'll create controversy, you dive in and say what must be said.

Jesus said to the *crowds:* ▪ ▪
"I *myself* am the *living* bread
come down from *heaven.* ▪ ▪
If anyone *eats* this bread ▪
he shall *live forever;* ▪ ▪
the bread *I* will give
is my *flesh,* ▪ for the *life* of the *world."* ▪ ▪ ▪

Rev. NAB says: "Whoever eats this bread lives forever."

Lower your pitch.

At *this* the Jews *quarreled* among themselves, ▪

Sincerely wondering.

saying, ▪ ▪ "How can he give us his *flesh* to eat?" ▪ ▪
Thereupon Jesus *said* to them: ▪ ▪

Speak to the questioner with urgency.

"Let me solemnly *assure* you, ▪
if you do *not* eat the flesh of the Son of Man ▪
and *drink* his *blood,* ▪
you have no *life* in you. ▪ ▪

Throughout the passage "he" and "the man": "Those" and plural verbs are more inclusive.

He who *feeds* on my *flesh* ▪
and *drinks* my *blood* ▪
has life *eternal,* ▪ ▪
and I will *raise* him up on the *last* day. ▪ ▪

Eye contact. Almost a whisper.

For my flesh is *real* food ▪
and my *blood* ▪ *real drink.* ▪ ▪

Fresh energy. Trying to win over the crowd.

The man who *feeds* on my flesh ▪
and *drinks* my blood ▪
remains in me ▪ and I in *him.* ▪ ▪
Just as the *Father* who has *life* ▪ sent *me* ▪
and I have life *because* of the Father, ▪ ▪
so the man who *feeds* on me ▪
will have life *because* of me. ▪ ▪

Lower energy. A summation.

This is the bread that came *down* from *heaven.* ▪ ▪

Contrast the manna of the "ancestors" with "this bread."

Unlike your *ancestors* ▪ who *ate* and *died*
nonetheless, ▪ ▪
the man who feeds on *this* bread ▪
shall live *forever."* ▪ ▪ ▪

AUGUST 25, 1991

TWENTY-FIRST SUNDAY IN ORDINARY TIME

LECTIONARY #123

READING 1 Joshua 24:1–2, 15–17, 18

A reading from the book of *Joshua* ▪ ▪ ▪

Slowly, with majesty.

Joshua gathered together *all* the tribes of Israel at *Shechem,* ▪ summoning their *elders,* ▪ their *leaders,* ▪ their *judges* and their *officers.* ▪ ▪ When they stood in *ranks* before *God,* ▪ Joshua *addressed* all the people: ▪ ▪

A challenge. *"Ancestors" is more inclusive.*

"If it does not *please* you to serve the *Lord,* ▪ *decide* today whom you *will* serve, ▪ the gods your *fathers* served beyond the *River* ▪ or the gods of the *Amorites* in whose *country* you are dwelling. ▪ ▪ As for *me* and

Boldly, with grateful pride.

my *household,* ▪ ▪ *we* will serve the *Lord."* ▪ ▪ ▪

But the people *answered,* ▪ ▪ *"Far* be it from us to forsake the *Lord* ▪ for the service of *other* gods. ▪ ▪ For it was the Lord, ▪ our *God,* ▪ who brought *us* and our

"Ancestors" is more inclusive. Imagine the miracles you describe.

fathers up out of the land of *Egypt,* ▪ out of a state of *slavery.* ▪ ▪ He performed those great *miracles* before our very *eyes* ▪ and *protected* us along our *entire journey* ▪ and among all the *peoples* through whom

Pause. Then speak simply and sincerely.

we *passed.* ▪ ▪ Therefore ▪ we *also* will serve the *Lord,* ▪ for *he* is our *God."* ▪ ▪ ▪

READING II Ephesians 5:21–32

Last of seven consecutive weeks we read from Ephesians.

A reading from the letter of *Paul* ▪ to the *Ephesians* ▪ ▪ ▪

Most important line. Slowly.

Defer to one another ▪ out of *reverence* for *Christ.* ▪ ▪ ▪

Wives should be submissive to their *husbands* as if to the *Lord* ▪ because the husband is *head* of his wife ▪ just as *Christ* is head of his *body,* ▪ the *church,* ▪ as

Without preachiness or condescension.

well as its *savior.* ▪ ▪ As the *church* submits to *Christ,* ▪ so *wives* should submit to their husbands in *everything.* ▪ ▪ ▪

A call to selfless service.

Husbands, ▪ *love* your wives, ▪ as *Christ* loved the *church.* ▪ ▪ He *gave* himself up for her to make her

Persuasive.

holy, ▪ *purifying* her in the bath of water by the power of the *word,* ▪ to present to himself a *glorious* church, ▪

READING I Old age and ill health have a way of clarifying vision. What really matters stands out against the backdrop of eternity. Now very old and sensing death looking over his shoulder, Joshua determines to hear a final affirmation of his people's fidelity to the Lord. It's a most impressive event you describe: "All the tribes" assembled before their aged leader to swear allegiance to their God. Take time with the opening narration, then, to establish the necessary sense of awe and majesty.

Joshua minces no words. His challenge is not coffee time conversation; it is oratory in the style of Churchill or Kennedy. Challenge your assembly with similar tones and energy.

Joshua's statement of loyalty to the Lord is spoken slowly, with fervent intensity. The people don't hesitate. Matching his intensity, but at a faster, more urgent pace, they assert their desire to cling to the Lord. Then, at a slower pace, they prove they have not forgotten God's goodness to them.

Their litany of God's saving actions is very important. Speak it as your own history, visualizing the events you describe. Pause before the last sentence; then speak in quiet simplicity like a child saying, "Of course I'm going home, that's where I live."

READING II Paul lived at a time much different from our own. Though often a visionary, Paul was not exempt from the cultural suppositions that distinguished his society. On the face of it, what he says about husband-wife relationships is not what we want to hear. For centuries his words justified abusive dominance of men over women. Though we still might like to edit his words, our focus can fall on the notions of mutuality, of subordination to one another implicit in this text and other texts by Paul. The first line states his thesis; it is his most palatable admonition. He asks *everyone* to "defer" not because of anyone's real or imagined superiority, but "out of reverence for Christ." Speak this line with great care and tenderness while slowly scanning the assembly.

Call wives to joyful *service* of their husbands and families. Avoid any hint of righteousness or preachiness; Paul is endorsing an ideal, not chiding anyone for failures.

Paul spends the most time advising husbands. His tone is intimate, supportive, calling for heroic selflessness. Speak like a father counseling his soon-to-be-married son. A new build starts on "Husbands should love their wives . . ." where Paul becomes more insistent, striving to be clear and understood. You owe your wife no less love than you give yourself, he stresses with a reasoning tone.

Paul concludes by quoting Genesis. Man and woman become "one [flesh]" in marriage. By loving each other, husband and wife love themselves. There's no room for dominance in that formula.

GOSPEL The passage starts on an angry note: "This talk is hard . . . can anyone take it seriously?" They are angry words of frustrated men and women who feel let down, perhaps betrayed, and thus question their role as disciples. The narrator senses Jesus' pain as the "murmuring" is described. And Jesus' question perhaps betrays an inner turmoil.

Jesus goes on to ask if a great sign would help their unbelief. It's a throwaway question, for Jesus is not proving himself; he asks for their voluntary acceptance of his words. There is energy in his assertion that he speaks spirit and life, but he sighs out his awareness that "some" will not believe.

The narrator picks up the heaviness of Jesus' heart in the parenthetical aside, while a sense of resignation characterizes Jesus' statement that faith is God-given. These disciples are less the masters of their destinies than they realize.

The severing of the bond between Jesus and "many of his disciples" can be spoken with a harsh, clipped delivery suggestive of the hostile attitude that caused them to break away. Then pause, as if to survey the faithful minority that remains, and ask the frank but painful question. Pause again, then speak Peter's answer while imagining his simplicity, honesty and understated faith.

holy and *immaculate,* ▪ without *stain* or *wrinkle* ▪

More intensity.

or *anything* of that sort. ▪▪ Husbands should *love* their wives as they do their own *bodies.* ▪▪ He who loves his *wife* loves *himself.* ▪▪ Observe that no one

Speak as if to say, "This is common sense."

ever *hates* his own *flesh;* ▪▪ *no,* ▪ he *nourishes* it and takes *care* of it as *Christ* cares for the *church*— ▪ for we are *members* of his *body.* ▪▪▪

"For this reason ▪ a man shall *leave* his father and mother, ▪
and shall *cling* to his *wife,* ▪
and the *two* shall be made into *one.*" ▪▪

A whispered secret.

This is a *great* foreshadowing; ▪▪ I mean that it refers to *Christ* and the *church.* ▪▪▪

GOSPEL John 6:60–69

A reading from the holy *gospel* according to *John* ▪▪▪

Anger and frustration.

Many of the *disciples* of Jesus remarked, ▪▪ "This sort of talk is *hard* to *endure.* ▪▪ How can *anyone* take it *seriously?*" ▪▪ Jesus was fully *aware* that his

Sympathetic narrator.

disciples were murmuring in *protest* at what he had said. ▪▪ "Does it *shake* your faith?" ▪ he asked them. ▪▪▪

"What, then, ▪ if you were to *see* the Son of Man *ascend* to where he was *before* . . . ? ▪▪

Most animated here.

It is the *spirit* that gives *life;* ▪▪
the *flesh* is *useless.* ▪▪
The words I *spoke* to you
are spirit and life. ▪▪

Resignation.

Yet among *you* ▪ there are some who do *not* believe." ▪▪

Narrator is sympathetic, perhaps angry at "refusal" and "handing over."

(Jesus knew from the *start,* of course, ▪ the ones who *refused* to believe, ▪ and the *one* who would hand him *over.*) ▪▪ He went *on* to say: ▪▪

No pause. Acceptance without bitterness.

"This is why I have *told* you
that *no* one can come to me ▪
unless it is *granted* him by the *Father.*" ▪▪▪

"That person" is more inclusive.

From *this* time on, ▪ many of his disciples *broke*

Suggest the hostility.

away ▪ and would not *remain* in his company

A painful question.

any longer. ▪▪ Jesus then said to the *Twelve,* ▪▪ "Do *you* want to leave me *too?*" ▪▪ *Simon Peter*

Quietly. Understated.

answered him, ▪▪ "*Lord,* ▪ to *whom* shall we go? ▪▪ *You* have the words of *eternal life.* ▪▪ We have come to *believe;* ▪▪ we are *convinced* that you are God's *holy* one." ▪▪▪

SEPTEMBER 1, 1991

TWENTY-SECOND SUNDAY IN ORDINARY TIME

LECTIONARY #126

READING I Deuteronomy 4:1–2, 6–8

A reading from the book of *Deuteronomy* ▪ ▪ ▪

Moses = figure of reverence and authority. Invite us to listen.

The Law brings fullness of life.

"Ancestors" is more inclusive.

Speak this command out of reverence for the Law.

An appeal to their national pride and their faith in God's goodness.

With just pride and confidence.

Moses told the people: ▪ ▪ "*Now,* Israel, ▪ hear the *statutes* and *decrees* which I am teaching you to *observe,* ▪ that you may *live,* ▪ and may *enter* in and take *possession* of the land which the *Lord,* ▪ the God of your *fathers,* ▪ is *giving* you. ▪ ▪ In your *observance* of the commandments of the Lord, your God, ▪ which I *enjoin* upon you, ▪ you shall not *add* to what I command you ▪ nor *subtract* from it. ▪ ▪ Observe them *carefully,* ▪ for thus will you give evidence of your *wisdom* and *intelligence* to the nations, ▪ who will *hear* of all these statutes and say, ▪ ▪ "This *great* nation is truly a *wise* and *intelligent* people. ▪ ▪ For *what* great nation *is* there ▪ that has gods *so close* to it as the Lord, our God, is to *us* ▪ *whenever* we call upon him? ▪ ▪ Or what great nation has *statutes* and *decrees* that are as *just* ▪ as this *whole law* which I am setting before you *today?*" ▪ ▪ ▪

READING II James 1:17–18, 21–22, 27

A reading from the letter of *James* ▪ ▪ ▪

First of five consecutive weeks we read from James.

Instant energy. "Every worthwhile *gift, (build) every* genuine *benefit."*

Urgency.

Every *worthwhile* gift, ▪ every *genuine* benefit comes from *above,* ▪ descending from the *Father* of the heavenly *luminaries,* ▪ who cannot *change* ▪ and who is *never* shadowed over. ▪ ▪ He wills to bring us to *birth* with a *word* spoken in *truth* ▪ so that we may be a kind of *firstfruits* of his creatures. ▪ ▪ ▪

Rouse us to action.

Don't hold back: You're speaking to friends.

Humbly *welcome* the word that has taken *root* in you, ▪ with its power to *save* you. ▪ ▪ *Act* on this word. ▪ ▪ If all you do is *listen* to it, ▪ you are *deceiving* yourselves. ▪ ▪ ▪

Slowly.

Looking after *orphans* and *widows* in their *distress* ▪ and keeping oneself *unspotted* by the *world* ▪ make for *pure* worship without *stain* before our *God* and *Father.* ▪ ▪ ▪

READING I We've said before that names that start a reading require emphasis. Moses' name is emphatic all by itself: He is the ultimate prophet, the likes of which has not "arisen in Israel." Speak his name with the reverence due this leader in the faith.

Moses uses three imperatives: "hear," "you shall not add," and "observe." Invite us to "hear the statutes and decrees." For the Jews the Law is a source of joy and freedom, not a burden. Reveal that attitude in the way you share the consequences of following the Law: "that you may live . . . and take possession."

The *sacredness* of the Law is conveyed in the command to "add" or "subtract" nothing from what is given. Your tone is more serious and instructive, like a teacher making sure everyone understands the rules.

With passion, mindful of the utter necessity of clinging to the commandments, you tell us to "observe them carefully." Moses sounds like a teacher again. He speaks with pride in the closing sentences: "What great nation is there that has gods so close to it as the Lord . . . is to us?" "What great nation has statutes and decrees that are as just as this whole Law?"

READING II We'll be listening to James for the next five weeks and hearing some of the New Testament's most animated (and poetic) dialogue together with some practical advice for ethical conduct. Today's pericope contains elements of James's ethical guidance.

Jump right in and address your assembly as if they were a group of friends with whom you can speak honestly, without worry of offending anyone if you choose the wrong word. That familiarity will let the introductory paragraph draw us in to listen without defensiveness. Stress the adjectives of the opening line to remind us that the things of this world can't compete with those that come "from above." The second sentence is explanatory but *insistent* in its assertion that God wants us to rank as "firstfruits" of all creation.

Now that rapport is established, the guidance flows naturally: "*Welcome* the word . . . *Act* on this word." If the word gets lost somewhere between your ears and your heart, you've wasted your time and fooled no one but yourself. The tone is not harsh, but it's as bold and as honest as friendship can make it.

The last paragraph must be spoken slowly. James provides specifics of moral conduct which could be shared as if in response to the question, "What is 'pure worship?'" The tone is gentle and encouraging, calling each of us to act justly through showing concern for "orphans and widows." Social justice being an act of worship may be a surprising concept. Persuade us, through the conviction in your voice, that commitment to the world's oppressed is truly pleasing to God.

GOSPEL Mark uses a clever device for creating suspense: By hinting at a confrontation he then delays, Mark sustains our interest through many details until the clash occurs. The first sentence is the hint. The way you nuance "the Pharisees and . . . experts" can signal the approaching conflict. Writing to a gentile audience that was unacquainted with Jewish customs, Mark explains the purification rituals at length (one of many clues in Mark that the original audience of the gospels was not Palestinian Jews). Anticipate Jesus' attitude toward that piety as you describe the customs by letting impatience with all their concern for "cups and jugs and kettles" color your tone.

Since Jesus responds with a harsh condemnation at the Pharisee's berating of Jesus' disciples, the tone of the Pharisees must be proportionately righteous when they question him. Imagine Jesus shaking his head as he recalls the accuracy of Isaiah's prophecy. The quote is for the benefit of the crowd as well as for the leaders, so make the assembly your crowd and speak forcefully about true and false worship. Jesus provides some powerful contrasts: "lip service" with "heart"; "dogmas" with "human precepts"; "God's commandment" with "human tradition."

Recognizing the human tendency to cling to narrow interpretations, Jesus urges the crowd to "hear . . . and *try* to understand" and to "heed" what they hear. Having said what does *not* cause impurity, Jesus slowly enunciates those activities that *do* render one impure. Don't belabor the list. Speak it candidly, aware that each of us is tempted.

GOSPEL Mark 7:1–8, 14–15, 21–23

A reading from the holy *gospel* according to *Mark* ▪ ▪ ▪

Signal the coming confrontation.

The *Pharisees* and some of the *experts* in the *law* ▪ who had come from *Jerusalem* ▪ gathered around *Jesus.* ▪ ▪ They had observed a few of his *disciples* eating *meals* without having *purified* ▪ —that is to say, ▪ *washed*—their hands. ▪ ▪ The *Pharisees,* ▪ and in fact *all* Jews, ▪ *cling* to the custom of their *ancestors* ▪ and *never* eat without *scrupulously* washing their hands. ▪ ▪ *Moreover,* ▪ they never eat *anything* from the market without first *sprinkling* it. ▪ ▪ There are many *other* traditions they observe ▪ —for *example,* ▪ the washing of *cups* and *jugs* and *kettles.* ▪ ▪ So the Pharisees and the scribes *questioned* him: ▪ ▪ "Why do your disciples not *follow* the tradition of our *ancestors,* ▪ but instead *take* food without *purifying* their *hands?*" ▪ ▪ He *said* to them: ▪ ▪ "How *accurately* Isaiah prophesied about you *hypocrites* when he wrote, ▪ ▪

Start hinting at Jesus' impatience with this legalism.

A return to the narrative. Hostility.

Address the assembly. Use the contrasts.

'This people pays me *lip* service ▪
but their *heart* is *far* from me. ▪ ▪
Empty is the reverence they do me ▪
because they teach as *dogmas* ▪ mere
human precepts.' ▪ ▪

Real anger.

You disregard *God's* commandment and *cling* to what is *human* tradition." ▪ ▪ ▪

Plurals make it inclusive: "Nothing that enters people . . . can make them impure."

Urgent. "They hear" is more inclusive.

He *summoned* the crowd again and *said* to them: ▪ ▪ "*Hear* me, ▪ *all* of you, ▪ and try to *understand.* ▪ ▪ *Nothing* that enters a man from *outside* can make him *impure;* ▪ ▪ that which comes *out* of him, ▪ and *only* that, ▪ constitutes impurity. ▪ ▪ Let everyone *heed* what he hears!" ▪ ▪ ▪

Less urgent but great candor.

"Person" is more inclusive.

"*Wicked* designs come from the deep *recesses* of the *heart:* ▪ ▪ acts of *fornication,* ▪ *theft,* ▪ *murder,* ▪ *adulterous* conduct, ▪ *greed,* ▪ *maliciousness,* ▪ *deceit,* ▪ *sensuality,* ▪ *envy,* ▪ *blasphemy,* ▪ *arrogance,* ▪ an *obtuse* spirit. ▪ ▪ All these *evils* come from *within* ▪ and *render* a man *impure.*" ▪ ▪ ▪

SEPTEMBER 8, 1991

TWENTY-THIRD SUNDAY IN ORDINARY TIME

LECTIONARY #129

READING I Isaiah 35:4–7

Poetry requires extra preparation and extra energy.

A reading from the book of the prophet ▪ *Isaiah* ▪▪▪

Say to those whose hearts are *frightened:* ▪▪
Be strong, ▪ *fear not!* ▪▪
Here is your *God,* ▪

Be convincing. Offer hope.

he comes with *vindication;* ▪▪
With divine *recompense*
he comes to *save* you. ▪▪

God can do it.

Then will the eyes of the blind be *opened,* ▪
the ears of the deaf be *cleared;* ▪▪

Mounting joy. Pace quickens.

Then will the lame *leap* like a *stag,* ▪
then the tongue of the dumb will *sing.* ▪▪

Use the contrasts.

Streams will burst forth in the *desert,* ▪
and *rivers* in the *steppe.* ▪▪

Ritardando: "The burning sands . . . springs of water."

The *burning* sands will become *pools,* ▪
and the *thirsty* ground, ▪ *springs* of *water.* ▪▪▪

READING II James 2:1–5

Second of five consecutive weeks we read from James.

A reading from the letter of *James* ▪▪▪

"Brothers and sisters" is more inclusive.

My brothers, ▪ your *faith* in our Lord Jesus Christ glorified ▪ must not allow of *favoritism.* ▪▪ *Suppose* there should come into your assembly ▪ a man *fashionably* dressed, ▪ with *gold rings* on his fingers, ▪▪

You're telling us to stop discriminating.

and at the same time a *poor* man dressed in *shabby* clothes. ▪▪ Suppose *further* you were to take *notice*

Overly courteous.

of the well-dressed man and say, ▪▪ "Sit *right here,* please;" ▪▪ whereas you were to say to the *poor* man, ▪▪ "You can *stand!*" ▪▪ or "Sit over *there* ▪ by my *footrest.*" ▪▪ Have you not in a case like this *discriminated* in your hearts? ▪▪ Have you not set yourselves up as *judges* who hand down *corrupt* decisions? ▪▪▪

READING I Some people use language the way musicians use notes and artists use paint. They make magic with words because on their way to saying something they create a thing of beauty. We call them poets, and Isaiah is one of them. He communicates his message with power and urgency through the images he conjures. This passage conveys only one message: Be strong in faith, for God will come to save! Though it consists of several distinct images of celebration, all of them coalesce to express that simple message.

Isaiah's prophecy speaks of the exile from which God "comes to save you." It also anticipates the time of the Messiah who will open eyes and ears and make bent limbs straight. What more do we need to rejoice than exiles returning home and the infirm being made whole? Only the awareness that those things are happening in our midst—not just thousands of years ago. Even *now* God comes to save, heal, refresh and restore. You *know* situations where God is doing those things—recall them as you read.

Like notes that must be sung and paints that must be brushed on before they mean anything, poetry can't express itself—it isn't beautiful until a voice gives it life. Isaiah's words could sound like the recitation of the phone book if you don't give them energy, excitement and vibrant joy.

"Be strong, fear not!" is an order given with a smile that immediately explains *why* it's given: because there is cause for rejoicing. Catch eyes in the assembly on the "blind," "deaf," and "lame" lines and speak hope and comfort to them about their own blindness or infirmity. Use the wonderful contrasts ("streams/desert," "sands/pools") and the words that sound like their meaning ("burning," "thirsty," "springs") to convince us that God can transform even the most arid life into rivers of grace.

READING II James is speaking to disciples who are still uncomfortable with the radical requirements of Christian living. There's no room in your new lives for "favoritism," he says, and then comically illustrates how that old attitude looked and sounded. James cleverly holds up a mirror to the community, but it's a fun-house mirror that exaggerates features and forces people to laugh at themselves at the same time they are chided.

Like "Once upon a time," "Suppose there should come" signals the start of a story, so your tone changes. Your instructions to the well-dressed man are all fawning and flattery, but your orders to the poor man are curt and dismissive. James's point is very serious. "Have you not . . . discriminated . . . set yourselves up as judges?" These are questions that require sustained eye contact and an attitude that says: Let's be honest and admit our failings.

The directness of his words, "Listen, dear brothers [and sisters]," comes out of his earlier folksiness. Instead of indictment he ends with a question—another clever technique. The answer is obvious, but he allows his listeners to consider its implications on their own.

GOSPEL One of Mark's trademarks is earthiness, which is marvelously exhibited in this miracle story. In the pagan region of Tyre and Sidon some people brought to Jesus a man with a speech impediment and begged him to heal the man. Biblical narration often forces us to uncover information at which the narrator only hints. The faith of the deaf man's friends and the urgency of their request can only be suggested by your tone and intensity.

Perhaps Jesus removing the man from the crowd reflects Jesus' sensitivity to the man whose cure he does not wish to make into a sideshow. The earthiness becomes palpable as Jesus puts his "fingers into the man's ears" and touches "his tongue" with spittle. The original storytellers of this miracle tale would not have shied away from these trenchant details. Speak them slowly and vividly. On the word, "Ephphatha!" (but not on its translation) release Jesus' strong emotion.

Excitement swells when the cure is manifest, and futile are the efforts to silence or contain it. Mark is impressed by the crowd's enthusiasm. Rather than trying to mimic their outburst, speak "He has done everything well!" in soft tones full of awe and longing.

"Brothers and sisters" is more inclusive. With excitement, knowing you speak of us.

Listen, dear brothers. ▪▪ Did not God choose those who are *poor* in the eyes of the world ▪ to be *rich* in *faith* ▪ and *heirs* of the *kingdom* he promised to those who *love* him? ▪▪▪

GOSPEL Mark 7:31–37

A reading from the holy *gospel* according to *Mark* ▪▪▪

A pagan district.

People of obvious faith.

"Begged" sounds like it means.

Suggest Jesus' concern and sensitivity.

Slowly, utilizing the graphic details.

"Ephphatha" = strong and intense. "Be opened" = soft and intense. Speak with amazement.

With a shrug at futility of trying to contain it.

Jesus left *Tyrian* territory and returned by way of *Sidon* to the *Sea* of *Galilee,* ▪▪ into the district of the *Ten Cities.* ▪▪ Some people brought him a *deaf* man who had a *speech* impediment ▪ and *begged* him to lay his *hand* on him. ▪▪ Jesus took him off by *himself* away from the *crowd.* ▪▪ He put his *fingers* into the man's *ears* ▪ and *spitting,* ▪ touched his *tongue;* ▪▪ then he looked up to *heaven* and emitted a *groan.* ▪▪ He said to him, ▪▪ *"Ephphatha!"* ▪ (that is, ▪ *"Be opened!"*) ▪▪ At *once* the man's ears were *opened;* ▪▪ he was *freed* from the impediment, ▪ and began to speak *plainly.* ▪▪ Then he enjoined them *strictly* ▪ not to *tell* anyone; ▪▪ but the more he ordered them *not* to, ▪ the more they *proclaimed* it. ▪▪ Their *amazement* went beyond *all* bounds: ▪▪ "He has done *everything* well! ▪▪ He makes the deaf *hear* and the mute *speak!"* ▪▪▪

SEPTEMBER 15, 1991

TWENTY-FOURTH SUNDAY IN ORDINARY TIME

LECTIONARY #132

READING I Isaiah 50:4–9

With quiet strength and gratitude.

A tribute of thanks to God, who made such courage possible. "Plucked," "buffets" and "spitting" sound like they mean.

Here's the heart of the message.

Growing bolder.

Who dares? Anyone?

"That person" is more inclusive.

Ritardando: "who . . . wrong?"

A reading from the book of the prophet ▪ *Isaiah* ▪ ▪ ▪

The Lord God *opens* my ear that I may *hear* ▪
And I have not *rebelled,* ▪
have *not* turned back. ▪ ▪
I *gave* my back to those who *beat* me, ▪
my *cheeks* to those who *plucked* my beard; ▪ ▪
My *face* I did not *shield*
from *buffets* and *spitting.* ▪ ▪ ▪

The Lord God is my *help,* ▪
therefore ▪ I am not *disgraced;* ▪ ▪
I [...]e *set* my face like *flint,* ▪
k[...]ing that I shall *not* be put to *shame.* ▪ ▪
He is [...] ▪ who *upholds* my *right;* ▪ ▪
if any[...]shes to *oppose* me, ▪
let us a[...]her. ▪ ▪
Who *dispute*[...]? ▪ ▪
Let him *con*[...]
See, ▪ the Lord [...] ▪ ▪
who will prove [...]

READING II James 2:14–18

Third of five consecutive weeks we read from James.

"Brothers and sisters" is more inclusive. Ask as if they were commonsense questions, then pause to await reply.

Your tone says: "Now here's an example."

A reading from the letter of *James* ▪

My brothers, ▪ what *good* is it to pr[...] without *practicing* it? ▪ ▪ *Such* faith has n[...] *save* one, ▪ *has* it? ▪ ▪ If a brother or sister has [...] to *wear* ▪ and no *food* for the day, ▪ and you s[...] them, ▪ ▪ *"Good-bye* and *good luck!* ▪ ▪ Keep wa[...] and *well fed,"* ▪ but do not *meet* their bodily needs, ▪ what *good* is that? ▪ ▪ So it is with the *faith* that does nothing in *practice.* ▪ ▪ It is thoroughly *lifeless.* ▪ ▪ ▪

READING I The speaker here is Isaiah's suffering servant, who readily acknowledges God's presence in the midst of suffering. Because God is part of that mystery, the servant has "not rebelled" and willingly accepts whatever God allows. There is stone-faced resignation and courage in the opening sentence that continues in the frank acknowledgment of past suffering confessed in the second sentence. The servant is paying tribute here not to his personal strength, but to the God-given fortitude that allowed him to endure this abuse without cowering in fear.

Sometimes friends, often spouses, can say to each other, "If you remain at my side, I can go through anything." For Isaiah's servant, God is friend *and* spouse, enabling the servant to "set [his] face like flint" and convincing him that he "will *not* be put to shame." Don't brag in those lines; speak instead with the deep conviction that the God who "is near" makes anything possible.

Your attitude becomes suddenly bolder in the last three sentences. Imagine challenging a group of people and when no one rises to "confront" you, you say: See, no one dares because "God *is* my help."

READING II We might be tempted to call people who profess faith without practicing it hypocrites, but James calls them "My brothers [and sisters]." Let that set your tone. None of us is guiltless in this regard, so your attitude must not be judgmental. You want to win over your listeners, not alienate them. The first sentences are conversational, honest and direct. James is convinced his point is pure common sense: "Such faith has no power . . . *has it?"*

He chides his listeners with a bit of humorous exaggeration. The dialogue he invents is spoken by a character who is obviously out of touch, blind or crassly insensitive, but not someone sinister. Somehow the person has [...]sed the boat on how a responsible Chris[...]sponds to someone in need. James's [...]n makes sure that the person [...]s the point again: that such a [...]*eless."*

[...]esponse to "such a per[...]nd animated banter between [...]thout hostility you challenge the [...] can prove my faith *through* my works; [...] *you* prove your faith *without* any works? (You might want to try that challenge first on yourself.)

GOSPEL Mark tells this story in three acts. The first presents Jesus and the disciples in conversation regarding mistaken notions of his identity—climaxed by Peter's confession of Jesus as "Messiah." The second act consists of two scenes: first, serious teaching about Jesus' inevitable suffering and then repudiation of Peter's too human reaction to that suffering. The final act brings the crowd onto the stage for a lesson on the cost of discipleship.

Careful attention to the atmosphere and pace of each "act" will bring vibrant life to your retelling of this familiar event. Imagine Jesus and the disciples walking together or camped under a tree when Jesus asks what people are saying about him. A politician running for office might ask the same question—eliciting immediate responses from his advisors. Jesus' question and Peter's reply are pivotal in Mark's gospel, and Jesus' order to keep silent is meant to avoid false interpretations of his messiahship.

Calling the group into a tighter circle, Jesus begins to teach "quite openly" about his passion. Not weighed down with fear or worry, Jesus' tone is neither heavy nor didactic. Peter is disappointed. We can almost hear him say: "How could you talk like that?" Wanting the disciples to hear the reprimand but not seeking to humiliate Peter, Jesus rebukes him, thus rejecting this false interpretation of what it means to be the Messiah.

The last "act" builds on the encounter with Peter. Like a gentle teacher who must make the point, Jesus speaks these words with an insistent but hopeful attitude.

No anger, but still a challenge. Jerusalem Bible says: "You say you have faith and I have good deeds; I will prove to you that I have faith by showing you my good deeds—now you prove to me that you have faith without any good deeds to show."

To *such* a person one might say, ▪▪ "*You* have faith and *I* have works ▪ —is *that* it?" ▪▪ *Show* me your faith *without* works, ▪ and *I* will show you the faith ▪ that *underlies* my works! ▪▪▪

GOSPEL Mark 8:27–35

A reading from the holy *gospel* according to *Mark* ▪▪▪

Start with a lighthearted mood that grows more serious.

Jesus and his *disciples* set out for the villages around *Caesarea Philippi.* ▪▪ On the *way* ▪ he asked his disciples this *question:* ▪▪ "*Who* do people say that I *am?*" ▪▪ They replied, ▪▪ "Some, ▪ *John* the *Baptizer,* ▪▪ others, ▪ *Elijah,* ▪▪ still *others,* ▪ one of the *prophets.*" ▪▪ "And *you,*" ▪ he went on to ask, ▪▪ "who do *you* say that I am?" ▪▪▪ *Peter* answered him, ▪▪ "You are the *Messiah!*" ▪▪▪ Then he *strictly* ordered them not to tell *anyone* about him. ▪▪▪

Testing the waters.

Quickly, without forethought. Now we hear the seriousness.

He then began to *teach* them that the Son of Man had to *suffer* much, ▪ be *rejected* by the elders, ▪ the *chief priests,* ▪ and the *scribes,* ▪ be put to *death,* ▪ and *rise* three days later. ▪▪ He said this quite *openly.* ▪▪ *Peter* then took him *aside* ▪ and began to *remonstrate* with him. ▪▪ At this he *turned* around and, ▪ *eyeing* the disciples, ▪ *reprimanded* Peter in turn: ▪▪ "Get out of my *sight,* you *satan!* ▪▪ You are not judging by *God's* standards ▪ but by *man's!*" ▪▪▪

Good but misguided intentions.

"Remonstrate" = "argue."

Rev. NAB says: "You are thinking not as God does, but as human beings do."

He summoned the *crowd* with his disciples and *said* to them: ▪▪ "If a man wishes to come *after* me, ▪ he must *deny* his very *self,* ▪ take up his *cross,* ▪ and *follow* in my steps. ▪▪ Whoever would *save* his life will *lose* it, ▪ but whoever *loses* his life for *my* sake and the *gospel's* ▪ will *save* it." ▪▪▪

Use of the plural "those who wish . . ." is more inclusive.

Tone is life-giving and hopeful.

SEPTEMBER 22, 1991

TWENTY-FIFTH SUNDAY IN ORDINARY TIME

LECTIONARY #135

READING I Wisdom 2:12, 17–20

A reading from the book of *Wisdom* ▪ ▪ ▪

They plan to attack and harass him.

[The *wicked* say:] ▪ ▪
Let us *beset* the *just* one, ▪ because he is
obnoxious to us; ▪ ▪
he sets himself *against* our doings, ▪

Self-righteousness.

Reproaches *us* for transgressions of the law ▪
and *charges* us with *violations* of our training. ▪ ▪

Quieter; whispered plotting.

Let us *see* whether his words be *true;* ▪ ▪
let us *find* out what will *happen* to him. ▪ ▪

Justifying their evil actions.

For *if* the just one be the son of *God,* ▪ *he* will
defend him ▪
and *deliver* him from the hand of his *foes.* ▪ ▪
With *revilement* and *torture* let us put him
to the *test* ▪
that we may have *proof* of his gentleness ▪
and *try* his *patience.* ▪ ▪

Mocking defiance.

Let us *condemn* him to a *shameful* death; ▪ ▪
for according to his *own* words, ▪ *God* will
take *care* of him. ▪ ▪ ▪

READING II James 3:16—4:3

Fourth of five consecutive weeks we read from James.

A reading from the letter of *James* ▪ ▪ ▪

Start slowly.

Change your tone.

Visualize the virtues lived out by someone.

Contrast "sown" and "cultivate."

Where there are *jealousy* and *strife,* ▪ there also are *inconstancy* ▪ and all kinds of *vile* behavior. ▪ ▪ *Wisdom* from above, ▪ by *contrast,* ▪ is *first* of all *innocent.* ▪ ▪ It is also *peaceable,* ▪ *lenient,* ▪ *docile,* ▪ rich in *sympathy* ▪ and the *kindly* deeds that are its fruit, ▪ *impartial* and *sincere.* ▪ ▪ The harvest of *justice* is *sown* in *peace* ▪ for those who *cultivate* peace. ▪ ▪ ▪

Without self-righteousness, for we all have these "cravings."

Where do the *conflicts* and *disputes* among you *originate?* ▪ ▪ Is it not your *inner* cravings that make *war* within your members? ▪ ▪ What you *desire* you do not *obtain,* ▪ and so you resort to *murder.* ▪ ▪ You

READING I The attitude depicted in this reading is as modern as it is ancient. Remember the colleague who doesn't participate in office gossip and the student who doesn't misbehave when the teacher leaves the room. Ever wonder if they really are as good as they seem; ever find within yourself the urge to topple them from their pedestals? Then you know the motives operating here.

The plotters in this passage are determined to discredit "the just one" in order to preserve their own sense of superiority. But of course they don't acknowledge their corrupt motives even to themselves. Self-righteousness infects the opening lines. "He is obnoxious to us . . . [Who does he think he is?]; he sets himself against our doings . . . [How dare he?], [He even] Reproaches . . . our training." [We'll show him!]

The die is cast by the time you reach "Let us see . . . ." Trying to bolster their evil resolve, the schemers wonder out loud "what will happen to him" as if convincing themselves they've performed a great service by putting the just one to the test. We've done nothing wrong, they imply, for if he is who he claims to be, "[God] will defend him."

READING II James is standing at the teacher's desk, lecturing about what flows in the veins of jealousy and in the veins of wisdom. In wisdom's veins are all good things, and James enumerates them the way a lover might list the virtues of the beloved or the way a eulogist might honor a departed friend. The trick is to read slowly and to visualize each virtue put into action by someone. James summarizes, saying that you can only "*cultivate* in peace" if you have first "*sown* in peace."

In the second paragraph he calls for some tough introspection. Be honest, he insists, "Is it not your *inner cravings* that make war . . . ?" When would you resort to this kind of tone? When you've warned someone repeatedly? When you care enough about the other person to be as blunt as necessary? James is certainly prompted by this last motive. He's direct because he cares. Imagine a situation when you would speak like this and you'll recognize the mix of emotions at play here: anger, regret, urgency, frustration. All four emotions are especially evident in the last sentence. When you consider the riches of wisdom that we pass up because "we do not ask" or "ask wrongly," you will speak with sufficient seriousness.

GOSPEL In Mark's gospel, Jesus makes three predictions of his passion, and each time he meets with a disappointing response from the disciples. Last week we saw Peter's unwillingness to hear of suffering and death. Today it is *all* the disciples who engage in a tug-of-war for preeminence.

Begin quietly to suggest that Jesus "did not want anyone to know about" his whereabouts. Jesus is teaching the disciples (a clue to the tone of the entire passage) about his betrayal, death and resurrection. These are important matters; speak slowly and significantly. The disciples receive the prediction with confusion and fear, evidenced by how they "failed to understand" but "were afraid to question him."

"Once inside the house" Jesus asks a seemingly innocent question, giving no hint of knowing about their contention. Speak "At this they fell silent . . ." as the fumbling disciples who must finally admit that they were arguing about who was most important. His suspicions confirmed, Jesus calls the disciples to him. Showing great patience and restraint, he deals with them as the spiritual children they are—challenging their understanding of primacy and then using a child to teach them further.

There's gentle intimacy in the description of Jesus "putting his arms around" the child. The disciples don't realize it but the child represents them. Whoever welcomes a servant like them welcomes Jesus, and whoever welcomes Jesus welcomes God.

Motivated by loving concern for your listeners.

Convince us so we don't miss out on Wisdom's treasures.

envy and you cannot *acquire,* ▪ so you *quarrel* and *fight.* ▪▪ You do not *obtain* because you do not *ask.* ▪▪ You *ask* and you do not *receive* because you ask *wrongly,* ▪ with a view to *squandering* what you receive on your *pleasures.* ▪▪▪

GOSPEL Mark 9:30–37

A reading from the holy *gospel* according to *Mark* ▪▪▪

They're leaving the mountain of the transfiguration. Use quiet tone.

A sensitive teacher sharing a hard but important lesson.

Jesus and his *disciples* came down the mountain ▪ and began to go through *Galilee,* ▪ but he did not want anyone to *know* about it. ▪▪ He was *teaching* his disciples in this vein: ▪▪ "The *Son* of *Man* is going to be delivered into the hands of men who will put him to *death,* ▪▪ *three days* after his death ▪ he will *rise.*" ▪▪ Though they failed to *understand* his words, ▪ they were *afraid* to question him. ▪▪▪

Question innocently, then start fumbling for reply. "Who was most the important" is an embarassed admission.

Gentle and intimate. "That person" is more inclusive than "he."

Tenderly.

They returned to *Capernaum* ▪ and *Jesus,* ▪ once inside the *house,* ▪ began to *ask* them, ▪▪ "What were you *discussing* on the way home?" ▪▪ At this they fell *silent,* ▪ for on the way they had been *arguing* about who was the most *important.* ▪▪ So he *sat* down and *called* the Twelve around him ▪ and said, ▪▪ "If anyone wishes to rank *first,* ▪ he must remain the *last* one of all ▪ and the *servant* of all." ▪▪ Then he took a little *child,* ▪ *stood* him in their midst, ▪ and putting his *arms* around him, ▪ said to them, ▪▪ "Whoever *welcomes* a child such as *this* ▪ for *my* sake ▪ welcomes *me.* ▪▪ And whoever welcomes *me* ▪ welcomes, *not* me, ▪ but *him* who *sent* me." ▪▪▪

SEPTEMBER 29, 1991

TWENTY-SIXTH SUNDAY IN ORDINARY TIME

LECTIONARY #138

READING I Numbers 11:25–29

A reading from the book of *Numbers* ▪ ▪ ▪

Amazing and overwhelming, like seeing a ghost.

Awe and majesty.

The *Lord* came down in the *cloud* ▪ and *spoke* to *Moses.* ▪ ▪ Taking some of the *spirit* that was on him, ▪ he *bestowed* it on the *seventy elders;* ▪ ▪ and as the spirit came to *rest* on them, ▪ they *prophesied.* ▪ ▪ ▪

A news report: accurate and impartial.

Loudly.

He's asking: "What's your real motive?"

An earnest prayer.

Now *two* men, ▪ one named *Eldad* and the other *Medad,* ▪ were *not* in the gathering ▪ but had been left in the *camp.* ▪ ▪ They *too* had been on the *list,* ▪ but had *not* gone out to the *tent;* ▪ yet the *spirit* came to rest on them *also,* ▪ and they *prophesied* in the camp. ▪ ▪ *So,* ▪ when a young man quickly told *Moses,* ▪ ▪ "*Eldad* and *Medad* are *prophesying* in the camp," ▪ *Joshua,* ▪ son of *Nun,* ▪ who from his *youth* had been Moses' *aide,* ▪ said, ▪ ▪ "*Moses,* my lord, ▪ *stop* them." ▪ ▪ But Moses *answered* him, ▪ ▪ "Are you *jealous* for *my* sake? ▪ ▪ Would that *all* the people of the Lord were *prophets!*" ▪ ▪ Would that the *Lord* might bestow his *spirit* on them *all!*" ▪ ▪ ▪

READING II James 5:1–6

Last of five consecutive weeks we read James.

A reading from the letter of *James* ▪ ▪ ▪

Make it a call to repentance. "Rotted" sounds like it means.

What happened to them will happen to you!

Recognize how worthless riches are.

Speak on behalf of the poor.

Controlling the anger.

Pause before "he does not resist you." "Just man" or "just one" is anyone among the innocent poor.

You *rich,* ▪ *weep* and *wail* over your impending *miseries.* ▪ ▪ Your wealth has *rotted,* ▪ your fine *wardrobe* has grown *moth-eaten,* ▪ your *gold* and *silver* have *corroded,* ▪ and their corrosion shall be a *testimony* against you; ▪ ▪ it will *devour* your flesh like a *fire.* ▪ ▪ *See* what you have *stored* up for yourselves against the *last* days. ▪ ▪ Here, ▪ *crying* aloud, ▪ are the wages you *withheld* from the farmhands who *harvested* your fields. ▪ ▪ The *shouts* of the harvesters have reached the ears of the *Lord* of *hosts.* ▪ ▪ You lived in wanton *luxury* on the earth; ▪ ▪ you *fattened* yourselves for the day of *slaughter.* ▪ ▪ You *condemned,* ▪ even *killed,* ▪ the *just* man; ▪ ▪ *he* does not *resist* you. ▪ ▪ ▪

READING I The sentence that opens today's reading suggests a momentous encounter between God and Moses. And how could we talk about a voice from "the cloud" as if it were a voice on the phone? The opening is both solemn and awe-inspiring: "And when the spirit came to rest on them . . . they prophesied."

But the second paragraph shatters that mood with earthly issues of status, rivalry and limited vision. The narration concerning the two men who "had been on the list" but were not present at the outpouring of the spirit is unemotional, though great care is taken to disclose the details fairly and accurately.

Surprise us with the urgency and disapproval with which the young man rushes to tell Moses that the two men "are prophesying in the camp." Joshua is perhaps an overzealous assistant loudly exhorting Moses to stop them.

Moses restores calm and reason by first challenging Joshua's motives ("Are you jealous for my sake?") and then asserting that this is a truly good thing, so good in fact that he wishes that "all the people of the Lord were prophets!" His last line is a prayer for the universal outpouring of God's spirit.

READING II How do we read this passionate writing? Like the hilltop prophet would be one way, but let's suggest another. Perhaps with controlled anger. Think of a time when you were truly, righteously angry: not just a time when you stubbed your toe or lost your temper because one of the children didn't obey, but angry at the core of your being over some injustice or repeated abuse. Chances are your voice was controlled and each word was carefully articulated as you confronted the one with whom you were angry. Sometimes people hear us best when we *don't* raise our voices.

You don't enjoy speaking these words of judgment, for you are trying to open eyes, not close hearts. There is regret over the "impending miseries" and a real desire to change hearts in the warning that the unjust rich will experience decay and destruction as surely as "the fine wardrobe [that] has grown moth-eaten" and the "gold and silver (that) have corroded."

James gives a voice to the wages withheld unjustly from the farmhands. You are speaking on behalf of those whose "shouts . . . have reached the ears of the Lord of hosts," but you are not one of that desperate, crying host. Display instead the passionate intensity of an advocate for the poor, whose task it is to force the rich to see themselves as they are: "You lived . . . you fattened . . . you condemned, even killed!" The evil of such behavior stands in stark and poignant contrast with "the just man [one]" (take a short pause) who "does not resist."

GOSPEL John's opening comment reveals the enticing attractiveness of the private club and the instinct for exclusion that creates an "us-them" mentality. Jesus squashes this immediately. The disciples are not an exclusive club, for "whoever is not against us is with us," he insists. "Do not try to stop him" is a plea for tolerance.

Jesus speaks tenderly as he explains that those who care for his disciples will not go unrewarded, reserving his anger for anyone who leads astray the simple believers. He thereby trains the apostles in true discipleship by showing concern not for his own reputation but for the welfare of his followers.

The second paragraph is an example of well-crafted rhetoric where a chant-like refrain ("Cut it off!") and three illustrations make a single point. Speak this entire section at a moderately fast pace using the same inflection for each "if . . . then" construction. Jesus makes one point here: If you want to be saved, remove all obstacles from your path. Urgency characterizes his repetitions, for he must persuade us that no effort is too great if it keeps us out of "Gehenna." Because he is cautioning against self-ensnarement, his tone is very direct. Don't shy away from the strong images of "worm" and "fire"— they remind us that our decisions have far-reaching consequences.

GOSPEL Mark 9:38–43, 45, 47–48

A reading from the holy *gospel* according to *Mark* ▪ ▪ ▪

John is questioning.

Strongly stated.

"No one" is more inclusive.

"Anyone" is more inclusive.

"Go unrewarded" is more inclusive.

"If anyone" . . . "his neck": "if those . . . their necks" is more inclusive.

John said to Jesus, ▪ ▪ *"Teacher,* ▪ we saw a man using *your* name to expel *demons* ▪ and we tried to *stop* him because he is not of our *company."* ▪ ▪ *Jesus* said in reply: ▪ ▪ "Do not *try* to stop him. ▪ ▪ No man who performs a *miracle* using *my* name ▪ can at once speak *ill* of me. ▪ ▪ Anyone who is not *against* us is *with* us. ▪ ▪ *Any* man who gives you a *drink* of *water* because you belong to *Christ* ▪ will *not,* ▪ I *assure* you, ▪ go *without* his *reward.* ▪ ▪ But it would be *better* if anyone who leads *astray* one of these simple *believers* ▪ were to be *plunged* in the sea with a great *millstone* fastened around his *neck.* ▪ ▪ ▪

Contrast "one" and "both."

Ritardando: "and the fire . . . extinguished."

"If your *hand* is your difficulty, ▪ *cut* it *off!* ▪ ▪ *Better* for you to enter life *maimed* ▪ than to *keep* both hands and enter *Gehenna,* ▪ with its *unquenchable* fire. ▪ ▪ If your *foot* is your undoing, ▪ *cut* it *off!* ▪ ▪ Better for you to enter life *crippled* ▪ than to be thrown into Gehenna with *both* feet. ▪ ▪ If your *eye* is your downfall, ▪ *tear* it *out!* ▪ ▪ Better for you to enter the kingdom of God with *one* eye ▪ than to be thrown with *both* eyes into *Gehenna,* ▪ where 'the *worm* dies *not* ▪ and the *fire* is *never* extinguished.'" ▪ ▪ ▪

OCTOBER 6, 1991

TWENTY-SEVENTH SUNDAY IN ORDINARY TIME

LECTIONARY #141

READING I Genesis 2:18–24

A reading from the book of *Genesis* ▪ ▪ ▪

God is concerned for humankind.

The Lord *God* said: ▪ ▪ "It is not *good* for the man to be *alone.* ▪ ▪ I will make a suitable *partner* for him." ▪ ▪ So the Lord God *formed* out of the *ground* various wild *animals* ▪ and various *birds* of the *air,* ▪ and he *brought* them to the man to see what he would *call* them; ▪ ▪ *whatever* the man called *each* of them would be its *name.* ▪ ▪ The man *gave* names to all the *cattle,* ▪ all the *birds* of the air, ▪ and *all* wild animals; ▪ ▪ but *none* proved to be the suitable *partner* for the man. ▪ ▪

Disappointment.

So the Lord God cast a *deep sleep* on the man, ▪ and *while* he was asleep, ▪ he *took* out one of his *ribs* ▪ and *closed* up its place with *flesh.* ▪ ▪ The Lord God then *built* up into a *woman* ▪ the rib that he had *taken* from the man. ▪ ▪ When he *brought* her to the man ▪ the man said: ▪ ▪

Awed and delighted.

"This one, ▪ at *last,* ▪ is *bone* of my *bones* ▪
and *flesh* of my *flesh;* ▪ ▪

Joy.

This one shall be called ▪ *'woman,'* ▪
for out of *'her man'* this one has been
taken." ▪ ▪ ▪

That is why a man *leaves* his father and mother ▪ and *clings* to his *wife,* ▪ and the *two* of them become *one* body. ▪ ▪ ▪

READING II Hebrews 2:9–11

First of seven consecutive weeks we read from Hebrews. Three sentence reading = slow reading.

A reading from the letter to the *Hebrews* ▪ ▪ ▪

Teaching tone. Dropping "men" is more inclusive. "Children" is more inclusive than "sons."

Jesus was made for a *little* while ▪ *lower* than the angels, ▪ that through God's gracious *will* ▪ he might taste *death* for the sake of all *men.* ▪ ▪ Indeed, ▪ it was *fitting* that, ▪ when bringing many sons to *glory,* ▪ God, ▪ *for* whom and *through* whom *all* things exist, ▪ should make their *leader* in the work of salvation ▪

READING I "It is not good for the man to be alone." God thinks and immediately conceives a solution: "I will make a suitable partner." The reading demands a God who is very human, warm and concerned.

There's excitement in the narrator's voice as God joyously births the "wild animals" and "birds of the air," for the narrator is as *anxious* as God to see if the new creatures will be suitable. Eagerly, God grants the man permission to *name* the animals (symbolizing God's relinquishing authority over the creatures to human beings). The way you narrate "the man gave names to all . . . but *none* proved . . . suitable" tells us that Adam was perhaps disappointed.

Suggest how anxious God is to find a proper partner for the man by speaking with urgent determination when narrating "So the Lord cast a deep sleep . . . " Then shift suddenly to a quieter, whispering tone as if tiptoeing around the man to keep from waking him as his rib is "built up into a woman."

Adam's delight is unabashed when God finally pairs him with the woman. He rejoices that the woman is "bone of my bones and flesh of my flesh," for she alone can bring wholeness and fulfillment to his life. The closing sentence overflows with Adam's joyful response to Eve.

READING II Carlo Caretto, philosopher and spiritual writer, says: "We are afraid to suffer, but we need to suffer. It is school. And it is the school of love. Suffering helps us enter into love." I don't like those words, and maybe you don't either. And maybe we'd have an easier time rejecting them had Jesus not modeled them so well.

The author of Hebrews reflects on Jesus' willingness, "for the sake of all," to enter the school of suffering. This is a tightly-knit package of good news. Read slowly, as if speaking to someone who does not know the Christian faith. Explain that Jesus' humanity ("for a little while" he was made "lower than the angels") and his earthly suffering are not sound reasons for rejecting faith in him. Justify God's allowing Jesus to suffer, and argue that it was an almighty God "through whom all things exist" who chose to work this way. Navigate carefully past the two parenthetical clauses of the second sentence, keeping the focus on Christ's being "perfect[ed] through suffering." And remember that "them" in the last sentence also means "us."

GOSPEL The Pharisees arrive and want to know "whether it was permissible for a husband to divorce his wife." To demonstrate that they have abandoned a divine precept in favor of human accommodation, Jesus asks what Moses prescribed. They respond somewhat arrogantly that Moses "permitted divorce." Yes, he did, Jesus rebuts, but only "because of your *stubbornness.*" Then he reminds them of God's original plan as articulated in Genesis. It is moving to hear Jesus speak so respectfully of the holy union between man and woman. Jesus' comments are for the crowd as well as for the Pharisees, so there's a gentleness in his tone that hardens only when he addresses the leaders again with "let no man [one] separate what God has joined."

Once back in the house, Jesus expands on his teaching for the curious disciples, who are eager to hear more. Jesus obliges, confiding a harder teaching for which the crowd was perhaps not yet ready.

There's a lot of action in the final scene where eager crowds, scolding disciples and the indignant Jesus vie for attention. Jesus wins and restores calm by insisting that the children be admitted. He genuinely enjoys their company and speaks of them caringly. Jesus wouldn't scold in the presence of these children. He says little because his actions ("he *embraced* and *blessed* them") speak louder than his words.

"Suffering" is the Passion of Jesus. Building to final announcement.

"Brothers and sisters" is more inclusive.

perfect through *suffering.* ▪▪▪ He who *consecrates* and those who *are* consecrated ▪ have one and the *same* Father. ▪▪ Therefore, ▪ he is not *ashamed* to call them *brothers.* ▪▪▪

GOSPEL Mark 10:2–16

A reading from the holy *gospel* according to *Mark* ▪▪▪

"Permissible . . . to divorce his wife," indirect quote spoken as Pharisee.

They think they have him.

Stern scolding.

Jesus softens. Tender and respectful.

Harder tone again. "One" is more inclusive.

Suggest disciples' eagerness for explanation.

He knows this is a new teaching for them.

Some *Pharisees* came up and as a *test* ▪ began to ask *Jesus* whether it was *permissible* for a husband to *divorce* his wife. ▪▪ In *reply* he said, ▪▪ "What command did Moses give you?" ▪▪ They answered, ▪▪ "Moses *permitted* divorce and the writing of a *decree* of divorce." ▪▪ But Jesus *told* them: ▪▪ "He *wrote* that commandment for you because of your *stubbornness.* ▪▪ At the *beginning* of creation God made them *male* and *female;* ▪▪ for this reason a man shall *leave* his father and mother ▪ and the *two* shall become as *one.* ▪▪ They are *no longer* two but *one* flesh. ▪▪ Therefore ▪ let no man *separate* what *God* has joined." ▪▪ Back in the *house* again, ▪ the disciples began to *question* him about this. ▪▪ He *told* them, ▪▪ "Whoever *divorces* his wife and marries *another* ▪ commits *adultery* against her; ▪▪ and the *woman* who divorces her *husband* and marries another ▪ *commits* adultery." ▪▪▪

A chaotic scene.

Holding back anger for children's sake.

Warmly; as if playing with children while he speaks.

People were bringing their little *children* to him ▪ to have him *touch* them, ▪ but the disciples were *scolding* them for this. ▪▪ Jesus became *indignant* when he noticed it and *said* to them: ▪▪ "*Let* the children *come* to me ▪ and do not *hinder* them. ▪▪ It is to just such as *these* that the *kingdom* of *God* belongs. ▪▪ I *assure* you that whoever does not *accept* the kingdom of God like a *little child* ▪ shall not *enter* into it." ▪▪ Then he *embraced* them and *blessed* them, ▪ placing his *hands* on them. ▪▪▪

[Shorter: Mark 10:2–12]

OCTOBER 13, 1991

TWENTY-EIGHTH SUNDAY IN ORDINARY TIME

LECTIONARY #144

READING I Wisdom 7:7–11

Suggest both the supplication *and the joy at being heard.*

Contrast "scepter" with "nothing."

Contrast "gold" and "silver" with "sand" and "mire."

I gladly sacrificed all for her.

Overwhelmed and overjoyed.

A reading from the book of *Wisdom* ▪ ▪ ▪

I *prayed,* ▪ and *prudence* was *given* me; ▪ ▪
I *pleaded,* ▪ and the spirit of *Wisdom* came to me. ▪ ▪ ▪
I *preferred* her to *scepter* and *throne,* ▪
And deemed riches *nothing* ▪ in *comparison* with her, ▪ ▪
nor did I liken any priceless *gem* to her; ▪ ▪
Because all *gold* ▪ in *view* of her, ▪ is a little *sand,* ▪
and before *her,* ▪ *silver* is to be accounted *mire.* ▪ ▪
Beyond *health* and *comeliness* I loved her, ▪
And I chose to have *her* rather than the *light,* ▪
because the *splendor* of her never *yields* to sleep. ▪ ▪
Yet *all* good things together *came* to me in her *company,* ▪
and countless *riches* at her hands. ▪ ▪ ▪

READING II Hebrews 4:12–13

Second of seven consecutive weeks we read from Hebrews. It's short, so go slowly.

Build: "It penetrates . . . it judges."

A healthy fear of the Lord.

A reading from the letter to the *Hebrews* ▪ ▪ ▪

God's *word* is *living* and *effective,* ▪ *sharper* than any two-edged *sword.* ▪ ▪ It *penetrates* and *divides* ▪ *soul* and *spirit,* ▪ *joints* and *marrow;* ▪ ▪ it *judges* the *reflections* and *thoughts* of the *heart.* ▪ ▪ Nothing is *concealed* from him; ▪ ▪ all lies *bare* and *exposed* to the *eyes* of him ▪ to whom *we* must render an *account.* ▪ ▪ ▪

READING I Convey an attitude of earnest supplication in the opening lines. The author of Wisdom confesses to praying, no, pleading for Wisdom, and the prayer was answered.

The author, speaking as King Solomon, goes on to explain that the prayer was so fervent because Wisdom was "preferred" to all earthly riches. Gems, even silver and gold, pale next to her; health and physical beauty are worth nothing next to her. Of course, "her" always refers to Lady Wisdom—a brilliant but mysterious personification of the spirit of the Lord.

Accentuate also the contrasting attitudes between "gold" (positive) and "sand" (negative) and "silver" (positive) and "mire" (negative).

After freely choosing to give up riches for the sake of Wisdom, the author finds Wisdom does not travel alone—she brings "all good things . . . and countless riches" with her.

READING II Anything that's "sharper than any two-edged sword" had best be handled carefully. That goes for any reading from scripture and for today's pericope (passage) in particular. You've noticed how short it is, so all the usual cautions apply: Read slowly lest you finish before the assembly has started listening; *use* the words and pay special attention to word color; pause to let the meaning sink in before moving on to the next idea.

Speak as if to people who have grown tired of the word, bored with its sound and unmoved by its message. Wake them up and convince them the word is not to be played with and not to be ignored! Speak of its power to achieve God's will, to "penetrate and divide" (both words sound like they mean) and to "judge." "Sharper" also sounds like it means and should be spoken quickly—creating the sound of a knife slicing the air. There is urgency about letting the word do its work in us so that what will lie "bare and exposed to the one to whom we must render an account" will not be anything of which to be ashamed. (Now time yourself and be sure you take at least thirty to forty seconds to deliver the reading.)

GOSPEL It would be easy to impute negative motives to the man who confronts Jesus today. After all, since childhood he has kept the commandments. What does he need from Jesus—an affirmation of his righteousness, maybe a reward? Mark wouldn't tell us Jesus "looked at him with love" if the man were on an ego trip. He is driven by the same goodness that motivated his lifelong adherence to the Law. Knowing he lacks something, he comes running to Jesus and throws himself at his feet breathlessly asking what more he must do to find "everlasting life." He even calls Jesus "Good Teacher," a rarely used title suggesting his great respect. Jesus seems to dismiss the epithet, but perhaps he's inviting the man to think further about what he's said.

The commandments are recited in summary fashion, not as a teaching. Relieved, the man informs Jesus he has kept them. Time stops as Jesus look(s) at him with love, a love based on the man's having kept all the commandments. Jesus' command to "go and sell" is not meant for everyone, but it is meant for this person. No one moves while he grows sad and then slowly walks away. Speak "many possessions" with Jesus' awareness of the weighty spiritual burden they so easily become.

Suddenly Jesus shatters the silence with the pronouncement: "How hard it is. . . ." Don't dilute Jesus' call for renunciation of worldly wealth. Stunned by Jesus' reversal of popular belief that wealth was a sign of God's approval, the disciples panic: "Then *who* can be saved?" Jesus responds with comfort and assurance, but this is Mark's gospel, so the assurance is given ("a hundred times as many homes . . . children and property—*and persecution besides"*) while pointing to the cross.

GOSPEL Mark 10:17–30

A reading from the holy *gospel* according to *Mark* ▪ ▪ ▪

With respect and sincerity.

Fast pace.

As *Jesus* was setting out on a *journey* ▪ a man came *running* up, ▪ *knelt* down before him and *asked* ▪ ▪ *"Good Teacher,* ▪ what must I *do* to share in *everlasting life?"* ▪ ▪ Jesus *answered,* ▪ ▪ "Why do you call me *good?* ▪ ▪ *No* one is good but *God* alone. ▪ ▪ You know the *commandments:* ▪ ▪

'You shall not *kill;* ▪ ▪
You shall not commit *adultery;* ▪ ▪
You shall not *steal;* ▪ ▪
You shall not bear *false witness;* ▪ ▪
You shall not *defraud;* ▪ ▪
Honor your *father* and your *mother.'"* ▪ ▪

A specific prescription for this man.

Jesus speaks directly.

"Children" is more inclusive. Stress the paradox.

He *replied,* ▪ ▪ "Teacher, ▪ I have *kept* all these since my *childhood."* ▪ ▪ Then Jesus *looked* at him with *love* ▪ and told him, ▪ ▪ "There is one thing *more* you must do. ▪ ▪ Go and *sell* what you have and give to the *poor;* ▪ ▪ you will then have treasure in *heaven.* ▪ ▪ *After* that ▪ come and *follow* me." ▪ ▪ At *these* words the man's face *fell.* ▪ ▪ He went away *sad,* ▪ for he had *many* possessions. ▪ ▪ Jesus *looked* around and said to his *disciples,* ▪ ▪ "How *hard* it is for the *rich* to enter the *kingdom* of *God!"* ▪ ▪ The disciples could only *marvel* at his words. ▪ ▪ So Jesus *repeated* what he had said: ▪ ▪ "My *sons,* ▪ how hard it is to *enter* the kingdom of God! ▪ ▪ It is *easier* for a *camel* to pass through a *needle's eye* ▪ than for a *rich* man to enter the kingdom of God." ▪ ▪ ▪

Baffled and alarmed.

"Human beings" is more inclusive.

They were completely *overwhelmed* at this, ▪ and *exclaimed* to one another, ▪ ▪ "Then *who* can be *saved?"* ▪ ▪ Jesus fixed his *gaze* on them and said, ▪ ▪ "For *man* ▪ it is *impossible* ▪ but not for *God.* ▪ ▪ ▪ With *God* ▪ *all* things are possible." ▪ ▪ ▪

Slowly.

Don't lose this warning.

Peter was *moved* to say to him: ▪ ▪ "We have put aside *everything* to follow you!" ▪ ▪ Jesus answered: ▪ ▪ "I give you my *word,* ▪ there is *no* one who has given up *home,* ▪ *brothers* or *sisters,* ▪ *mother* or *father,* ▪ *children* or *property,* ▪ for *me* and for the *gospel* ▪ who will not *receive* in this *present* age ▪ a *hundred* times as many *homes,* ▪ *brothers* and *sisters,* ▪ *mothers,* ▪ *children* and *property*— ▪ ▪ and *persecution* besides— ▪ and in the *age* to *come,* ▪ *everlasting life."* ▪ ▪ ▪

[Shorter: Mark 10:17–27]

OCTOBER 20, 1991

TWENTY-NINTH SUNDAY IN ORDINARY TIME

LECTIONARY #147

READING I Isaiah 53:10–11

Short reading means slow reading.

A reading from the book of the prophet ▪ *Isaiah* ▪▪▪

Speak as narrator. "Him" is God's servant.

[But the Lord was *pleased*
to *crush* him in *infirmity.*] ▪▪

Stress voluntary self-offering.

If he *gives* his life as an *offering* for sin, ▪
he shall see his *descendants* in a *long* life, ▪
and the *will* of the *Lord* shall be *accomplished*
through him. ▪▪▪

Speak as God promising reward.

Because of his affliction ▪
he shall see the *light* in *fullness* of days; ▪▪

Gratitude and love.

Through his *suffering,* ▪ my servant shall justify
many, ▪
and *their* guilt he shall bear. ▪▪▪

READING II Hebrews 4:14–16

Third of seven consecutive weeks we read from Hebrews. Short reading means go slowly.

A reading from the letter to the *Hebrews* ▪▪▪

Tone of celebration.

State your case firmly.

Let's be joyous and grateful that we can do this.

We have a *great* high priest who has passed through the *heavens,* ▪ *Jesus,* ▪ the *Son* of *God;* ▪▪ let us hold *fast* to our profession of faith. ▪▪ For we do not have a high priest who is unable to *sympathize* with our *weakness,* ▪ but one who was *tempted* in *every* way that *we* are, ▪ yet *never* sinned. ▪▪ So let us *confidently* approach the throne of *grace* ▪ to receive *mercy* and *favor* ▪ and to find *help* in time of *need.* ▪▪▪

READING I It's sometimes helpful, but today it's essential: Study the gospel of the day first. Jesus teaches some hard lessons about suffering and service. James and John want assurances of preeminence and rank in the kingdom: Jesus promises *suffering,* and the title he bestows is *"servant."* Isaiah incorporates both these themes in the fourth of the five "Suffering Servant" oracles. Your careful and poignant rendering of this passage will prepare our ears and hearts for the gospel teaching.

The first sentence is starkly blunt and ugly if not properly understood. God is not "pleased" by the random suffering of an individual but by the generous and free self-offering of the servant whose "suffering . . . shall justify many." Stress the words "gives" and "offering." The "will" of the Lord "accomplished through him" is a loving, forgiving will, not one bent on destruction or revenge. Help us hear that when you speak.

The second paragraph states the consequences of the servant's faithful endurance both for himself and for the many: The servant shall see light in "fullness of days" and bear the "guilt" of many people. Speak of those consequences the way St. Paul so often speaks of Jesus' death and resurrection—as the cause of great joy and gratitude. "Many," don't forget, includes you and all to whom you speak.

READING II Let's hold on to what we believe, the author of Hebrews boldly admonishes, for we are not the followers of someone who has no idea what it is like to be human, what it is like to be weak. No! Our high priest was tempted like we are, yet (and this is why we rejoice) he "never sinned." Because he never sinned he is in a position to help us in our own times of weakness. So, come on! "Let us confidently approach" our loving Lord who sits on the very "throne of grace." At his hands we will receive "mercy," and we will "find help" when we're most in need.

Because the passage is so brief you must read slowly, but don't let your slow pace stifle the tone of joy and appreciation that suffuses the piece. You're a cheerleader of sorts, and you cheer for the Christ of the gospel who came "to serve [and] to give his life in ransom for the many."

GOSPEL It's an animated scene Mark presents today. A director staging this scene might have the disciples and Jesus seated around a dinner table, playing cards or otherwise engaged in some mundane activity that absorbed Jesus' attention. In the midst of that activity Zebedee's sons would approach to say they want Jesus to "grant [their] request." Filling his mouth with food or drawing another card, Jesus would ask "What is it?" The brothers, sensing the ripeness of the opportunity, would draw closer, one leaning over the other, even finishing each other's sentences, as they state their request: "See to it (what boldness!) that we sit one at your right, the other at your left."

Extending our imagined scenario, Jesus would not stop what he was doing. He'd play his cards and off-handedly comment that they "do not know what [they] are asking." Without looking, he would ask, as if it were nothing of the life-or-death question that it is, whether they can "drink the cup [he] shall drink or be baptized in the same bath of pain." The two then would fall over each other to eagerly assert, "We can!" Now Jesus reveals that he has listened more intently and with greater interest than he let on. He looks the men square in the eyes and, with a smile and nodding head, he agrees, "the cup I drink of you *shall* drink, the bath . . . you shall *share*."

His eyes hold them for several moments sharing silent communion. Then, releasing them, he informs them that who sits where is not something that he can decide.

Maybe the brothers had Jesus to themselves for a private moment or perhaps they questioned brazenly in front of their brethren. Either way, they've created a storm Jesus must calm. We hear the anger of "the other ten" in the narration that they "became indignant at James and John." Jesus intervenes immediately, and gathering the disciples to himself, he begins to teach them. His tone is patient and gentle, for he knows these men will pay with their lives for the privilege of learning from him.

This scenario contains no poignant melodrama, no violins weeping in the background. It's very ordinary and mostly understated, but it's also the way people work. Contrasting the disciple's intensity with Jesus' composure serves a purpose. There are seldom horns swelling behind important conversations. They just happen; later we look back and realize they changed our lives.

GOSPEL Mark 10:35–45

A reading from the holy *gospel* according to *Mark* ▪▪▪

Zebedee's sons, ▪ *James* and *John*, ▪ approached *Jesus*. ▪▪ *"Teacher,"* ▪ they said, ▪▪ "we want you to grant our *request*." ▪▪ "What *is* it?" ▪ he asked. ▪▪ They replied, ▪▪ *"See* to it that we sit, ▪ *one* at your *right* and the *other* at your *left*, ▪ when you come into your *glory*." ▪▪ Jesus *told* them, ▪▪ "You do not *know* what you are *asking*. ▪▪▪ Can you drink the cup *I* shall drink ▪ or be baptized in the same bath of *pain* as I?" ▪▪ "We *can*," ▪ they told him. ▪▪ Jesus said in *response*, ▪▪ "From the *cup* I drink of you *shall* drink; ▪▪ the bath I am *immersed* in you *shall share*. ▪▪ But sitting at my *right* or my *left* ▪ is not *mine* to give; ▪▪ *that* is for those for whom it has been *reserved*." ▪▪▪ The *other* ten, ▪ on *hearing* this, ▪ became *indignant* at James and John. ▪▪ Jesus called them *together* and *said* to them: ▪▪ "You know how among the *Gentiles* those who seem to exercise *authority* ▪ *lord* it over them; ▪▪ their *great* ones make their importance *felt*. ▪▪ It *cannot* be like that with *you*. ▪▪ *Anyone* among you who aspires to *greatness* ▪ must *serve* the rest; ▪▪ whoever wants to rank *first* among you ▪ must serve the *needs* of *all*. ▪▪ The *Son* of *Man* has not come to *be* served ▪ but to *serve*— ▪ to give his *life* ▪ in *ransom* for the *many*." ▪▪▪

They're not shy.

Boldly.

Pause.

He's not looking at them.

"We can:" again, boldness.

Jesus addresses them directly and lovingly.

They're angry and jealous.

Patient and loving.

Some urgency.

No regret; happy to show the way.

[Shorter: Mark 10:42–45]

OCTOBER 27, 1991

THIRTIETH SUNDAY IN ORDINARY TIME

LECTIONARY #150

READING I Jeremiah 31:7–9

A reading from the book of the prophet ▪ *Jeremiah* ▪▪▪

Isaiah is speaking to defeated people who are being restored.

Thus says the *Lord;* ▪▪
Shout with *joy* for Jacob, ▪
exult at the head of the *nations;* ▪▪
Proclaim your *praise* and say: ▪▪
The Lord has *delivered* his people, ▪
the *remnant* of Israel. ▪▪

Rejoicing.

Behold, ▪ I will bring them *back*
from the land of the *north;* ▪▪

Slower.

I will *gather* them from the *ends* of the world, ▪
with the *blind* and the *lame* in their midst, ▪
The *mothers* and those with *child;* ▪▪
they shall return as an *immense* throng. ▪▪

Contrast the sadness of "tears" with the reassurance of "console" and "guide."

They departed in *tears,* ▪
but I will *console* them and *guide* them; ▪▪
I will lead them to *brooks* of *water,* ▪
on a *level* road, ▪ so that none shall *stumble.* ▪▪

Tremendous love and pride. Ritardando: "Ephraim . . . first born." "Israel" and "Ephraim" are synonymous.

For I am a *father* to Israel, ▪
Ephraim is my *first-born.* ▪▪▪

READING II Hebrews 5:1–6

Fourth of seven consecutive weeks we read from Hebrews.

A reading from the letter to the *Hebrews* ▪▪▪

"People" is more inclusive than "men."

Slowly, noting the balances and contrasts.

Still persuading.

Every high priest is taken from among *men* ▪ and made their *representative* before *God,* ▪ to offer *gifts* and *sacrifices* for sins. ▪▪ He is able to deal *patiently* with erring sinners, ▪ for he is *himself* beset by weakness, ▪ and so must make sin offerings for *himself* ▪ as *well* as for the people. ▪▪ One does not take this honor on his *own* initiative, ▪ but *only* when called by *God* ▪ as *Aaron* was. ▪▪ Even *Christ*

READING I Jeremiah's song is as joyous as the time that preceded it was miserable. The Israelites are returning from exile—a time of national shame as well as personal anguish. But the page is being turned on that tragic chapter of their history: Jeremiah is announcing a new exodus, a time of deliverance and regeneration, a time of promises fulfilled. Only someone who has suffered greatly could rejoice as fully as these verses command.

What would need to end in your life to inspire such joy within you—long illness, depression, a broken relationship, grieving over a loved one? All that and more is expressed in Jeremiah's words and must be evident in your voice as you proclaim. The tone of your voice alone should be enough to tell people that there is something to celebrate here. Adults don't let the fact that infants can't understand words stop them from speaking to their children, because they know the tone of their voices communicates the love or disapproval they wish to convey. Speak with an unmistakable tone of celebration and triumph.

The reading need not start with a "shout," but it must start with intensity and a smile. Jeremiah tells you to "exult," "proclaim" and "praise." You can't do those things without expending energy or without eye contact with the assembly. Contrast that high energy with the compassionate, tender references to "the blind and the lame . . . mothers and those with child." Expectant mothers need much reassurance; God's voice offers it to them and to any of us who are bent or broken.

READING II This is the second of five weeks during which we hear the author of Hebrews' reflections on the priesthood of Jesus. Last week we were reminded that, though he never sinned, Jesus was tempted in every way we are and is thus able to "sympathize with our weakness." Today the analogy between Jesus and human high priests is elaborated.

Imagine yourself lecturing to a group who knows nothing about an issue you hold dear—world peace, the environment, family life, homeless people,—and realize that you must win their hearts before you can change their minds. Our author seems to know that we are guided a step at a time to the realization that Jesus is our "[high] priest forever." As reader, be like the "priest" described here: patient, aware of your own weaknesses, humble about the call you have received. The subdued energy of this passage contrasts with the high energy of today's first reading.

Concentrate on the contrasts in the author's reasoning: "He is able to deal patiently" with sinners, for he is "himself beset by weakness." He must make "sin offerings for *himself* as well as for the *people*." "One does not take this honor on his *own* initiative, but only when called by *God*." "Even *Christ* did not glorify himself; . . . he *received* it." The quotes that end the passage are expressions of love and pride; let your voice convey these emotions.

GOSPEL Perhaps the most remarkable feature of this passage is the behavior of the crowd. So eager are they to please Jesus, to ingratiate themselves with him, that they adjust their allegiances according to their perception of Jesus' mood. They scold Bartimaeus "to make him keep quiet" when they think he is a nuisance to Jesus, but quickly become solicitous when Jesus takes note of him and orders them to call him over. They turn their angry reprimands into encouragement ("You have nothing to fear. Get up! He is calling you!"), as if they hope that helping Bartimaeus will give them a share in the blessing he will receive. The vacillating crowd serves as a foil for Bartimaeus, who never wavers in his resolve to be heard. Their scolding just makes him shout "all the louder." Accentuate the fickle moods of the crowd in your rendering of their dialogue.

Jesus' question to Bartimaeus, "What do you want . . ." provides the occasion for a profession of faith in Jesus' power to heal. Let your voice be full of faith as you say, "Rabboni, I want to see." The blind man is healed, and immediately recognizes the "road" he must take. Though the road leads to Jerusalem and to death, he instantly starts "to follow him."

did not glorify himself with the office of high priest; ▪ ▪
he *received* it from the One who *said* to him, ▪ ▪
"You are my *son;* ▪ ▪
today I have *begotten* you"; ▪ ▪
just as he says in *another* place, ▪ ▪

Spoken with pride.

"You are a *priest forever,* ▪
according to the order of *Melchizedek.*" ▪ ▪ ▪

GOSPEL Mark 10:46–52

A reading from the holy *gospel* according to *Mark* ▪ ▪ ▪

Jesus is headed for Jerusalem—and death.

By inserting "meaning" before "son of Timaeus," the passage will be easier to understand.

Crowd is intolerant and annoyed.

Build the intensity.

"Threw," "jumped," "came" suggest an eruption of activity.

Ritardando: "and started . . . up the road."

As Jesus was leaving *Jericho* with his disciples and a *sizable* crowd, ▪ there was a *blind* beggar ▪ *Bartimaeus* ▪ ("*son* of Timaeus") ▪ sitting by the *roadside.* ▪ ▪ On *hearing* that it was *Jesus* of *Nazareth,* ▪ he began to *call* out, ▪ ▪ "*Jesus,* ▪ Son of *David,* ▪ have *pity* on me!" ▪ ▪ Many people were *scolding* him to make him keep *quiet,* ▪ but he shouted all the *louder,* ▪ ▪ "*Son* of *David,* ▪ have *pity* on me!" ▪ ▪ ▪ Then Jesus *stopped* and said, ▪ ▪ "*Call* him over." ▪ ▪ So they *called* the blind man over, ▪ *telling* him as they did so, ▪ ▪ "You have nothing whatever to *fear* from him! ▪ ▪ *Get* up! ▪ He is *calling* you!" ▪ ▪ ▪ He *threw* aside his cloak, ▪ *jumped* up and *came* to Jesus. ▪ ▪ Jesus *asked* him, ▪ ▪ "What do you want me to *do* for you?" ▪ ▪ "*Rabboni,*" ▪ the blind man said, ▪ ▪ "I want to *see.*" ▪ ▪ Jesus said in reply, ▪ ▪ "Be on your *way!* ▪ ▪ Your *faith* has healed you." ▪ ▪ *Immediately* he received his *sight* ▪ and started to *follow* him up the road. ▪ ▪ ▪

NOVEMBER 1, 1991

ALL SAINTS

LECTIONARY #667

READING I Revelation 7:2–4, 9–14

A reading from the book of *Revelation* ▪ ▪ ▪

This is a vision. You must "see" the images before you describe them.

Increase the volume.

Be impressed by the great number.

I, ▪ *John,* ▪ saw *another* angel come up from the *east* ▪ holding the *seal* of the *living God.* ▪ ▪ He *cried* out at the *top* of his voice to the four *angels* ▪ who were given power to *ravage* the land and the sea, ▪ ▪ "Do *no harm* to the land or the sea or the *trees* ▪ until we *imprint* this seal on the *foreheads* of the *servants* of our God." ▪ ▪ I heard the *number* of those who were so marked— ▪ ▪ *one hundred* and *forty-four thousand* from every *tribe* of Israel. ▪ ▪ ▪

This number is even more awesome.

An impressive and moving spectacle.

A hymn of praise.

"Praise and glory . . . might": each a distinct image.

Quietly.

After this ▪ I saw before me a *huge crowd* which no one could *count* ▪ from every *nation,* ▪ *race,* ▪ *people,* and *tongue.* ▪ ▪ They stood before the *throne* and the *Lamb,* ▪ dressed in *long white robes* ▪ and holding *palm branches* in their hands. ▪ ▪ They cried out in a *loud voice,* ▪ ▪ *"Salvation* is from our *God,* ▪ who is seated on the *throne,* ▪ *and* from the *Lamb!"* ▪ ▪ All the *angels* who were standing around the throne ▪ and the *elders* and the *four living creatures fell* down before the throne to *worship* God. ▪ ▪ They said: ▪ ▪ *"Amen!* ▪ *Praise* and *glory,* ▪ *wisdom,* ▪ *thanksgiving,* and *honor,* ▪ *power* and *might* ▪ to *our God forever* and *ever.* ▪ ▪ *Amen!"* ▪ ▪ ▪

Look at assembly as you ask.

Caught off guard.

With pride and suggestion that "This could happen to you."

Ritardando: "in the . . . Lamb."

Then one of the *elders* asked me, ▪ ▪ "Who do you think these *are,* ▪ all dressed in *white?* ▪ ▪ And *where* have they *come* from?" ▪ ▪ I *said* to him, ▪ ▪ "Sir, ▪ *you* should know better than *I.*" ▪ ▪ He then *told* me, ▪ ▪ "These are the ones who have *survived* the great period of *trial;* ▪ ▪ they have *washed* their robes and made them *white* ▪ in the *blood* of the *Lamb.*" ▪ ▪ ▪

READING I Today is the harvest festival of the church. We acknowledge and honor those holy men and women who've gone before us. And we remind ourselves, still struggling, that we can follow in their footsteps. All of us will be harvested into heaven if we are sealed and washed in the blood of the Lamb.

John's vision has this promise in mind. A militant and struggling infant church, faced with persecution and the specter of martyrdom, looks to heaven for hope. John sees and announces it with near-frenzied joy, a joy that intensifies almost as soon as it begins. The first sentence gives you time to fix the vision in your mind, but then you must race to keep up with it. (That means you create the *illusion* of speed by the excitement you generate, not by actually rushing the words.)

"Do no harm . . ." is spoken with an authoritative voice that can command cosmic forces. Being "sealed" signifies being protected by the one whose mark you bear. So there is a solicitous tone in this part of the vision.

Suddenly the vision expands. "Every nation, race, people, tongue . . ." (four distinct images) is included, singing hymns of praise before "the throne and the Lamb." They wear white and hold palms symbolizing victory and they "cry out!"—which tells you *how* to read.

The "elder's" voice is kind, paternal, wise. There is pride in his description of those who survived persecution and whose robes have been made "white in the blood of the lamb." That last comment is doubly important, for it says that these have been made saints—not by their own work but by the work of the "lamb"—and that the same can happen to us.

READING II God has made us God's own children but the world does not recognize it. Later we shall be changed but we don't know into what. Whatever it will be, we will resemble Christ. Knowing this we have no choice but to be pure as Christ is. That's a simple message. It only takes three verses to tell. Yet it's a powerful message. You will have to work to bring out its power. Short and straightforward readings like this give the impression that their proclamation requires little effort. Not so.

"See what *love*" God has shown in giving us the title *"children* of *God."* "Yet *that* is what we *are!"* you insist. Then you explain, so speak slowly and with emphasis.

The question of "what we shall later be . . ." gives way to the excitement of knowing we will be like *Christ.* But, of course, there's no time like the present. If we're going to resemble Christ, let's start now by keeping "pure." You challenge and inspire with a joyous tone on that line. It will be even more powerful if besides an announcement it's also a prayer.

GOSPEL Try speaking each beatitude simply, quietly, with an awareness of how life-altering each is. At certain points you might imagine some of your listeners standing up and leaving (doubtless some left Jesus when he spoke). That image can add urgency to the beatitude that follows. You never have to raise your voice for hilltop projection. A quiet intensity will serve the scripture better. On the final beatitude you might gesture to the entire assembly and, here, increase your volume suggesting that in each of us the moral revolution, though not complete, has begun.

The beatitudes do many things. They comfort those who sorrow. They bring the hope of joy to those who've forgotten how it tastes. And they challenge us to be different from the world in which we live. With thought and practice you can achieve all three goals in your proclamation. Do it by first letting them comfort and challenge your own heart and give it a taste of kingdom joy.

READING II 1 John 3:1–3

Short reading = slow reading.

A reading from the first letter of *John* ▪ ▪ ▪

With genuine delight.

See what *love* the Father has *bestowed* on us ▪
in letting us be called *children* of *God!* ▪ ▪

Insistent.

Yet ▪ that in *fact* ▪ is what we *are.* ▪ ▪

An explanation.

The *reason* the world does not *recognize* us ▪
is that it *never* recognized the *Son.* ▪ ▪

Eye contact with assembly.

Dearly *beloved,* ▪
we *are* God's children *now;* ▪ ▪
what we shall *later* be ▪ has not *yet* come
to light. ▪ ▪
We know that when it *comes* to light ▪

Lower volume but retain intensity. Make it a prayer.

we shall be *like him,* ▪
for we shall *see* him as he *is.* ▪ ▪

More inclusive: "Everyone" becomes "all." "Himself" becomes "themselves." The verbs become plural.

Everyone who has this *hope* based on *him* ▪
keeps himself *pure,* ▪ as *he* is pure. ▪ ▪ ▪

GOSPEL Matthew 5:1–12

A reading from the holy *gospel* according to *Matthew* ▪ ▪ ▪

When Jesus saw the *crowds* ▪ he *went* up on the mountainside. ▪ ▪ After he had *sat* down ▪ his disciples *gathered* around him, ▪ and he began to *teach* them: ▪ ▪

Slowly, one image at a time.

"How *blest* are the *poor* in *spirit:* ▪ the reign of
God is theirs. ▪ ▪

Quietly, humbly. You are asking all *from those who listen.*

Blest *too* ▪ are the *sorrowing;* ▪ they shall be
consoled. ▪ ▪
[Blest are the *lowly;* ▪ they shall *inherit* the
land.] ▪ ▪
Blest are they who *hunger* and *thirst* for
holiness; ▪
they shall have their *fill.* ▪ ▪
Blest are they who *show mercy;* ▪ ▪ *mercy* shall
be *theirs.* ▪ ▪

Keep three goals in mind: to comfort, challenge, share joy.

Blest are the *single-hearted,* ▪ for they shall
see God. ▪ ▪
Blest too the *peacemakers;* ▪ they shall be
called *sons* of God. ▪ ▪

"Sons and daughters" is more inclusive.

Blest are those *persecuted* for *holiness'* sake; ▪
the *reign* of God is *theirs.* ▪ ▪
Blest are *you* ▪ when they *insult* you and
persecute *you* ▪ and utter every kind of
slander against you because of *me.* ▪ ▪

Intense joy, but with an awareness of the cost.

Be *glad* and *rejoice,* ▪ for your *reward* in heaven
is *great."* ▪ ▪ ▪

NOVEMBER 3, 1991

THIRTY-FIRST SUNDAY IN ORDINARY TIME

LECTIONARY #153

READING I Deuteronomy 6:2–6

A reading from the book of *Deuteronomy* ▪ ▪ ▪

"Moses" spoken with deep respect. "Fear" = a healthy sense of God's awesome grandeur.

"And thus . . .": Highlight this consequence of obedience.

Other consequences of fidelity: Stress them. "Your ancestors" is more inclusive.

Joyous proclamation.

Slowly: "heart . . . soul . . . strength."

Eye contact with assembly.

Moses told the people: ▪ ▪ *Fear* the Lord, your *God,* ▪ and *keep,* ▪ *throughout* the days of your lives, ▪ all his *statutes* and *commandments* which I *enjoin* on you, ▪ ▪ and thus have *long* life. ▪ ▪ *Hear* then, Israel, ▪ and be *careful* to observe them, ▪ that you may grow and prosper the *more,* ▪ in keeping with the *promise* of the Lord, ▪ the God of your *fathers,* ▪ to give you a *land* flowing with *milk* and *honey.* ▪ ▪ ▪ *"Hear,* ▪ O *Israel!* ▪ ▪ The *Lord* is our *God,* ▪ the Lord *alone!* ▪ ▪ Therefore, ▪ you shall *love* the Lord, your God, ▪ with all your *heart,* ▪ and with all your *soul,* ▪ and with *all* your *strength.* ▪ ▪ Take to *heart* these words which I *enjoin* on you today." ▪ ▪ ▪

READING II Hebrews 7:23–28

A reading from the letter to the *Hebrews* ▪ ▪ ▪

Fifth of seven consecutive weeks we read from Hebrews.

Contrast the "old" priesthood with priesthood of Jesus.

High point. Joy and gratitude.

Under the *old* covenant there were *many* priests ▪ because they were prevented by *death* from *remaining* in office; ▪ ▪ but *Jesus,* ▪ because he remains *forever,* ▪ has a priesthood which does *not* pass away. ▪ ▪ Therefore ▪ he is *always* able to *save* those who approach God through *him,* ▪ since he forever *lives* to make *intercession* for them. ▪ ▪ ▪

"When he offered himself": reverence and gratitude for Christ's death. Slowly.

"The word of the oath" = the oath sworn by God that the Son would be priest "forever." Strong finish, with conviction.

It was *fitting* that we should have such a high priest: ▪ ▪ *holy,* ▪ *innocent,* ▪ *undefiled,* ▪ *separated* from sinners, ▪ *higher* than the *heavens.* ▪ ▪ Unlike the *other* high priests, ▪ he has no *need* to offer sacrifice *day* after *day,* ▪ first for his *own* sins ▪ and then for those of the *people;* ▪ ▪ he did that *once* for *all* ▪ when he offered *himself.* ▪ ▪ For the *law* sets up as high priests ▪ men who are *weak,* ▪ ▪ but the word of the *oath* which came *after* the law ▪ appoints as priest the *Son,* ▪ made *perfect* forever. ▪ ▪ ▪

READING I Certain moments and words burn themselves into your consciousness: the exchange of marriage vows, the birth of a child, a parent's death. Such events and words become a part of us; we don't forget them lest we forget who we are. Nations also experience such times and words: "We hold these truths to be self-evident. . . ." In our faith history there are many such utterances, and today you will proclaim one of the foremost: the *Sh'ma,* "Hear, O Israel! The Lord is our God, the Lord alone!" The *Sh'ma* expresses the Jewish people's fervent faith in one God and in their uncompromising love of God. Today it becomes your statement of faith as well.

Remember who Moses is and the solemn authority with which he speaks. Solemn doesn't mean sad or lifeless; it means ceremonious, dignified, sacred. Moses urges the people to be careful to observe the Law because he knows that their growth and prosperity depend on it. Make it sound like the life-or-death decision that it is.

Your intensity and volume increase for the recitation of the *Sh'ma;* make it as passionately prayerful as you can. We are told to love the Lord with "heart," "soul" and "strength." There is no "begging" in the final sentence; there's an implied "If you know what's good for you" in the tone. What else is there to do but "take these words . . . to heart"?

READING II You come in halfway through the telling of a joke, and you try to guess how it began as you continue listening. Then, suddenly, the joke ends and everyone laughs, but you're still trying to figure out what it was you missed—one of life's small vexations, to be sure. But a larger vexation occurs when scripture is read and we can't shake that same uncomfortable feeling that we've missed something. Today's pericope from Hebrews can give that feeling unless you take measures to prevent it.

Three suggestions: First, for your own preparation, read the passages from Hebrews from the previous two weeks. Second, note how the author contrasts human high priests with "the great high priest," Jesus. Third, let your tone suggest that you are picking up in the middle of things and are continuing a certain line of reasoning. Begin as if stating: "As I was saying, 'under the *old* covenant . . .'" Some obvious contrasts immediately emerge: There were many priests because death kept them from remaining in office. Now Jesus remains forever and his priesthood "does *not* pass away."

When you tell us it was fitting that we have "such a high priest," you're referring to the description of the first paragraph and also to what we heard in the previous weeks' passages. List Jesus' attributes slowly, with joy and pride. Don't let your tone sound as if you were criticizing "the other high priests." Instead, insist that Jesus is superior because he had no sins of "his own" for which to offer sacrifice and because he "offered himself" *as* the sacrifice! Your job throughout is to *persuade* us that the former priesthood (consisting of "men who are weak") has been replaced by the priesthood of "the Son, made perfect forever."

GOSPEL Artists learn to communicate with symbols. In a movie a character's wickedness might be suggested by the music played when he or she enters; in a painting that characteristic could be hinted by the uses of light and shadow; while in a story or poem inclement weather or the response of animals might warn of a character's sinister intent. Readers can employ vocal devices to telegraph attitudes not overtly stated by the words. Not until the closing sentences do we learn of Jesus' approval of the scribe whom he attests to be "close to the reign of God." Unless you start telegraphing it from the first sentence, your listeners won't realize until it's over that Jesus shares the stage today with a saint.

Introduce the scribe with a positive tone. His question is sincere, void of the intent to trick Jesus—so often hidden in the questions of his adversaries. Realizing he's been given a wonderful opportunity, Jesus pauses and quotes the best known and most repeated prayer in Judaism. He can tell the crowd, without actually saying it, that legalistic religious observances mean nothing compared to love of God and neighbor.

The scribe hears exactly what he hoped to, and his heart leaps at Jesus' affirmation of his intuitions. Then, as if making sure he heard Jesus correctly, he repeats the formula with growing strength and conviction. Relief and joy (even love) fill Jesus' voice as he invites this insightful religious leader to discipleship in "the reign of God." Then the narrator summarizes: "No one had the courage to ask him any more questions."

GOSPEL Mark 12:28–34

A reading from the holy *gospel* according to *Mark* ▪ ▪ ▪

A sincere, learned man seeking a sincere and learned answer.

Addressing first the scribe (quietly) then incorporating the crowd (louder).

One of the *scribes* came up to Jesus, and *asked* him, ▪ ▪
"Which is the *first* of all the *commandments?*" ▪ ▪
Jesus replied: ▪ ▪ *"This* is the first: ▪ ▪ ▪
'*Hear,* O Israel! ▪ ▪ The *Lord* our God is Lord
alone! ▪ ▪
Therefore you shall *love* the Lord your God
with all your *heart,* ▪
with all your *soul,* ▪
with all your *mind,* ▪
and with *all* your *strength.*' ▪ ▪ ▪
This is the *second,* ▪ ▪
'You shall love your *neighbor* as *yourself.*' ▪ ▪

Now quieter again. Speaking directly to scribe.

He's been waiting *to say this. Lovingly.*

Narrator is pleased with the outcome.

There is no other commandment *greater* than *these.*" ▪ ▪ The scribe *said* to him: ▪ ▪ *"Excellent,* Teacher! ▪ ▪ You are *right* in saying, ▪ ▪ 'He is the *One,* ▪ there is *no* other than he.' ▪ ▪ *Yes,* ▪ 'to *love* him with all our *heart,* ▪ with *all* our *thoughts* ▪ and with all our *strength,* ▪ and to love our *neighbor* as *ourselves*' ▪ is worth *more* than any *burnt* offering or *sacrifice.*" ▪ ▪ Jesus *approved* the insight of this answer and *told* him, ▪ ▪ "You are not *far* from the *reign* of *God.*" ▪ ▪ ▪ And *no one* had the *courage* ▪ to ask him any *more* questions. ▪ ▪ ▪

NOVEMBER 10, 1991

THIRTY-SECOND SUNDAY IN ORDINARY TIME

LECTIONARY #156

READING I 1 Kings 17:10–16

A reading from the first book of *Kings* ▪ ▪ ▪

"Zarephath" = Zĕr-ah-fat.

Elijah ▪ [the prophet] ▪ went to *Zarephath.* ▪ ▪ As he *arrived* at the *entrance* of the city, ▪ a *widow* was gathering *sticks* there; ▪ ▪ he *called out* to her, ▪ ▪ *"Please* ▪ bring me a small cupful of *water* to *drink."* ▪ ▪ She left to *get* it, ▪ and he called out *after* her, ▪ ▪ *"Please* bring me a *bit* of *bread."* ▪ ▪ "As the Lord, your God, *lives,"* ▪ she answered, ▪ ▪ "I have *nothing* baked; ▪ ▪ there is only a *handful* of flour in my jar ▪ and a little *oil* in my jug. ▪ ▪ Just *now* I was collecting a couple of *sticks,* ▪ to go in and *prepare* something for *myself* and my *son;* ▪ ▪ when we have *eaten* it, ▪ we shall *die."* ▪ ▪ ▪ "Do not be *afraid,"* ▪ Elijah said to her. ▪ ▪ *"Go* and *do* as you propose. ▪ ▪ But *first* make me a little cake and *bring* it to me. ▪ ▪ *Then* you can prepare something for *yourself* and your *son.* ▪ ▪ For the *Lord,* ▪ the God of *Israel,* says, ▪ ▪ 'The *jar* of *flour* shall not go *empty,* ▪ nor the *jug* of *oil* run *dry,* ▪ until the *day* when the Lord sends *rain* upon the earth.'" ▪ ▪ She left and *did* as Elijah had said. ▪ ▪ ▪ She was able to *eat* for a *year,* ▪ and *he* and her *son* as well; ▪ ▪ the jar of flour did *not* go empty, ▪ nor the *jug* of *oil* run *dry,* ▪ as the Lord had *foretold* through Elijah. ▪ ▪ ▪

"Please" gets her attention; then speak request.

Stress "after." "A bit of bread": spoken as if calling from a distance.

More concerned about inability to provide than her own plight.

He asks without embarrassment because he knows the promise he will make.

God's loving assurance to a worthy daughter.

Impressed with her faith.

Almost incredulous.

READING II Hebrews 9:24–28

A reading from the letter to the *Hebrews* ▪ ▪ ▪

Sixth of seven consecutive weeks we read from Hebrews.

"Sanctuary" = the Jerusalem temple.

Christ did not enter into a sanctuary made by *hands,* ▪ a mere *copy* of the *true* one; ▪ ▪ he entered heaven *itself* ▪ that he might appear before God *now* ▪ on *our* behalf. ▪ ▪ Not that he might *offer* himself there *again* and *again,* ▪ as the *high priest* enters year after *year* into the *sanctuary* ▪ with *blood* that is not his *own;* ▪ ▪ were that *so,* ▪ he would have had to suffer *death* ▪ *over* and *over* from the *creation* of the *world.* ▪ ▪

Stress contrast between high priest's repeated offerings and Jesus' "once for all" sacrifice.

READING I Elijah, the prophet who conversed with Jesus during the Transfiguration and whose return was promised before the coming of the Messiah, makes a rare appearance today.

During a tragic three-year drought, Elijah reaches a city that is on the verge of becoming a mass grave for its starving populace. Look for and highlight the words that suggest the desolation oi that place: "widow," "sticks," "handful of flour," "a little oil," etc. Without introduction Elijah asks help of the widow, who unhesitatingly complies. Use the word "Please" (followed by a pause) to get the woman's attention before telling her what you want. The second request accentuates "a bit of bread," for now you are calling from a distance, trying to catch the woman before she's out of earshot. Apparently much happens between the lines: Why does the woman respond so readily? How does she know about Elijah's God? A relationship is forming that can't be suggested if you rush the dialogue.

The woman has long since become resigned to her inevitable fate. There is no melodramatic self-pity in her declaration that once she and her son have eaten, "we shall die." She speaks with noble courage, even seems embarrassed by her inability to be hospitable despite facing her own death. Had the woman been distraught, Elijah's request for "a little cake" would have seemed crassly insensitive. He reassures her, asks for food in tranquil tones, then surprises her with the promise of God's provident care.

The narrator is impressed that "She left and did . . ." and marvels at the literal fulfillment of Elijah's prophecy. Help us to marvel as well.

READING II Our own century provides an example of the unsettling aftershocks that result from changes in religious structures and directions. In the wake of the changes wrought by Vatican II, many felt disoriented, left behind, missing the old and puzzled by the new. Sensitive leaders knew good pastoring required careful explanations, gentle coaxing and ready answers to many questions. The author of Hebrews is a good pastor who understands how challenging it is to accept new ideas. Though scholars dispute whom the author is addressing, it is clear that the author is demonstrating that the priesthood of Christ is in the tradition of the Jewish priesthood, and yet it is for all time and for all people, never to be ended. That requires carefully crafted arguments spoken with confidence and tinged with *joy.*

Move slowly throughout the passage,

remembering this is a written *homily* that is meant to teach and persuade. In a homily the assembly is always of primary importance, so never lose contact with your listeners; it is to them and because of them that you speak. Tell them that Christ has entered heaven, not the earthly Temple in Jerusalem that is only a copy of the true sanctuary, and that there Christ intercedes for us. Then outline the difference between Jesus' intercession and that made by human high priests: The latter repeated their sacrifices "year after year" because they could not definitively remove sins, whereas Christ took sins away "once for all by his sacrifice."

You conclude with hope-filled faith in the promise of Christ's second coming. If we hadn't before, your announcement of his coming "to bring salvation" should make us await him *"eagerly."*

GOSPEL Jesus displays much emotion as he speaks of hypocrites. He characterizes them as posturing peacocks who strut for the public seeking places of honor while at the same time taking advantage of defenseless widows. With righteous anger Jesus assigns to them "the *severest* sentence."

A radical mood shift occurs in the second half of this passage. With an ironic style, Jesus turns the victim into the hero. One of the victimized widows of the first paragraph becomes Jesus' paradigm of sacrificial giving. There is a hushed tone in this paragraph, as if Jesus does not want to be seen observing "the crowd putting money into the collection box," nor to be overheard praising the widow's generosity. There is no juxtaposition of good poor and bad rich here. The wealthy are not wolf-like predators who devour widows, but generous benefactors who give "sizable" amounts—so speak of them without judgment. But sizable amounts don't necessarily reveal values and priorities, and Jesus makes sure his disciples know that. Bluntly, like a teacher with his students, he tells them what he wants them "to observe." The widow offered the most, he says admiringly, because she held nothing back. If your heart is truly where your treasure is, then the widow left no doubt about the location of hers.

Your tone says: "This would be absurd."

"We" or "all" is more inclusive.

Joyous expectation of Jesus' triumphant return.

But now he has *appeared,* ▪ at the *end* of the ages ▪ to *take* away sins *once for all* by his *sacrifice.* ▪▪ Just as it is *appointed* that men die *once,* ▪ and *after* death be *judged,* ▪▪ so *Christ* was offered up *once* to take away the sins of *many;* ▪▪ he will appear a *second* time ▪ not to take away *sin* ▪ but to bring *salvation* ▪ to those who eagerly *await* him. ▪▪▪

GOSPEL Mark 12:38–44

A reading from the holy *gospel* according to *Mark* ▪▪▪

Jesus is a teacher advising his students.

Mocking their self-importance and their posturing.

In the course of his *teaching* Jesus said: ▪▪ "Be on *guard* against the *scribes,* ▪ who like to *parade* around in their *robes* ▪ and accept marks of respect in *public,* ▪ *front* seats in the *synagogues,* ▪ and places of *honor* at banquets. ▪▪ These men *devour* the savings of *widows* ▪ and recite *long* prayers for *appearance'* sake; ▪▪ it is *they* who will receive the *severest* sentence." ▪▪▪

Quietly.

With approval and respect.

"That this poor . . . to the treasury": almost whispered to keep from being overheard.

Admiring her and challenging them (us).

Taking a *seat* opposite the *treasury,* ▪ he observed the *crowd* putting money into the *collection* box. ▪▪ Many of the *wealthy* put in *sizable* amounts; ▪▪ but one poor *widow* came and put in two small *copper* coins ▪ worth about a *cent.* ▪▪ He called his *disciples* over and *told* them: ▪▪ "I want you to *observe* that this poor widow contributed *more* than all the *others* who donated to the treasury. ▪▪ *They* gave from their *surplus* wealth, ▪ but *she* gave from her *want,* ▪ *all* that she had to *live* on." ▪▪▪

[Shorter: Mark 12:41–44]

NOVEMBER 17, 1991

THIRTY-THIRD SUNDAY IN ORDINARY TIME

LECTIONARY #159

READING I Daniel 12:1–3

A reading from the book of the prophet ▪ *Daniel* ▪ ▪ ▪

"That time" = time of great tribulation.

At that *time* there shall arise
Michael, ▪ the great *prince,* ▪
guardian of your people; ▪ ▪
It shall be a time *unsurpassed* in distress ▪
since nations *began* until *that* time. ▪ ▪

Shift tone from describing distress to giving reasons for hope.

At that time your people shall *escape,* ▪
everyone who is found written in the *book.* ▪ ▪
Many of those who *sleep*
in the *dust* of the earth ▪ shall *awake;* ▪ ▪

Build from "sleep" to "awake" to "forever."

Some shall live *forever,* ▪

Sharp contrast between "some" and "others."

others shall be an everlasting *horror* and
disgrace. ▪ ▪

Rousing conclusion.

But the *wise* shall shine *brightly* ▪
like the *splendor* of the *firmament.* ▪ ▪
And those who lead the many to *justice* ▪
shall be like the *stars* ▪ *forever.* ▪ ▪ ▪

READING II Hebrews 10:11–14, 18

A reading from the letter to the *Hebrews* ▪ ▪ ▪

Last of seven consecutive weeks we read from Hebrews.

Use the contrasts: "every other priest" with "Jesus" and "those same sacrifices" with "one sacrifice."

Mounting energy. A sense of satisfaction.

Mood shifts to gratitude. Ritardando: "no further offering for sin."

Every *other* priest stands ministering *day* by *day,* ▪ and offering again and *again* those *same* sacrifices ▪ which can *never* take away sins. ▪ ▪ But *Jesus* offered *one* sacrifice for sins ▪ and took his seat *forever* at the *right* hand of *God;* ▪ ▪ now he waits until his *enemies* are placed beneath his *feet.* ▪ ▪ ▪ By *one* offering he has forever *perfected* those who are being *sanctified.* ▪ ▪ Once sins have been *forgiven,* ▪ there is no *further* offering for sin. ▪ ▪ ▪

READING I The prophet Daniel understood that people experiencing great distress sometimes hold on to nothing more than beautiful words of hope crafted by the poetic soul. Daniel speaks remarkable words today to people needing images that will keep them afloat during dark times *"unsurpassed* in distress." His words are remarkable not only for the beauty and richness of their imagery but also because they clearly articulate, for the first time in scripture, belief in life after death. As a sign of hope, Daniel offers the angel Michael, Israel's guardian and "great prince." The mere speaking of his name should inspire confidence and dispel fears. Dark and light are blended on the canvas you are painting, for as soon as you've announced the upheaval of "that time," you declare that "everyone who is found written in the book" shall "escape." Picture those who need your words of comfort staring at you with frightened faces. Speak slowly, with quieter intensity, of those "who sleep" and "shall awake" and "live forever," for while you are rousing the imagination you are soothing the heart.

The last four lines are almost sung—a final offering of joyous hope describing the reward that awaits the wise and just. In lives darkened with fear, this poetry shines "like the stars."

READING II A mediocre lector might think: Oh no, another passage taken hopelessly out of context, full of technical, unemotional language and so short you're finished before you get started. A fine lector might think: Here's a clearly written, well-structured passage that loses little from being removed from its context. Technical, yes, but it suggests emotions that, if not overtly articulated, are clearly implied. Let's get to work!

Which lector are you? We'll assume the latter. So, let's get to work: Review the passages from Hebrews read in recent weeks. Today is your summation: The sacrifices of "every other priest" (speak slowly, with deliberate precision), despite being offered "day by day" and "again and again (with mounting energy you make a point that to you is obvious and well established), are unable to "take away sins." "But Jesus" (slowly building intensity) offered only "one sacrifice" and (higher energy) can now sit at God's right hand (you smile with satisfaction) waiting for his enemies to be fully vanquished! Whether in a courtroom or in a friendly debate, you've made your point.

Now comes the response that you yourself feel and that you want to elicit from your listeners: gratitude. Christ's "one offering" was his death, and through it *we* "are being sanctified." That takes a slow and tender reading. You are no longer courtroom lawyer, but friend or parent or confessor assuring a loved one that God's mercy really does forgive, and once forgiven, "there is no further offering for sin."

GOSPEL Apocalyptic writing often uses dark and startling imagery in juxtaposition with a core message of consolation to announce the victory of light over darkness. Mark incorporates both elements in this passage. There's no shortage of frightening imagery: "trials of every sort," darkened sun and lightless moon, falling stars and shaken heavens. All these converge to present a world in desperate need of salvation, and Mark provides that, too, in the image of "the Son of Man coming in the clouds."

It's crucial that the description of the Son of Man sound not like a continuation of the list of calamities that will befall the earth but like an intervention by a loving God on behalf of the terrified populace. The triumphant Christ will "dispatch his messengers" not to destroy but to gather the "chosen." They will leave no stone unturned, searching from "earth" to "sky" in their effort to rescue God's people. Suggest a time-consuming search and allow time for the images to do their work by moving slowly through these lines.

A sudden shift occurs at "the fig tree." From cosmic concerns we narrow our focus to a single tree. Your tone adjusts accordingly, becoming more conversational and didactic. But only for a moment, for immediately the scene widens again as Jesus draws our attention back to the skies and, with a quickening tempo, cautions us to be alert and ready. He speaks with the urgency of one who understands the consequences of missing the time for either sowing or reaping.

A fascinating coda ends this text. There's a note of finality in Jesus' "but my words will not." Then, as if sensing an unspoken question from his disciples (in *every* generation), he warns against efforts to pin down exact times. The point is that we keep eyes on "heaven" waiting for the Son, who will lead us to the Father.

GOSPEL Mark 13:24–32

A reading from the holy *gospel* according to *Mark* ▪ ▪ ▪

High energy and intensity, but don't rush.

Jesus said to his *disciples:* ▪ ▪ "During that period ▪ after *trials* of *every* sort ▪ the *sun* will be *darkened,* ▪ the *moon* will not shed its *light,* ▪ *stars* will *fall* out of the skies, ▪ and the heavenly *hosts* will be *shaken.* ▪ ▪

"People" is more inclusive than "men."

Then men will see the *Son* of *Man* coming in the *clouds* ▪ with great *power* and *glory.* ▪ ▪

The dawn of hope in that time of darkness.

He will dispatch his *messengers* ▪ and assemble his *chosen* from the four *winds,* ▪ from the *farthest* bounds of *earth* and *sky.* ▪ ▪ ▪

Slower, less intense.

Learn a *lesson* from the *fig* tree. ▪ ▪ Once the *sap* of its branches runs *high* ▪ and it begins to sprout *leaves,* ▪ you know that *summer* is near. ▪ ▪

Intensity climbs again.

In the *same* way, ▪ when you *see* these things happening, ▪ you will *know* that *he* is near, ▪ *even* at the *door.* ▪ ▪

Eye contact with assembly.

I *assure* you, ▪ *this* generation will not *pass away* until *all* these things take place. ▪ ▪

Ritardando: "my words will not." A solemn warning.

The *heavens* and the *earth* will pass away, ▪ but my *words* will *not.* ▪ ▪ ▪

"As to the exact *day* or *hour,* ▪ *no* one knows it, ▪ neither the *angels* in heaven nor even the *Son,* ▪ but *only* the *Father."* ▪ ▪ ▪

NOVEMBER 24, 1991

LAST SUNDAY IN ORDINARY TIME, CHRIST THE KING

LECTIONARY #162

READING I Daniel 7:13–14

A reading from the book of the prophet ▪ *Daniel* ▪▪▪

This apocalyptic vision is meant to inspire awe.

As the *visions* during the night *continued,* ▪▪
I saw
One ▪ like a *son* of *man* ▪ *coming,*
on the *clouds* of *heaven;* ▪▪

"Ancient One" = God.

When he reached the *Ancient One* ▪
and was *presented* before him, ▪

Enumerate slowly.

He received *dominion,* ▪ *glory,* ▪ and *kingship;* ▪▪
nations and peoples of *every* language *serve* him. ▪▪

With pride.

His *dominion* is an *everlasting* dominion
that shall *not* be taken *away,* ▪

Ritardando: "his kingship shall not be destroyed."

his *kingship* shall not be *destroyed.* ▪▪▪

READING II Revelation 1:5–8

A reading from the book of *Revelation* ▪▪▪

A hymn of praise requiring joyful energy.

Jesus Christ is the faithful *witness,* ▪ the *firstborn* from the dead ▪ and *ruler* of the kings of earth. ▪▪

Gratitude for the price Christ paid.

To him who *loves* us and *freed* us from our sins by his *own blood,* ▪ who has made us a *royal* nation of *priests* in the service of his *God* and *Father*— ▪

Climax of praise.

to *him* be *glory* and *power* ▪ *forever* and *ever.* ▪▪ *Amen.* ▪▪▪

Excitement.

See, ▪ he *comes* amid the *clouds!* ▪▪
Every *eye* shall *see* him, ▪

Painful memory of his suffering and of those who still reject him.

even of those who *pierced* him. ▪▪
All the *peoples* of the earth
shall lament him *bitterly.* ▪▪
so it is to *be.* ▪▪ *Amen!* ▪▪

"Alpha and Omega" = "beginning and end." Affirmation of Christ's glorious triumph.

The Lord *God* says, ▪▪ "I am the *Alpha* and the *Omega,* ▪ the One who *is* and who *was* and who is to *come,* ▪▪ the *Almighty!"* ▪▪▪

READING I Even people who dislike hearing others recount their dreams can't help but be drawn in by the telling of one that's especially fascinating because of its arresting images, its awe-inspiring tone, its departure from anything familiar or predictable. Such is the vision Daniel shares today.

Notice first that he is describing a continuing experience; we have come in the midst of his telling and have already missed much. His expansive tone is established, his audience is spellbound, his energy is at full-throttle—he's only stopped to catch his breath before concluding the narration of his "visions during the night." Imagine that everyone has come to church today specifically to hear you retell these visions the way a group might gather to hear someone's report of a UFO sighting or a near-death experience. They're here because they want to be; they're listening because they want to know. So tell them.

"I saw One like a Son of Man" (awe fills your voice) "coming, on the *clouds* of heaven" (not only is that in itself miraculous, but clouds are a symbol of divine presence, so what you are glimpsing is heaven itself). He approached "the *Ancient* One" (a title for the Everlasting God) and "he received . . ." (the list of honors and titles is staggering, signifying the majesty of this Son of Man to whom so much is given and from whom nothing shall be "taken away"). "His dominion . . ." (spoken like a humble subject eager to serve this king) and ". . . his kingship shall not be destroyed."

All that remains is for you to fill a minute with this story and to let the story fill you with profound awe.

READING II Remember the solemnity we've come to celebrate. You've been chosen to sing a hymn of praise to the Christ who reigns over us as "the Almighty" king. There are three verses to your song. Verse one is a doxology that acknowledges Jesus' love for us ("To him who loves us"), lists the consequences of that love (he "freed us from our sins *by his own blood"*), and ends with praise ("to him be glory and power forever and ever!"). The sections of this verse create their own distinct feelings: first affection, then bittersweet awareness of the price Christ paid for loving us, and finally enthusiastic, joyful worship.

Verse two alludes to the prophecy from Daniel we hear in today's first reading. There's a finger pointed to the sky in this section as John directs our attention to the one who will be seen by all—both those who loved him and those who killed him. "All the peoples" refers to unbelievers who persecute the church and are thus hostile to Christ. They shall lament bitterly. To underscore the solemnity of that prophecy John repeats his "so be it" with a redundant "Amen!"

The last verse of your song proclaims God's eternal sovereignty over all humankind. No matter the whims of earthly kings, no matter their designs against the church of Christ, the "One who is and was" reigns even over them, and they had best beware for he is to come again! Amen!

GOSPEL Christ doesn't appear very kingly here, bound at the wrists and waiting the sentence that will tell if he lives or dies. But this is the king we serve, and we need to be reminded that his notion of lordship included washing feet and laying-down his life.

When we encounter this scene during Holy Week, its purpose and impact are perhaps different from what they are today. Pilate is important then as a more passive than active player in the drama that propels Jesus to his death. The dialogue serves John's end of showing Jesus in charge of his own destiny, capable but unwilling to resist the fate that awaits him. Today the scene harmonizes with the Apocalyptic visions of Daniel and John that focus us on a heavenly king who comes in glory. They fix our eyes on the skies and the clouds. Jesus reinforces that by telling us his kingdom "does not belong to this world." He downplays his present predicament because the "truth" of who he is has not yet been fully revealed or understood.

Don't read this passage with the intensity of Good Friday because it is so brief here. What matters here is the image of a king who dies willingly for the sake of his subjects. Pilate asks "Are you the king . . . ?" He is not only a Roman official but a person who seeks to understand Christ's identity. When Jesus questions, "Are you saying this on your own . . . ?" he could be asking any one of us. There is poetry in Jesus' words. There is also dignity and majesty in this king who cares more about truth than saving his own life.

GOSPEL John 18:33–37

A reading from the holy *gospel* according to *John* ▪ ▪ ▪

Down-played. Not angry.

Pilate said to Jesus: ▪ ▪ "Are you the *king* of the Jews?" ▪ ▪ Jesus *answered,* ▪ ▪ "Are you saying this on your *own,* ▪ or have others been *telling* you about me?" ▪ ▪ *"I am no Jew!"* ▪ Pilate retorted. ▪ ▪ "It is your own *people* and the *chief priests* who have handed you over to me. ▪ ▪ What have you *done?*" ▪ ▪ Jesus answered: ▪ ▪

Mute his reaction.

Pointing to realities that transcend the moment.

"My *kingdom* does not belong to *this* world. ▪ ▪
If my kingdom *were* of this world, ▪
my *subjects* would be fighting
to *save* me from being handed over to the Jews. ▪ ▪
As it is, ▪ my kingdom is not *here.*" ▪ ▪ ▪

A question, not an accusation.

At this *Pilate* said to him, ▪ ▪ "*So,* then, ▪ you *are* a king?" ▪ ▪ Jesus replied: ▪ ▪

He does not deny it, but points to a different sort of kingship.

"It is *you* who say I am a king. ▪ ▪
The reason I was *born,* ▪
the reason why I *came* into the world, ▪
is to *testify* to the *truth.* ▪ ▪

Eye contact. Call assembly to commitment.

Anyone *committed* to the truth ▪ *hears* my voice." ▪ ▪ ▪

PRONUNCIATION GUIDE

Aaron	àr"-*n
Abba	ab"-a, a-ba"
Abel Meholah	a"-b*l mi-ho"-la
Abiathar	a-bi"-a-thêr
Abijah	a-bi"-ja
Abilene	a-bi-le"-ne
Abishai	a-bi"-shi, a-bi"-sha-i
Abiud	a-bi"-*d
Abner	ab"-nêr
Abraham	a"-bra-ham
Abram	a"-bram
Achaia	a-ki"-ya, a-ka"-ya
Achim	a"-kim
Advocate	ad"-vo-kat
Ahaz	a"-haz
aloes	a"-loz
Alpha	al"-fa
Alphaeus	al-fe"-us
Amalek	am"-a-lek
Amalekites	a-mal"-e-kitz
Amaziah	a-ma-zi"-a
Amminadab	a-min"-a-dab
Ammonites	a"-mo-nitz
Amon	a"-mon
Amorites	a"-môr-itz
Amos	a"-mos
Amoz	a"-moz
Anna	a"-na
Annas	a"-nas
Antioch	an"-te-ok
Apollos	a-pol"-os
Arabah	âr"-a-ba
Aramaean	âr-a-me"-an
Archelaus	âr-ke-la"-us
Arimathaea	âr-i-ma-the"-a
Asa	a"-sa
Asher	a"-shêr
Attalia	a-ta-li"-a
Azariah	a-za-ri"-a
Azor	a"-zôr
Baal-shalishah	ba"-al-sha"-li-sha, bal" ...
Babel	ba"-b*l
Babylon	ba"-bi-lon
Barabbas	bâr-ab"-as
Barnabas	bâr"-na-bas
Barsabbas	bâr-sa"-bas
Bartholomew	bâr-thol"-om-yu
Bartimaeus	bâr-ti-me"-us
Baruch	bàr"-uk
Beelzebul	be-el"-za-b*l
Bethany	beth"-a-ne
Bethel	beth"-el
Bethlehem	beth"-le-hem
Bethphage	beth"-fa-je
Bethsaida	beth-sa"-i-da
Boaz	bo"-az
Caesarea	sez-a-re"-a
Caiaphas	ki"-ya-fas, ka"-a-fas
Cana	ka"-na
Canaan	ka"-nan
Canaanite	ka"-na-nit
Capernaum	k*-pêr"-na-um
Cappadocia	ka-pa-do"-sha
Carmel	kâr-mel"
Cephas	se"-fas
Chaldaeans	kal-de"-anz
Chloe	klo"-e
Chronicles	kron"-i-k*lz
Chuza	ku"-za
Cilicia	si-lis"-ya, si-lish"-a
Cleopas	kle"-o-pas
Clopas	klo"-pas
Colossians	ko-losh"-anz
Corinth	kôr"-inth
Corinthians	kôr-in"-the-anz
Cornelius	kôr-nel"-yus
Cretans	kre"-tans
Cushite	k*sh"-it
Cyrene	si-re"-ne
Cyrus	si"-rus
darnel	dâr"-nel
Damascus	da-mas"-kus
Decapolis	di-ca"-po-lis
denarius, -rii	de-nâr"-e-us, de-nâr"-e-e
Deuteronomy	dyu-têr-on"-o-me
drachmas	drak"-maz
Ebed-melech	e-bed-mel"-ek
Ecclesiastes	e-kle-ze-as"-tez
Elamites	el"-a-mitz
Eldad	el"-dad
Eleazar	el-e-a"-zèr
Eli	e"-li
Eli, Eli, lama sabachthani	a"-le, a"-le, la"-ma sa-bak-ta"-ne
Eliab	e-li"-ab
Eliakim	e-li"-a-kim
Elijah	e-li"-ja
Elisha	e-li"-sha
Eliud	e-li"-ud
Eloi, Eloi, lama sabachthani	a"-loy, a"-loy, la"-ma sa-bak-ta"-ne
Emmanuel	e-man"-yu-el
Emmaus	e-ma"-us
Ephah	e"-fa
Ephesians	e-fe"-zhanz
Ephphatha	ef"-a-tha
Ephraim	e"-fra-im, ef"-r*m
Ephrata	e"-fra-ta
Ephrathah	e"-fra-tha,-ta
Euphrates	yu-fra"-tez
Ezekiel	e-zek"-e-el
Ezra	ez"-ra
Gabbatha	ga"-ba-tha
Galatia	ga-la"-sha
Galatians	ga-la"-shanz
Galilean(s)	ga-li-le"-an(z)
Galilee	ga"-li-le
Gehazi	ge-ha"-ze, ge-ha"-zi
Gennesaret	ge-nes"-a-ret
Gethsemane	geth-sem"-a-ne
Gibeon	gi"-be-an
Gilgal	gil"-gal
Golgotha	gol"-ga-tha
Gomorrah	ge-môr"-a
Habakkuk	hab"-a-kuk, ha-bak"-uk
Hadad-rimmon	ha"-dad-rim"-on
Hades	ha"-dez
Hebron	he"-bron
Hellenists	hel"-*n-ists
Herodians	he-ro"-de-anz
Hezekiah	he-ze-ki"-a
Hezron	hez"-ron
Hilkiah	hil-ki"-a
Hittite	hit"-it
Horeb	ho"-reb
Hosea	ho-za"-a, ho-ze"-a
Hur	hûr
Iconium	i-ko"-ne-um
Immanuel	i-man"-yu-el
Isaac	i"-zak
Isaiah	i-za"-a
Iscariot	is-kàr"-e-ot
Israel	iz"-ra-el, iz"-re-el
Israelites	iz"-re-*l-itz"
Ituraea	i-tu-re"-a
Jairus	ji"-rus
Javan	ja"-van
Jechoniah	jek-o-ni"-a
Jehoshaphat	je-hosh"-a-fat, je-hos"-a-fat
Jeremiah	jàr-a-mi"-a
Jericho	jàr"-i-ko
Jerusalem	je-ru"-sa-lem
Jesse	jes"-e
Jethro	jeth"-ro
Joanna	jo-an"-a
Job	job
Joel	jo"-*l
Jonah	jo"-na
jonquil	jon"-kwil
Joram	jôr"-am
Joses	jo"-ses
Joset	jo"-set
Joshua	josh"-yu-a
Josiah	jo-si"-a

Jotham	jo"-tham
Judah	ju"-da
Judaism	ju"-de-izm
Judas (Iscariot)	ju"-das (is-kàr"-e-ot)
Judea, Judaea	ju-de"-a
Justus	jus"-tus
Kedron	ked"-ron
Lazarus	la"-za-rus
Lebanon	leb"-a-non
Levi	le"-vi
Levite(s)	le"-vit(z)
Leviticus	le-vit"-i-cus
Libya	lib"-e-a
Lud	lud
Lysanius	li-sa"-ne-us
Lystra	lis"-tra
Maccabees	mac"-a-bez
Macedonia	ma-sa-do"-ne-a
Magdala	mag"-da-la
Magdalene	mag"-da-l*n
Malachi	mal"-a-ki
Malchiah	mal-ki"-a
Malchus	mal"-kus
Mamre	mam"-re
Manasseh	ma-nas"-e
manna	ma"-na
Massah	mas"-a
Matthat	math"-at
Matthew	math"-yu
Matthias	ma-thi"-as
Medad	me"-dad
Medes	medz
Megiddo	me-gid"-o
Melchizedek	mel-kiz"-e-dek
Meribah	mêr"-i-ba
Mesopotamia	me"-so-po-ta"-me-a
Micah	mi"-ka
Midian	mid"-e-an
Moriah	mo-ri"-a
Moshech	mo"-shek
myrrh	mûr
Naaman	na"-a-man
Nahshon	na"-shon
Nain	na"-in
Naphtali	naf"-ta-li
Nathan	na"-than
Nathanael	na-than"-y*l
Nazara	na"-za-ra
Nazarene	na"-za-ren
Nazareth	na"-za-reth
Nebuchadnezzar	neb"-yu-kad-nez"-êr
Nehemiah	ne-he-mi"-a
Nicanor	ni-ka"-nôr
Nicodemus	ni-ko-de"-mus
Nicolaus	ni-ko-la"-us
Nineveh	ni"-ne-v*
Nun	nun
Obed	o"-bed
Omega	o"-me-ga, o-me"-ga
Onesimus	o-nes"-i-mus
Ophir	o"-fer
Pamphylia	pam-fi"-le-a
Parmenas	pâr"-me-nas
Parthians	pâr"-the-anz
Patmos	pat"-mos, pat"-mos
Perez	pêr"-ez
Perga	pêr"-ga
Persia	pêr"-zha
Phanuel	fan"-yu-el
Pharaoh	fàr"-o
Pharisees	fàr"-i-sez
Philemon	fi"-li-mon
Philippi	fi-lip"-i
Philippians	fi-lip"-e-anz
Phrygia	fri"-je-a
phylacteries	fi-lak"-t*-rez
Pisidia	pi-si"-de-a
Pontius Pilate	pon"-shus pi"-l*t
Pontus	pon"-tus
Portico	pôr"-ti-ko
Praetorium	pre-tôr"-e-um
Prochorus	pro-kôr"-us, pro"-ko-rus
proselytes	pro"-sa-litz
Put	put
Qoheleth	ko-hel"-eth
Quirinius	kwi-rin"-e-us
Rabbuni	ra-bu"-ne
Rehab	ra"-hab
Ram	ram
Rehoboam	re-o-bo"-am
Rephidim	ref"-i-dim
Rosh	rosh, rosh
Rufus	ru"-fus
Sabaoth	sa"-ba-ot, sa"-ba-oth
Sadducees	sad"-ju-sez
Salem	sa"-lem
Salmon	sal"-mon
Salome	sa-lo"-me
Samaria	sa-màr"-e-a
Samaritan(s)	sa-màr"-i-tan(z)
Sanhedrin	san"-hi-drin, san-he"-drin
Saul	sol
Scythian	sith"-e-an
Seba	se"-ba
Shaphat	sha"-fat
Sharon	shàr"-*n
Shealtiel	she-al"-te-el
Sheba	she"-ba
Shebna	sheb"-na
Shechem	she"-kem, shek"-am
Sheol	she"-ol
Shinar	shi"-nar
Shunem	shu"-nem
Shunammitess	shu"-na-mi"-tes
Sidon	si"-d*n
Sidonian	si-do"-ne-an
Silas	si"-las
Siloam	si-lo"-am, si-lo"-am
Silvanus	sil-va"-nus
Simeon	sim"-e-*n
Sinai	si"-ni
Sion	si"-*n, zi"-*n
Sirach	si"-rak
Sodom	sod"-*m
Solomon	sol"-o-m*n
Sosthenes	sos"-the-nez
Sovereignty, -ties	sov"-rin-te(z)
Susanna	su-za"-na
Sychar	si"-kâr
Syria	se"-rea
Syrian	se"-re-an
Talitha kum	ta-li"-tha kum
Tamar	ta"-mâr
Tarshish	târ"-shish
Tarsus	târ"-sus
tetrarch	tet"-rârk
Thaddaeus	tha"-de-us, tha-de"-us
Theophilus	the-of"-i-lus
Thessalonians	thes"-a-lo"-ne-anz
Thessalonika	thes"-a-lo"-ne-ka
Tiberias	ti-be"-re-as
Tiberius Caesar	ti-be"-re-us se"-zêr
Timaeus	ti-me"-us
Timon	ti"mon
Titus	ti"-tus
Trachonitis	tra"-ko-ni"-tus
Tubal	tu"-bal
Tyre	tir
Ur	ûr
Uriah	yu-ri"-a
Uzziah	*-zi"-a
wadi	wa"-de
Zacchaeus	za-ke"-us
Zadok	za"-dok
Zarephath	zàr"-a-fat
Zealot	zel"-*t
Zebedee	zeb"-i-de
Zebulon, Zebulun	zeb"-yu-lon
Zechariah	zek"-a-ri"-a
Zedekiah	zed"-a-ki"-a
Zephaniah	zef"-a-ni"-a
Zerah	ze"-ra
Zerubbabel	ze-ru"-ba-bel
Zion	zi"-*n
Ziph	zif

Key:

Accented syllable is marked by "

fate	evil	bite	hope	jute
fat	bet	bit	hop	but
târ	hêr	fîr	ôr	tûrn
alas *las	wanted want*d	easily eas*ly	book b*k	pull p*ll
shàre			cow	
extra			boy	

LECTOR TRAINING PROGRAM

This Is the Word of the Lord

Do you want to be a better lector?

Only for those who want to become excellent lectors!

These entertaining and challenging presentations are by Michael Sparough, SJ, nationally known leader of the Fountain Square Fools. Use privately or together with the other lectors to review the lessons on preparation, volume and the microphone, pacing and pauses, eye communication and much, much more.

The tapes enable the reader to go over difficult points again and again. The booklet provides the texts. The evaluation sheet helps to applaud the strengths and to identify the opportunities for growth. ISBN 0-930467-96-5.

Note: *Tapes and booklet are protected by copyright and may* not *be duplicated.*

Set of three audiocassettes,
booklet and worksheet: $24.00

Twelve 15-minute lessons on three audiocassettes

A 27-page booklet to guide you step-by-step

The "Lector-Checker" for evaluating actual performance

Order from your bookstore or from LTP: 1-800-933-1800.

A WELL-TRAINED TONGUE

by Ray Lonergan

Give this book to lectors NOW— *hear the results later!*

LTP publishes *A Well-Trained Tongue* to assist you in your ministry of proclaiming the word of God. Both beginners and veteran lectors—in groups or working alone—can use this popular book.

Two dozen short lessons provide introductory notes and challenging exercises. The renowned author deals with all the problems of lectors with creativity and encouragement. 8½ × 11, 105 pages. ISBN 0-930467-39-6.

$6.95

Could you use a unified course of study to improve your skills?

Order from your bookstore or from LTP: 1-800-933-1800.